The First Epistle of Paul
The Apostle
to the
CORINTHIANS

CALVIN'S COMMENTARIES

CALVIN'S COMMENTARIES

The First Epistle of Paul
The Apostle
to the
CORINTHIANS

Translator
JOHN W. FRASER

Editors
DAVID W. TORRANCE
THOMAS F. TORRANCE

Wm. B. Eerdmans Publishing Company
Grand Rapids, Michigan

PUBLISHED . . . 1960

Sixth reprinting, November 1980

ISBN 0-8028-2049-2

Published in Great Britain by Oliver and Boyd, Edinburgh

INTRODUCTION

Chief Editions of John Calvin's Commentary on St Paul's First Epistle to The Corinthians

I. *Latin.*

First edition, 1546, dedicated to the Lord James, of the House of Burgundy, and Lord of Falais, 24 January 1546. Strassburg Vendelinus Rihelius.

Another edition, 1551, with the same dedication. (Because of Calvin's dispute with Bolsec at Geneva, this dedication was removed from subsequent editions.) Composite edition, Geneva, Girard.

Another edition, 1556, dedicated to the Italian, Galliazo Carracciolo, 24 January 1556. Composite edition, R. Stephanus.

Included also in composite editions of the Commentaries on all Paul's Epistles, Geneva; Crispinus 1557, Thomas Curteus 1565, Crispinus 1572, Eustace Vignon 1580 and 1600.

Works, Volume 5 Part 3, Geneva, Vignon and Chouet, 1617.

Works, Amsterdam Edition, Volume 7, 1667.

Commentaries of John Calvin on the New Testament, edited by A. Tholuck, Volume 5, Berlin 1834.

Corpus Reformatorum. Volume LXXVII. *Johannis Calvini Opera quae supersunt Omnia.* Volume XLIX. *Opera Exegetica et Homiletica.* Volume XXVII. Brunswick 1892.

II. *French.*

Commentaire de M. Iean Calvin sur la premiere Epistre aux Corinthiens, Chez Iean Girard, 1547.

In composite editions of the Commentaries on all Paul's Epistles, Printed by Estienne Anastase, 1560; Conrad Badius, Geneva, 1561, 1562; Sebastian Honoratus, Lyons, 1563.

III. *English.*

A Commentary upon S. Paules Epistles to the Corinthians, written by M. Iohn Caluin, and translated out of Latine into Englishe, by Thomas Tymme, Minister. London, 1573.

Calvin Translation Society. Translated by the Rev. John Pringle, Edinburgh, 1848.

The present translation has been made from the Latin in the C.R. text, checked by that of Tholuck. It has also been compared at various points with the French edition printed in 1562 by Conrad Badius, from the copy available in the National Library of Scotland, Edinburgh.

Use of Scripture

For the English text at the head of each section the Revised Version is used. As far as the actual Commentary is concerned, because Calvin often paraphrases Scripture or uses freedom in quoting it, the R.V. is quoted when it agrees with his Latin, otherwise his Latin is translated. Sometimes there is a blend of both R.V., and a translation of the Latin. At the beginning of the commentary on each verse, the R.V. is generally followed, but when required, for clarity, Calvin's Latin is translated.

Scripture References

Calvin has not given the Bible references of all the passages and verses he has quoted or referred to. The Translator has added many references, inserting them in the body of the commentary, and as footnotes in the Theme.

Note on Adultery in Roman Law

The translator is indebted to Professor M. G. Fisher, C.B.E., Q.C., M.A., LL.B., Dean of the Faculty of Law, University of Edinburgh, for the information included in the note on p. 146.

Abbreviations Used

C.R. Corpus Reformatorum, as above.
Tholuck, Edition of A. Tholuck as above.
C.T.S. Calvin Translation Society, as above.
Vulgate (WW) Latin Vulgate, revised by John Wordsworth, and Henry J. White. *Editio Minor* by Henry J. White, Oxford/British and Foreign Bible Society, London, 1911.
Vulgate (Clem) Latin Vulgate, Clementine Edition. *Biblia Sacra* (Tournai, 1938, 1947).

Banchory   JOHN W. FRASER
 Kincardineshire
 April 1958

JOHN CALVIN'S DEDICATION TO THE COMMENTARY ON ST PAUL'S FIRST EPISTLE TO THE CORINTHIANS[1]

TO THAT HONOURABLE GENTLEMAN, THE LORD JAMES OF BURGUNDY, LORD OF FALAIS, AND BREDA, ETC.

IN this commentary of mine, I have attempted to expound an epistle of Paul's, that is no less difficult than valuable. Many people have been asking for it, and have indeed been making urgent appeals for it for a long time, but now that it is published I only wish that it may equally satisfy their hopes and wishes. I am saying this not in order to get some reward for my work in the form of praise, for such ambition ought to be far from the servants of Christ; but because I want it to bring benefit to everybody, and it cannot do that if it is not acceptable. I have indeed laboured with the utmost faithfulness and diligence, so that without any obtrusiveness the work might be of the greatest value to the Church of God. How far I have succeeded, my readers will judge from actual experience of the work.

At least I believe that I have achieved this much, that this Commentary will be of unusual help in gaining a thorough grasp of Paul's thought. Certainly, most honourable Sir, I am so sure that you will find it thoroughly acceptable, that it is even necessary for me to warn you not to allow yourself to be swept off your feet by an excessive affection for me. Even if that should happen, I shall nevertheless value your judgement so highly that I shall consider my labour to have been highly successful, if it has gained your unstinted approval.

Further, although I dedicated it to you, it was not only because I was hoping that it would be pleasing to you, but for many other reasons, the most important being that your personal life perfectly bears out one of the themes of Paul's letter. For, while at the present time, there are far too many people who turn the Gospel into a cold and academic philosophy, thinking that they have done all that is required of them, and done it properly, if they nod their heads in assent to what they are told, you, on the other hand, are a conspicuous example to us of that living power, which Paul insists upon so much. I mean that when we look at you, we realise what is meant by that

---

[1] After 1551 this was omitted from editions of the commentary because of the dispute that arose between Calvin and the Sieur de Falais over Bolsec.

spiritual vigour, which, Paul affirms, ought to burst forth in the Gospel. I am, of course, not mentioning that for your personal satisfaction, but because I think that it is of great importance from the point of view of example.

You belong to the first rank of the nobility, you obtained and enjoy a high and honourable station in life, and you are well endowed with property and wealth (states that are all swarming with corruptions today!). Now it would certainly have been an important thing in itself, if you, in those circumstances, had not only led a self-controlled and temperate life, but had also kept your family under control with a proper and wholesome discipline. Both of these you have, in fact, carried out to the full. For your behaviour has been such that everyone was presented with clear evidence to let him see that there is not a shred of self-seeking about you.

While it was necessary for you to keep your splendour, you did it in such a way that, while you maintained a moderate standard of living, there was no suggestion of niggardliness; and yet it was quite plain that you avoided rather than sought after, a magnificent style of life. You have shown yourself so courteous and considerate to all, that everybody was forced to praise your unassuming behaviour. There was, in fact, not the slightest evidence of pride or arrogance to give offence to anyone. As far as your family is concerned, suffice it to say, in a word, that it has been managed in such a way as to reflect the mind of its Lord and His way of life, just as a mirror reflects a person's image. That in itself would have given people a clear and remarkable example of virtue to imitate.

But there is something that I consider far more important. You have been wrongly charged before the Emperor by the misrepresentations of ungodly men, and that, for no other reason except that immediately the Kingdom of Christ begins to make headway anywhere, it drives them to madness and frenzy. But (and this is what is so important) you have maintained a stout-heartedness that has not weakened, and you are now living as an exile from your native land, with every bit as much esteem as you had previously, when you honoured it with your presence. I am not going to mention other factors, because it would be tedious to carry on further. Indeed Christians should always have been regarding it as something more than merely common and customary, not only to leave estates, castles, and noble positions without a pang, for the sake of Christ, but also to be ready and willing to despise, in comparison with Him, everything that is looked upon as very precious on earth. However, nearly all of us are easy-going and indifferent into the bargain, so that that particular virtue is especially deserving of our admiration. Therefore, when we can see it so clearly in you, I only wish that it may waken up many people, so that they may want to copy it, and, instead of going on for ever hiding in their nesting-places doing nothing, may one day come out into the open bringing whatever spark of the Christian spirit they may have.

Now, when men attack you by frequently bringing fresh charges against you, they make it quite plain that they are violent enemies of religion, and they will gain nothing from this except to make themselves more and more detestable by indulging so flagrantly in lying. Surely any man in his senses realises that they are mad dogs, seeing that they wanted to tear you in pieces, and now, when they cannot bite you, avenge themselves by barking at you. It is a good thing that they do so at a distance, for that means they are doing no harm. But even if the wrongs done by ungodly men have resulted in the loss of much of your possessions, they have not meant any such lessening in the real glory with which believers regard you. But, as a Christian should, you take a wider view than that. For you are satisfied with nothing else but the heavenly glory, which is laid up for us with God, and which will be brought to light, as soon as our outer nature perishes.

Farewell, most worthy Sir, and your noble wife. May the Lord Jesus keep you both safe for a long time to come, for the spreading of His Kingdom; and may He always have the victory in you over Satan, and the whole host of His enemies.

GENEVA, 24th January, 1546

JOHN CALVIN'S
SECOND DEDICATORY EPISTLE

GREETINGS TO A NOBLEMAN,
WHO IS EVEN MORE OUTSTANDING FOR HIS VIRTUES,
THAN FOR HIS NOBLE BIRTH,
THE LORD GALLIAZO CARRACCIOLO
ONLY SON AND LAWFUL HEIR
OF THE MARQUIS OF VICO

I WISH that when this commentary was first published, I had no knowledge of, or, on the other hand, had been thoroughly acquainted with, the man, whose name previously appeared on this page, for I am now forced to delete it. I am certainly not afraid that he will accuse me of being fickle, or complain that I have snatched away what I had given to him; for, having deliberately sought not only to keep as far away as possible from me personally, but also to have no dealings with our church, he has left himself with no grounds for protesting. Yet it is with reluctance that I depart from my usual practice, and remove somebody's name from my writings; and I am sorry that that person has fallen from the high position which I had given to him, for it means that he is not giving the good example to others, which I had hoped he would. But since the cure for this evil does not lie in my hands, let him, as far as I am concerned, lie buried in oblivion, for even now I am anxious to say no more about him, and so do no further damage to his reputation.

But as for you, most honourable Sir, I should have had to find some pretext for now substituting your name for his, if I did not venture to take this liberty, relying on your incredible kindness and love towards me, which are well known to all our friends. To turn again to my desires, I wish I had known you ten years ago, for then there would be no reason for making any change now. This change is all to the good as far as an example to the Church at large is concerned, because, not only will we feel no loss by forgetting about the person who has withdrawn himself from us, but we will be compensated, in you, by an example which is far richer, and, indeed, preferable in every way. For, although you are not seeking after popular applause, being content to have God as your only witness; and although I have no intention of singing your praises, yet my readers must not be kept completely in the dark about what would be useful and beneficial for them to know. You were a man born into a noble family; you had a great

4

reputation and great riches as well; you were blessed with a wife of the noblest birth and the highest virtue, with many children, with peace and harmony in your home; you were indeed blessed in all the circumstances of your life. But in order to cross over into Christ's camp, of your own free will you left your native land, you abandoned a fertile and pleasant domain, a splendid inheritance, and a house as delightful as it was spacious; you deprived yourself of a household used to a magnificent style of living; you cut yourself off from father, wife, children, relations and kindred; and, after saying farewell to so many worldly attractions, and being content with our impoverished circumstances, you adopt our frugal way of life, the standard of ordinary folk, just as if you were one of ourselves. While I relate all these things to other people, yet I do not by any means forget the benefit which I personally receive. For if I set your virtues before the eyes of my readers here, as in a mirror, so that they can copy them, it would be a shame for me, who have them before my very eyes, not to be the more deeply affected, in view of the fact that I see them so clearly every day. But because I really do know from experience how much your example means for the strengthening of my own faith and devotion, and because all the children of God who are here acknowledge, along with me, that they have derived extraordinary benefit from it, I considered that it would be worth while for me to make it known, so that a wider circle of people might reap the same advantage. Otherwise, it would be foolish to speak at length in praise of a man, whose nature and temperament are as far removed from ostentatiousness as one can imagine, and, more, to do so in the presence of foreigners in far-away places. Therefore if many people, who knew nothing of you before, because they were at a distance from you, have this admirable example set before them, and will be prepared to leave the nesting-places, to which they are too inclined to cling, and copy it, I shall be amply rewarded for the things I have written.

Indeed Christians ought always to have regarded it as something more than merely common and customary, not only to leave estates, castles, and noble positions without a pang, if it is impossible to follow Christ otherwise; but also to be ready and willing to despise, in comparison with Him, everything that is looked upon as very precious on earth. But we are all of us so easy-going, or, rather, so indifferent, that while many nod their heads in formal assent to the teaching of the Gospel, scarcely one in a hundred, perhaps the possessor of some insignificant little farm, will allow himself to be torn from it, for the sake of the Gospel. Hardly a person is to be prevailed upon, except with the greatest reluctance, to give up the slightest advantage, which shows how far men are from being prepared to renounce life itself, as they ought to be. More than anything else my wish is that all would resemble you in self-denial, the first of all the virtues. For you are the person best fitted to testify of me, and I in turn of you, how little pleasure we find in the companionship of those, who, after leaving their native land, end up by making it quite plain that they have brought with them the same outlooks, as they had there.

But since it is better for my readers to make further reflection on these things in their own minds, rather than that I should put them into words, I now turn to pray that God, who, until now, has encouraged you by the wonderful power of His Spirit, may equip you with invincible steadfastness right to the end. For I am well aware of the way in which God has disciplined you with many hard struggles, but, with your remarkable insight, you have concluded from them, that a stern and heavy warfare still lies in front of you. And since many experiences have taught you how really necessary it is for a hand to be stretched out to us from heaven, you will be ready to join me in making earnest appeal to God for the gift of perseverance. As for myself, I shall pray to Christ, our King, to whom the Father has given supreme authority, and in whose hands all the treasures of spiritual blessings have been placed, asking Him to keep you safe, so that we may have you for a long time with us for the spreading of His Kingdom; and that He may continue to use you to obtain the victory over Satan and his followers.

24th January, 1556, ten years after this
commentary was first published

THE THEME OF PAUL'S
FIRST EPISTLE TO THE CORINTHIANS

THIS letter is of value in many different ways; for it contains a number of important subjects. As they are dealt with, successively in their order, the discussion itself will make it plain how necessary it is to know about them. And indeed that will come out very clearly in this very account. I shall try to present it briefly, but, at the same time, to give a complete summary of it, without missing out any of the main points.

It is well known that *Corinth* was a rich and famous city of Achaia. When L. Mummius destroyed it,[1] he did so simply because its advantageous situation made him distrust the place. But people of a later day rebuilt it for the very same reason that had made him demolish it, while the same topographical advantages caused it to be restored in a short time. Since it was near the Aegean Sea on one side, and the Ionian Sea on the other, and since it was on the isthmus linking Attica and the Peloponnesus, it was ideally suited for the importing and exporting of goods.

Luke tells us in Acts that, after Paul had taught there for a year and a half, he was forced, by the outrageous behaviour of the Jews, to sail from there to Syria.[2] In Paul's absence false apostles had infiltrated into the place. They did not come (in my opinion at any rate) to upset the Church with obviously unorthodox teaching, or to damage the orthodox teaching intentionally, as it were. There were three reasons for their coming. First of all, being proud of their brilliant and showy oratory, one should rather say, being swollen-headed about their empty and bombastic language, they were out to treat the simplicity of Paul and even the very Gospel, with contempt. Secondly, because of their ambition, they aimed at breaking the Church up into different factions. Finally, indifferent to everything except the good opinion they wanted people to have of them, they came in order to make it their business to increase their own reputation, rather than to promote the Kingdom of Christ and the well-being of the people.

Again, since Corinth was in the grip of those vices, with which commercial cities are usually infested, luxury, arrogance, vanity, pleasures, insatiable covetousness, self-seeking; those vices had penetrated also into the very Church, so that discipline had greatly deteriorated. More seriously, there was already a falling away from the pure

---

[1] 146 B.C.   [2] Acts 18.11, 18.

7

teaching, so that one of the fundamentals of the faith, the resurrection of the dead, was being called in question. And yet in the midst of so much corruption of every kind, they were pleased with themselves, as if everything connected with them was perfectly in order. These are the tricks which Satan usually employs. If he cannot stop the spread of teaching, he creeps up secretly to make an attack upon it. If he cannot suppress it by lies which contradict it, and prevent it from coming into the open, he prepares concealed pits for its destruction. Finally, if he cannot alienate men's minds from it at one fell swoop, he causes them to give it up by degrees.

Now, I have good reason for thinking that those worthless fellows, who had caused trouble in the Corinthian church, were not open enemies of the truth. We know that Paul does not overlook false doctrines in other letters. The letters to the Galatians, Colossians, Philippians and Timothy are all short; yet in all of them, not only does he strongly attack the false apostles, but at the same time he also points out the ways in which they are causing damage to the Church. And he was perfectly justified; for not only must believers be warned about the men of whom they ought to beware, but they must also be shown the evil against which they ought to be on their guard. I cannot therefore credit it that in a letter as long as this one, he meant to pass over in silence what he drives home so painstakingly in other and much shorter letters. Besides that he deals with many faults of the Corinthians, some of them, indeed, quite trifling, so it appears that he did not intend to miss out anything about them that called for reproof. And, if that were not so, he is wasting a lot of words in joining issue with those preposterous teachers or chattering speechmakers. He condemns their ambition; he takes them to task for turning the Gospel into a man-made philosophy; he denies that they have the power of the Spirit to give results, because, with their preoccupation with empty, bombastic language, they were only pursuing 'the dead letter'; but there is not a single word about corrupt teaching. I am therefore quite sure that they did not openly detract from the substance of the Gospel in any respect; but since they were burning with a misguided and passionate desire for prominence, I think that they had devised a new method of teaching, that was not consistent with the simplicity of Christ; and they hoped that it would make them the objects of people's admiration. This is what inevitably happens to all those who have not yet got rid of self-concern, so as to enter on the Lord's work with absolutely no encumbrances: The first step in serving Christ is to forget about ourselves, and think about the glory of the Lord alone, and about the salvation of men. Further, no person will ever be fit for teaching, if he has not first absorbed the power of the Gospel, so that he speaks, not so much with his lips, but from his very heart. What therefore happens in the case of those who have not been born again by the Spirit of God, having had no experience of the power of the Gospel in their own hearts, and having no idea what it means that we must be *new creations*?[1] Their preaching is dead, when it should be alive and producing results; and in order to be in the public eye themselves they disguise the Gospel, dressing it in different clothes, so that it may look like a worldly philosophy.

And it was easy for the people, whom we are now considering, to do all that at Corinth. For merchants are usually taken in by outward appearances; and not only do they allow themselves to be cheated by the very same deception, which they themselves practise on others, but in a way they also enjoy it. In addition they have sensitive ears, so that they cannot bear to be censured too severely, with the result that if they come across teachers, who are soft and let them off lightly, they reciprocate, by way of reward, by flattering them. I agree that this happens everywhere, but it is more common in rich, commercial cities. On the other hand, Paul, who in other respects was a god-like man, and stood out because of the admirable qualities he had, made a poor show of it, however, as far as pleasing outward graces were concerned, and he was not bursting with ostentation, seeking to blow his own trumpet. In fact, because his heart was really under the influence of the Spirit, there was not a scrap of ostentation about him, he was incapable of flattery, and was not concerned about pleasing men. He had one end in view, viz. that he and all others being restored to order, Christ might reign. Since the Corinthians had a liking for teaching that was clever rather than beneficial, they had no relish for the Gospel. Since they were eager for new things, Christ was already out of date to them. At any rate, if they had not yet actually fallen into those errors, they were already naturally inclined towards seductive things of that sort. So it was easy for the false apostles to get a hearing among them, and to adulterate the teaching of Christ. For it certainly is adulterated, when its natural purity is so spoiled, and, as it were, painted a different colour, that it is on a level with any worldly philosophy. Therefore, in order to suit the Corinthians' taste, they added seasoning to their teaching, with the result that the true flavour of the Gospel was ruined. We are now in a position to understand why Paul was induced to write this letter.

I shall now summarize the argument, by making brief notes about each of the chapters in turn.

Paul begins the *first chapter* by congratulating them, and that has the effect of encouraging them to carry on as they started. In this way he

---

[1] II Cor. 5.17.

9

mollifies them before going any further, so that they might be more willing to receive his teaching. But at once he strikes a sterner note, making the transition to reproof, as he refers to the disagreements which were troubling their church. Wanting to cure this evil, he urges them to turn from pride to humility. For he casts aside all the wisdom of the world, so as to set up the preaching of the Cross alone. At the same time he also humbles them individually, by telling them to take note of the kind of people whom the Lord has, for the most part, adopted and brought into His flock.

In the *second chapter* he cites the example of his own preaching, which, humanly speaking, was poor and insignificant, but which was remarkable because it had the power of the Spirit. And he goes on to develop the thought that the Gospel contains a heavenly and secret wisdom. It is something that neither man's natural ability, however acute and penetrating, nor his physical senses, can grasp; something about which human argument can give no conviction; something which needs no flowery language and word-pictures. It is only by the revelation of the Spirit that it comes to be known by the minds of men, and to be sealed in their hearts. Finally, he concludes, not only that the preaching of the Gospel is poles apart from human wisdom, since it consists in the humiliation of the Cross, but also that mere human judgement cannot determine what its real value is. Paul does that in order to turn them away from a misplaced confidence in their own understanding, which gives wrong assessments of everything.

At the beginning of the *third chapter* he applies what he has just said, to them. For Paul complains that being carnal men they were scarcely fit to learn even the first principles of the Gospel. In this way he points out that the distaste for the Word, which was so strong in them, did not come from any defect in the Word itself, but from their ignorance; and, at the same time, he gives a tacit warning, that they need to have their minds renewed, so that they may begin to assess things properly.

He then shows the place that ought to be given to the ministers of the Gospel. The honour due to them should not detract in the slightest degree from the glory that is due to God; for there is one Lord, and they are all His servants; He alone has the power in His hands, and He alone gives the results; they are all simply His instruments.

At the same time he shows that they ought to be aiming at building up the church. He takes the opportunity to explain the correct and proper method for making a good job of the building, viz. to have Christ as the one and only foundation, and to make the whole structure appropriate to that foundation. And here, having affirmed in passing that he was a skilled master-builder, he warns those who are left to continue the work to keep the building in conformity with the foundation all the way through to its completion.

He also urges the Corinthians not to allow themselves to be defiled by corrupt teachings, since they are the temples of God. And in that closing part of the chapter he again reduces the pride of human wisdom to nothing, so that only the knowledge of Christ may be in evidence among believers.

At the beginning of *chapter four* he explains what the office of a genuine apostle is, and, rejecting their corrupt judgement, that prevented them from recognizing him as an apostle, he appeals to the day of the Lord. Then, seeing that they despised him because of his humble appearance, he shows that that should in fact be more of an honour to him than a disgrace. He goes on to cite instances from his actual experience, which make it plain that he was not concerned about his own glory, or his own material gain, but had faithfully done Christ's business and nothing else. In due course he points out the way in which the Corinthians ought to honour him (i.e. vv. 14-16). In the concluding part of the chapter he commends Timothy to them, until he comes himself. And at the same time he announces that on his arrival he will make it quite plain that he puts no value at all upon all the hot-air with which the false apostles were singing their own praises.

In *chapter five* Paul takes them to task because they had silently tolerated an incestuous union between a man and his step-mother. And he tells them candidly that, instead of their being so boastful, an enormity such as this ought to make them hang their heads in shame. He moves on from that to general instruction to the effect that offences like that should be punished with excommunication, so that indulgence in sin may be checked, and that the uncleanness may be limited to one person, and not spread further to affect the rest.

The *sixth chapter* has two main parts. In the first he condemns their practice of causing annoyance to each other, and bringing great discredit upon the gospel, by bringing their disputes into the law-courts, which were presided over by unbelievers. In the second part, he condemns promiscuous sexual indulgence, which had reached such a pitch, that it was looked upon as almost a legitimate thing to do. He does, in fact, start off with a grave threatening note, and he then goes on to produce arguments in support of the warning that he gives.

Chapter seven contains a discussion on virginity, marriage and celibacy. As far as we can gather from what Paul says, the Corinthians had become strongly influenced by the superstitious notion that virginity is an outstanding, almost an angelic virtue, so that they despised marriage as if it were something unclean. In order to get rid of this mistaken view, Paul teaches that each individual must know what his particular gift is; and in this connexion must not try to do something he has not got the ability to do; for everybody is not called to the same state. Accordingly he points out who can abstain from marriage, and what his object should be in abstaining from it. On the other hand he advises who ought to be married, and what the true basis of Christian marriage is.

In *chapter eight* he forbids them to get involved with idol-worshippers and their unclean sacrifices, or to practise anything at all that might cause injury to somebody with a weak conscience. They were making excuses for themselves on the pretext that when they associated themselves with idol-worshippers they never went with wrong ideas in their heads, since in their own hearts they acknowledged *one God*, which, of course, made them look upon idols as worthless things that men make. Paul dismisses this excuse on the grounds that everyone ought to be concerned about his brothers, and, on the other hand, that there are many weak people, whose faith would be destroyed by insincerity like that.

In the *ninth chapter* he makes it plain that he is asking no more of them than what he has done himself, so that he might not seem to be unfair in imposing on them a principle which he does not keep himself. For he reminds them how he voluntarily refrained from using the liberty which the Lord had allowed him, so as not to cause offence to anyone; and how, as far as neutral things are concerned, he adopted different attitudes, as it were, in order to accommodate himself to all sorts of men. He reminds them of those two facts, so that they may learn by his example, that no-one ought to be so wrapped up in himself, as not to take pains to adapt himself to his brothers for the promotion of their edification.

Because the Corinthians were highly delighted with themselves, as I said at the beginning, he starts *chapter ten* by using the example of the Jews to warn them not to deceive themselves with a false sense of security. For he shows that, if they are swollen-headed by reason of external things, and the gifts of God, the Jews also had similar reasons for boasting. Yet it proved to be of no advantage at all in their case, because they made wrong use of the blessings they received. After frightening them with this warning, he quickly returns to the subject which he had dealt with earlier (i.e. idol-worship, v. 14), and shows how inconsistent it is for those who share in the Lord's Supper to partake in the table of demons; for that is a disgraceful and intolerable way of being defiled. Finally, he concludes that we should accommodate ourselves to others in all our actions, so that we cause offence to no-one.

In the *eleventh chapter* he seeks to purge their gatherings for worship of certain bad practices, which were hardly in keeping with Christian seemliness and order, and he tells them that great dignity and restraint must be observed in these gatherings, where we stand in the sight of God and the angels. But his main criticism is directed against their corrupt administration of the Supper. But, in addition, he gives the method for correcting the abuse which had crept in; viz. by calling them back to our Lord's original institution as the one sure standard and permanent rule for its correct administration.

But since many of them were making wrong use of spiritual gifts for their own ends, he deals in *chapter twelve* with the purpose for which God gives them to us, and also with the right and proper way to use them, viz. that by serving each other, we may grow together into the one body of Christ. He illustrates his teaching by drawing an analogy with the human body. Although the body has different members, all with different functions, there is yet such a well-balanced arrangement and inter-dependence (*communio*) that what has been given to the individual members is employed for the benefit of the whole body. Therefore he concludes that love is our best guide in this connexion.

And so he pursues that theme at length in *chapter thirteen*, giving a fuller explanation of what he means. But it all amounts to this: love (*caritas*) ought to be the controlling factor in everything. He takes the opportunity that presented itself to make a digression to sing the praises of love, so that he might be all the more persuasive in making people want to have it, and also in encouraging the Corinthians to put it into practice.

In *chapter fourteen* he begins to give more precise details about how the Corinthians had gone wrong in the use of spiritual gifts. And, since they were putting such a great deal of emphasis on ostentation, he teaches them that in everything they do edification must be their one concern. That is why he prefers prophecy to all the other gifts, since it is more beneficial; whereas the Corinthians thought that tongues were more valuable, purely on the ground of their empty showiness. He also lays down the proper order for doing things. At the same time he condemns the fault of holding forth noisily in unknown tongues, to the benefit of nobody; for it meant that while that was going on teaching and exhortations, which always ought to be given priority, were being pushed aside.

After that he forbids women to teach in public, as it is unseemly.

In the *fifteenth chapter* he attacks a most pernicious error. Even if we can hardly credit it that it made an assault upon all the Corinthians, yet it had gained a hold over the minds of some of them to such a degree that a remedy was clearly needed. But it seems that Paul purposely put off mentioning this matter until the end of the letter; for if he had started off with it, or if he had turned to it immediately after he began, they would have thought that they were all being condemned. He therefore shows that the resurrection hope is so necessary that if it is cut out, then the whole Gospel collapses in utter ruin. Having established the hope by the use of powerful arguments, he goes on to show the basis on which it rests, and how it will take place (i.e. vv. 35-50 and 51 ff). In a word, he carries out a full and careful discussion of this question.

Chapter sixteen has two parts. In the first part he encourages them to give help to the Jerusalem brethren in their need. At that time they were being hard pressed by famine, and were suffering cruel treatment at the hands of unbelievers. The apostles had given Paul the task of encouraging the Gentile churches to provide relief for them. Paul therefore instructs them to set aside whatever they felt they would like to contribute, so that it might be conveyed to Jerusalem immediately.[1]

He brings the letter to a close with a friendly exhortation, and with joyous greetings.

We can gather from this, as I said at the beginning, that this letter is full of the most valuable teaching, for it contains various discussions on a number of glorious themes.

[1] So Calvin here. But see 16.3.

CHAPTER ONE

PAUL, called to be an apostle of Jesus Christ through the will of God, and Sosthenes our brother, unto the church of God which is at Corinth, even them that are sanctified in Christ Jesus, called to be saints, with all that call upon the name of our Lord Jesus Christ in every place, their Lord and ours: Grace to you and peace from God our Father and the Lord Jesus Christ. (1-3)

1. *Paul, called to be an apostle.* Paul begins nearly all his letters in this way, to gain authority, and acceptance for his teaching. He obtains authority for himself from the role, imposed upon him by God, of being an apostle of Christ, sent by God; acceptance, by bearing witness to his love towards those to whom he writes. For it is easier for us to have faith in a man whom we consider to be genuinely well disposed towards us, and faithfully caring for our interests. Therefore in this greeting he claims authority for himself, when he describes himself as an apostle of Christ, and indeed called by God, that is, set apart by the will of God.

But two things are required in anyone who would be heard in the Church and occupy the position of a teacher; he must be called by God to that office, and be faithful in carrying out its duties. Paul is claiming here that both apply to him. For this name apostle means that he carries out the duties of an ambassador for Christ conscientiously, and proclaims the pure teaching of the Gospel. But because no-one ought to take this honour on himself, but must be called to it, he adds that he had not rushed thoughtlessly into it, but had been appointed to it by God.

Let us learn then to take both of these into account when we wish to know whom we ought to have as ministers of Christ: a call, and faithfulness in fulfilling that office. Since no-one can by right arrogate to himself the description and office of minister unless he is called, so it is not enough that a person be called, if he does not also give satisfaction in carrying out his work. The Lord does not choose ministers to be dumb idols, or to act dictatorially under pretext of their call, or to make their own whim their law. Rather, at the same time He lays down what kind of men they ought to be, and puts them under His laws. In short, He chooses them for the ministry, that in the first place they may not be idle, and secondly, that they may confine themselves within the limits of their office. Therefore, since the apostleship depends on the call, if a man wishes to be thought of as an apostle, he must show that he really is one, and so indeed must everyone who desires that men should trust him, or pay heed to his teaching. For since Paul relies upon those grounds for claiming his authority, it would be insolence on the part of any man to wish to have the position without them!

But it should be noted that it is not enough for a man to lay claim to having the title to a call, as well as to being faithful in carrying out the duties of his office, unless he really gives proof of both. For it often happens that those who boast most about their titles are the very people, who, in fact, have none; as, for instance, the false prophets of long ago, who claimed with great arrogance that they were sent by the Lord. And today what else do the Romanists make a great fuss about, but 'ordination from God and an inviolable succession all the way from the apostles themselves'? But in the end it appears that they are lacking completely in all those things about which they are so elated. Here, therefore, it is not boasting, but the real thing, that is needed. But since it is common for good and bad to assume the name, we must come to the test, to learn who may truly call himself an apostle, and who may not. God attested the call of Paul himself by many divine words, and then confirmed it with miracles. The faithfulness had to be assessed in this way: was he, or was he not, proclaiming the pure teaching of Christ? As to the twofold call, that of God and that of the Church, see my *Institute* (4.3.11).

Apostle. Although this word has a general significance by its derivation, and furthermore is sometimes taken in a wide sense, to refer to all ministers without distinction, nevertheless it belongs, as a particular designation, to those who were set apart by the Lord's commission to publish the Gospel in the whole world. But it was important that Paul be counted in their number for two reasons, first, because much more deference was paid to them than to other ministers of the Gospel, and secondly, because they alone, strictly speaking, had the authority to institute all churches.

By the will of God. Since the apostle is accustomed to acknowledge gladly his indebtedness to God for every good thing he receives, he does so particularly with reference to his apostleship, so that he may remove every suggestion of arrogance from himself. And there is no doubt that, as a call to salvation is of grace, in the same way a call to the office of apostle is also of grace, as Christ teaches in these words: 'Ye did not choose me, but I chose you' (John 15.16). At the same time, however, Paul implies that all who try to overthrow his apostleship, or to oppose it in any way, oppose the ordering of God. For Paul does not make an empty boast here about honorary titles, but purposely defends his apostleship from being disparaged in a malicious way. For, since his authority must have been sufficiently clear to the Corinthians, there was no need to mention the will of God specifically, if unjust men had not been trying, by indirect means, to overthrow his God-given position of honour.

And Sosthenes our brother. This is the Sosthenes who was ruler of the synagogue at Corinth, and whom Luke mentions in Acts 18.17. But Paul included his name here because the Corinthians must have had an understandable regard for one whom they knew to be steadfast in his devotion to the Gospel. Therefore, it is now a greater honour for him to be called the brother of Paul, than, as before, ruler of the synagogue.

2. *To the church of God which is at Corinth.* Perhaps it may seem an extraordinary thing that he should give the name, *the Church of God*, to that company of people, in which so many faults prevailed that Satan held more powerful sway than God. But he certainly did not wish to flatter the Corinthians, for he speaks by the Spirit of God, who is not accustomed to flatter. But in the midst of such filth, what sort of likeness to a church is any longer presented? My answer is: Since God had there said to Paul (Acts 18.9): 'Do not be afraid, I have many people in this city', Paul recalled that promise, and conferred on a few good people the great honour of recognizing them as the Church in the midst of so many unrighteous people. Later on, despite the fact that somehow or other many vices, and various corruptions of teaching and manners had crept in, some marks of the true Church were nevertheless still apparent. We should give close attention to this verse, however, lest we should expect in this world a Church without spot or wrinkle, or immediately withhold this title from any gathering whatever, in which everything does not satisfy our standards. For it is a dangerous temptation to think there is no Church where perfect purity is lacking. The point is that anyone who is obsessed by that idea, must cut himself off from everybody else, and appear to himself to be the only saint in the world, or he must set up a sect of his own along with other hypocrites.

Why then should Paul have recognized the Church at Corinth? No doubt it was because he saw among them the teaching of the Gospel, baptism and the Lord's Supper, the marks by which the Church ought to be determined. For while some had begun to be uncertain about the resurrection, yet that error had not permeated the whole body, and so neither the name nor the reality of the Church is wiped out on that account. Although some defects had crept into the administration of the Supper, discipline and moral tone had greatly declined, the simplicity of the Gospel was despised, they had surrendered themselves to ostentation and display, they were broken up into various parties

17

through the ambition of their ministers; nevertheless, because they held on to the fundamental teaching—the One God was worshipped by them and was invoked in the name of Christ—they rested their confidence of salvation in Christ, and they had a ministry that was not wholly corrupt. For those reasons the Church still continued to exist among them. Hence wherever the worship of God is unimpaired, and that fundamental teaching, of which I have spoken, persists, there, we may without difficulty decide, the Church exists.

Sanctified in Christ Jesus, called to be saints. Paul reminds them of the blessings which God had bestowed on them, as if he were reproaching them, because, in response, they do not even show that they are grateful. For what could be more discourteous than rejecting an apostle, by whose service they had been set apart as God's own property?

Here, however, he shows, by the use of these two epithets, who are included among the true members of the Church, and who properly belong to her communion. For if you do not reveal yourself as a Christian by holiness of life, you will certainly be able to conceal yourself in the Church, but all the same you will not belong to it. Therefore, all who wish to be reckoned among the people of God must be sanctified in Christ. Moreover, the word 'sanctification' denotes separation. This takes place in us when, by the Spirit, we are born again into newness of life, to serve, not the world, but God. For since we are by nature unholy the Spirit sets us apart to God. Because this really takes place when we are ingrafted into the body of Christ, outside of which there is only defilement, and since the Spirit is given to us from Christ only, and not from any other source, Paul rightly says that we are sanctified in Christ, when, through Him, we cleave to God, and in Him are made 'new creations' (II Cor. 5.17).

What comes next, *called to be saints,* I take to mean: 'as you have been called into holiness'. But that can be taken in two ways. First, we may understand Paul as saying that the cause of sanctification is the call of God, because God Himself has chosen them; that is to say, it depends on His grace, and not on men's goodness. The alternative meaning is: it is consistent with our profession that we be holy, because that is what the teaching of the Gospel aims at. Although the first meaning seems to suit the context better, it makes little difference which way you take it, as those two meanings are in close agreement with each other, for our holiness flows from the source of divine election, and it is also the goal of our calling.

Therefore, we must maintain that we are righteous, not in the least by our own efforts, but by God's call; because He alone sanctifies those who were by nature unclean. And I think it very probable that when

Paul points, as if with his finger, to the open fountain of holiness, it is to go a step higher, to the gracious purpose of God Himself, by which Christ also came forth to us. Besides, as we are called by the Gospel to blamelessness of life, it must therefore become a reality in us, so that our calling may be effectual. But someone will object that there were not many like that among the Corinthians. My answer is that the weak are not excluded from this number, for here God merely begins His work with us, and brings it to completion little by little indeed, adding to it by degrees. I would further answer that Paul looks rather at the grace of God at work in them, than at their own faults, that he might make them feel ashamed of their negligence in not doing what was required of them.

Together with all who call. This epithet is also one that is common to all believers. For since calling on the name of God is one of the main ways in which faith is exercised, so it is by this duty that the faithful are mainly to be adjudged. Notice also that Paul says that Christ is called on by the faithful; and in this way His divinity is established, for invocation is one of the primary evidences of the worship of God. Therefore, in this context invocation, by synecdoche (κατὰ συνεκδοχήν), means a total profession of faith in Christ, just as in many passages of Scripture it is generally taken to cover the complete worship of God.

Some explain it as profession alone, but this does not seem to me to carry much weight, and it is out of keeping with scriptural use. Now, I have put those small words 'ours' and 'their' in the genitive, as referring to Christ. Others, taking them as referring to place, render them in the ablative. I have followed Chrysostom in what I have done. This rendering will perhaps seem harsh, because the words 'in every place' appear in the middle, but there is nothing harsh about this construction in Paul's Greek. My reason for preferring this reading to that of the Vulgate is that if you explain it as referring to place, the additional phrase will be not only unnecessary, but inapposite. For what place would Paul call his own? They take him to mean Judaea; but on what grounds? Then, to what place would he be referring as that of others? They maintain that all the other places in the world are left; but that, too, is not very suitable. Indeed the meaning which I have given is most fitting, for, since he had referred to 'all who everywhere call on the name of Christ our Lord', he adds, 'both theirs and ours', in order to make it quite clear that Christ is undoubtedly the common Lord of all who call upon Him, whether they are Jews or Gentiles.

In every place. Paul has added this contrary to his usual practice, for in his other letters he mentions, in the greeting, only those to whom he is addressing the letters. But it appears that he wished to anticipate the misrepresentations of unjust men, to prevent them saying that he was adopting a high and mighty attitude towards the Corinthians, and claiming for himself an authority, which he would not dare to assume towards other churches. As will soon be evident, he had also been unjustly charged with the reproach, that he was constructing little nesting-places for himself, as if to get out of the light, or secretly to cut himself off from the rest of the apostles. To rebut this lie, he seems therefore to be purposely putting himself in a commanding position, from which he might make his voice heard far and wide.

3. *Grace to you and peace.* Readers may find an exposition of this prayer in the beginning of my commentary on the Letter to the Romans. For I do not wish to burden them with repetitions.

I thank my God always concerning you, for the grace of God which was given you in Christ Jesus; that in every thing ye were enriched in him, in all utterance and all knowledge; even as the testimony of Christ was confirmed in you: so that ye come behind in no gift; waiting for the revelation of our Lord Jesus Christ; who shall also confirm you unto the end, that ye be unreproveable in the day of our Lord Jesus Christ. God is faithful, through whom ye were called into the fellowship of his Son Jesus Christ our Lord. (4-9)

4. *I always give thanks to my God.* After showing, in the greeting, that his authority rests on the role that had been imposed upon him, Paul now procures acceptance for his teaching, by expressing his love towards them. In this way he mollifies them beforehand, so that they may listen to his rebukes with patience. Indeed he gives them cause for confidence in his love, first, in his rejoicing in their blessings just as much as if they had been bestowed on himself, and secondly, in affirming that he is well disposed towards them, and has good hope for their future. Moreover, he modifies his rejoicing, so as to give them no grounds for taking pride in themselves, since he regards God as the source of all the blessings they received. Consequently, since those came from His favour, all the praise must go to Him. In other words he is saying: 'I congratulate you in all sincerity, but in such a way as to ascribe the praise to God.'

I have explained in my commentary on the Letter to the Romans, what Paul means by calling God 'his God'.

Further, as Paul did not want to flatter the Corinthians, he did not give them praise to which they were not entitled. For though all the people did not deserve such praise, and though they spoiled many gifts of God by ambition, he could not ignore, as if they had little value, the gifts themselves, which did, in themselves, deserve the greatest respect. Again, because the gifts of the Spirit are bestowed for the upbuilding of all, he is justified in reckoning them as gifts common to the whole Church. But let us see what he does praise in them.

On account of the grace etc. Grace is a general term, for it embraces every kind of blessing, which they had obtained by means of the Gospel. For the word grace means here, not the favour of God, but, by metonymy, the gifts which He freely lavishes upon men. Paul then passes to particular instances, when he says 'in everything ye were enriched', and he explains 'everything' as the teaching and Word of God. For Christians should abound in those riches, which ought to be all the more honoured and the more highly valued by us, in proportion as they are disregarded by people at large.

I preferred to keep the phrase 'in Him' rather than change it to 'by Him' because in my opinion it is more vivid and forceful. For we are enriched in Christ, because we are members of His body, and we have been ingrafted into Him; and, furthermore, since we have been made one with Him, He shares with us all that He has received from the Father.

6. *Even as the testimony of Christ was confirmed in you.* Erasmus' rendering is different, 'by those things the testimony of Christ was confirmed among you', meaning, by knowledge and by the Word. The words have a different ring about them, and if they are not twisted, the meaning is simply that God set His seal to the truth of His Gospel among the Corinthians, in order that it might be all the better established among them. But that could have been done in two ways, either by miracles, or by the inward testimony of the Holy Spirit. Chrysostom seems to take it to be by way of miracles, but I take it in a wider way. First of all, it is certain that the Gospel must be confirmed in our case by faith, because so long as it is received by us by faith, then indeed 'we set our seal to the fact that God is true' (John 3.33). Though I admit that miracles ought to be of value in confirming it, a higher source must nevertheless be sought, viz. that the Spirit of God is the earnest (*arrha*) and seal. Therefore my explanation of these words is that the Corinthians were rich in knowledge, inasmuch as from the beginning God had made His Gospel yield results among them. Further He did not do this in one way only, but as much by the inward working of the Spirit, as by the excellence and variety of gifts, by miracles, and by all the other things that help. The testimony of Christ or concerning Christ is Paul's way of describing the Gospel, for its whole purpose is to lay open to us Christ, 'in whom are hidden all the treasures of knowledge' (Col. 2.3). If anyone prefers to take it in an active sense, because the primary author of the Gospel is Christ, so that the apostles are no more than secondary or less important witnesses, I have no great quarrel with him. The former explanation is more

pleasing to me however. I admit that a little later (chapter 2.1) 'the testimony of God' must, undoubtedly, be taken in an active sense, because the passive would be unsuitable. But here it is different; and furthermore, that passage confirms my opinion, because immediately he adds what it means: 'to know nothing but Christ' (2.2).

7. *So that you are deprived of no gift.* Ὑστερεῖσθαι means to be without something which in fact you really need. Paul means therefore that the Corinthians are rich in all the gifts of God, and indeed lack for nothing. It is as if he said, 'Not only has the Lord considered you worthy of the light of the Gospel, but He has richly provided you with all the qualities which can help believers to make progress in the way of salvation.' For Paul calls *gifts* (*charismata*) the spiritual qualities which are, so to speak, means of salvation to believers. On the other hand, it may be objected that believers are never so rich as not to feel that they lack some graces, so that they are forced always to be 'hungry and thirsty' (Matt. 5.6). For who is not far from perfect? My answer is: since they are sufficiently provided with necessary gifts, and whenever they are in need the Lord comes opportunely to satisfy them, Paul therefore credits them with such wealth. For the same reason he adds, 'waiting for the revelation', meaning that he does not think of them as having such wealth that nothing is left to be desired, but as having only what will suffice until they will have reached perfection. The present participle 'waiting' I take to mean, 'in the meantime while you are waiting'. So the meaning will be: 'So you are lacking no spiritual gift in the meantime, while you are waiting for the day of perfect revelation, in which Christ our Wisdom will be made fully manifest.'

8. *Who will also confirm you.* The relative here applies not to Christ but to God, although the name of God is the more remote antecedent. For the apostle is continuing to express his joy, and just as he told them above what he felt about them, so now he shows what hope he has for their future; not only to make them feel even more assured of his affection for them, but also to encourage them, at the same time, by his own example, to lay hold of the same hope. It is as if he said: 'Even if you are in a state of suspense because you are expecting a salvation that has still to come, you ought to be certain, nevertheless, that the Lord will never give you up, but, on the contrary, that He will increase what He has begun in you, so that when that day will come, in which all must appear before the judgement seat of Christ (II Cor. 5.10) we may then be found blameless.'

Blameless. Paul teaches, in the letters to the Ephesians and Colossians, that the goal of our calling is that we might appear pure, and free from blame in the presence of Christ (Eph. 1.4; Col. 1.22). But we must note that such cleanness is not completed in us straight away, but rather it is

for our own good to go on making a daily practice of penitence, and
to go on being cleansed of our sins, which make us liable to the
punishment of God, until at last we put off, with 'the body of death'
(Rom. 7.24), all the uncleanness of sin. Of the day of the Lord we
shall speak in chapter 4.

God is faithful. When the Scripture calls God faithful it often means
His steadfastness, and His constant uniformity of character (*perpetuum
tenorem*), so that whatever God begins He carries through to completion.
Paul himself says (Rom. 11.29) 'the calling of God is irrevocable'.
Therefore, in my opinion, the meaning of this passage is that God is
unwavering in His purpose. Since that is so, He does not, therefore,
make fun of us in calling us, but He will maintain His work for ever.
Accordingly, because we experienced God's blessings in the past, we
should always have good hope for the future. But Paul turns his
attention higher, for he argues that the Corinthians cannot be thrown
aside, because they were once called by the Lord 'into fellowship with
Christ'. But in order to know what value this argument has, let us
notice first of all that everyone ought to see in his own calling evidence
of his election. Then, though one cannot judge with the same certainty
about another person's call, yet we must always decide, making our
judgement in love, that as many as are called, are called to salvation;
I mean both effectually and fruitfully. Paul was directing these words
to people in whom the Word of God had taken root, and in whom
some fruit was appearing as a result.

Should anyone object that many, who once received the Word,
afterwards fall away, I answer that the Spirit alone is the faithful and
sure witness to each person of his election, and on that perseverance
depends. I would reply further that this did not, however, prevent
Paul from being persuaded, in the judgement of love, that the call of
the Corinthians would be firm and unshakable, since he saw among
them signs of God's fatherly goodwill. Besides, those tokens do not
tend, by any means, to produce a mere sense of carnal security; for the
Scripture often warns us about our own weakness indeed, to drive
such a sense of security from us; but the purpose of those things is
rather to establish our confidence in the Lord.

Now, it was important for Paul to write this to prevent them from
being dejected when they came face to face with all the faults, that he
will reveal to them later on. All this could be summed up in the following way: sincere Christians should entertain good hopes about all who
have come onto the right way of salvation, and are staying the course,
even though they are still beset by many maladies. From the time he
is enlightened by the Spirit of God in the knowledge of Christ, each
one of us should, indeed, be quite convinced, that he has been adopted

by the Lord into the inheritance of eternal life. For effectual calling ought to be evidence to believers of God's adoption. In the meantime, however, we must all walk 'in fear and trembling' (Phil. 2.12). I shall make further reference to this matter in chapter 10.

Into the fellowship. Instead of this Erasmus has given the rendering, 'into partnership' (*consortium*). The Vulgate has 'society' (*societatem*). I have, however, preferred 'fellowship' (*communionem*), because it expresses better the force of the Greek word κοινωνία. For the whole purpose of the Gospel is that Christ be made ours, and that we be ingrafted into His body. But when the Father gives Him to us as a possession, He also imparts Himself to us in Christ, and because of this we really come to share in every blessing. Paul's argument is therefore: since you have been brought into fellowship with Christ through the Gospel, which you have received by faith, there is no reason for you to be afraid of the danger of death, since you have been made partakers of Him who rose, the Victor over death. In short, when the Christian looks at himself he can only have grounds for anxiety, indeed despair, but because he is called into fellowship with Christ, he can think of himself, in so far as assurance of salvation is concerned, in no other way than as a member of Christ, thus making all the blessings of Christ his own. In this way, he will lay hold of the certain hope of final perseverance (as it is called), if he looks upon himself as a member of Christ, who cannot possibly fail.

Now I beseech you, brethren, through the name of our Lord Jesus Christ, that ye all speak the same thing, and that there be no divisions among you; but that ye be perfected together in the same mind and in the same judgement. For it hath been signified unto me concerning you, my brethren, by them which are of the household of Chloe, that there are contentions among you. Now this I mean, that each one of you saith, I am of Paul; and I of Apollos; and I of Cephas; and I of Christ. Is Christ divided? was Paul crucified for you? or were ye baptized into the name of Paul? (10–13)

10. *Now I beseech you, brethren.* So far Paul has been treating the Corinthians gently, because he knew that they were far too sensitive. Now, after preparing their minds for rebuke, acting like a good, experienced surgeon, who touches the wound gently when a painful remedy must be used, Paul begins to handle them more severely. All the same he uses a good deal of moderation here too, as we shall see. This is the substance of what he is saying: 'It is my fervent hope that the Lord has not in vain bestowed so many gifts on you, without wishing to bring you to salvation. On the other hand, you ought also to be taking pains yourselves to prevent such excellent qualities being

24

polluted by your vices. Therefore see that you agree with one another. I have every justification for asking you to agree among yourselves, for I have received a report that you disagree even to the point of hostility; that factions and partisanship are fermenting among you, wrecking the true unity of faith.' But since mere exhortation might perhaps not be persuasive enough in their case, he turns to imploring them, for he begs them earnestly, in the name of Christ, as they love Him, to seek for harmony.

That ye all speak the same thing. In encouraging them to seek unity Paul expresses himself in three different ways. First of all, he asks for such agreement among them that all have one voice. Then he asks for the removal of the evil by which unity is torn asunder and destroyed. Thirdly, he describes the nature of true harmony, viz. that they might agree among themselves in mind and will. What Paul has put second is actually first in order, viz. that we should beware of divisions for, when we are, then something else will follow, viz. that we are in harmony. Then, finally, a third thing will certainly ensue, which is mentioned first here, that we all speak as if with one voice; and that is very desirable indeed, as the fruit of Christian harmony. Let us therefore take note that there is nothing more out of keeping for Christians than their being divided from each other. For the most important principle of our religion is this, that we be in concord among ourselves. Moreover, on this agreement the safety of the Church rests and depends.

But let us see what Paul looks for in Christian unity. If anyone wishes more exact distinctions, Paul wants them first of all to agree together in one mind; then in one judgement; and thirdly he wishes them to declare their agreement openly in words. But since my rendering is somewhat different from Erasmus' version, I would, in passing, bring to the attention of my readers that Paul uses a participle here, which means things which are fitly and suitably joined together. For the verb καταρτίζεσθαι, from which that participle κατηρτισμένος comes, properly means, 'to be joined', and 'to be united', in the same way as the members of the human body are joined together in a very well-balanced arrangement.

For *judgement* (*sententia*) Paul has γνώμην. But I take it here as referring to the will, so that the whole of the soul is brought into play, when the first clause (in one mind) is made to refer to faith, and the other (in one judgement) to love. Therefore Christian unity will be established in our midst, not only when we are in close agreement about teaching, but when we are also in harmony in our endeavours and wills, and so are of one mind in every respect. In the same way Luke bears witness to the faithful of the early Church, saying that they had 'one heart and one soul' (Acts 4.32). That will certainly be found wherever the Spirit of Christ reigns. When Paul tells them to speak the same thing, which is the fruit of unity, he is bringing out even more clearly how complete the agreement ought to be, viz. that not even in words should any diversity appear. This is certainly difficult to do, but all the same it is necessary among Christians, from whom there is asked not only one faith, but also one confession.

11. *For it hath been signified unto me.* Since general exhortations have often little effect, he begins to explain that what he had said applies in actual fact to them. Paul makes this application therefore, in order that the Corinthians might know that he has not made mention of agreement for nothing. For he shows, not only that they have turned aside from holy unity, but that they had fallen into disputes, which are more serious than differences of opinion. And in case he might be accused of being very credulous, in giving a ready ear to untrue complaints, he speaks well of those who had given him the information. They must have been highly regarded, since he did not hesitate to cite them as competent witnesses against the whole Church. But although it is by no means certain whether *Chloe* is the name of a place or a woman, it seems to me more likely that it is the name of a woman. I consider therefore that it was a well-ordered household that had told Paul of this malady in the Corinthian Church, wanting him to cure it. But to think, as many people do, following the lead of Chrysostom, that Paul refrained from using actual names, so as not to get them into trouble, seems absurd to me. For he does not say that any particular members of the household had reported this to him, but he rather refers to them all, and there is no doubt that they were very willing to be named. Further, in case he should irritate them by being too severe, he has mitigated the reproof by speaking in such a way as to win respect; and he has done so, not in order to make light of their trouble, but to make them more teachable, and so understand the seriousness of their malady.

12. *Now this I mean, that each one of you saith etc.* Some people think that there is an instance of imitation (μίμησις) here, as if Paul were repeating their actual words. Although the manuscripts vary in regard to the particle ὅτι, I think however that it is the conjunction ὅτι (because, for) rather than the relative pronoun ὅτι (which), so that there is merely an explanation of the preceding sentence here, as follows: The reason why I say that there are disputes among you, is because each one of you is glorying in the name of a man. But someone will object that those assertions do not in themselves give any indication of disputes. I reply that where divisions are rife in religion, it is bound to happen that what is in men's minds will soon erupt in real conflict. For while nothing is more effective for joining us together, and there is

nothing which does more to unite our minds, and keep them peaceful, than agreement in religion, yet if disagreement has somehow arisen in connexion with it, the inevitable result is that men are quickly stirred up to engage in fighting, and there is no other field with fiercer disputes. Therefore Paul is justified in bringing forward as sufficient proof of disputes the fact that the Corinthians were working in sects and factions.

I belong to Paul etc. He now mentions by name faithful servants of Christ, Apollos, who had been his successor at Corinth, and also Peter himself. Then he adds his own name to theirs lest he might otherwise appear to be doing more for his own cause, than for that of Christ. Yet, it is unlikely that there were any parties which were attached to one particular minister of those three, at the expense of the other two, since they were bound together in their ministry by a sacred agreement. But as he suggests later on (I Cor. 3.4 ff), he transferred to himself and Apollos what was applicable to others. He did that in order that they might find it easier to consider the issue itself, detached from consideration of the personalities involved.

But someone will point to the fact that he also mentions here those who publicly confessed that they 'belonged to Christ'. Did this also call for rebuke? I reply that in this way clearer expression is given to the really bad situation that develops from our wrong in giving our devotion to men. If that happens then Christ must necessarily rule only in a part of the Church, and believers have no alternative but to separate themselves from others, if they do not want to deny Christ.

But since this verse is twisted in various ways, it is only right that we should decide more exactly what Paul means here. He wishes to maintain that in the Church authority belongs to Christ alone, so that we may all be dependent on Him; that He alone may be called Lord and Master among us, so that the name of no other person may be set up in rivalry to His. Therefore Paul condemns those who draw away followers after themselves, and so split the Church into sects, for he looks upon them as enemies who destroy our faith. Accordingly he does not allow men to have such predominance in the Church, that they usurp the Lordship of Christ. Those men are not to be honoured in such a way as to detract, even in the slightest degree, from the dignity of Christ. Ministers of Christ must have their due honour, of course. They are also masters in their own way; but this qualification must always be kept in mind, that what belongs to Christ might remain unimpaired, viz. that He is nevertheless the one and only Master, and is to be thought of as such. For that reason good ministers make the following things their aim: to serve Christ, all of them alike, claiming for Him alone dominion, authority and glory; to fight under His banner; to obey Him alone, and to bring others under His sway. If anyone is mastered by ambition, he wins followers, not for Christ, but for himself. Therefore this is the source of all evils, this is the most harmful of all diseases, this is the deadly poison in all churches—when ministers are devoted to their own interests rather than to Christ's. In short, the unity of the Church rests mainly on this one thing: that we all depend on Christ alone, and that men therefore take, and remain in, a lower place, so that nothing may detract from His position of pre-eminence.

13. *Is Christ divided?* This intolerable evil followed from the divisions that existed among the Corinthians. For only Christ ought to rule in the Church. And since the purpose of the Gospel is that we might be reconciled to God through Him, it is necessary first of all, that we should all be bound together in Him. Only a very few of the Corinthians, wiser than the others, continued to acknowledge Christ as their Master. All of them however boasted that they were Christians. In that way Christ was being torn to pieces. For we ought to be one body, if we want to be kept together under Him, as under the Head. For if we are split into different bodies we also break away from Him. To glory in His name in the midst of disagreements and parties is to tear Him in pieces. That cannot in fact be done. For never will He Himself turn away from unity and harmony, because 'He cannot deny Himself' (II Tim. 2.13). Having placed this contradictory situation before them, Paul wishes to make the Corinthians understand that they are alienated from Christ, because of their divisions. For He reigns in our midst, only when He is the means of binding us together in an inviolable union.

Was Paul crucified for you? Paul uses two powerful arguments to show how unworthy it is to wrest from Christ His place of honour as sole Head of the Church, sole Teacher, sole Master; or to take away any part of that honour from Him and transfer it to men. The first reason is that we have been redeemed by Christ on the principle that we are not under our own jurisdiction. Paul uses this very argument in his Letter to the Romans 14.9, when he says, 'For to this end Christ died and rose again, that He might be Lord both of the living and the dead'. Therefore let us live to Him, and die to Him, because we are His always. Again, in chapter 7.23 of this letter he writes: 'You have been bought with a price, do not become slaves of men.' Therefore, since the Corinthians had been purchased by the blood of Christ, they were, in a sense, renouncing the blessing of redemption, so long as they were making other people their heads. This is a remarkable piece of teaching: 'No authority lies with us to let ourselves pass under subjection to men, since we are the Lord's own property.' Therefore he accuses the Corinthians here of the greatest ingratitude, because they were alienating themselves from that Head, by whose blood they had been redeemed; however ignorantly they may have done so.

Further, this verse wrecks the wicked invention of the Papists, which they use to try to bolster up their system of indulgences. For from the blood of Christ and the martyrs they make up that counterfeit treasury of the Church, which, they teach, is dispensed by indulgences. They pretend that by their deaths the martyrs meritoriously gained something for us in the sight of God, so that we might ask help from this source to obtain remission of our sins. They will deny that that makes the martyrs our redeemers. But nothing is clearer than that the one thing follows from the other. It is a question of reconciling sinners to God; it is a question of obtaining forgiveness; it is a question of appeasing the wrath of the Lord; it is a question of atoning for offences. They boast that all that is to be done partly by the blood of Christ, and partly by the blood of the martyrs. Therefore they make the martyrs partners with Christ in winning our salvation. But here Paul is denying strongly that any other but Christ was crucified on our behalf. The martyrs did indeed die for our benefit, but (as Leo says) it was to give an example in steadfastness, not to acquire the gift of righteousness for us.

Or were you baptized into the name of Paul? His second argument is taken from the profession of baptism. For we enlist into the service of Him, in whose name we are baptized. In this way we are bound to Christ, in whose name our baptism is consecrated. From this it follows that the Corinthians can be accused of faithlessness and desertion, if they yield themselves in subjection to men.

Notice that the nature of baptism is like a bond of mutual contract, for as the Lord by that symbol receives us into His household, and adds us to His people, so we put ourselves under the obligation of faithfulness to Him, and may never have any other spiritual Lord. Accordingly, as God on His part makes a covenant of grace with us, in which He promises remission of sins and new life, so on our part there is an oath to wage spiritual warfare, by which we promise allegiance to Him forever. Paul does not deal with the first part here, because the context did not call for it; but in dealing with baptism it should not be omitted. In fact Paul is not so much accusing the Corinthians of desertion, because of their leaving Christ and turning to men, but he is pointing out that the very fact that they are not holding fast to Christ, and Christ alone, would make them breakers of the covenant.

The question is asked: what does it mean to be *baptized in the name of Christ?* I reply that this way of speaking means not only that baptism is founded on the authority of Christ, but also that it rests on His power, and in a sense consists in that; and finally that the whole effect of it depends on the fact that the name of Christ is invoked in it. But another question will be asked. Why does Paul say that the Corinthians have been baptized in the name of Christ, when Christ Himself directed the apostles to baptize in the name of the Father, and the Son, and the Holy Spirit? My answer is that in dealing with baptism our first consideration is the fact that God the Father, having placed us by His unmerited goodness in His Church, receives us by adoption into the fellowship of His sons. Secondly, because no union is possible for us with Him except by reconciliation, we need Christ to restore us to the Father's favour by His blood. Thirdly, because we are consecrated to God by baptism, we also need the intervention of the Holy Spirit, whose function it is to make us new creatures. It is indeed His special work to wash us in the blood of Christ; but because we only obtain the mercy of the Father, or the grace of the Spirit, by Christ alone, we have good grounds for calling Him the proper object (*scopum*) of baptism, and we associate baptism with His name in particular. Yet this does not in the least cut out the names of the Father and the Spirit. For when we wish to speak briefly about the efficacy of baptism we mention the name of Christ alone; but when we want to be more precise we must bring in the names of the Father and the Spirit also.

I thank God that I baptized none of you, save Crispus and Gaius; lest any man should say that ye were baptized into my name. And I baptized also the household of Stephanas: besides, I know not whether I baptized any other. For Christ sent me not to baptize, but to preach the gospel: not in wisdom of words, lest the Cross of Christ should be made void. For the word of the cross is to them that are perishing foolishness; but unto us which are being saved it is the power of God. For it is written, I will destroy the wisdom of the wise, And the prudence of the prudent will I reject. Where is the wise? where is the scribe? where is the disputer of this world? hath not God made foolish the wisdom of the world? (14-20)

14. *I thank God.* In these words Paul sharply rebukes the perverseness of the Corinthians, for it made it necessary for him to avoid, to some extent, the holy and honourable administration of baptism. Indeed Paul would have acted within his rights, and in accordance with the nature of his office, if he had baptized a great many people. But he rejoices that it fell out differently, and he is aware that it was done by God's providence, in case they might make it a ground for taking pride in him, or in case he might bear some resemblance to those ambitious men, who were, in this way, on the look-out for followers. But what if he had baptized many? There would have been nothing wrong in it; but (as I have said) a severe reproach against the Corinth-

ians and their false apostles is involved in the fact that a servant of the Lord had to rejoice that he had to refrain from a work, otherwise good and valuable, to prevent it becoming a means of causing harm to them.

17. *For Christ sent me not etc.* Paul takes up a possible objection against him, viz. that he had not carried out what he should have done, in view of the fact that Christ commands His apostles to baptize as well as teach. Therefore he replies that these functions did not have equal priority as far as his office was concerned; rather, the task of teaching had been laid upon him as the principal one, to which he must devote himself. For when Christ says to the apostles, 'Go, preach and baptize' (Matt. 28.19; Mark 16.15), He joins baptism to teaching, simply as an addition or appendage, so that teaching always holds the first place.

Two things however must be noticed here. The first is this, that the apostle does not here deny that he had a command to baptize. For the words, *Go, baptize,* apply to all the apostles, and he would have been presumptuous in baptizing even one man without having been given the authority to do so. What he does here is simply to point out the chief thing in his calling. The second point is this: he does not by any means lessen the worth and effect of baptism here, as some think. For Paul is not dealing with the efficacy of baptism here, and does not make this comparison in order to detract from its efficacy in any way. But since the gift of teaching belonged to a few, while many were allowed to baptize, and further, since many could be taught at one time, while baptism could only be administered to individuals one at a time, Paul, who excelled in the ability to teach, was pursuing the work which it seemed more necessary for him to do, and he was leaving to others what they could do better. Again, if readers will consider all the circumstances more closely, they will see that tacit irony underlies this, for he wittily bites at those who seek a little glory at the expense of another person's labour, under the pretext of a religious ceremony. For Paul's labour in the building of that church had been incredible. Certain easy-going teachers had come after him, who had drawn disciples into their sects by the sprinkling of water. Paul therefore surrenders the title of honour (*honoris*) to them, and asserts that he is content to have the onerous work (*onere*).

Not in the wisdom of words. This anticipates and refutes two objections. For those misguided teachers could infer that Paul, who had no gift of eloquence, was making a ridiculous boast in claiming that the role of teacher had been laid on him. For that reason he says, by way of concession, that he was not a born orator, who might blazon himself in a splendour of words, but a minister of the Spirit, a servant, who, with unpolished and ordinary speech, might bring down the wisdom of the world. Again, someone might object that he was seeking after glory in proclaiming the Gospel, just as much as others were seeking it by baptizing. To that he answers briefly that since the method of teaching, which he followed, was free of all brilliance, and revealed not a trace of ambition, it could not be suspect on that score. If I am not mistaken, we can also clearly gather from this the principal feature of the controversy which Paul was having with the bad and unfaithful ministers of the Corinthians, viz. since they were swollen with ambition, they wanted to rush the people into admiration of them, and did it by ingratiating themselves with them by a show of words and a mask (*larva*) of human wisdom.

From this main evil two others follow. (1) By those things, which we might call disguises, the simplicity of the Gospel was deformed, and Christ was clothed, as it were, in a new and foreign garb, so that the pure and genuine knowledge of Him was hidden from view. Further (2) because men's minds were turned to the brilliancy and fineness of words, to clever speculations, to an empty show of rather uplifted teaching, the power of the Spirit vanished, and nothing was left except the dead letter. The majesty of God, which shines out in the Gospel, was blanked out, and, instead, only purple and fruitless pomp was visible.

Therefore, in order to censure those corruptions of the Gospel, Paul makes a transition here to the manner of his preaching. He asserts that his way of preaching is right and legitimate, although it is, at the same time, diametrically opposed to the ostentation of those self-seeking men. It is as though he said: 'I know how much those easy-going teachers of yours coax you with their high-sounding language. For my part, not only do I confess that my preaching is done in a style that is unpolished, clumsy, and far from cultivated, but I even glory in it. For it ought to have been like that, and indeed this method was prescribed to me by God.'

By the *wisdom of words* he does not mean verbal legerdemain (λογοδαιδάλιαν), which is mere empty talk, but true eloquence, which consists in skilful choice of subjects, in clever arrangement, and fineness of style. He declares that he did not have that, indeed that for his preaching it was neither suitable nor useful.

Lest the Cross of Christ should be made void. As Paul had so often before set the name of Christ in contrast to the proud wisdom of the flesh, so he now plants the Cross of Christ right in the centre, in order to dethrone all the haughtiness and superiority of that wisdom. For all the wisdom of believers is concentrated in the Cross of Christ. And is there anything more contemptible than a Cross? Therefore he who would be truly wise in the things of God must necessarily stoop to the humility of the Cross. This will only be done by first of all renouncing his own understanding of things, and all the wisdom of the world. Indeed Paul is teaching here not only what sort of men the disciples of Christ ought to be, and the proper way by which they ought to learn, but also what the method of teaching should be in the school of Christ. 'The Cross of Christ would have been rendered useless,' he says, 'if my preaching had been tricked out with eloquence and brilliance.' He has used the Cross of Christ for the benefit of salvation, which must be sought from Christ crucified. But the teaching of the Gospel, which calls us to that benefit, ought to suggest the nature of the Cross, so that, instead of being glorious, it might rather be despised and worthless, in the eyes of the world. The meaning therefore is that if Paul had used the acuteness of a philosopher and clever speeches in his dealings with the Corinthians, the power of the Cross of Christ, in which the salvation of men consists, would have been buried, because it cannot reach us in that way.

Two questions are raised here. (1) Does Paul, in this verse, completely condemn the wisdom of words as something in opposition to Christ? (2) Does he mean that the teaching of the Gospel must always be kept distinct from eloquence, so that they cannot come together, and that the preaching of the Gospel is spoiled, if any suggestion of eloquence is used to dress it up attractively?

To the first question I answer that Paul would not be so very unreasonable as to condemn out of hand those arts, which, without any doubt, are splendid gifts of God, gifts which we could call instruments for helping men carry out worth-while activities. Therefore there is nothing irreligious about those arts, for they contain sound learning, and depend on principles of truth; and since they are useful and suitable for the general affairs of human society, there is no doubt that they have come from the Holy Spirit. Further, the usefulness which is derived and experienced from them ought not to be ascribed to anyone but God. Therefore what Paul says here is not to be taken as disparaging to the arts, as if they were working against religion.

The second question is a little more difficult. For Paul says that the Cross of Christ is made void, if it is mixed up in any way with the wisdom of words. My answer to that is that we must pay attention to those to whom Paul is speaking. For the ears of the Corinthians were itching with a foolish eagerness for high-sounding talk. Therefore they needed to be called back to the humility of the Cross more than other people, so that they might learn to lay hold of Christ alone, and the Gospel in its simplicity, free from any adulteration. However I think that in some measure this viewpoint has a permanent validity, viz. that the Cross of Christ is made void, not only by the wisdom of the world, but also by the brilliance of words. For the preaching of Christ is bare and simple; therefore it ought not to be obscured by an overlying disguise of words. The characteristic work of the Gospel is to bring down the wisdom of the world in such a manner, that, deprived of our own understanding we become completely docile, and do not consider knowing, or even desire to know anything but what the Lord Himself teaches. As far as the wisdom of men is concerned, we shall have to give fuller consideration, later on, as to the way it is opposed to Christ. But I shall speak briefly about eloquence here, giving it as much attention as the passage demands.

We realize that from the beginning God has so arranged it, that the Gospel should be handled stripped of any support from eloquence. Could not He who designs the tongues of men for eloquence, be Himself skilful in speech if He wished? While He could be so, He did not choose to be so. I can find two most important reasons for His unwillingness. The *first* is that the majesty of His truth might be all the clearer in the setting of unpolished and unrefined language, and the efficacy of His Spirit might penetrate the minds of men, by itself, without external aids. The *second* reason is that He might put our obedience and teachableness the better to the test, and, at the same time, instruct us in the way of true humility. For the Lord admits only little ones to His school. Therefore the only persons capable of heavenly wisdom are those who are content with the preaching of the Gospel, though it may be worthless in appearance, and who have no wish that Christ be covered over with a disguise (*larvatum*). Therefore the teaching of the Gospel had to be made to serve the purpose of drawing believers away from all arrogance and haughtiness.

But what if someone in our day speaks in rather brilliant fashion, and makes the teaching of the Gospel sparkle with his eloquence? Should he be rejected on that account, as if he spoiled it, or obscured the glory of Christ? I answer first of all that eloquence is not in conflict with the simplicity of the Gospel at all, when, free from contempt of the Gospel, it not only gives it first place, and is subject to it, but also serves it as a handmaid serves her mistress. For, as Augustine says, 'He who gave Peter, the fisherman, also gave Cyprian, the orator.' He means by that, that both men are from God, although the one, who is much the superior in authority, lacks any attractiveness of speech, while the other, who sits at his feet, is famous for his outstanding eloquence. We must not condemn or reject the kind of eloquence which does not aim at captivating Christians with an outward brilliancy of words, or at intoxicating them with empty delights, or at tickling their ears with its jingle, or at covering up the *Cross of Christ* with its ostentation. No, we must not condemn or reject it, because, on the other hand, its aim

is to call us back to the original simplicity of the Gospel, to set on high
the preaching of the Cross and nothing else by humbling itself of its
own accord, and, finally, to carry out, as it were, the duties of a herald,
to obtain a hearing for those fishermen and uneducated common
people, who have nothing attractive about them except the power of
the Spirit.

In the second place I reply that the Spirit of God has also an eloquence
of His own. It shines with a splendour that is natural to it, peculiar to
itself, to use a better word, intrinsic (as they say), more than with
assumed rhetorical ornaments. Prophets have such eloquence, particularly Isaiah, David and Solomon. Moses also has a sprinkling of it.
Indeed even if the writings of the apostles are not so polished, yet a few
tiny sparks of it flash out at times there too. It follows that the eloquence, which is in keeping with the Spirit of God, is not bombastic
and ostentatious, and does not make a lot of noise that amounts to
nothing. Rather, it is genuine and efficacious, and has more sincerity
than refinement.

18. *For the word of the cross.* Paul makes a concession in the first
clause. For, since it was easy to object that the Gospel is regarded with
contempt everywhere, if it is made known in such a bare and insignificant way, Paul of his own accord grants as much. But when he adds
that that is the view of those who are perishing, he means that very
little value must be put on their opinion. For who would want to
condemn the Gospel at the cost of perishing? Therefore this sentence
ought to be understood like this: 'The preaching of the Cross is
regarded as foolishness by those who are perishing, just because it does
not have the attractiveness of human wisdom to commend it. Be that
as it may; in our view, however, the wisdom of God is shining from
it.' Paul, however, is indirectly censuring the bad judgement of the
Corinthians, who were easily attracted by the alluring words of self-
seeking teachers, and yet looked scornfully on the apostle of God, who
was endowed with the power of God for their salvation, and they did
so simply because he devoted himself to the preaching of Christ. How
the preaching of the Cross is the power of God unto salvation, I bring
out in my comments on Romans 1.16.

19. *For it is written, etc.* By using the testimony of Isaiah Paul proves
still further how wrong it is that the truth of the Gospel should be
hampered by the prejudice arising from the fact that the wise men of
the world laugh at it, indeed hold it up for contempt. For it is plain
from the prophet's words that their opinion counts for nothing in the
eyes of God. The words are taken from Isaiah 29.14, where the Lord
declares that He will avenge Himself, because of the hypocrisy of the
people, with this particular kind of punishment, that 'wisdom will

perish from the wise' etc. Now that applies to the situation with which Paul is dealing, in this way: It is nothing new or unusual for men, who otherwise seem to be outstanding in their discretion, to make such absurd judgements. For the Lord has been accustomed to punish in this way the arrogance of those who rely with confidence on their own natural ability, and desire to be their own guides and the guides of other people. In this way He once destroyed the wisdom of the leaders of Israel. If this happened to that people, whose wisdom the other nations were supposed to look up to, what will be the fate of others?

We ought however to compare the words of the prophet with those of Paul, and to examine the whole matter still more closely. Although the prophet uses neuter verbs when he says 'wisdom will perish and prudence will vanish', while Paul converts them into the active, making God the subject, they agree fully in meaning however. For God attests that He will bring about this great wonder, so that all may be moved to astonishment. So 'wisdom perishes' but it is by God's act of destruction; 'wisdom vanishes', but it is spread over and obliterated by God. Now the second verb (ἀθετεῖν), which Erasmus renders *reiicere*, 'to reject', is ambiguous, and is sometimes taken to mean, 'to efface' (*delere*), or 'blot out' (*expungere*), or 'obliterate' (*obliterare*). That is the sense I prefer to take it in, so as to correspond to the word of the prophet, 'to vanish' or 'be hidden'. Nevertheless this reason had a greater influence with me, viz. that the idea of rejecting did not agree with the subject matter, as will soon be apparent. Let us look into the meaning, therefore. The prophet wants to make it very clear that they will no longer have governors, with rightful qualifications for ruling, because the Lord will take away from them sound judgement and intelligence. For just as he threatens the whole people with blindness in another passage (Isa. 6.10), so here it is the leaders, and it is just as if He were plucking out the eyes from the body.

However that may be, a great difficulty arises from the fact that the terms 'wisdom' and 'prudence' are taken by Isaiah in a good sense, but Paul quotes them with quite a different purpose in mind, as if the wisdom of men is condemned by God because it is perverse, and their prudence rejected because it is futile. I agree that that is the usual explanation, but as it is certain that the words of the Holy Spirit are not twisted into other meanings by the apostles, I prefer to depart from the common opinion of the interpreters, rather than accuse Paul of distorting the truth. And in other respects the genuine meaning of the prophet's words do not fit in badly with Paul's intention. For if even the wisest become foolish when the Lord takes away a right spirit, how much faith will be placed in the wisdom of men? Further, since God's usual way of avenging is to strike with blindness those who are bound to their own way of understanding, and are exceedingly wise in their own eyes, it is not surprising that when carnal men rise up against God, to make His eternal truth give place to their presumptuousness they become fools, and futile in their thinking. Now we see how apposite is Paul's use of this testimony. Isaiah declares that the punishment of God on all those who honoured God with what they produce themselves, is that 'wisdom would vanish from their wise men'. Paul makes use of this testimony of Isaiah's in order to prove that the wisdom of this world is useless and valueless, when it lifts itself up against God.

20. *Where is the wise man? where is the scribe?* This taunting note is added by way of illustration of the prophet's testimony. Paul has certainly not taken this sentence from Isaiah, as is commonly thought, but is expressing his own thought. For the passage in Isaiah, 33.18, which people refer to, has no similarity or relation at all to the present argument. For since Isaiah is there promising the Jews delivery from the yoke of Sennacherib, in order to show them all the more clearly what a great blessing from God that is, he then goes on to remind them of the wretched condition of those who are oppressed by the tyranny of foreigners. He says that they live in a constant state of agitated uncertainty, as they think of themselves being threatened by scribes and treasurers, weighers of tribute and counters of towers. More than that, he says that the Jews had been in such critical situations, that they are moved to gratitude in recalling them to mind. It is therefore a mistake to think that this sentence is taken from the prophet.

The words 'of this world' ought to be taken not only with the last term ('disputer') but should also be connected with the other two nouns ('wise man' and 'scribe'). For he calls the wise of this world those who are not enlightened in wisdom by the Word of God through the Spirit, but, being endowed with worldly insight only, place their trust in that.

It is usually accepted that the word 'scribes' means teachers. For, since סָפַר means in Hebrew 'to tell' or 'recount', and the noun derived from it סֵפֶר means a 'book' or 'volume', they call men of learning and those familiar with books, סוֹפְרִים. For that reason also *sopher regis* often occurs for a chancellor or secretary. Then the Greeks, following the etymology of the Hebrew word, translated it γραμματεῖς, *scribes*.

Paul appropriately calls disputers those who display sharpness in handling thorny problems and intricate questions. So, generally speaking, he brings down all the natural ability of men, so that it counts for nothing in the kingdom of God. And he has good grounds for speaking so.vehemently against human wisdom. For no words can describe how difficult it is to tear away from men's minds their misplaced confidence in the flesh, so that they may not arrogate to themselves more than is due. But it is going too far, if, relying even in the slightest degree on their own wisdom, they dare to form or pass judgements on their own.

Hath not God made foolish the wisdom of the world? By *wisdom*, Paul means here whatever man can comprehend, not only by his own natural mental ability, but also by the help of experience, scholarship, and knowledge of the arts. For he contrasts the wisdom of the world, with the wisdom of the Spirit. It follows that whatever knowledge a man may come by, apart from the enlightening of the Holy Spirit, is included in the wisdom of this world. He says that God has made all that ridiculous, or condemned it as foolish. You must think of that as done in two ways. For whatever knowledge and understanding a man has counts for nothing unless it rests upon true wisdom; and it is of no more value for grasping spiritual teaching than the eye of a blind man for distinguishing colours. Both of these must be carefully attended to, that (1) knowledge of all the sciences is so much smoke apart from the heavenly science of Christ; and (2) that man with all his shrewdness is as stupid about understanding by himself the mysteries of God as an ass is incapable of understanding musical harmony. For, in this way, Paul gives the lie to the consuming pride of those who exult in the wisdom of this world, so that they despise Christ and the whole teaching of salvation, thinking that they are happy if they cling to the things of this world. He also checks the arrogance of those who, trusting in their own capability, seek to penetrate into heaven.

At the same time an answer is given to the question, how it comes about that Paul throws to the ground, in this way, every kind of knowledge which exists apart from Christ, and, as it were, tramples under his feet what is well known to be the chief gift of God in this world. For what is more noble than the reason of man, by which he stands out far above all other animals? How greatly deserving of honour are the liberal sciences, which refine man in such a way as to make him truly human! Besides, what a great number of rare products they yield! Who would not use the highest praise to extol statesmanship, by which states, empires and kingdoms are maintained?—to say nothing of other things! I maintain that the answer to this question is obvious from the fact that Paul does not utterly condemn, either the natural insight of men, or wisdom gained by practice and experience, or education of the mind through learning; but what he affirms is that all those things are useless for obtaining spiritual wisdom. And it is certainly madness for any one to presume to ascend to heaven, relying on his own acumen, or the help of learning; in other words, to investigate the secret mysteries of the Kingdom of God, or force his way through to a knowledge of them, for they are hidden from human perception. Let us therefore take note that we ought to confine to the circumstances of the present case what Paul teaches here about the futility of the wisdom of this world, viz. that it remains on the level of this world but does not reach to heaven at all. It is also true, in other ways, that apart from Christ every branch of human knowledge is futile, and the man, who is well grounded in every aspect of learning, but is yet ignorant of God, has nothing. Furthermore, this must also be said, in all truth, that these fine gifts of God: quickness of mind, shrewd judgement, liberal sciences, knowledge of languages, all are in some way spoiled, whenever they fall into the hands of ungodly men.

For seeing that in the wisdom of God the world through its wisdom knew not God, it was God's good pleasure through the foolishness of the preaching to save them that believe. Seeing that Jews ask for signs, and Greeks seek after wisdom: but we preach Christ crucified, unto Jews a stumblingblock, and unto Gentiles foolishness; but unto them that are called, both Jews and Greeks, Christ the power of God, and the wisdom of God. Because the foolishness of God is wiser than men; and the weakness of God is stronger than men. (21-25)

21. *For since the world did not know.* The right order of things was surely this, that man, contemplating the wisdom of God in His works, by aid of the innate light of his own natural ability (*ingenita sibi ingenii luce*), might come to a knowledge of Him. But because this order has been inverted by man's perverseness God's will is, first of all, to make us foolish in our own eyes, before He begins to instruct us in the way of salvation. Thereafter, as evidence of His wisdom, He brings before us what has a certain appearance of foolishness. The ingratitude of men deserved this inversion of things. Paul describes as the wisdom of God, the fashioning of the whole world, which is splendid evidence of His wisdom, for it presents it so clearly to us. In the things that He has created God therefore holds out to us a clear mirror of His wonderful wisdom. As a result, any man, who has even a spark of sound judgement, and pays attention to the earth and the other works of God, is bound to burst out in admiration of Him. If men were led to true knowledge of God by observation of His works, they would come to know God in a way that is wise, or by a way of acquiring wisdom that is natural and appropriate to them. But because the whole world learnt nothing at all from what God revealed of His wisdom in created things, He then set about teaching men in another way. It must be put down to our own fault that we do not reach a saving knowledge of God, before we are emptied of our own understanding.

Paul makes a concession when he calls the Gospel the *foolishness of preaching*, for that is precisely the light in which it is regarded by those 'foolish wise men' (μωροσόφοις), who, intoxicated by a false confidence, have no fears about subjecting the inviolable truth of God to their own feeble censorship. And besides, there is no doubt that human reason finds nothing more absurd than the news that God became a mortal man, that life is submissive to death, that righteousness has been concealed under the likeness of sin, that the source of blessing has been subjected to the curse, that by this means men might be redeemed from death and be made sharers in blessed immortality, that they might gain possession of life, that, sin being abolished, righteousness might reign, that death and the curse might be swallowed up. All the same, we know that the Gospel is, in the meantime, hidden wisdom, which surpasses the heavens in its height, and at which even the angels are astonished. This is a very fine passage, and from it we can plainly see how great is the blindness of the human mind, which, surrounded by light, perceives nothing. For it is true that this world is like a theatre in which the Lord shows to us a striking spectacle of His glory. However, when such a sight lies open before our eyes, we are quite blind, not because the revelation is obscure, but because we are 'alienated in mind' (*mente alienati*, Col. 1.21), meaning that not only the will but also the power for this activity fails us. For notwithstanding that God shows Himself openly, yet it is only by the eye of faith that we can look at Him, bearing in mind that we receive only a slight inkling as to His divine nature, but enough to put us in the position of being without excuse (Rom. 1.20).

Therefore, since Paul says here that God cannot be known from things He has made, we must take him to mean that a pure knowledge of God cannot be obtained. So that no-one can fall back on the excuse of ignorance, men make progress in the universal school of nature to the point that they are impressed with some awareness of deity, but they have no idea what God's nature is. On the contrary their thinking immediately falls away to nothing, and so light shines in darkness. It follows therefore that men do not go wrong by mere ignorance, so as to be free of the charge of contempt, negligence and ingratitude. So it is indeed true that 'all have known God (*Deum novisse*), but did not give glory to Him' (Rom. 1.21); and, on the other hand, nobody, under the guidance of nature, has ever made such progress as to come to know God (*Deum cognosceret*). If anyone puts forward philosophers as exceptions to this, I reply, that in their case especially there is a conspicuous example of our weakness. For you cannot find one of them who has not constantly fallen away from that principle of knowledge which I have already mentioned, to wanderings and misleading speculations. They are mostly sillier than old wives! When Paul says that 'believers are saved', this corresponds with verse 18, that 'the gospel is the power of God for salvation' (Rom. 1.16). Again, by contrasting believers, whose number is small, with a blind and foolish world, Paul is reminding us that we are wrong to be upset by their small number, since they have been set apart 'for salvation' by act of God.

22-23. *Seeing that Jews ask for signs etc.* This explains the previous sentence, i.e. he is showing in what way the preaching of the Gospel is thought of as foolishness. However, not only does he explain it, but he also enlarges on it by saying that the Jews do more than put small value on the Gospel, for they detest it as well. 'The Jews', Paul says, 'want to have evidence of the divine power before their eyes in the form of miracles. The Greeks love what has the attraction of acuteness, and so pleases human cleverness. We in fact preach Christ crucified, and, at first glance, there seems to be nothing in that but weakness and foolishness. Therefore it is a stumblingblock to the Jews, to see Him, seemingly forsaken by God. The Greeks think it is like a fable to hear that this was the way of redemption.' In my opinion Paul means by the term *Greeks*, not simply the heathen or Gentiles, but those who were educated in the liberal sciences, or who were outstanding because of their superior intelligence. However, by synecdoche, all the others are also included in it.

Then he draws a distinction between the Jews and the Greeks. When the Jews attacked Christ in their extravagant zeal for the Law, they raved in a storm of fury against the Gospel—just as hypocrites always do when they are fighting for their own wrong beliefs (*superstitionibus*). The Greeks, on the other hand, swollen with pride, despised Him as if He was insipid.

The fact that Paul finds fault with the Jews for being so eager in desiring signs does not mean that it is wrong in itself to demand them. But he shows where they were wrong, in the following points, (1) by their repeated urgent demands for miracles they were, in a sense, pressing God under their laws; (2) through the dullness of their understanding they were wanting to have palpable contact with Him in open miracles; (3) being mesmerized by the miracles themselves they looked on them with astonishment; (4) in short, no miracles would satisfy them, but every day they were on the continual, eager look-out for new ones. For Hezekiah is not rebuked because he readily consented to be encouraged by a sign (II Kings 19.29; 20.8). Even Gideon was not reproached, though he sought a double sign (Judges 6.37, 39). But, on the other hand, Ahaz is condemned because he rejected the sign offered him by the prophet (Isaiah 7.12). Therefore, why were the Jews doing wrong in seeking for miracles? Because they were not seeking them for a good purpose; they were putting no limit to their demands; and were not making good use of them. For while faith ought to be helped by miracles, they were only trying hard for a way to remain in their unbelief. While it is unlawful to lay down the law to God, in their monstrous desire they knew no licence. While miracles ought to guide us to knowledge of Christ, and the spiritual grace of God, they were an obstacle to the Jews. For this reason also, Christ Himself rebukes them, saying, 'a perverse generation seeks for a sign' (Mark 8.12). For there were no bounds to their curiosity, and their persistent demanding; and as often as they had obtained miracles, they were none the better for them.

24. *Both Greeks and Jews.* Paul shows by this antithesis how badly Christ is received, and that this does not come about by His fault, or by the natural inclination of mankind, but that its cause lies in the perverseness of those who had not been enlightened by God. For no stumblingblock prevents the elect of God, whether Jews or Gentiles, from coming to Christ, so as to find assurance of salvation in Him. Paul contrasts power with the stumblingblock, which arose from the humility of Christ, and he sets wisdom over against foolishness. The substance of it is therefore this: 'I know that nothing but signs can have any effect on the stubbornness of the Jews, and that in reality only an empty kind of wisdom can soften the scornful contempt of the Greeks. We ought, however, to place no importance on this fact, seeing that, no matter how our Christ offends the Jews with the humility of His Cross, and is laughed to scorn by the Greeks, He is, nevertheless, for all the elect, of every nation, both the power of God for salvation, for overcoming these stumblingblocks, and the wisdom of God for taking away what masquerades (*larvam*) as wisdom.'

25. *For the foolishness of God.* When the Lord deals with us in such a way that He seems to act in an absurd way because He does not make His wisdom plain to see, nevertheless what appears to be foolishness surpasses in wisdom all the shrewdness of men. Further, when God hides His power and seems to act in a weak way, what is imagined to be weakness is nevertheless stronger than any power of men. But we must always take note, in looking at these words, that there is a concession, as I noted a little earlier. For anyone can see quite clearly how improper it is to ascribe either foolishness or weakness to God, but it was necessary to use such ironic expressions in rebutting the insane arrogance of the flesh which does not hesitate to strip God of all His glory.

For behold your calling, brethren, how that not many wise after the flesh, not many mighty, not many noble, are called: but God chose the foolish things of the world, that he might put to shame them that are wise; and God chose the weak things of the world, that he might put to shame the things that are strong; and the base things of the world, and the things that are despised, did God choose, yea and the things that are not, that he might bring to nought the things that are: that no flesh should glory before God. But of him are ye in Christ Jesus, who was made unto us wisdom from God, and righteousness and sanctification, and redemption: that, according as it is written, He that glorieth, let him glory in the Lord. (26–31)

26-27. *Look at your own call etc.* Because there is doubt about the mood of the Greek verb (βλέπετε), the indicative suiting the context just as well as the imperative, I leave it to the reader to decide which he prefers. However the meaning is obviously the same in both moods, for by using the indicative 'you see', Paul would be calling them to witness, as it were, something obvious, and be confronting them, as it were, with something on the spot. But, on the other hand, by using the imperative he would be rousing them up, as if they were listless, to consider this very matter.

Call can be taken collectively as the company of those called, like this: 'You see the kind of persons, in your fellowship, whom the Lord has called.' But I am more inclined to think that the manner of their calling is being pointed out. And that is a most powerful argument, because it follows from it, that if they despise the humility of the Cross, then, in a sense, they are nullifying their call; for in their call God had maintained His method of taking away all honour from human wisdom and power and glory. Therefore Paul tacitly accuses them of ingratitude, because, forgetting both the grace of God, and themselves, they treat the Gospel of Christ with scorn.

Two things must be observed here, however. (1) He wished to use the example of the Corinthians to confirm the truth of what he had said. (2) He wished to warn them that they must be completely divested of all pride, if they were paying proper attention to the kind of procedure which the Lord had followed in calling them. Paul says He did it 'to put the wise and high-born to shame', and 'to destroy the things that are'. Both expressions are very suitable, for strength and wisdom vanish when they are put to shame; and what has existence must be destroyed. He means that God preferred to call the poor and foolish and the obscure of birth, before the great and wise and high-born. Had God treated all on equal terms, that would never have sufficed for the breaking of human arrogance. So He pushes aside those who appeared to be superior, so that He might really reduce them in standing.

D   43

However, it would be foolish for anyone to infer from this that God has overthrown the glory of the flesh in this way, so that the great and wise might be debarred from the hope of salvation. There are some irresponsible people who not only make this an excuse for insulting the great, as if they were abandoned by God, but, when they compare them with their own situation, also despise them. Let us remember however that this was said to the Corinthians, who, although they had no great standing in the world, were proud all the same, even when they had no occasion to be so. Therefore in putting the strong and wise and great to shame, God does not exalt the weak and uneducated and worthless, but brings all of them down to one common level. Therefore let those who are contemptible in the eyes of the world turn this over in their minds: 'How unassuming we should be, when even those who are held in high regard by the world are left with nothing! If the radiance of the sun is eclipsed, what is to happen to the stars? If the light of the stars is put out, what is to become of the things of darkness?' The purpose of those questions is, that those who have been called by the Lord, seeing that they count for nothing in the eyes of the world, might not take advantage of these words of Paul's to plume their feathers. On the contrary, remembering his exhortation in Romans 11.20, 'Thou standest by thy faith. Be not highminded, but fear,' they may walk in God's sight with thoughtfulness, fear and humility.

On the other hand Paul does not say here that no high-born or powerful people were called by God, but that there were a few. He gives the reason for this: that the Lord, in preferring the contemptible to the great, might bring down the pride of men. The same God, through the mouth of David, exhorts kings to kiss Christ (Ps. 2.12); and also announces through the lips of Paul (I Tim. 2.1-4) that He wishes all men to be saved, and that His Christ is set forth for all men, the insignificant as well as the great, kings and ordinary citizens too. He Himself has given us actual proof of that; shepherds are the first to be called to Christ; then afterwards come the philosophers; uneducated and despised fishermen hold the most honourable place, but, later, kings and their advisers, senators and orators are received into their school.

28. *The things that were not.* Paul uses similar words in Romans 4.17, but with a different sense. For there, describing the universal call of the godly, he says that we are nothing before we are called. That must be understood to be the truth as God sees it, even if we seem to count for something in the eyes of men. Here, however, the nothingness (οὐδένεια) of which he speaks ought to be taken as referring to the opinion of men. This is clear from the subordinate clause, where he says this must be done so that the things that are might be abolished. For nothing

exists except in appearance because in reality we are all nothing. Therefore you must explain those 'things that are' as 'those which appear'; so this passage corresponds to these statements: 'He raiseth up the poor . . . from the dunghill' (Ps. 113.7); 'He raises on high those who are cast down' (Ps. 146.8); and others of a similar nature. From those quotations it is perfectly clear that those people are very foolish who suppose that there is some merit or worthiness in men, which may precede the election of God.

29. *That no flesh should glory.* Even if, as in many passages of scripture, the word 'flesh' means all men here, yet it has a particular connotation in this verse, for the Spirit, in speaking of men with contempt, curbs their pride; as in Isaiah 31.3, 'The Egyptian is flesh not spirit.' But this is a thought worth remembering: that nothing is left us in which we may really glory. For that reason Paul adds the phrase 'in the presence of God'. For many people take delight in the wrong kind of glorying, i.e. in the eyes of the world, but it is only for a short time and it quickly fades away like smoke. Yet, with these words all men are put to silence, when they come into the presence of God; as Habakkuk says (2.20), 'Let all flesh keep silent before God.' Therefore let anything that is worthy of praise be looked upon as given to us by God.

30. *But of him are ye in Christ Jesus.* In case they might think that some of his sayings did not refer to them Paul now shows how they do apply to them, in that they have no life except from God. For the emphasis lies in the verb 'you are', as if he said, 'Your origin is from God,, who calls those things that are not, disregarding those things which appear to be. Your existence (*subsistentia*) is in fact founded on Christ, so that you have no cause for pride.' And he is not speaking of our creation only, but of that spiritual being (*essentia*) into which we are born again by God's grace.

Who was made unto us wisdom from God etc. Since there are many who, while they do not wish to withdraw deliberately from God, do however seek something apart from Christ, just as if He alone did not contain all things in Himself, Paul tells us, in passing, what, and how great, are the treasures with which Christ is provided, and in doing so he seeks to describe at the same time our mode of existence (*modus subsistendi*) in Christ. For when Paul calls Christ our righteousness, the opposite must be understood about us, that in us there is nothing but sin; and so it is with the other terms in this sentence. For here he ascribes to Christ four titles which sum up all His perfection, and every benefit that we receive from Him.

First Paul says that He has been made our *Wisdom.* By this he means that we obtain absolute perfection of wisdom in Him, because the

Father has revealed Himself fully in Him for us, so that we may not desire to know anything apart from Him. There is a similar passage in Colossians 2.3: 'In Him all the treasures of wisdom and knowledge are hidden.' We shall say more about this in the next chapter.

Secondly. Paul says that He has been made unto us for *Righteousness*. By this he means that in His name we are accepted by God, because He atoned for our sins by His death, and His obedience is imputed to us for righteousness. For since the righteousness of faith consists in remission of sins and free acceptance, we obtain both through Christ.

Thirdly. Paul calls Him our *Sanctification*. He means by that, that we, who are in ourselves unholy by nature, are born again by His Spirit into holiness, that we may serve God. From this we also gather that we cannot be justified freely by faith alone, if we do not at the same time live in holiness. For those gifts of grace go together as if tied by an inseparable bond, so that if anyone tries to separate them, he is, in a sense, tearing Christ to pieces. Accordingly, let the man who aims at being justified by God's free goodness through Christ take note that this cannot possibly be done, unless at the same time he lays hold of Him for sanctification; in other words he must be born anew by His Spirit to blamelessness and purity of life. Men find fault with us, because in preaching the free righteousness of faith, we seem to be calling men away from good works. But this passage clearly refutes them, by showing that faith lays hold of regeneration just as much as forgiveness of sins in Christ.

On the other hand notice that while those two offices of Christ are united, they are yet distinguishable from each other. Therefore we are not at liberty, indeed it would be wrong, to confuse what Paul expressly separates.

Fourthly. Paul teaches that He was given to us for *Redemption*. By that he means we are delivered by His goodness from all slavery to sin, and from all the misery which flows from it. So redemption is the first gift of Christ to be begun in us, and the last to be brought to completion. For salvation begins when we are extricated from the labyrinth of sin and death. In the meantime however we sigh for the final resurrection day, yearning for redemption, as it is put in Romans 8.26. But if someone asks how Christ has been given to us for redemption, I reply that He made Himself the price of redemption.

Finally let us seek not the half, or some part, but the totality of the benefits in Christ which are listed here. For Paul does not say that He has been given to us as something to add on to, or to be a buttress to righteousness, holiness, wisdom and redemption, but he ascribes to Christ alone the complete fulfilment of them all. But since there is scarcely another passage in Scripture which gives a clearer description of all the offices of Christ, it can also give us the best understanding of the force and nature of faith. For, since Christ is the proper object of faith, everyone who knows what benefits Christ gives to us, also learns what faith is.

31. *He that glories, let him glory in the Lord.* Notice God's purpose in lavishing everything upon us in Christ. It is that we might claim nothing for ourselves, but acknowledge that He gives us everything. For God does not strip us and leave us naked, but clothes us with glory at once, but with this one condition, that whenever we wish to boast we must turn away from ourselves. To sum up, man, reduced to nothing in his own eyes, knowing that goodness exists in God alone and nowhere else, and having given up eagerness for his own glory, is not only moved, but also aspires with his whole being to promote the glory of God alone. And this is clearer from the context of the passage of the prophet from whom Paul has borrowed this text. For there the Lord, after denying to all men the right to boast in strength, wisdom and wealth, commands them to glory only in knowledge of Him (Jer. 9.23, 24). But He wishes to be known (*cognosci*) in such a way that we may know (*sciamus*) that it is He who acts in justice, righteousness, and mercy. For this knowledge produces in us both trust in Him and fear of Him. Therefore the man who really glories in God is the man who has acquired such an attitude of mind that he claims nothing for himself, but rather desires to exalt God alone; who is satisfied with His grace; who finds all his happiness in His fatherly love; who, in a word, is content with God alone. I say 'really glories' because hypocrites also boast in Him, but in the wrong way (as Paul asserts in Romans 2.17) when, swollen-headed with His gifts, or elated by an ungodly confidence in the flesh, or misusing His Word, they nevertheless use His name as a cover for themselves.

CHAPTER TWO

And I, brethren, when I came unto you, came not with excellency of speech or of wisdom, proclaiming to you the mystery of God. For I determined not to know anything among you, save Jesus Christ, and him crucified. (1-2)

1. *And I, when I came etc.* Having begun to speak of his own method of teaching, Paul proceeded almost at once to deal with the general character of evangelical preaching. Now he turns to himself again, to show that whatever is to be despised in him is bound up with the nature of the Gospel itself, and in a sense is inseparable from it. Therefore he acknowledges that he did not have the help of human eloquence or wisdom, the provision of which might enable him to accomplish something. But he goes on to add, that from the very fact that he admits his lack of those resources, the power of God, which does not need such aids, is all the more evident in his ministry. He introduces that truth a little later on. But, in the meantime, having conceded that he was without human wisdom, he nevertheless maintains that he proclaimed the 'testimony of God' (*testimonium Dei*).[1] Although some interpreters explain the 'testimony of God' in a passive sense, I have no doubt, however, that the opposite is what the apostle has in mind: that the 'testimony of God' is that which takes its origin in God, viz. the teaching of the Gospel, of which He is the Author and Witness. Paul now distinguishes between *speech* and *wisdom* (λόγον ἀπὸ τῆς σοφίας). This confirms what I mentioned before, that so far he has been speaking not about mere empty chattering, but about the whole culture of human learning.

2. *For I determined not to know anything among you etc.* Since the Greek κρίνειν often means ἐκλέγειν, i.e. to select something as valuable, I think that no-one of sound judgement will deny that my rendering is a likely one, provided that it is consistent with the (Greek) construction. Yet, if we render it, 'I did not value any part of knowledge,' there would not be any harshness about it. But if you supply something that is missing, the sentence will run quite well, like this: 'I considered it of first importance not to know anything by my own efforts, or merely for the sake of having knowledge.' However, I do not reject out of hand a different interpretation, that Paul affirms that he esteemed nothing as knowledge, or as a substitute for knowledge except Christ

[1] Calvin accepts a well-supported variant reading, μαρτύριον τοῦ θεοῦ.

alone. If so, the Greek preposition ἀντί would have to be supplied, as it often is. But whether the first interpretation is the one that is approved, or whether the second is more satisfying, it amounts to this: 'The reason why I lacked embellishments of speech, and did not argue with more refinement and subtlety, was because I did not strive after those things, in fact I rather disdained them, because only one thing mattered to me—to proclaim Christ with simplicity.'

In adding *crucified* Paul does not mean that he proclaimed nothing about Christ except the Cross, but the very humiliation of the Cross did not keep him from proclaiming Christ. It is as if he said, 'The disgrace of the Cross will not prevent me from looking up to Him who is the source of salvation, or make me ashamed of finding all my wisdom summed up in Him—Him, I say, whom proud men treat with disdain, and reject on account of the reproach of the Cross.' Therefore what he says must be explained in this way: 'No knowledge was of such importance to me, as to make me desire to know anything other than Christ, even if He was crucified.' This little phrase is by way of being an addition (αὔξησιν) to cause more irritation to those arrogant teachers, who already had a poor opinion of Christ, for their great desire was to be applauded for their reputation for some sort of higher wisdom. This is a beautiful verse, and from it we may learn what faithful ministers ought to teach, and what we must be learning throughout our life; and in comparison with that everything else is to be counted as *dung*.

And I was with you in weakness, and in fear, and in much trembling. And my speech and my preaching were not in persuasive words of wisdom, but in demonstration of the Spirit and of power: that your faith should not stand in the wisdom of men, but in the power of God. (3-5)

3. *And I was with you in weakness.* Paul gives a full explanation of what he merely touched on before, that there was nothing splendid or distinguished about him in men's eyes, to make him a notable figure. However, he concedes to his opponents what they were seeking, in such a way as to make those very things, which they thought tended to lessen the reputation of his ministry, to redound to its highest commendation. He appeared to be someone worthy of less honour, because he was so insignificant and humble, according to the flesh. Nevertheless he shows that the power of God was all the more evident in his ability to do so much, although he did not have the support of any human aids. But he is thinking not only of those boasters, who, to gain a name for themselves, were busying themselves merely with ostentation; but of the Corinthians who were astonished at their empty displays. So such a reminder ought to have had a great deal of effect

among them. They knew that Paul brought no human qualities which might help him to make progress, or by which he might ingratiate himself in men's favour. Nevertheless they had seen the wonderful success which the Lord had given to his preaching. Indeed, further, they had seen, one might say with their own eyes, the Spirit of God present in his teaching. Therefore since they had neglected his simplicity, and longed feverishly for wisdom of some kind or another, that would be more grandiose and more polished, and since they were captivated by outward appearances, and more than that, by an assumed disguise, rather than by the living Spirit, did they not make their own love of display plain enough? Paul is therefore quite right in bringing his first visit back to their minds, lest they might turn away from God's power, which they had once experienced.

By weakness Paul generally means, here and several times afterwards, whatever can detract from the standing and dignity of someone in the estimation of other people. Fear and trembling are the results of this weakness. However, there are two ways in which we can explain these two words. One explanation is that, having pondered the magnitude of the task which he continued to undertake, he was perturbed, and it was not without very great anxiety that he was busy in the discharge of it. The other explanation is that, because he was surrounded by many dangers, he was in perpetual fear and constant anxiety. Either suits the context quite well, but in my judgement the second is the simpler. Indeed modesty like that is proper for the servants of the Lord, so that, conscious of their own weakness, and on the other hand, looking with respect at the difficulty, and also the excellence of such a task, they might approach it with reverence and engage in it with fear. For those who present themselves with confidence, and a very superior air, or who exercise the ministry of the Word in a careless fashion, as if they were equal to the task, know neither themselves nor the task itself.

But since Paul here links fear with weakness, and weakness means whatever could bring him into contempt, it follows that here fear relates to dangers and difficulties. But it is quite certain that this fear was such that it did not prevent Paul from carrying out the Lord's work, as the facts confirm. Nor are the servants of the Lord so dull as not to see threatening dangers, nor so insensitive as not to be affected by them. No! and in fact they must be seriously apprehensive for two main reasons: (1) that, humbled in their own eyes, they might learn to lean and rest completely on God alone; and (2) that they might be trained in true self-denial. Paul, therefore, was not without a sense of anxiety, but he controlled it, so that he nonetheless continued to be undaunted in the midst of crises, so that with unconquerable perseverance and strength he drew on himself all the insults of Satan and the world; and in brief, so that he forced his way through all resistance.

4. *And my preaching was not in persuasive words.* When he says 'the persuasive words of human wisdom' Paul means choice oratory, which strives and exerts itself with artifice rather than truth; and at the same time he means the appearance of acuteness, which attracts the minds of men. He is justified in attributing persuasiveness ($\tau\grave{o}$ $\pi\iota\theta\alpha\nu\acute{o}\nu$) to human wisdom. For, by its majesty, the Word of the Lord urges us, as by a violent force, to give obedience to it. On the other hand human wisdom has its charms with which it insinuates itself; and has its showy ornament, as it were, by which to win over the minds of its hearers to itself. Over against this Paul sets 'demonstration of the Spirit and power', which most interpreters confine to miracles. But I understand it in a wider sense, viz. as the hand of God stretching itself out to act powerfully through the apostle in every way. He seems to have put 'Spirit and power' either by hypallage ($\kappa\alpha\theta$' $\acute{v}\pi\alpha\lambda\lambda\alpha\gamma\acute{\eta}\nu$) for spiritual power; or, surely in order that he might point out by means of signs and effects how the presence of the Spirit had been apparent in his ministry. And his use of the word $\acute{\alpha}\pi o\delta\epsilon\iota\xi\iota\varsigma$ or demonstration is apposite. For our dullness, when we look closely at the works of God, is such, that when He uses inferior instruments, His power is concealed as if by so many veils, so that it is not clearly evident to us. On the other hand, in promoting Paul's ministry, because no human or worldly help was at work, the hand of God stretched itself out, as it were, bare; certainly His power was more visible.

5. *That your faith might not be in the wisdom of men.* 'To be' is used here for 'to consist'. Paul means therefore that the Corinthians have this benefit, from the fact that he had preached Christ among them without relying on human wisdom, but solely on the power of the Spirit, that their faith was founded, not on men, but on God. If the apostle's preaching had been supported by the power of eloquence alone, he could have been overthrown by superior oratory. Further, that truth which relies on brilliance of oratory no-one will call genuine. Indeed it can be helped by it, but it ought not to depend on it. On the other hand, what stands on its own, independent of all support, must be more powerful. For this reason it is a striking commendation of Paul's preaching that heavenly power shone out in it so much, that it had the upper hand over so many hindrances, without any assistance from the world. It follows therefore that they must not allow themselves to be moved away from his teaching, when they know he had been supported by God's authority. Besides, Paul is speaking of the faith of the Corinthians here in such a way that this sentence is of universal application. Therefore we should know that the character-

istic of faith is to rest in God alone, and not to depend on men. For its assurance must be so great that it does not collapse even if assailed by all the contrivances of hell, but holds out staunchly, and withstands all attacks. This cannot be done unless we are firmly convinced that God has spoken to us, and that what we believe is no fabrication of men. But though faith ought properly to be founded on the Word of God alone, there is nothing out of place about adding this second support— that believers know by the effect of its power that the Word which they hear has its origin with God.

> *Howbeit we speak wisdom among the perfect: yet a wisdom not of this world, nor of the rulers of this world, which are coming to nought: but we speak God's wisdom in a mystery, even the wisdom that hath been hidden, which God foreordained before the worlds unto our glory: which none of the rulers of this world knoweth: for had they known it, they would not have crucified the Lord of glory: but as it is written, Things which eye saw not, and ear heard not, And which entered not into the heart of man, Whatsoever things God prepared for them that love him. (6–9)*

6. *We speak wisdom.* In order that he might not appear to despise wisdom, as uneducated and ignorant men despise learning, with all the fierceness of the uncultured, Paul adds that he did have the genuine wisdom, but that it is appreciated only by those capable of judging. He means by 'perfect', not those who had attained to a full and complete wisdom, but those who have a sound and uncorrupted judgement. For the Hebrew םָּת, which the Greek translators always rendered by τέλειος, means whole, complete. But in passing he reproaches those who had no liking for his preaching, and points out that it was their own fault. It is as if he said, 'If my teaching does not suit any, in that way they now produce proof enough that their understanding is perverted and corrupted, because it is always recognized as the highest wisdom by men of sound thinking and good judgement.' On the other hand, though Paul's preaching had been presented to all, it had not always been assessed at its proper value. That is why he appeals to sound and impartial judges, who might declare the teaching, which was uninteresting to the world, to be genuine wisdom. In the meantime, by the words, *we speak*, he lets it be known that he is bringing forward a splendid example of wonderful wisdom, lest anyone might object that he was boasting of some unknown thing.

A wisdom not of this world. He again repeats, by anticipation, what he had already allowed, that the Gospel is not human wisdom, lest anyone might object that there are few supporters of that teaching, indeed that it was despised by those of the most outstanding mental ability. Therefore Paul acknowledges, of his own accord, the objection which could be made, but in such a way that he surrenders no part of his position in doing so.

Or of the rulers of this world. By *rulers of the world* he means those who are eminent in the world because of some talent. For there are sometimes those who are not so acute in thinking, but are looked up to nevertheless because of their personal standing. But that we may not be alarmed by their outward appearances (*larvis*) the apostle adds that they are to be destroyed or to perish. For it is not right that a matter of eternal significance should depend on the authority of those who are passing away and perishing, unable to give perpetuity even to themselves. It is as if he said: 'When the Kingdom of God is revealed, let the wisdom of this world depart, and let what is transitory yield to what is eternal. For the rulers of this world have their distinction, but such as is destroyed in a moment. What is this in comparison with the heavenly and incorruptible Kingdom of God?'

7. *The wisdom of God in a mystery.* The reason he gives for the small value put on the teaching of the Gospel by the rulers of this world is that it is wrapped up in mysteries, and for that reason concealed. For the Gospel towers over the insight of the human mind so that those who are considered intellectually of the first rank may look as high as they like, but they never reach its eminence. In the meantime, however, they look down upon its insignificance as if it were prostrate at their feet. In consequence the more haughtily they despise it the further are they from knowing it; more than that, they are standing at so great a distance from it that they are prevented from seeing it.

Which God appointed before the ages for our glory. Because Paul had said that the Gospel is a hidden thing there was a danger that believers, hearing this, and being frightened by the difficulty, might run away from it and lose heart. Therefore he faces this danger and declares that nevertheless the Gospel had been appointed for us, for our enjoyment of it. Lest anyone, I say, might consider that the hidden wisdom has nothing to do with him, or even that it is wrong for him to look at it, because it is not within the range of human comprehension, Paul teaches that it has been imparted to us by the eternal purpose of God. Yet he had something greater in mind, for by a tacit comparison he places in a clearer light the grace which has been laid open for us by the coming of Christ, and which puts us in a higher position than our fathers who lived under the Law. I have said more about this at the end of the last chapter of Romans. *First* of all, then, he argues from what God has ordained. For if God established everything to some purpose, it follows that we will lose nothing in hearing the Gospel, which He intended for us, for when He speaks to us He accommodates Himself to our capacity. What Isaiah says relates to this (45.19): 'For I have not spoken in a hiding place, or in a dark corner. Not in vain did I say to the seed of Jacob, "Seek me".' *Secondly*, in order to make the Gospel attractive, and to awaken in us a longing to come to know it, Paul also concluded that God's purpose was to give it to us for our glory. In those words also he seems to compare us with the fathers, whom our Heavenly Father did not regard as worthy of that honour, for He delayed it until the coming of His Son.

8. *None of the rulers of this world knew.* If you add, 'by their own ability', nothing more is asserted of them than of men generally, and of the very humblest of the people; for what do all of us, from the greatest of us to the least of us, achieve in that way? Of course we might perhaps say that rulers ought to be censured for blindness and ignorance more than others, because in this world they alone appear to be clear-sighted and wise. However I prefer to take it more simply, following the frequent usage of Scripture which is accustomed to use the universal affirmative of those things which are ἐπὶ τὸ πολύ, i.e. which occur generally; and also to use the universal negative of those things which only occur ἐπὶ ἔλαττον, i.e. very seldom. In that light, there was no incongruity (with what Paul says) if there were a few outstanding men, above others in rank, who at the same time were possessed of the genuine knowledge of God.

For if they had known. The wisdom of God was shining forth clearly in Christ, but the rulers did not perceive it there. In the crucifying of Christ the lead was taken, on the one hand by the chief men of the Jews, whose reputation for righteousness and wisdom was outstanding, and, on the other hand, by Pilate and the Roman Empire. This is a clear example of the extreme blindness of all those who are wise only according to human standards. However this argument of the apostle might appear to be weak. 'Why! Do we not see every day people who are not unacquainted with the truth of God, but who oppose it with deliberate malice? Even though such open rebellion were not perceived by our eyes, what else is the sin against the Holy Spirit, however, but wilful stubbornness against God, when a man, knowingly and willingly, not only works against His Word, but also takes up arms against it? That is why Christ testifies that the Pharisees and those associated with them knew Him (John 7.28), when He strips them of the excuse of ignorance, and accuses them of ungodly cruelty in persecuting Him, the faithful Servant of the Father, on no grounds except their hatred of the truth.'

I answer that there are two kinds of ignorance. The one springs from thoughtless zeal, and it does not simply reject the good, but rather thinks it is evil. Although nobody sins in ignorance in such a way as not to be accused of a bad conscience in the sight of God, there being always a mixture of hypocrisy, or pride or scorn; sometimes, however, judgement and all understanding are so stifled in a man's mind that nothing except plain ignorance is apparent, not only to others but also to himself. Paul was like that before he was enlightened. The reason for his hatred of Christ, and his hostility to His teaching, was that, in ignorance, he was dragged away by a perverted zeal for the law. Indeed he was not without hypocrisy, or innocent of pride, so that he might be excusable in God's sight, but those vices were so completely buried by ignorance and blindness, that he did not even notice or feel them himself.

The other kind of ignorance is more like madness and derangement than mere ignorance. For those who rise up of their own accord against God are, as it were, frenzied, for they see and yet do not see. Indeed the general conclusion must be that unfaithfulness is always blind. But this is what matters: sometimes blindness covers over malice so that a man does not have any awareness of his own evil, just as if he were senseless. This is the position with those who deceive themselves with a good intention, as they call it, but with what is in fact a foolish fancy. Sometimes malice gets the upper hand so that, despite the protests of conscience, a man rushes into such wickedness with something like fury. Accordingly, it is no wonder that Paul says that the rulers of the world would not have crucified Christ if they had known the wisdom of God. For the Pharisees and scribes did not know the teaching of Christ to be true, so as not to wander, as dazed men, in their own darkness.

9. *But as it is written, Things which eye has not seen etc.* Almost all agree that this passage is taken from Isaiah 64.3 (LXX 4); and, because at first glance the meaning is clear and easy, interpreters do little in way of explaining it. On closer inspection however two very great difficulties appear. The first is that the words, which are used by Paul, do not agree with the words of the prophet. The second is that Paul seems to be working on different lines to the prophet, and so to be misapplying his statement.

We will deal first with the words then. Because they are ambiguous, interpreters explain them in different ways. Some put it in this way. 'From of old men have not heard or understood with their ears, and no eye has seen a god except thee, who acts (*faciat*) in such a way toward the man who looks for him.' Others interpret the words as addressed to God, in this way: 'Eye has not seen, nor ear heard, O God except thee, what thou doest (*facias*) for those who look for thee.' A literal rendering of the prophet's words is as follows: 'From of old men have not heard, nor understood with their ears, eye has not seen a god (or, O God)ᐟ except thee (*oculus non vidit Deum (vel Deus) praeter te, faciet*), he will do (or will prepare) for him who looks for him.' If we read אֱלֹהִים (God) in the accusative (*Deum*) the relative who (*qui*) will have to be supplied. And at first glance this exposition seems to suit the prophet's context better, because the verb that follows is in the third person, but it is further from Paul's meaning, and that ought to carry more weight with us than other reasons. For who better than the Spirit of God will be a sure and faithful interpreter of this prophetic declaration, which He Himself dictated to Isaiah, seeing it was He who explained it by the mouth of Paul? However, so that we may resist the unjust charges of wicked men, I maintain that the nature of the Hebrew construction allows this as the prophet's true meaning: 'O God, neither has eye seen, nor has ear heard, but thou alone knowest what thou art accustomed to do for those who look for thee.' The sudden change of person is no difficulty. We know it to be so customary for the prophets to do this that we need not be detained by it. If the first interpretation pleases some better they will be in no position to blame us or the apostle for departing from the simple meaning of the words, for we supply less than they do, because they are forced to add a term of similitude to the verb 'acts' (making it read 'who acts in such a way').

Although the prophet does not include what follows about 'the entering of those things into the heart of man', the phrase does not strike a different note from the clause 'except Thee'. For, since he ascribes this knowledge to God alone, he excludes from it not only the physical senses of man, but also all the ability of the mind. Therefore, although the prophet makes reference only to sight and hearing, he implicitly includes all the faculties of the mind. Certainly those are the two media by which we obtain knowledge of those things which reach the understanding. In using the phrase 'those who love Him', Paul is following the Greek interpreters, who translated it so because they were misled by the similarity of one letter to another[1]; but as that made no difference to the point of this verse he did not wish to depart from the common reading, for again and again we see how much he gives

---

[1] The confusion is of a כ and ב. The Hebrew of Isa. 64.3, last phrase, is: יַעֲשֶׂה לִמְחַכֵּה־לוֹ. The corresponding verse in LXX is 4 and reads ἃ ποιήσεις τοῖς ὑπομένουσιν ἔλεον. Calvin is wrong here. He is referring to the Hebrew מְחַכֵּה from Piel חִכָּה to wait. He assumed LXX translators misread it as Piel participle of a rare word to love, חָבַב (used once only Deut. 33.3). So Calvin says מְחַבֵּב has been read for מְחַכֵּה. But LXX has used ὑπομένειν to wait, agreeing with Hebrew. Paul has a change in his Greek reading ὅσα ἡτοίμασεν ὁ θεὸς τοῖς ἀγαπῶσιν αὐτόν. Tr.

way to the accepted text. Therefore, although the words are not the same, there is no real difference of meaning.

Now I come to the subject matter. In this passage the prophet remembers how wonderfully God always came to His people's assistance when they were in need, and exclaims that His favours to the godly are beyond the comprehension of the human mind. But someone will say, 'What has this to do with spiritual teaching, and the promises of eternal life, which Paul is discussing here?' There are three ways in which this question may be answered. It will not be out of place to say that the prophet, having mentioned earthly benefits, was led on by thinking of these to a general statement, and indeed to glory in the spiritual blessedness, which is laid up in heaven for believers. I prefer however to understand simply the favours of God, which are daily bestowed on believers. In dealing with them we ought always to look beyond their immediate aspect, and pay attention to their cause. Moreover, the cause is the free goodness of God, by which He has adopted us into the number of His sons. The man who wants to assess those things properly, will not look upon them in their nakedness, but will clothe them with God's fatherly love as with a garment, and in this way he will be led from temporal gifts to eternal life. It can also be said that this is an argument from less to greater. For if man's mind cannot attain to the measuring of God's earthly gifts, how much less will it reach the height of heaven? But I have already shown which interpretation satisfies me most.

But unto us God revealed them through the Spirit: for the Spirit searcheth all things, yea, the deep things of God. For who among men knoweth the things of a man, save the spirit of the man, which is in him? even so the things of God none knoweth, save the Spirit of God. But we received, not the spirit of the world, but the Spirit which is of God; that we might know the things that are freely given to us by God. Which things also we speak, not in words which man's wisdom teacheth, but which the Spirit teacheth; comparing spiritual things with spiritual.
(10-13)

10. *But God has revealed them to us.* Having concluded that all men are blind, and having deprived the human mind of the power to rise up to knowledge of God, Paul now shows how the faithful are delivered from this blindness, viz. by the Lord honouring them with a special enlightenment of the Spirit. Therefore, the duller the human mind is for understanding the mysteries of God, and the greater its uncertainty, the surer is our faith, which is supported by the revelation of the Spirit of God. In this we recognize the boundless goodness of God who makes use of our defect for our good.

For the Spirit searches everything. This is added for the encouragement of believers that they might rest more securely in the revelation, which the Spirit of God gives them. It is as if he said: 'Let it be enough for us that we have the Spirit of God as witness, for in God there is nothing too deep for Him to penetrate.' For that is what 'searches' means here. By 'the deep things' you must understand, not secret judgements, which we are not allowed to investigate, but the whole teaching of salvation. This would have been set before us in the Scriptures uselessly, if God does not lift up our minds to Him by His Spirit.

11. *For who among men knows.* Paul wishes to teach two things here: (1) that the teaching of the Gospel can only be understood by the witness of the Holy Spirit; and (2) that the assurance of those who have such witness from the Holy Spirit is as strong and firm as if they were actually touching with their hands what they believe, and that is because the Spirit is a faithful and reliable witness. Paul proves this by the likeness (*similitudine*) of our spirit. For everyone knows his own thoughts well. But others do not know what is hidden in his heart. Similarly the purpose and will of God are such that they are hidden from all men; for who was His Counsellor? It is therefore a 'Holy of Holies', inaccessible to men. But yet if the Spirit of God Himself brings us into it, that is, if He makes us surer of those things which are otherwise hidden from our perception, there will be no more room for hesitation. For nothing that is in God Himself, escapes His Spirit.

On the other hand this similitude does not seem to be altogether suitable. For since speaking is a characteristic mental activity, men convey their thoughts and feelings to each other, so that they come to know each other's minds well. Why may we not therefore understand from the Word of God what His will is? For while by pretence and lies men often obscure, rather than reveal, their real state of mind, that is not the way with God, whose Word is absolute truth and His own living image. But we must consider to what extent Paul wished to draw out this similitude. The inner thought of a man, of which others know nothing, is clear to him alone. If, later, he reveals it to others, that does not alter the fact that his spirit alone knows what is in him. For it might be that he does not use persuasive language; it might even be that he does not properly convey what he really means. If he does however achieve both of those, that does not make any difference to this other statement, i.e. it is still the case that only his own spirit is truly familiar with it. There is, however, this important difference between the thoughts of God and men. On the one hand men understand each other; on the other hand the Word of God is a kind of hidden wisdom, to whose loftiness the weak human mind does not reach. So light shines in darkness, until the Spirit opens the eyes of the blind.

The spirit of the man. Note that here the spirit of man means the soul (*anima*) in which the power of understanding, as it is called, resides. For Paul would not have been precise if he had said that the understanding of man knows, that is, the faculty itself, but not the soul. For the soul possesses the power of understanding.

12. *But we have not received the spirit of the world.* Using contrast, Paul enlarges on that assurance which he had already mentioned. He says, 'The Spirit of revelation which we receive does not belong to the world, so that He is earth-bound like a snake, so that He is subject to futility, so that He wavers, alters, is now one thing then another, or holds us in suspense or perplexity. But He is from God, and so is above all the heavens, is of genuine and unchangeable truth, and beyond every possibility of doubt.'

This is a very clear passage for refuting the diabolical principle of sophists that believers are in a continual state of perplexity. They desire to raise doubts in believers' minds, whether they are living in the grace of God or not, and the only assurance of salvation they allow is what depends on moral or probable inference. However, by this they destroy faith in two ways. For, first, they want us to doubt if we are in a state of grace, and then again, their suggestions make us uncertain about final perseverance. But here the apostle announces in a general way that the elect have been given the Spirit by whose witness they know for a certainty that they have been adopted to the hope of eternal salvation. There is no doubt that if the sophists wish to maintain their principle they must deprive the elect of the Holy Spirit, and make the Spirit Himself also subject to uncertainty. Both of these are in open conflict with Paul's teaching. Therefore we may know that this is the nature of faith, that conscience has, by the Holy Spirit, a sure witness of God's goodwill towards itself, and relying on this, it confidently calls on God as Father. So Paul lifts our faith above the world, so that from its exalted position it can look down upon all carnal arrogance. Otherwise it will always be agitated and hesitant, because we see how audaciously human cleverness exalts itself; and the sons of God must tread upon this pride by an opposite kind of pride, heroic magnanimity.

That we might know what things have been given to us by Christ.[1] The word *know* has been used in order to bring out better the assurance of confidence. However let us note that it is not obtained in a natural way, or laid hold of by our mental power of comprehension, but it depends altogether on the revelation of the Spirit. Paul speaks of

[1] So Latin. Greek, 'by God'.

'those things which are given by Christ'. They are the blessings which
we obtain from His death and resurrection, viz. that having been
reconciled to God through the remission of sins which has been effected,
we know that we have been adopted into the hope of eternal life.
Further, we know that being sanctified by the Spirit of regeneration,
we are being made new creatures in order that we might live to God.
Paul says in Ephesians 1.18 what amounts to the same thing: 'That you
may know what is the hope of your calling.'

13. *And we speak of those things, in words taught, not by human wisdom,
but by the Holy Spirit.* Paul is referring to himself, for he is still concerned with commending his ministry. But it is a remarkable tribute
to his own preaching when he says that it consists of the secret revelation
of the greatest of things: the teaching of the Holy Spirit, the totality
of our salvation, the priceless treasures of Christ. He does so that the
Corinthians might know how much it ought to be valued. In the
meantime he returns to what he conceded before, that his preaching
was not embellished with any veneer of words, that it did not have a
sparkling elegant style, but he was content to preach only what he was
taught by the Holy Spirit.

By the words 'taught by human wisdom', Paul means those which
savour of human learning, and are polished according to the rules of
the rhetoricians; or are purposely and proudly overloaded with philosophy in order to rush hearers into admiration. But the words 'taught
by the Spirit' are suitable for a style which is sincere and simple, rather
than empty and ostentatious, and one more in keeping with the dignity
of the Spirit. For in order that there may be eloquence, we must always
be on the alert to prevent the wisdom of God being spoiled by a forced
and common brilliancy. But Paul's way of teaching was such that in
it the power of the Spirit shone forth, pure and simple, without any
external assistance.

Spiritual things with spiritual (πνευματικοῖς πνευματικὰ συγκρίνοντες).
I have no doubt that the Greek verb συγκρίνεσθαι is used here for *aptare*,
i.e. to adjust or adapt. For since this is sometimes the meaning of the
word (according to a quotation from Aristotle by Budaeus), so σύγκριμα
is also used for what is joined or bound together. And certainly
that suits Paul's context far better than 'to compare', as others have
rendered it. He says therefore that he adjusts or adapts spiritual things
to spiritual, when he accommodates the words to the reality. In other
words he properly combines that heavenly wisdom of the Spirit with
plainness of speech, and in such a way that it shows openly the very
power of the Spirit Himself. In the meantime he reprimands others,
who with an assumed elegance of style, and a great show of cleverness,
strive after men's applause, as either completely lacking in the genuine

truth, or corrupting the spiritual teaching of God with an unbecoming veneer.

Now the natural man receiveth not the things of the Spirit of God: for they are foolishness unto him; and he cannot know them, because they are spiritually judged. But he that is spiritual judgeth all things, and he himself is judged of no man. For who hath known the mind of the Lord, that he should instruct him? But we have the mind of Christ.
(14–16)

14. *But the natural man.* By the *natural man* (*animalis homo*) Paul means, not, as is generally assumed, a man enslaved to gross desires, or, as they say, to his own sensuality, but any man endowed only with the powers of nature. This is clear from the opposite term, for he contrasts *the natural* with *the spiritual.* Since *the spiritual* refers to the man whose mind is directed by the illumination of the Spirit, there is no doubt that *the natural* means the man left in purely natural endowments (*in puris naturalibus*) as they are called. For the soul (*anima*) is bound up with nature, but the Spirit springs from a supernatural gift (*ex dono supernaturali*).

Paul takes up again what he had touched on before. For he wants to take away a stumbling-block which could upset the weak, viz. the fact that so many were rejecting the Gospel with contempt. He shows that we should take no account of the contempt that arises from ignorance, and therefore it ought not to prevent us from pressing on in the race of faith; unless we perhaps choose to shut our eyes to the splendour of the sun, on the grounds that the blind do not see it! But he would be a most ungrateful man, who refuses a special favour, of which God thinks he is worthy, on the ground that every one else does not have it, when, on the contrary, its very rarity puts it at a premium.

For to him they are foolishness, and he cannot understand them. Paul is saying this: 'All those whose wisdom is on a purely human level have no taste for the teaching of the Gospel. But how does this come about? It is due to their blindness. How then can this detract from the majesty of the Gospel?' In short, when ignorant people disparage the Gospel, because, in forming their own estimate of its value, they simply echo other people's assessment, Paul makes use of that as an argument for a greater heightening of its worth. For he teaches that it is despised because it is unknown to men; and that it is unknown because it is at once too profound, and too lofty to be grasped by the human mind. What a wonderful wisdom this is, which so far surpasses all human knowledge, that men cannot have even the slightest taste of it! But although Paul here tacitly blames human pride for the fact that men presume to condemn as foolishness what they do not understand, at the same time however he shows how great is the feebleness, or rather the dullness of the human mind, when he says that it is not capable of spiritual understanding. For he teaches that it is due not only to the stubborn pride of the human will, but also to the impotence of the mind, that man by himself cannot attain to the things of the Spirit. He would have been saying no more than the truth if he had said that men do not wish to be wise, but he goes further, and says that they do not even have the power. From this we conclude that faith is not something that depends on our decision, but it is something given by God.

Because they are spiritually judged. That is, the Spirit of God, from whom the teaching of the Gospel comes, is the only true interpreter for opening it up to us. It follows that in passing judgement on it the minds of men must necessarily be in darkness, until they are enlightened by the Spirit of God. The inference from this is that all men are by nature without the Spirit of God; otherwise the argument would fall to the ground. Of course, the light of reason, such as it is, which is a necessity of life for all of us, is from the Spirit of God. But here we are speaking of that special revelation of heavenly wisdom, of which God thinks only His sons are worthy. Because of that there is all the less ground for tolerating the ignorance of those who think that the Gospel is offered to men universally in such a way that it is free to all without distinction to lay hold of salvation by faith.

15. *But the spiritual man judges all things.* Having taken away the natural man's ability to judge, he now teaches that only the spiritual are proper judges of this matter; because only the Spirit of God knows Himself, and it is His personal function to separate His own things from those of others; to approve what is His own, and to strip everything else of trustworthiness. The meaning is therefore this: 'In this connexion there is no place for the discernment of the flesh! It is the spiritual man alone who has such a firm and sound knowledge of the mysteries of God, that he really distinguishes truth from falsehood, the teaching of God from the fabrications of men, and he is deluded very little.' On the other hand, 'nobody judges him', because the assurance of faith is not under the control of men, so as to be reduced to ruins at their pleasure, when in fact it is superior to the angels themselves. Notice that this prerogative is assigned, not to the man personally, but to the Word of God, which the spiritual take as a guide, when they are judging, and which, indeed, is declared to them by God, so that they really understand it. When that happens a man's conviction is made firm, because it is above the uncertainty of human judgement.

Notice, further, the word for judging. The apostle means by it, not only that we are enlightened by the Spirit to perceive the truth, but that we are also equipped with a spirit of discernment so as not to be suspended in doubt between truth and error, but to be able to decide what we should avoid and what we should follow.

But here we may ask, who is the spiritual man, and where are we to find a man endowed with so much light, that he is capable of judging everything, when we are well aware of the fact that we are always beset with a great deal of ignorance, and are liable to the danger of going wrong, and, more than that, when even the most excellent of men repeatedly fall and come to grief? The answer is easy: Paul does not make this ability apply to everything, as if he delivers all who are renewed by the Spirit of God from every kind of error; but he simply wishes to teach that human intelligence is useless for assessing the teachings of religion, and that the right to judge in this way belongs to the Spirit of God alone. Therefore, a man judges aright and with assurance, according to whether he is born again, and according to the measure of grace bestowed on him – and no more.

He himself is judged by no-one. I have already explained why Paul says that the spiritual man does not lie under the judgement of any man, viz. because the truth of faith, which depends on God alone, and is founded on His word, does not stand or fall according to the pleasure of men. What he says later on, that the spirit of one prophet is subject to other prophets, is not at variance with this thought. For the reason for that subjection is simply that each of the prophets pays attention to the others, and does not despise or refuse their revelations, in order that the truth of God, which had been ascertained, might finally remain fixed and be accepted by all. In this passage, however, Paul places the knowledge of faith, which has been received from God, above the height of heaven and earth, so that it might not be assessed by the judgement of men.

However, ὑπ' οὐδενὸς can be read in the neuter, i.e. 'by nothing', so that it is taken to refer to a thing and not to a man. In this way the contrast will be more complete; the spiritual man, to the extent he is endowed with the Spirit of God, judges everything, but is judged by 'no thing', because he is subject to no human wisdom or reason. And in this way Paul would free the consciences of the godly from all ordinances, laws and censures of men.

16. *For who has known . . .?* It is likely that Paul was looking at what is found in the 40th chapter of Isaiah. The prophet asks there, 'Who has been God's counsellor? Who has weighed His Spirit (Isa. 40.13); or has helped Him both in the creation of the world, and in His other works; and, finally, who has a sure grasp of the motive for His works?' In the same way Paul wishes to teach by the use of this question, how far removed from the minds of men is His secret counsel

which is contained in the Gospel. Therefore this confirms the preceding statement.

But we have the mind of Christ. It is not certain whether he speaks about believers in general, or only about ministers, for either meaning suits the context quite well. However I prefer to take it as referring especially to himself and other faithful ministers. He says, therefore, that the servants of the Lord are taught under the direction of the Spirit, what is far removed from human understanding, in order that they might speak fearlessly as it were from the mouth of the Lord. Afterwards this gift spreads by degrees to the whole Church.

CHAPTER THREE

And I, brethren, could not speak unto you as unto spiritual, but as unto carnal, as unto babes in Christ. I fed you with milk, not with meat; for ye were not yet able to bear it: nay, not even now are ye able; for ye are yet carnal: for whereas there is among you jealousy and strife, are ye not carnal, and walk after the manner of men? For when one saith, I am of Paul; and another, I am of Apollos; are ye not men? (1-4)

1. *And I, brethren.* He begins to apply what he had said about carnal men to the Corinthians themselves, so that they might understand that it was their own fault that the teaching of the Cross had little attraction for them. It is likely that too much self-confidence and pride still clung to their commercial minds, so that it was only with considerable reluctance and very great difficulty that they were embracing the simplicity of the Gospel. The result was that they neglected the apostle, and the divine efficacy of his preaching, and paid more attention to those teachers who were noisy and very ostentatious. Therefore, in order to curb their insolence the better, he asserts that they were to be counted among those, who, having been overwhelmed by the mind of the flesh, were not able to receive the spiritual wisdom of God. Indeed he softens the harshness of his reproach by calling them 'brothers', but for all that he makes it a frank matter of reproach against them, that their minds were suffocated by the darkness of the flesh so much, that it formed a hindrance to his preaching among them. How then can they be credited with sound judgement, when as yet they are not fit and ready even for hearing? But he does not mean that they were completely carnal, without even a spark of the Spirit of God, but that they were still much too full of the mind of the flesh, so that the flesh prevailed over the Spirit, and, as it were, extinguished His light. Although they were not entirely without grace, yet they had more of the flesh than of the Spirit in their lives, and that is why he calls them *carnal.* That is plain enough from his adding immediately, that they were 'babes in Christ' (*pueros in Christo*), for they would not have been babes, if they had not been begotten, and this begetting is the work of the Spirit of God.

Babes in Christ. This description is sometimes used in a good sense, as, for example, by Peter, who entreats us to be like 'new born babes' (I Pet. 2.2); and in that statement of Christ's, 'unless you become children like·these, you will not enter the Kingdom of God' (Luke

18.17).[1] Here, however it bears a bad sense, because it refers to the understanding. For we must be 'children in malice, but not in mind', as he says in chapter 14.20. This distinction clears up any question of ambiguity. Ephesians 4.14 corresponds to this: 'That we may not be children, carried about by every wind of doctrine, and made the sport of men's tricks, but that we may grow daily etc.'[2]

I fed you with milk. Here one may ask if Paul presented a different Christ to different people. I answer that this refers to his manner or form of teaching, rather than to the substance of what he taught. For the same Christ is milk for babes, and solid food for adults. The same truth of the Gospel is handled for both, but so as to suit the capacity of each. Therefore a wise teacher has the responsibility of accommodating himself to the power of comprehension of those whom he undertakes to teach, so as to begin with first principles when instructing the weak and ignorant, and not to move any higher than they can follow. In short, he must instil his teaching bit by bit, for imparting too much would only result in loss. But these rudiments will contain whatever is necessary for knowledge, no less than the fuller instruction given to the stronger. In this connexion read Augustine's 98th *Homily on John*. So this proves false the trumped-up excuse of some who, because they fear danger, make only some stammering and indistinct reference to the Gospel, and allege that in this Paul is their example. In the meantime they make known a Christ so far away, and indeed hidden by many coverings, that the result is that they are always keeping their followers in a state of fatal ignorance. I say nothing about their bringing in many corruptions; their presenting not merely half of Christ, but a Christ torn in little pieces; not only their disguising what is gross idolatry, but also their establishing it by their own example; and their immediate spoiling of any good thing they said by a lot of lies. It is plain enough how unlike Paul they are; for milk is nourishment and not poison, and it is food which is suitable and beneficial for children until they grow bigger.

For you were not yet fit for it. So that they may not flatter themselves too much on their own acuteness, Paul shows, first of all, what he discovered in them at the beginning, then he adds something that is more disagreeable, that the same faults are still present among them. For at least they ought to have cast aside the flesh when they put on Christ; and so we see Paul complaining that the progress to which his teaching was entitled, was hampered. For if the hearer causes no delay because of his slowness, it is the duty of a good teacher to be always moving higher, until perfection has been reached.

[1] This is a conflation of Luke 18.17 and Matt. 18.3.
[2] This represents a free rendering rather than an exact citation of Eph. 4.14.

3. *For you are yet carnal.* So long as the flesh, that is, natural corruption, rules in a man, it takes possession of his mind so that the wisdom of God is denied entry. Because of that, if we wish to make any progress in the school of the Lord, we must first renounce our own understanding and our own will. Although there was some glimmer of religion in the Corinthians, for the most part, however, it was being extinguished.

For since there are among you. The proof is from the effects. For since jealousy, disputes and factions are fruits of the flesh, we can be sure that, wherever they are to be seen, there flourishes the root. These evils held sway among the Corinthians; therefore from that Paul shows clearly that they were carnal. He also uses the same argument in Galatians 5.25: 'If you live by the Spirit, walk also by the Spirit.' For since they wished to be considered spiritual, he calls them to look at their works, by which they were denying the profession of their lips. But notice the fitting order which Paul adopts here. For from jealousy are born disputes, which, once they are inflamed, break out into dangerous sects. Moreover, the mother of all these evils is ambition.

You walk after the manner of men. From this it is plain that the word *flesh* is not to be restricted merely to the lower desires, as sophists make out, calling the source of it sensuality; but it is predicated of the whole nature of man. For those who follow the guidance of nature are not governed by the Spirit of God. Those, according to the apostle's definition, are carnal, so that the flesh and man's natural ability are absolutely synonymous. Therefore Paul has good reason for asking elsewhere, that we be 'new creations in Christ' (II Cor. 5.17).

4. *For when one says etc.* Paul now tells us the precise form that the divisions took (and he does so by speaking as if he were one of the Corinthians, so giving more force to his description), viz. that each was boasting in his own particular teacher as if Christ were not the one teacher of all. Further, where people continue to be in the grip of a desire to please people like that, the Gospel makes little or no progress. However we must not take it that they made open profession of this in so many words, but the apostle finds fault with the misguided devotion, by which they were mastered. Nevertheless, as empty chattering usually goes with showing favour to people for the sake of one's own ends, it is likely that they did disclose their distorted outlook by what they said, singing the extravagant praises of their own teachers, at the same time as they were pouring contempt on Paul, and those like him.

What then is Apollos? and what is Paul? Ministers through whom you believed; and each as the Lord gave to him. I planted, Apollos watered;

but God gave the increase. So then neither is he that planteth anything, neither he that watereth; but God that giveth the increase. Now he that planteth and he that watereth are one: but each shall receive his own reward according to his own labour. For we are God's fellow-workers: ye are God's husbandry, God's building. (5-9)

5. *Who then is Paul?* Paul now begins to discuss the view that must be held about ministers, and the purpose for which they have been ordained by the Lord. But he names himself and Apollos rather than others to avoid being accused of jealousy. 'What else is the task of all ministers', he asks, 'but to bring you to faith by their preaching?' From this Paul infers that there ought to be no boasting in any man for faith allows no glorying except in Christ alone. It follows that those who extol men excessively deprive them of their true greatness. For the most important thing of all is that they are ministers of the faith, i.e. they gain followers not for themselves but for Christ. But although he appears to lessen the authority of ministers in this way, he does not however give it less than its due. For he is saying a great deal when he says that we obtain faith by their ministry. Moreover, the seal of approval is very clearly set on the efficacy of teaching by others (*externae doctrinae*), when it is called the instrument of the Holy Spirit; and pastors are being honoured with no ordinary description when God is said to use them as ministers to dispense the incomparable treasure of the faith.

As the Lord gave to each. [Calvin's Latin: *et sicut unicuique Dominus dedit.* Greek: καὶ ἑκάστῳ ὡς ὁ κύριος ἔδωκεν]. In Paul's Greek the particle of comparison, ὡς, *as*, is placed after ἑκάστῳ, *to each*; but the order has been inverted. Therefore so that the meaning might be clearer, I preferred 'as to each' (*sicut unicuique*) rather than 'to each as' (*unicuique sicut*). Besides, in some copies the particle καί, *and*, is missing, so that it runs into one, thus, 'ministers through whom you believed, as the Lord gave to each'. If we take that reading, the second clause will be added in explanation of the first, so that Paul might bring out what he meant by 'minister'. It is as if he were to say, 'Ministers are those whose labour God employs; not those who are equal to anything relying on their own strength, but those who are governed by His hand, as instruments.'

However, the reading which I have adopted, is, in my opinion, nearer the truth. If we follow it, the sentence will be richer, for it will consist of two clauses, as follows. In the first place ministers are those who place their services at Christ's disposal, so that you might believe in Him. Further, they have nothing of their own to be proud about, seeing that they do not accomplish anything on their own, and have no power for any undertaking except by the gift of God, and each according to his own measure; which shows that whatever an individual has, has its source in another. Finally, he binds them all together as if by a common bond, seeing that they stand in need of one another's help.

6. *I have planted, Apollos has watered.* Paul makes it clearer what that ministry was like by the use of a metaphor, by which the nature of the Word and the value of preaching are most appositely illustrated. In order that the earth may bear fruit, ploughing and sowing and all the other agricultural processes are necessary. But when all these have been done the labour of the farmer would be futile, if the Lord did not 'give the increase' from heaven by the influence of the sun, and more than that, by His own wonderful and secret power. Therefore, although the attentiveness of the farmer is not ineffective, and the seed he casts is not unproductive, nevertheless, it is only by the blessing of God that they are made to yield. For what is more astonishing than that the seed rots and then germinates? Similarly the Word of the Lord is seed, fruitful by its very nature. Ministers are, as it were, cultivators, who plough and sow. Then other aids follow, irrigation for example. Ministers are responsible for those tasks also, when, having sown the seed in the earth, they give as much aid as they can to the earth itself, until it brings forth what it has conceived. But the actual bringing of their labour to fruitfulness, is in very truth a miracle of divine grace, not a product of human industry.

Observe, however, from this passage how necessary the preaching of the Word is, and how necessary that it be done continually. Indeed it would be no more difficult for God to bless the earth without the attention of men, so that it might bring forth food on its own, than to draw out, or rather force out, its produce by means of a great deal of application on the part of men, and much sweat and frustration. But because the Lord has so appointed it that man should toil, and the earth should respond to his cultivating, let us act accordingly. Similarly there is nothing to hinder God from being able to implant faith in sleeping men, without their doing anything, if He so wished. But He has determined otherwise, viz. that faith is born of hearing. Therefore the person who is sure that he can come to faith by disregarding this means, acts just as if the farmers, giving up the plough, neglecting sowing and leaving all cultivation, were to open their mouths and expect food to fall into them from heaven.

We learn now what Paul has in mind about the continual preaching of the Word. It is clear that sowing is not enough, if the seed is not brought on by the frequent use of other helping agents. Therefore he who has already received the seed still needs watering, and it must not be left off until he has reached fullness of growth, in other words, until the end of his life. Apollos, then, who succeeded Paul in the ministry of the Word in Corinth, is said to have watered what Paul had sown.

7. *Neither is he that planteth anything.* It is clear, from what has already been said, that their work is not unimportant. Therefore we must see why Paul depreciates it in this way. First of all, indeed, it is right to note that he is accustomed to speak of ministers, as of the sacraments, in two ways. For sometimes he thinks of a minister as ordained by the Lord first of all for the regeneration of souls, thereafter for feeding them unto eternal life, for remitting sins, for renewing of the minds of men, for setting up the Kingdom of Christ and the destruction of Satan's. Accordingly, Paul assigns to the minister not only the duty of planting and watering, but also provides him with the power of the Holy Spirit so that his labour might not be unproductive. Similarly, in another passage (II Cor. 3.6) he calls himself a minister of the Spirit, not of the letter, for he writes the Word of the Lord in their hearts.

On the other hand he sometimes thinks of the minister as a servant, not a master; as an instrument, not the hand; finally, as a man, not God. Accordingly he leaves him nothing but his work, and indeed that is dead and useless, unless the Lord gives effective power to it by His Spirit. The reason for this view is that, when it is simply a question of the ministry, we ought not to pay attention to a man so much, but also to God working in him by the grace of the Spirit. This does not mean that the grace of the Spirit is always tied to the word of man, but that Christ puts forth His own power in the ministry which He instituted, in such a way that it is evident that it was not instituted in vain. In this way Christ does not take away or reduce anything which belongs to Himself in order to transfer it to a man. For He is not separated from the minister, but rather His power is made known as efficacious in the minister. But since, through the depravity of our judgement, we sometimes take advantage of this fact to make too much of men, we must make a distinction in order to correct this fault: the Lord must be placed separately on one side, and the minister on the other. It is then plain how needy man is in himself, and how completely lacking in power he is.

Therefore we should learn from this passage that ministers are put alongside the Lord for comparison. The reason for this comparison is that men, putting little value on the grace of God, are far too lavish in extolling ministers; and so they snatch away what is God's and transfer it to themselves. However, Paul always maintains the fullest sense of proportion, for when he says that 'God gives the increase', he means that the work of men themselves is not without success. We shall see in another passage that the same reasoning also applies to the sacraments. Therefore, although our Heavenly Father does not reject our work in

cultivating His soil, and does not allow it to be unfruitful, He nevertheless desires its success to depend on His blessing alone, so that all the
praise might remain His. Therefore if we want to gain any benefit
from our working, our striving, and our pressing on, we should be
aware that we shall make no progress unless He prospers our work, our
exertions, and perseverance, so that we may commit ourselves and
whatever we do to His grace.

8. *Now he who plants and he who waters are one.* By taking another
factor into account Paul shows that the Corinthians are wrongly taking
advantage of the names of their teachers in the interests of their parties
and factions. They are wrong because those teachers are striving with
united efforts for one thing, and they cannot be torn apart and separated
in any way except at the cost of deserting their duty at the same time.
'They are one', Paul says. In other words, they are so connected that
their union does not permit of separation, because one goal ought to
be set before the eyes of every one of them, because they are serving
the one Lord, and because they are engaged in the same work. Therefore if they devote their labour to the faithful cultivation of the Lord's
field, they will promote unity, and they will help each other with
common 'give and take'. That is a very different matter from their
names being standards for stirring up controversies. This is a fine
passage for encouraging ministers to seek unity. Meanwhile, however,
Paul indirectly reproves those ambitious teachers who were providing
the cause for divisions, and thereby making it plain that they were not
servants of Christ, but slaves of vain-gloriousness; and that they did
not toil at planting or watering, but rather at uprooting and burning.

Each shall receive his own reward. Paul teaches here what goal all
ministers should have before them: not being on the look-out for the
applause of the crowd, but pleasing the Lord. He does this in order to
call back to the judgement seat of God those ambitious teachers who
were intoxicated by the glory of the world and were thinking of
nothing else; and also in order to warn the Corinthians of the worth-
lessness of that empty acclamation which an elegant style and hollow
ostentation draw out. At the same time he reveals his own untroubled
conscience by these words, because he dares to look forward to the
judgement of God undaunted. For the reason why ambitious men try
to recommend themselves to the world is that they have not learned to
give themselves up to God; and Christ's heavenly Kingdom is not
before their eyes. Therefore, as soon as God does appear among them,
that foolish desire for winning men's approval vanishes.

9. *For we are God's fellow-workers.* This is the best argument. We
are engaged in the Lord's business, and it is to Him that we have hired
our labour. Therefore since He is faithful and fair He will not dis-

appoint us of our reward. For that reason the man who looks to men or depends on their recompence, is making a mistake. Here an extra-ordinary thing is said about the ministry, that, while God is able to carry things out by Himself, He takes us, insignificant men that we are, to Himself as helpers, and uses us as instruments. Certainly the Papists' wrong use of this text for establishing the freedom of the will is exceedingly foolish, for Paul does not teach here what men are capable of by their natural powers, but what the Lord does through them by His grace. Some give this explanation: Paul, who was God's workman, was a fellow-worker with his colleagues, i.e. the other teachers. That view seems harsh and forced to me, and in fact no reason compels us to have recourse to this subtle distinction. For it agrees very well with the apostle's intention that, while it is God's own function to build His temple or cultivate His vineyard, He receives ministers into a working association with Himself. He, by Himself, acts through them in such a way that they, in turn, work with Him for a common end. In regard to the reward of works, see my *Institutes* 3.18.

God's husbandry, God's building. These can be explained in two ways: active and passive. The active meaning is: you have been planted in the Lord's field by the labour of men in such a way that the Heavenly Father Himself is the real Farmer, the one who undertakes this planting. Again, you have been built up by men in such a way that He Himself is the real Master-builder. On the other hand the passive sense is: we have laboured in cultivating you, in sowing the Word of God in your midst, in watering. But we did not do that for our own sake, or that the fruit might come to be ours; but we have devoted our obedience to the Lord. In our eagerness to build you up, we have not been driven by a regard for our own advantage, but by a concern that you may be God's planting and building.

The second interpretation seems to me to be the better one. For I think that Paul wished to express here that true ministers do not labour for themselves but for the Lord. From this it follows that the Corin-thians were wrong in yielding themselves to men, when, by right, they belong to God alone. And in the first place he indeed calls them His husbandry, maintaining the metaphor already begun; then, in order to make a transition and widen his discussion, he takes up another metaphor, from architecture.

According to the grace of God which was given unto me, as a wise master-builder I laid a foundation; and another buildeth thereon. But let each man take heed how he buildeth thereon. For other foundation can no man lay than that which is laid, which is Jesus Christ. But if any man buildeth on the foundation gold, silver, costly stones, wood, hay,

stubble; each man's work shall be made manifest: for the day shall declare it, because it is revealed in fire; and the fire itself shall prove each man's work of what sort it is. If any man's work shall abide which he built thereon, he shall receive a reward. If any man's work shall be burned, he shall suffer loss: but he himself shall be saved; yet so as through fire.
(10–15)

10. *As a wise master-builder.* This is a most suitable metaphor, and therefore it occurs frequently in the Scriptures, as we shall see a little later on. Here indeed the apostle reveals his own faithfulness with much confidence and assurance. It had to be affirmed like that, not only in face of the disparagement of the wicked, but also of the pride of the Corinthians, who had already begun to treat his teaching with contempt. Therefore, the more they pushed him down, the higher does he rise, and as if he were on the highest of platforms, he proclaims that he had been the first master-builder of God among them, in laying the foundations, that he had fulfilled this role with wisdom, and that it is left to others to continue in the same way, and complete the superstructure, taking the work on the foundations as the standard. Let us take note that Paul says these things, first of all, in order to commend his teaching, which he saw being despised by the Corinthians; and secondly to curb the arrogance of others who, wanting to make a name for themselves, were eager for a new kind of teaching. Therefore he warns them not to attempt anything foolish in God's building. He prohibits them from doing two things. They must not attempt to lay another foundation; and they must not raise a superstructure that is out of keeping with the foundation.

According to the grace. Paul always takes great care not to divert to himself the least little bit of the glory that belongs to God. For he carries everything back to God, and leaves nothing for himself, except the fact that he was an instrument. But while he humbly submits to God in this way, he indirectly reproves the arrogance of those who thought nothing of obscuring the grace of God, so long as they themselves were well thought of. And he even hints that in that empty display for which they were much admired, there was nothing of the grace of the Spirit. As for himself, he truly frees himself from men's contempt, on the ground that he had been under the direction of God.

11. *For other foundation can no man lay.* This sentence has two parts: (1) that Christ is the one and only foundation of the Church; and (2) that the Corinthians have been properly founded on Christ by Paul's preaching. For it was necessary that they be brought back to Christ alone, for their ears were itching with an eagerness for novelty. It was a matter of great importance that Paul should be known as the principal

73

and (if I may say so) fundamental master-builder, from whose teaching they could not depart without forsaking Christ Himself. To sum up: the Church must quite definitely be founded on Christ alone; and Paul had carried out his role in this respect among the Corinthians so faithfully that his ministry could leave nothing to be desired. It follows that whoever may come after him cannot serve the Lord conscientiously, or be heard as ministers of Christ, in any other way than by taking pains to make their teaching like his, and to maintain the foundation which he has laid.

From this we can come to a certain conclusion about those who, when they follow true ministers, do not trouble to adapt themselves to their teaching, and to follow up a good beginning in order to make it perfectly plain that they are not undertaking something new. We can conclude that they are not working faithfully to build up the Church, but rather are its demolishers. For what is more destructive than confusing believers well grounded in pure doctrine, with a new kind of teaching, so that they are not sure where they stand and turn this way and that? On the other hand the fundamental doctrine, which it is forbidden to overthrow, is that we might learn Christ. For Christ is the one and only foundation of the Church. But there are many who use the name of Christ as a blind, and drag out the universal truth of God by the roots.

We must therefore note how the Church is properly built up on Christ; viz. if He alone is set up for righteousness, redemption, sanctification, wisdom, satisfaction, cleansing, in short for life and glory; or, if you prefer it briefer, if He is preached in such a way that His office and virtue are understood in the way they are presented at the end of the first chapter. Now, if Christ is not properly known, and is given merely the name of Redeemer, while at the same time righteousness, sanctification and salvation are sought elsewhere, He is ejected from the foundation, and counterfeit stones are substituted in His place. There is an example of this in what the Papists do, when they strip Him of almost all His adornments, and leave Him almost nothing but the bare name. Such persons therefore are a long way from being founded on Christ. For since Christ is the foundation of the Church, because He is the one and only source of salvation and eternal life, because in Him we know God the Father, because the fountain of all our blessings is in Him, then if He is not acknowledged as such, He immediately ceases to be the foundation.

But it may be asked whether Christ is only a part, or originator, of the teaching about salvation, as the foundation is only a part of the building. For if that were the case, believers would only make a beginning in Christ, and would be brought to completion without any connexion with Him, and indeed Paul seems to hint at that. My answer is that that is not the meaning of what he says, otherwise he would be contradicting himself when he says in Col. 2.3 that 'all the treasures of wisdom and knowledge are hidden in Him'. Therefore the man who has 'learned Christ' (Eph. 4.20) is already replete in the whole heavenly teaching. But since Paul's ministry was concerned with establishing the Corinthians, rather than with raising in their midst the highest part of the roof of the building, he only shows here what he had done, viz. that he had preached Christ, pure and simple. For that reason, thinking of what he had done, Paul calls Christ *the foundation*, but that does not mean to say, however, that he excludes Him from the rest of the building. In a word, Paul does not set any other kind of teaching in contrast to knowledge of Christ; he is rather pointing out the relationship between Him and the other ministers.

12. *But if anyone builds on this foundation.* He persists with the metaphor. It was not sufficient that the *foundation* had been laid, if the whole superstructure did not correspond to it. For since it would be absurd to build up cheap material on a golden foundation, so it is a wicked thing to bury Christ under other people's superimposed doctrines. Therefore, he means by 'gold, silver and jewels' teaching that is not only in keeping with Christ, but is also a superstructure in harmony with such a foundation. Moreover do not let us imagine that this teaching is drawn from sources other than Christ, but rather we must understand that we have to continue to teach Christ, until the building is completed. However we must pay attention to the order of doing things, so that a start may be made with general doctrine, and the more essential of the chief points, as the foundation. After that there follow reproof, exhortations, and whatever is needed for perseverance, strengthening and progress.

Since there is complete agreement about Paul's meaning so far, it follows, on the other hand, that the teaching which is described as 'wood, stubble and hay' does not conform to the foundation; teaching, that is, which is fabricated in men's minds, and then thrust upon us as oracles of God. For God wants His Church to be built up by the pure preaching of His Word, not by human fictions; and that is how you would describe whatever does nothing in the way of upbuilding. In that category are speculative questions which generally cater more for ostentation or some foolish desire, rather than the salvation of men.

Paul makes it known that at the last the quality of each person's work will be made manifest; even if it is concealed for the time being. It is as if he said, 'It can indeed happen that bad workmen are deceiving, so that the world does not make out at all how faithfully or dishonestly each has done his work. But what is now, as it were, submerged in

F   75

darkness must finally come to light. And what is now splendid in men's eyes must be overthrown before the face of God, and be regarded as worthless.'

13. *For the day will uncover it.* The Vulgate[1] has 'the day of the Lord'. But it is likely that the genitive was added by someone by way of explanation. For the meaning is quite adequate without that addition. For the description 'the day' is properly given to that time when darkness and obscurity are scattered, and truth is brought to light. Therefore the apostle declares that it cannot always be concealed, who have undertaken the Lord's work under false pretences, or who have carried out their duties faithfully. It is as if he said, 'Darkness will not always prevail; at last the light will shine out and will show everything up.' I acknowledge that that day is God's day, not man's. But the metaphor is more pleasing if you simply read 'the day', because Paul suggests in this way that the true servants of God are not always precisely distinguished from false workers, because good and bad points are covered by the cloak of night; yet that night will not last for ever. For ambition is blind, the favour of men is blind, the applause of the world is blind, but God will dispel this darkness later, in His own time. Take note that Paul always shows that he has the confidence that a good conscience brings; and with an unassailable greatness of mind he despises perverse judgements. Paul does so, first of all, to call back the Corinthians from the ambitious seeking of men's approval to a sound standard of judgement; and, secondly, to establish the faithfulness of his own ministry.

Because it will be revealed in fire. Having spoken of the teaching in metaphorical language, Paul now also uses metaphor in describing the actual means by which the teaching is examined as *fire*, so that the two different parts under comparison may be consistent with each other. Here, then, the fire is the Spirit of the Lord, who by His examination tests which teaching is like gold, and which like stubble. The nearer the teaching that God gives is brought to this fire, the clearer will it be. On the other hand what is produced in men's minds will vanish immediately, as stubble is consumed by fire. There also seems to be an allusion to 'the day', which he has mentioned. It is as though he said: 'At that time those things which a useless ambition concealed in the Corinthians like a dark night, will be brought to light by the splendour of the sun. More than that, there will at the same time be a powerful heat, not only for drying up and cleansing filth, but also for burning up all imperfections.' For, although men think they have acute powers of discernment, their acuteness nevertheless does not penetrate beyond the surface, which, generally, has no depth beneath

---

[1] Sixtus' and Clem. edns. Not WW.

it. The apostle makes appeal only to that day which examines every-thing to the depths of its being, not only by its brightness, but also by the fiery flame.

14. *If any man's work remains, he shall receive a reward.* He means that those who depend on men's estimation, so that they are satisfied if men pass them as acceptable, are foolish, because the work will receive praise and reward only after it has withstood the day of the Lord. Therefore Paul commands true ministers to pay attention to that day. (In regard to rewards see my *Institutes* 3.18.) For he declares, by using the word 'remains', that doctrines fly about as if they were not fixed, or better, they glisten for a short time like bubbles, until they are brought to face a serious test. From this it follows that all the plaudits of the world must be considered worthless, for God's judgement will soon expose their emptiness.

15. *If any man's work shall be burned.* It is as if he said: 'Let no-one flatter himself because, in men's opinion, he is rated among the eminent master-builders. For as soon as the day dawns, all his work must be completely ruined, if it is not approved by the Lord.' This, then, is the standard by which everyone's ministry must be tested.

Some explain this as referring to teaching, so that $\zeta\eta\mu\iota o\hat{\upsilon}\sigma\theta\alpha\iota$ is 'perishing' and nothing else. What follows after they refer back to the foundation, because the Greek $\theta\epsilon\mu\acute{\epsilon}\lambda\iota o\varsigma$ (foundation) is masculine. But they do not pay enough attention to the whole context. For in this passage Paul does not subject his own teaching to testing, but that of others. Therefore mention of the foundation at this point will be out of place. He has just said that 'each man's work will be tested by fire'. He then passes to an alternative, which ought not to be carried back beyond that general statement. But it is certain that there Paul was speaking only of the building which had been erected on the founda-tion. Already in the first alternative he promised a reward to good master-builders, whose work will have been approved. Therefore the antithesis in the second alternative fits in very well, viz. those who have mixed stubble, or wood, or straw will be disappointed of the praise for which they look.

But he himself will be saved etc. There is no doubt that Paul is speaking of those who, while always retaining the foundation, mix hay with gold, stubble with silver, wood with precious stones. In other words, they build on Christ, but because of the weakness of the flesh they give way to some human viewpoint, or through ignorance they turn aside to some extent from the strict purity of the Word of God. Many of the saints were like that, Cyprian, Ambrose, Augustine and others. You can also add, if you like, from those nearer our own day, Gregory and Bernard, and others like them, whose purpose it was to build on

Christ, but who, however, often turned away from the right method of building.

Paul says that men like that can be saved, but on this condition: if the Lord wipes off their ignorance, and purifies them from all uncleanness; and that is what the phrase 'as if by fire' means. Therefore he wants to suggest that he himself does not deprive them of the hope of salvation, provided that they willingly accept the loss of the work they have done, and are cleansed by God's mercy, as gold is purified in the furnace. Moreover, even if God sometimes purifies His people by sufferings, I take 'fire' to mean here the testing by the Spirit. In that way God corrects and destroys the ignorance of His people, by which they were controlled for a time. I know very well that many refer this to the Cross, but I am sure that my interpretation will satisfy all of sound judgement.

We must conclude by making a reply, in passing, to the Papists, who argue from this passage in support of purgatory. Their view is that sinners, whom God forgives, pass through the fire in order to be saved. So in that way they suffer punishment from God, in order that His justice might be satisfied. I omit their innumerable comments about the amount of punishment and about release from it. But I ask, who in fact are those who pass through the fire? Paul is quite definitely speaking about ministers only. 'But', they say, 'the same consideration applies to all.' As to that, God is certainly the best judge, not we! But even allowing them that, also, how childishly they fasten on the word fire. But what is the purpose of the fire but the consuming of hay and straw, and, on the other hand, the testing of gold and silver? Do they mean that doctrines are separated out by the fire of their purgatory? Who has ever learned from it how truth differs from falsehood? Also when will that day come in whose light every man's work will be shown up? Did it begin with the world's beginning, and will it last on continuously until its end? If stubble, hay, gold and silver are used metaphorically, as they are bound to allow, what sort of agreement will there be between the different clauses, if fire is not used metaphorically? No more about such worthless trifles, for their absurdity stares us steadily in the face! For I think that the apostle's real meaning is quite settled already.

Know ye not that ye are a temple of God, and that the Spirit of God dwelleth in you? If any man destroyeth the temple of God, him shall God destroy; for the temple of God is holy, which temple ye are. Let no man deceive himself. If any man thinketh that he is wise among you in this world, let him become a fool, that he may become wise. For the wisdom of this world is foolishness with God. For it is written, He that taketh the wise in their craftiness: and again, The Lord knoweth the reasonings of the wise, that they are vain. Wherefore let no one glory in men. For all things are yours; whether Paul, or Apollos, or Cephas, or the world, or life, or death, or things present, or things to come; all are yours; and ye are Christ's; and Christ is God's. (16–23)

16. *Do you not know etc.?* After giving advice to the teachers about their task, Paul now turns to the pupils so that they too might take heed to themselves. He had said to the teachers: 'You are the master-builders of God's house.' Now he says to the people: 'You are the temples of God. It is your responsibility to take care that you are not defiled in any way.' Now, what he has in mind is that they do not give themselves dishonourably into men's hands. Indeed he confers a rare honour on them, in speaking in this way, but he does it in order to show their guilt more clearly. For since God has consecrated them as a temple for Himself, at the same time He has appointed them as keepers of His temple. They are therefore violating a sacred trust in abandoning themselves to men. He calls all of them, together, the one temple of God. For every single believer is a living stone for the erecting of God's building. However, individuals also are sometimes called temples. A little later Paul uses the same idea again, but for another purpose. In that passage he is dealing with chastity, but here he is urging them to maintain to the last their faith in the obedience of Christ, and Christ alone. The use of the question gives greater emphasis, for, in calling upon them as witnesses, he is suggesting that he is speaking to them about something of which they were well aware.

And the Spirit of God etc. This is the reason why they are the temple of God. Therefore the 'and' should be read as 'because'. That is common enough, as, for example, where the poet says, 'You have heard it, and it has been reported.' Paul says: 'You are the temples because He dwells in you by His Spirit; for no unclean place can be God's dwelling-place.' In this passage we have clear evidence for affirming the divinity of the Holy Spirit. For if He were a created being, or simply something given to us, He could not, by indwelling us, make us the temples of God. At the same time we understand how God communicates Himself to us, and the chain by which we are bound to Him, viz. His pouring into us the power of His Holy Spirit.

17. *If any man destroys the temple of God him shall God destroy.* Paul adds a grave warning: because the temple of God ought to be most sacred, then whoever spoils it will not escape with impunity. But he is now speaking of that kind of violation when men push themselves into God's place so that they might lord it in the Church. For just as

faith, which is devoted to the pure teaching of Christ, is called elsewhere 'spiritual chastity', so it also consecrates us for the right and pure worship of God. For as soon as we are infected by the concoctions of men, the temple of God is defiled as if by filth, and that is because the sacrifice of faith, which God declares is His alone, is then offered to created things.

18. *Let no man deceive himself.* Here Paul puts his finger on the root of the trouble, since all the damage originated in their thinking far too highly of themselves. Therefore he strongly advises them not to be carried away by a wrong idea, in claiming any wisdom as their own. By that he means that all who rely on their own understanding are deceiving themselves. But in my opinion he is addressing the taught as much as the teachers. For the hearers were better disposed towards, and lent an ear to, those ambitious men. And because they were too fastidious in taste, the result was that the simple Gospel was milk and water to them. The teachers, wanting to be well thought of, cared for nothing but show. Therefore Paul warns both of them: 'Do not let one of you flatter himself on his own wisdom, rather, let him who thinks he is wise, become a fool in this world.' To put it another way: 'Let him who has a high place in the world because of a reputation for wisdom, take himself in hand, and empty himself, and become a fool in his own eyes.'

Moreover, by these words the apostle does not ask us to make a total surrender of the wisdom which is either innate or acquired by long experience. He only asks that we subjugate it to God, so that all our wisdom might be derived from His Word. 'To become a fool in this world', or in our own eyes, means this: when we prefer to yield to God and to embrace with fear and reverence whatever He teaches, rather than to follow what seems acceptable to us.

The meaning of the phrase 'in this world' is just as if he had said: 'according to the reasoning or opinion of the world.' For this is the wisdom of the world: if we think we, in ourselves, are equal to taking counsel about everything, to governing ourselves, to administering all our undertakings; if we depend on no-one else; and if we need no-one to direct us, but are capable of managing our own affairs.

Therefore, on the other hand, 'a fool in this world' is someone who renounces his own understanding, and, as if he were blind, allows himself to be guided by the Lord; who, lacking confidence in himself leans entirely on the Lord; who bases all His wisdom on Him; who yields himself, obedient and willing to learn, to God. Our wisdom must vanish by this method, so that God's will may have sway over our lives; and we must be emptied of our own understanding, so that we may be filled with the wisdom of God. 'In this world' can either be joined to the first clause, or the second. However, since the meaning is much the same, the reader can make his own choice.

19. *For the wisdom of this world.* This is an argument from the contrary. The confirmation of the one means the destruction of the other. Therefore since the wisdom of this world is foolishness with God, it follows that the only way we can be wise in God's sight is to be foolish in the world's. We have already explained what Paul means by the wisdom of this world: for natural insight is a gift of God. The arts men naturally pursue, and all the disciplines by which wisdom is acquired are also gifts of God. But they have their definite limits, for they do not penetrate into the heavenly Kingdom of God. Accordingly they ought to be maid-servants, not mistresses. Besides that, they must be looked upon as useless and worthless until they are subordinated completely to the Word and Spirit of God. But if they set themselves up against Christ they must be considered injurious pests. If they maintain that they are capable of anything by themselves, they must be regarded as the worst of hindrances.

Therefore the wisdom of this world is, to Paul, that which wrongly assumes lordship to itself, and refuses to be directed by the Word of God, or to be humbled so that it might be completely subjected to Him. Therefore, until it comes about that a man acknowledges that he knows nothing except what he has learnt from God, and, having rejected his own understanding, puts himself under the direction of Christ alone, he is wise from the world's point of view, but he is foolish in God's eyes.

For it is written: He taketh the wise in their craftiness. Paul supports what he has said by two texts from Scripture. The *first* of these is taken from Job 5.13. There the wisdom of God is exalted because in its presence no earthly wisdom can stand its ground. There is no doubt that in that context the prophet is speaking about the cunning and the designing. But since the wisdom of man is always like that when it is divorced from God, Paul quite rightly adapts it to mean that however much wisdom men acquire by themselves it counts for nothing in God's sight. The *second* is from Psalm 94.11, where, after David claimed for God the function of, and the authority for, teaching all, he adds that 'He knows the thoughts of all to be empty'. Therefore no matter how highly they are valued by us they are futile in God's judgement. This is an excellent passage for bringing down the confidence of the flesh; for here God declares from above that whatever the mind of man conceives and purposes is simply nothingness.

21. *Wherefore let no one glory in men.* Since nothing is more worthless than man, how little security there is in leaning upon an insubstantial shadow! Therefore he makes a valid inference from the pre-

ceding sentence in saying that there must be no glorying in men, since there we see how the Lord deprives all men of grounds for boasting. However this conclusion depends on all he has been teaching in the preceding argument, as we shall soon see. For since we belong to Christ alone, Paul is quite right in teaching us that a pre-eminence given to men, which involves a diminution of Christ's glory, is sacrilege.

22. *All things are yours.* He adds a reference to the position and standing that teachers ought to be given, viz. such that does not detract from the unique office of Teacher that belongs to Christ. Therefore since Christ is the one and only Teacher of the Church, since He alone and in all circumstances must be listened to, it is necessary to distinguish the others from Him. Christ Himself has also borne witness to Himself in similar terms in Matthew 23.8, and the Father is not commending any other person to us in this word: *Hear Him* (Matt. 17.5). Therefore since He alone is endowed with authority to rule us by His Word, Paul says that other men are ours, in other words, that God has appointed them in order that we might have the benefit of them, but not that they might be dictators to our consciences. Therefore he shows, on the one hand, that they are not useless, and, on the other hand, he keeps them in their place, so that they might not be swollen-headed, and so be in opposition to Christ.

As far as the present passage is concerned Paul is using hyperbole in what he adds about death, life and so on. Yet he wanted to argue from the greater to the less, as it were, as follows: 'Since Christ has placed life, death and everything else under us, can there be any doubt that he also made men subject to us, to help us by what they do for us; certainly they are not to be overbearing and despotic.'

Further, in light of this someone might make the point, that the writings of both Paul and Peter are subject to our judgement, seeing that they were men, and they are not exempt from the common lot of others. My answer is that while Paul does not in the least spare himself and Peter, he advises the Corinthians to distinguish between the man himself and the dignity and character of the office. It is as if he said, 'As for myself, seeing that I am a man, I wish to be judged only as a man, in order that Christ alone might be the conspicuous one in my ministry.' Still, we must on the whole maintain, that all who exercise the office of the ministry, from the greatest to the least, are ours, so that we are at liberty not to accept what they teach until they make it plain that it is derived from Christ. For they must all be tested and obedience must be given to them only when they have shown that they are true servants of Christ. But so far as Peter and Paul are concerned, the Lord has given more than enough evidence, so that there is no shadow of doubt that their teaching has its source in Him. In consequence, when we cherish and revere, as a declaration from heaven, whatever they have made known, we are hearing not so much them, as Christ speaking in them.

23. *Christ is God's.* This subjection (of Christ to God) refers to the humanity of Christ; for, in clothing Himself with our flesh He took to Himself the form and condition of a slave, so that He might make Himself obedient to the Father in every respect (Phil. 2.7, 8). And in order that we may cleave to God through Him, it is certain that He must have God as Head. But we must note the purpose Paul had in mind when he added this. For he advises us that our fullest happiness consists in our union with God who is the chief good. That is actually effected when we are gathered together under the Head whom the Heavenly Father has set over us. In similar terms Christ said to His disciples (John 14.28): 'You must rejoice, because I am going to the Father, for the Father is greater than I.' For there he sets Himself forth as the Mediator by whom believers may come to the original source of all blessings. It is certain that those who leave that one Head, are deprived of such a great benefit. That is why this arrangement, that those wishing to remain under the rule of God place themselves under Christ alone, fits in well with the tenor of this passage.

CHAPTER FOUR

Let a man so account of us, as of ministers of Christ, and stewards of the mysteries of God. Here, moreover, it is required in stewards, that a man be found faithful. But with me it is a very small thing that I should be judged of you, or of man's judgement: yea, I judge not mine own self. For I know nothing against myself; yet am I not hereby justified: but he that judgeth me is the Lord. Wherefore judge nothing before the time, until the Lord come, who will both bring to light the hidden things of darkness, and make manifest the counsels of the hearts; and then shall each man have his praise from God. (1-5)

1. *Let a man consider us in this way.* Since it was a matter of grave concern to see that the church was torn into harmful factions in this way, because of people's likes and dislikes, Paul begins to discuss the ministry of the Word still further. Three things are to be considered here in their order. *First* of all Paul defines the office of a pastor of the Church. *Secondly* he shows that it is not enough for anyone to present a title, or even venture on the work, but he must also be faithful in carrying out the duties of the office. *Thirdly*, since the Corinthians' judgement of him was quite distorted, he calls both them and himself back to the judgement seat of Christ.

First then, he shows the place that must be given to any teacher of the Church. In dealing with this he exercises restraint in what he is saying so that he does not throw over the dignity of the ministry, or, on the other hand, make more of men than is justified. Both of these positions are extremely dangerous; because contempt for the Word is born of a down-grading of ministers; while, on the other hand, if they are given far more importance than they deserve, ministers take advantage of their freedom and do just as they like, working against the Lord. Now, Paul's moderation lies in his calling them ministers of Christ. In doing so he means that they should not be attending to their own work, but to that of the Lord, who has hired their services. He also suggests that they have not been appointed to govern the Church imperiously, but to be under the supreme power of Christ. In short they are servants, not masters.

The addition, *stewards of the mysteries of God*, describes the character (*genus*) of the ministry. By that, he means that their function is confined to dispensing the secret things of God. In other words they hand over to men, 'from hand to hand' as we say, not what suits their own taste, but what the Lord has committed to their charge. He might put it like this: 'God chose them to be ministers of His Son in order that He might disseminate His heavenly wisdom to men through them. For that reason they must confine themselves strictly to that task.' However, he seems to take the Corinthians to task indirectly, for, having neglected the heavenly mysteries, they had begun to follow, far too eagerly, after strange things, which men concocted, and that was why they rated their teachers only by the standard of worldly learning.

Paul does honour to the Gospel in calling its content the mysteries of God. Further, since the sacraments are connected with these mysteries as appendages, it follows that those who are responsible for dealing with the Word, are also authorized to dispense them.

2. *Moreover it is required in ministers.* It is as if he said: 'It is little use being a steward (*dispensator*), if the stewardship (*dispensatio*) is wrong.' Now the rule governing true stewardship, is to carry out the duties faithfully. We should pay careful attention to this passage for we see how, in an arrogant way, the Papists wish that everything they do and teach should be authoritative, merely on the pretext of their being called 'pastors'. But so far from Paul being satisfied with the mere title, the rightful call is not even enough for him, unless the person who has been called carries out the duties of the office faithfully. Therefore, as often as the Papists present us with the camouflage of a name in order to maintain the despotic sway of their idol, let us make reply that Paul requires more than this in ministers of Christ. Yet, if everything is properly taken into account, you will find that the Pope and his entourage lack not only faithfulness in carrying out the duties of the office, but also the ministry itself.

But this passage joins issue not only with bad teachers, but also with all those who have some other end in view than the glory of Christ, and the upbuilding of the Church. For it is not the case that everyone who teaches the truth is consistently faithful, but only the person who desires from the bottom of his heart to serve the Lord and to advance the Kingdom of Christ. And indeed Augustine helpfully assigns to hirelings a middle position between wolves and good teachers. Further, in that passage Augustine speaks more clearly, indeed, than Paul about the fact that Christ also requires wisdom from a good steward. But the meaning is the same. For Christ means by 'faithful', integrity of conscience, which ought to go with sound and prudent deliberation. Paul means by a 'faithful minister' someone who, with knowledge as well as uprightness of heart, fulfills the role of a good and genuine minister.

3. *But with me it is a very small thing.* It remained for Paul to bring

his faithfulness right into the centre of the picture so that the Corinthians might make up their minds about him from that. But because their judgement was corrupt, he turns that down, and appeals to the judgement seat of Christ. The Corinthians were going wrong because they were fascinated by outward appearances, and did not pay heed to the true and proper marks of distinction. Therefore he very boldly testifies that he despises a judgement that is twisted and blind like theirs. In this he rightly pricks the vanity of the false apostles who were on the look-out for the approval of men and nothing else, and considered themselves happy if they were the objects of men's admiration. He is also severe in his censure of the Corinthians' arrogance, for it was the source of their blindness in judgement.

But it may well be asked what right Paul had, not only to reject the condemnation of one Church, but also to exempt himself from the judgement of men. This may be asked in view of the fact that it is the common lot of all pastors to be judged by the Church. My answer is that it is the mark of a good pastor to allow both his teaching and his life to be examined by the judgement of the Church, and it is the sign of a good conscience when he does not avoid the light of examination. For instance Paul himself was definitely ready to submit to the judgement of the Church at Corinth, and to be called to give account both of his life and teaching, if there had been among them a proper means of inquiry; for he often grants them this power, and of his own accord earnestly presses them to be willing to judge aright. But when a faithful pastor sees that he is overborne by hostile and wrongly-directed desires, and that no place is given to fairness and truth, then, regardless of what men think, he ought to appeal to God and have recourse to His judgement seat, especially when he cannot secure the undertaking of a true and proper hearing.

Therefore let the servants of the Lord remember that they must act in this way, let them allow their teaching and life to be brought to the test, and more than that, let them put themselves forward voluntarily; and, if there is any complaint against them, let them not refuse to reply. But if they see that they are condemned without a hearing, and judgement is passed without their case being heard, let them lift themselves to this level of greatness, where, by disdaining what men think, they wait undaunted for God to be their Judge. Long ago, when the prophets had to deal with unbending people, who dared to despise the Word of God confronting them in the prophets, they put themselves in a commanding position like that, so as to trample on that devilish obstinacy, which, as is well known, overthrows the sovereign sway of God and the light of truth. But when someone is offered the chance of defending himself, or at least when he needs to clear himself, and he appeals to God as a subterfuge, he will not assert his innocence in that way, but will rather betray his very great impudence.

Or of man's judgement. [Latin: *aut ab humano die.* Greek: ἢ ὑπὸ ἀνθρωπίνης ἡμέρας.] Even if others explain this differently my view is that it is easier to take the word 'day' metaphorically to mean 'judgement', because there are days appointed for administering justice, and parties are cited for a certain day. Paul calls it 'man's day' when judgement is pronounced, not according to the truth or the Word of God, but according to the fancy or thoughtlessness of men; when, in fact, God is not on the bench. Paul is saying: 'Let men sit in judgement as much as they like, it is enough for me that God will rescind whatever decision they have made.'

Yea, I judge not mine own self. The meaning is: 'I do not dare to judge myself, even though I am the one who knows myself best; how then will you, who do not know me nearly so well, judge me?' And he proves that he does not venture to judge himself, by saying that although he may not be personally aware of any wrong at all, that does not mean, however, that he is innocent in God's eyes. He therefore concludes that what the Corinthians claim for themselves, belongs to God alone. He says, 'When I have made a thorough examination of myself, I realize that my vision is not penetrating enough for me to see what the inner recesses of my being are really like. That is why I leave this to God, for only He is able to judge, and only He has the right to do so. As for you, on what ground will you lay claim to be able to do more?'

However, because it would be nonsense to debar all kinds of judgement, e.g. those of individuals about themselves, of each person about his brother, or of all together about their pastor, we must understand that Paul is not referring here to human actions, which can be adjudged good or bad according to the Word of the Lord, but to the worth of each person, which ought not to be assessed by the decision of men. It is God's prerogative to determine the value of each person, and what honour he deserves. The Corinthians, however, despised Paul, and were thoughtlessly setting others up in a high position, as if the examination which belonged to God alone, was a matter of their jurisdiction. This is the 'man's day' which he has already mentioned, viz. when men mount the judgement seat, and, as if they were gods, anticipate the day of Christ, who has been appointed sole Judge by the Father; when they allot to each one his position of honour, putting some in a high place, and relegating others to the lowest seats. But what principle governs their distinctions? They pay attention to what appears on the surface and nothing else, and so what is noble and honourable to them is often an abomination in the sight of God.

If anyone makes the further objection that ministers of the Word can be distinguished in this world by their works, as trees by their fruits, I acknowledge that that is indeed true, but we must consider those with whom Paul had to deal. They were men who were simply out for ostentation and show in judging, and who were arrogating to themselves that power, from which Christ Himself abstained when He was in this world, of assigning to each one his place in the Kingdom of God. Therefore he does not prevent us from making up our minds about those whom we have come to know to be faithful, and whom we commend as such; nor does he forbid our deciding who are bad workmen according to the Word of God. But he condemns the effrontery that is evident when some, governed by ambition, are put before others, not because they deserve it, but because proper account is not taken of all their circumstances.

4. *For I know nothing against myself.* Let us note that Paul is speaking here not about his whole life, but only about his carrying out of the duties of the apostleship. For if he had really been conscious of nothing wrong in himself, the complaint he makes in Romans 7.19 would not be genuine, viz. the evil which he would not that he does; and that he is prevented by sin from yielding himself totally to God. Therefore, Paul was aware of sin dwelling in himself and confessed it. But when it comes to his apostleship, and that is what he is dealing with here, he had conducted himself with so much integrity and faithfulness that his conscience did not accuse him in any way. This is no ordinary testimony, and it clearly shows how upright and holy of heart he was. But he denies that he is justified by that, i.e. that he is innocent and free from all guilt in the sight of God. Why? Because God is definitely far more penetrating in perception than we are, and therefore what appears dazzling and beautiful to us is filthy in His eyes. There is an excellent and very beneficial warning here not to measure the strictness of God's justice by our own ideas. For our perception is poor, but God is penetrating beyond measure. We are far too lenient in what we think about ourselves, but God is a very strict Judge. Therefore what Solomon says is true (Prov. 21.2): 'Every way of a man is right in his own eyes: But the Lord weigheth the hearts.'

Papists take advantage of this passage in order to shake the assurance of faith to its foundations, and indeed I confess that if their teaching were accepted we could only be in a state of wretched anxiety all our life. For what sort of peace of mind shall we possess, if it were decided from our works whether we are acceptable to God? I hold, therefore, that from the main foundation of the Papists there springs nothing but constant disturbance of consciences. On that account we teach that we must have recourse to the free promise of mercy which is offered to us in Christ, so that we may know with certainty that we are reckoned righteous by God.

5. *Wherefore judge nothing before the time.* It is evident from this conclusion that Paul was condemning, not every kind of judgement whatever, but only the hasty and rash judgement of matters without proper examination. For the Corinthians were not looking with un-prejudiced eyes at each person's character, but, being in the grip of ambition, they made the mistake of elevating one person and down-grading another, and took upon themselves what is more than men have right to do, the determining of each person's merit. Let us know then how much *is* allowed us, what is even now subject to examination by us, and what must be deferred until the day of Christ, and let us not attempt to go beyond these limits. For there are some things that are now plain to see, and others that are lying buried and hidden until the day of Christ.

Who will bring to light. If this is a true and proper statement about the day of Christ, it follows that the affairs of this world are never so well ordered that many things are not enveloped in darkness; that never is there so much light that many things do not remain obscure. I am speaking about the life and actions of men. In the second part of the sentence he explains what is the cause of the darkness and disorder, so that everything is not plain now. It is, of course, because there are extraordinary secret places and very deep recesses in the human heart. Therefore, until the thoughts of the hearts are disclosed, there will always be darkness.

And then shall each man have his praise from God. It is as if he said: 'Now you Corinthians act as if you were superintendents of the public games, for you give some the crown, and others you send away in disgrace. But this right and this function belong to Christ. You are doing this before the time, before it is clear who deserves a crown. The Lord indeed has appointed a day in which He will make it known.' This statement springs from the confidence of a good conscience, which also gives this benefit that, when we leave the matter of our praise in God's hands, we discount the acclamation of men and the hollow words they use.

Now these things, brethren, I have in a figure transferred to myself and Apollos for your sakes; that in us ye might learn not to go beyond the things which are written; that no one of you be puffed up for the one against the other. For who maketh thee to differ? and what hast thou that thou didst not receive? but if thou didst receive it, why dost thou glory, as if thou hadst not received it? Already are ye filled, already ye

89

*are become rich, ye have reigned without us: yea and I would that ye
did reign, that we also might reign with you.* (6–8)

6. *I have in a figure transferred etc.* We may infer from this, that it
was not those who were devoted to Paul who were founders of the
parties, for it is quite certain that they had received no instructions to
do so, but rather it was those who, moved by ambition, had put
themselves in the hands of the ostentatious teachers. But because he
could make particular reference to his own name and that of his
brethren more freely and with less odium, he preferred to illustrate
from his own case the fault that was in others. At the same time, in
what must be an annoying way to them, he finds fault with the founders
of the parties, and points with his finger at the sources from which
this fatal separation took its rise. For he suggests that if they had
been content with the good teachers, this evil would not have befallen
them.

That in us you might learn. Other manuscripts have 'that in you'.
Both readings are quite suitable, and no difference of meaning is involved. For Paul wishes to say: 'For the sake of example I have transferred these things to myself and Apollos, so that you might apply this
pattern to yourselves. Learn therefore in us, i.e. in the example in our
lives, which I have placed before you as a mirror.' Or 'learn in you,
i.e. apply this example to yourselves'.

But what does he want them to learn? That no one be puffed up
against the other for his teacher, i.e. that they should not be swelled-
headed about their teachers, and should not misuse their names to keep
sects alive, and to split the Church with disagreements. And note that
pride or self-glorification is the cause and starting point of all controversies, when each person, claiming for himself more than he is entitled
to have, is eager to have others in his power.

The phrase, 'beyond that which is written', can be explained in two
ways, as referring either to what Paul has written, or to the scriptural
proofs which he has adduced. But because this is not very important,
readers are free to choose whichever they prefer.

7. *For who maketh thee to differ?* The meaning is: 'Whoever the man
is who is eager for prominence and disturbs the Church with his
ambition, let him come out into the open. I shall ask him who puts
him before other people, i.e. who has given him this right of being
taken out of the rank that others have, and of being superior to others.'
Now this whole argument depends on the arrangement which the
Lord has established in His Church, that members of the Body of
Christ should cohere together, and that each one of them should be
content with his own place, his own rank, his own function, and the

honour he himself is given. If one member wants to give up his place to jump into another's place, and take possession of his office what will be the fate of the whole Body? Let us therefore realize that the Lord has placed us together in the Church, and He has allotted to each his station, in such a way that under one Head we may help each other. Let us also realize that we have been given so many differing gifts that we may serve the Lord unassumingly and humbly, and apply ourselves to advance the glory of Him who has bestowed on us everything we have. Therefore the best method of correcting the ambition of those who wanted to be superior, was to call them back to God, so that they might know that not one of them had a say as to whether he was put in a high or a humble position, for God alone does that. They should also know that God does not grant so much to anyone that he is promoted to the place of the Head; but He distributes His gifts in such a way that He alone receives the glory in everything.

'To make to differ' is taken here to mean 'to make outstanding'. Augustine often puts this text to skilful use in contending, against the Pelagians, that whatever excellence there is in men is not implanted by nature, so that it can be attributed to nature or heredity, nor is it procured of our own free will so as to put God under our control, but it flows from His mercy which is pure and free. For there is no doubt that here Paul places the grace of God over against the merit or worthiness of men.

What hast thou? This bears out what is said in the previous phrase. For the man who has nothing that can mark him out as superior to others can have no right to set himself above them. For what is more futile than boasting without any justification for it? But no man has anything in his own resources to make him superior; therefore whoever puts himself on a higher level is foolish and impertinent. The true basis of Christian humility is, on the one hand, not to be self-satisfied, for we know that we have no good in ourselves at all; and, on the other hand, if God has implanted any good in us, to be, for that reason, all the more indebted to His grace. In a word, we must not boast in anything (as Cyprian says), because we possess nothing.

Why dost thou glory, as if thou hadst not received it? Note that no room is left for taking pride in ourselves, when it is by the grace of God we are what we are. And that is what we had in the first chapter, that Christ is the source of all our blessings, so that we may learn to glory in the Lord, and we do not do that until we give up our own glory. And God only gets what is His right when we have been emptied, so that it may be plain that anything commendable in us comes from outside ourselves.

8. *Already are ye filled.* He has curbed their ill-founded confidence

in earnest, and in plain language. Now he makes fun of it, speaking ironically, and this because they were so highly delighted with themselves as if their happiness was complete. Step by step he also proceeds to bring out their insolence. First he says that they are filled, and this refers to what is past. Then he adds that they are rich, which applies to the future. Lastly he says that they have undertaken to reign—and that goes a lot further than either of the other two. It is as if he said: 'What will become of you when you seem not only to be full for the present, but also rich for the future, and more than that, rulers?'

At the same time he tacitly charges them with ingratitude, because they were bold enough to look down upon him, or rather upon those at whose hands they had obtained everything. He says, 'without us'. 'For Apollos and I mean nothing to you now, although it was by our work that the Lord bestowed everything upon you. What bad manners it is to make the gifts of God something to preen yourself about, at the same time looking down your nose at those through whom you have received them!'

And I would that ye did reign. He makes it plain here that he does not begrudge them their happiness. that is to say if they have any; and that even from the beginning he did not desire to rule over them, but only to bring them into the Kingdom of God. On the other hand, however, he means that the kingdom, in which they were boasting, is imaginary, and that their exultation is spurious and harmful. For the only true glorying is that which all the sons of God enjoy under Christ their Head, and each one according to the measure of grace given to him.

For by these words, *that we also might reign with you,* he means: 'In your own eyes you are so illustrious that you do not hesitate to despise me and those like me, but take note how futile your boasting is. For you can have no glory in God's eyes in which we do not share; for, if having the Gospel of God is something that brings you glory, how much more to us, by whose ministry it was brought to you? Indeed this foolish attitude is common to all proud people, with the result that, when they lay hold of everything for themselves, they deprive themselves of every blessing, and more than that, renounce the hope of eternal salvation.'

For, I think, God hath set forth us the apostles last of all, as men doomed to death: for we are made a spectacle unto the world, and to angels, and to men. We are fools for Christ's sake, but ye are wise in Christ; we are weak, but ye are strong; ye have glory, but we have dishonour. Even unto this present hour we both hunger, and thirst, and are naked, and are buffeted, and have no certain dwelling place; and we toil, working with our own hands: being reviled, we bless; being persecuted, we endure; being defamed, we intreat: we are made as the filth of the world, the offscouring of all things, even until now.

I write not these things to shame you, but to admonish you as my beloved children. For though ye should have ten thousand tutors in Christ, yet have ye not many fathers: for in Christ Jesus I begat you through the gospel. (9-15)

9. *For I think etc.* It is uncertain if he is speaking about himself alone, or whether he includes Apollos and Sylvanus, for he sometimes calls men like them apostles. I prefer however to take it as referring to himself alone. If anyone wishes to give it wider application, I have no great objection, provided that he does not understand it, like Chrysostom, to mean that all the apostles have been relegated to the least significant place, as if they were in disgrace. For there is no doubt that he means by 'last' those who had been admitted to the apostolic order after the resurrection of Christ. But he admits that he is like those who are exhibited to people just before they are dragged off to death. For the meaning of *set forth* is illustrated in those who were led through the streets in a triumph for the sake of a show, and then dragged off to prison to be strangled. He brings that out more clearly when he adds that he had been made a spectacle. He says: 'It is my lot to show the spectacle of my afflictions to the world, like those who are condemned either to fight with wild beasts, or to the gladiatorial games, or to some other kind of torture, and then brought before the gazing throng; and for me it is not a case of just a few spectators, but of the whole world.' Note Paul's wonderful steadfastness, for when he saw that he was treated by God like this he did not break down or lose heart. For he did not put it down to the high-handedness of the world that he was, as it were, led forth in disgrace to the games in the arena, but he ascribes it all to the providence of God.

The last part of the sentence, *to angels and to men*, I take to mean clearly: 'I present myself as a provider of sport and as a spectacle not only to the earth but also to heaven.' This passage has usually been explained as meaning devils, since it seemed absurd that it should refer to the good angels. But Paul does not mean that all who are witnesses of his misfortune are delighted with what they see. He simply wants to say that God guides his life in such a way that he seems to have been appointed to provide sport for the whole world.

10. *We are fools for Christ's sake.* This contrast is shot through with irony and cutting remarks, for it was manifestly intolerable and indeed absurd that the Corinthians should be happy in every way, and enjoying fame according to human standards, at the same time as they were seeing their teacher and father suffering distress because of utter dis-

grace, and misfortunes of every kind. There are those who think that
Paul humbles himself in this way so that he may in all seriousness credit
the Corinthians with having the things, which, by his own admission,
he does not have himself. Those who hold that view can quite easily
be refuted by the little clause which follows immediately after.

Therefore, he is being ironical in conceding that the Corinthians are
wise in Christ, and strong and illustrious. It is as if he said: 'You desire
to keep a reputation for wisdom along with the Gospel, whereas I have
been able to preach Christ to you only by becoming a fool in this
world. Now, when I have willingly put up with being a fool or
having that reputation, turn it over in your minds whether it is fair
that you wish to be looked upon as wise. You can hardly say these two
things go well together: that I, who have been your teacher, am a fool
for Christ's sake, while you remain wise.' It follows that being wise
in Christ has not got a good connotation here, for he laughs at the
Corinthians in their desire to mingle Christ and human wisdom together, because, in effect, they were wanting to join things which are
totally dissimilar.

The reasoning in the phrases which follow is similar: 'You are
strong', he says, 'and renowned; in other words you glory in the
riches and resources of the world, and you cannot tolerate the shame
of the Cross. Meanwhile is it reasonable that I should be obscure and
contemptible, and subject to many infirmities in your interest?' But
this complaint is all the more indignantly made, because he was indeed
weak and contemptible among them. In short, he mocks at their
vanity, because things were turned upside down when sons and pupils
were wanting to be famous and renowned, while the father remained
in obscurity, and also exposed to all the insults of the world.

11. *For to this hour.* Here the apostle paints a vivid picture of his own
circumstances, so that the Corinthians may learn from his example to
give up their high-mindedness, and, submissive in heart, embrace the
cross of Christ, along with him. He shows consummate skill, for, in
reminding them of those things which had made him contemptible,
he establishes his own unparalleled fidelity and untiring eagerness for
spreading the Gospel; and, on the other hand, he tacitly censures his
rivals, who, without giving any such evidence, were nevertheless
wanting to be given the first place.

12. The words themselves are all quite clear, except that we must
note the distinction between these two participles λοιδορούμενοι καὶ
βλασφημούμενοι (being reviled and being evilly spoken about). λοιδορία
(reviling) means that most cruel sort of biting wit, which gives a man,
not just a slight scratch, but a deep bite, and damages his character by
open insult. Therefore there can be no doubt that λοιδορεῖν means to

wound a man with abusive words as with some sharp instrument; and so I have rendered it 'provoked by abusive words'. βλασφημία is reproach in plainer words, when anybody is severely and cruelly slandered.

When he says that he undergoes persecution by enduring it and prays for his slanderers, he means not only that he is brought down and humbled by God through the Cross, but that he is also endowed with a willingness to be so humbled. In this, perhaps, he censures the false apostles, who were so effeminate and soft that they could not bear to be touched even with someone's little finger. In speaking of their work, he adds 'with our own hands' to make it clearer how contemptible his occupation was. He could have said: 'Not only do I make a living for myself by my own labour, but by humble work, using my own hands.'

13. *As the execrations of the world.* Paul uses two terms. The first of these means a man who was devoted to the gods by public execrations, to make atonement for the city. The Greeks sometimes call such men καθαρμοί, more often, καθάρματα,[1] because they take on themselves all the crimes and guilt of the city, and so cleanse the rest of the inhabitants. In adding the preposition περί[2] (around) Paul seems to have been thinking of the expiatory rite itself, since those wretched men, who were devoted to execrations, were led around the streets, so that they might take away, with themselves, the evil lurking in every corner of the city, and so make for a more complete cleansing.

The plural might seem to suggest that Paul is not speaking of himself alone, but of the others who were his colleagues, and who were no less looked down upon by the Corinthians. But there is no compelling reason for including more than himself in what he says.

The other term, περίψημα (scraping), is used for sawdust, scrapings of any sort, and also for floor-sweepings. But consult the annotations of Budaeus concerning both terms.

We must see how this applies to the meaning of the passage before us. In order to describe his own extreme degradation Paul says that he is deserving of the curses of the whole world like a man appointed to be a propitiatory sacrifice, and that, like off-scourings, he is distasteful to everybody. However, he does not suggest, by the first simile, that he himself is an expiatory sacrifice for sins, but he simply means that so far as disgrace and insults are concerned, there is no difference between him and the man on whom the execrations of everybody are heaped.

14. *I write not these things to shame you.* Since what he has just said was cutting in its irony, so that it might hurt the feelings of the Corinth-

---

[1] καθαρμοί=cleansings or expiations. καθάρματα=what is thrown away after cleansing, i.e. off-scourings; also, an outcast.

[2] The Greek is: περικαθάρματα τοῦ κόσμου.

ians, he now faces up to their displeasure in declaring that he did not say these things with the intention of making them ashamed, but rather to admonish them with a father's love. It is indeed certain that it is the effect and nature of a father's correction to make his son feel ashamed. For the beginning of repentance is the sense of shame of which the son is aware, when he is reproached for his sin. Therefore, in reproving his son, the father's aim is to make him feel dissatisfied with himself. We see that what Paul has been saying up to now, has tended to make the Corinthians ashamed of themselves. Yes, and indeed a little later on he will make it known that he reminds them of their faults in order that they may begin to be ashamed. But here he only wishes to say that it is not his intention to heap disgrace upon them, or to bring their sins out into the open for all to see, so that they could be discredited. For the person who admonishes in a friendly way takes special pains to see that all the shame should remain a matter between himself and the person whom he warns, and so be disposed of. But the man who upbraids in a malicious way exposes the sin of another, and produces shame in him, so as to make him the object of everybody's reproach. Therefore Paul is simply saying that he had not said what he had, with the intention of upbraiding or of damaging their good name; but rather, that with fatherly affection he has been reminding them forcibly of what was lacking in them.

But what is the purpose of this admonishing? It is just this: that the Corinthians, who were swollen-headed with bombastic ideas, which were nevertheless empty, might learn to glory in the humiliation of the cross along with Paul; and that they might not despise him any longer on those very grounds on which he was thoroughly worthy of glory in the eyes of God and the angels. In short, the purpose of it all was that they might put aside their former arrogance, and place more value on the *stigmata* of Christ on him, than on the empty and spurious ostentation of the false apostles. Now, teachers should learn from this, that such moderation must always be used in reproofs, so as not to hurt men's feelings by excessive harshness; and, as the well-known proverb puts it, honey or oil must be mixed with vinegar. But, most of all, they must take care not to appear to taunt those whom they are reproving, or to be taking a delight in their disgrace. No! and more than that, they must take pains to make it plain that they are out for nothing but the promotion of their welfare. For what will a teacher accomplish by mere shouting, if he does not season the sharpness of his rebuke with that moderation of which I spoke? Therefore if we want to do any good by correcting men's faults, it is right to make it plain to them that our criticisms come from a friendly heart.

15. *For though you should have ten thousand tutors.* Paul had said that

he is a father. He now shows that that description is peculiarly his own in relation to them, because he alone has begotten them in Christ. In using this comparison, however, Paul has in mind the false apostles, to whom the Corinthians were yielding all authority, so that Paul himself now counted for almost nothing among them. Accordingly he advises them to consider what honour ought to be given to a father and what to a tutor. It is as if he said: 'You pay great respect to those new teachers. I do not object, provided you bear in mind that I am your father, and they are only tutors.' But in claiming this authority for himself he means that he has a different attitude altogether from the men, whom they regarded so highly. He could have put it like this: 'They take pains in teaching you. Good and well! But a father's love, a father's care, a father's goodwill are all quite different from those of a tutor.' But what if he is also making allusion to that immaturity of faith, which he has already exposed? For although the Corinthians were giants in pride, they were children in faith, and that is why it was justifiable to despatch them to tutors. He also finds fault with the absurd, and indeed malicious, method of those teachers, in keeping their pupils occupied with first principles only, in order to have them always in bondage to their instruction.

For in Christ. This is the reason why he alone must be regarded as the father of the Church at Corinth: because he had begotten it. And he describes spiritual generation here most appositely in saying that he has begotten them in Christ, who is the only source of life; but indeed Paul states that the Gospel is the formal cause. Let us therefore take note that in God's eyes we are truly begotten, when we are ingrafted into Christ, outside of whom nothing but death is to be found. But in fact this must be done through the Gospel, for, since we are flesh and grass by nature, the Word of God is the 'incorruptible seed' by which we are renewed unto eternal life, as Peter teaches from Isaiah (I Pet. 1.23-25; Isa. 40.6-8). Take away the Gospel and we shall all remain accursed and dead in the sight of God. That same Word, by which we are begotten, is afterwards milk for rearing us, and is also solid food for our continual sustenance.

Someone may object in these terms: 'Seeing that new sons are begotten to God in the Church every day, why does Paul deny that those who have succeeded him are fathers?' The answer is easy: here he is speaking about the beginning of the Church. For even if many had been begotten by the ministry of others, this honour remained unimpaired to Paul alone, that he had founded the Corinthian Church. Again, if anyone asks: 'Should not all pastors be looked upon as fathers? Why then does Paul deprive all the others of this title so as to lay claim to it for himself alone?' My answer is: He speaks here in a comparative way. Accordingly, however appropriate the title of fathers might be for them in other respects, yet in comparison with Paul they were nothing but tutors. We must also bear in mind what I referred to a little ago, that he is not speaking about all of them (for, as far as men like himself were concerned, men like Apollos, Sylvanus and Timothy, men who were eager to advance the Kingdom of Christ, there would have been no difficulty about calling them fathers, and bestowing the greatest honour upon them), but he finds fault with those who, through misdirected ambition, were transferring to themselves the glory that belonged to another. Such were the men who snatched away the honour due to Paul, so as to blazon themselves in the spoils.

Today, indeed, the condition of the Universal Church is like that of the Corinthian Church then. For how few there are who care for the churches with fatherly affection, in other words who do not look for a personal reward, and devote themselves to their welfare! Meantime there are a great many tutors, who hire out their services for what they can get in return, and who do so, as if they were engaged on a task for a limited time, and in order to keep the people for the time being under their own control and in admiration of themselves. However, even so, it is a good thing when there are many tutors, who do good, at least in some ways, by teaching, and do not destroy the Church by the corrupting effect of false teaching. When I make complaint about the large number of tutors, I do not mean the Papist priests (for I do not consider them worthy of inclusion in this number), but those who agree with us in doctrine, and yet busy themselves looking after their own affairs rather than Christ's. All of us, indeed, wish to be thought of as fathers, and we demand the obedience of sons from others; but of how many can you say that they are outstanding because they show that they really are fathers?

There is still another and more difficult question. Since Christ forbids us to call anybody father on the earth because we have one Father in heaven (Matt. 23.9), how does Paul dare to apply the name of father to himself? I answer: properly speaking God alone is the Father, not only of our soul, but also of our body. However, in view of the fact that, in so far as the body is concerned, He grants the name of 'father' to those to whom He gives children, but retains for Himself alone the right and title of 'father' in regard to souls, I confess that for this reason He has the special title of 'the Father of spirits', and is to be distinguished from earthly fathers, as the apostle says in Heb. 12.9. However, because He alone begets souls by His own power, then regenerates them and makes them alive, but yet makes use of the ministry of His servants for this purpose, there is no harm in calling them fathers with regard to this ministry, for in doing so God's honour is left intact. The Word (as we have said) is the spiritual seed. By it and by His power God alone brings our souls to new birth, but He does not exclude the labour of ministers. If you would carefully consider what God does by Himself, and what He wishes to be done by ministers, you will easily understand in what sense He alone deserves the honour of father, and how far this name is suitable for ministers, without any violation of His right.

> I beseech you therefore, be ye imitators of me. For this cause have I sent unto you Timothy, who is my beloved and faithful child in the Lord, who shall put you in remembrance of my ways which be in Christ, even as I teach everywhere in every church. Now some are puffed up, as though I were not coming to you. But I will come to you shortly, if the Lord will; and I will know, not the word of them which are puffed up, but the power. For the kingdom of God is not in word, but in power. What will ye? shall I come unto you with a rod, or in love and a spirit of meekness? (16–21)

16. *I beseech you.* He now also expresses in his own words what he is wanting to get from them by his fatherly correction, viz. that, just because they are his sons, they do not break off relationship with their father. Could anything be more reasonable than for sons to take pains to be as like their father as possible? And yet he is giving up something of his own right when he urges them to this by asking rather than by commanding. But how far he means them to be imitators of himself, he makes plain in another passage, when he adds, as he was 'of Christ' (I Cor. 11.1). This qualification must always be maintained, so that we do not follow any man, except in so far as he leads us to Christ. But we know what Paul is dealing with here. Not only were the Corinthians avoiding the humiliation of the Cross, but they were also making their father an object of contempt, because he forgot the glory this world has to offer, and was glorying rather in the reproaches he suffered because of Christ; and they were thinking themselves and others fortunate, in having nothing which, by the world's standards, could be called contemptible. Therefore he advises them to follow his example and yield themselves in obedience to Christ, so as to endure everything.

17. *For this cause.* The meaning is: 'In order that you may know what my way of life is really like, and whether I am a fit example to follow, listen to what Timothy has to say, for he will be in a position to give reliable evidence in this connexion.' Now, two things produce confidence in a man's evidence, (1) his knowledge of the things about which he has to tell, and (2) his fidelity. Paul informs them that Timothy has both. For when he calls him his dearly beloved son, he

reveals that he knows Paul intimately, and is well acquainted with all his circumstances. He then calls him faithful in the Lord. He also commits two things to Timothy's charge. First he has to recall to the Corinthians' minds what they ought to have remembered of their own accord, and in this he tacitly finds fault with them. Secondly Timothy has to let them know how unvarying and consistent Paul's way of teaching is in every place.

But it is very likely that Paul had been attacked by the misrepresentations of the false apostles, as though he claimed more power for himself over the Corinthians than over others, or conducted himself quite differently in other places; for he had good reason for wanting this to be made known to them. Therefore a wise minister ought to determine what his method of teaching is to be, and to persist with this plan, so that no such objection could be brought against him, without his having a ready defence, based on the actual situation, as Paul had.

As though I were not coming to you. It is the custom of the false apostles to take advantage of the absence of good men to grow insolent and boast about themselves unchecked. Paul points out that they cannot bear his presence, and he does so to expose their bad conscience and to curb their assertiveness. Indeed it does sometimes happen that, when the opportunity to be insulting presents itself, shameless and brazen-faced men rise up openly against the servants of Christ; however they never come forward to a fair contest as if they had nothing to hide; rather by their underhand tricks they betray their own lack of confidence.

19. *But I will come to you shortly.* Paul says: 'They are making a mistake in pluming their feathers during my absence, as if that will go on for a long time, for they will soon be aware of how hollow their elation has been.' But he is not so much frightening them, as if he would strike them with lightning on his arrival, but rather bringing pressure to bear upon and attacking their consciences, because, no matter how they pretend otherwise, they know very well that Paul is equipped with power from God.

The phrase, *if the Lord will,* tells us that we ought not to make any promises to others about the future, or to make any personal plans, without adding this qualification: in so far as the Lord will allow. Hence James is quite right in ridiculing the foolhardiness of men in planning what they will do at the end of ten years, when, in fact, they have no certainty about living for one whole hour (James 4.15). Now, although we are not bound to be constantly using such expressions, all the same it is better to take care to become accustomed to them, so that again and again we may actively consider that all our plans must be subjected to the will of God.

And I will know, not the word. By 'word' we must understand that babbling in which the false apostles took delight; for their strength lay in a certain aptness and charm of speech, but they were quite lacking in the zeal and efficacy of the Spirit. By the word 'power' Paul means the spiritual efficacy with which those, who administer the Word of God earnestly, are endowed. The meaning therefore is: 'I shall see whether they have such great grounds for being so haughty, and I shall certainly not judge them by their great flow of words, on which they themselves place the whole of their glory, and on which they rely to lay claim to everything for themselves. If they want to have any credit in my eyes they must reveal that power, which distinguishes the true servants of Christ from impostors (*larvatis*); otherwise I shall have no time for them and their showiness. Therefore they are putting their trust in their eloquence in vain, when it will mean as much to me as smoke.'

20. *For the Kingdom of God is not in word.* Because the Lord governs His Church with His Word, as with a sceptre, the administration by the Gospel (*evangelii administratio*) is often called the Kingdom of God. Here we must understand by the Kingdom of God whatever aims at this, and is appointed for this purpose: that God may reign in our midst. Paul says that this Kingdom does not consist in word (*sermone*); for there is nothing wonderful about anyone being adept at speaking fluently when he is producing nothing but an empty jingle! Let us therefore learn that a merely superficial attractiveness and skill in teaching is like a body which is well-formed and healthy in colour, while the *power* (*virtutem*), of which Paul speaks here, is like the soul. We have already seen that the nature of evangelical preaching is such that it is full of a certain genuine majesty. This majesty shows itself when a minister goes into action more with power (*virtute*) than with words (*sermone*). In other words, he devotes himself actively to the Lord's work, not relying confidently on his own ability or eloquence, but equipped with spiritual weapons, which are zeal in protecting the glory of the Lord, desire for setting up the Kingdom of Christ, eagerness for up-building, fear of the Lord, undefeatable steadfastness, and other gifts needed. Without them preaching is dead, and has no force at all, no matter how brilliant and colourful it may be to the last. For that reason he says in II Cor. 5.17 that nothing less than a new creation will suffice in Christ. And that thought has the same object in view. For he does not want us to remain content with any outward shams (*externis larvis*), but to persevere in the inward power (*internae virtuti*) of the Holy Spirit.

Although he curbs the ambition of the false apostles with these words, at the same time, however, he charges the Corinthians with distorted judgement, because they were forming their opinion of the servants of Christ from their least important qualities. This is a remarkable thought; one which applies just as much to us as to them. As far as many people are concerned, where is the Gospel, of which we are proud, where is newness of life, where is spiritual efficacy, but in speech (*lingua*)? And that is not the position with the people only. For how many there are who are making use of the Gospel to gain favour and renown as if it were some purely secular branch of knowledge, and whose one concern it is to speak with taste and acuteness! It is not my belief that *power* should be restricted to miracles, because from the contrast here it is easy to conclude that it has a wider application.

22. *What will ye?* The person who divided the epistles into chapters ought to have made this the beginning of the fifth chapter. For up to this point Paul has reproved the Corinthians' foolish pride, their empty confidence, their judgement which was distorted and spoiled by ambition, but now he mentions the vices which were troubling them, and which ought to have been making them ashamed of themselves. It is as if he said: 'You are swollen-headed, just as if your affairs were on an excellent footing, but it would be better for you to acknowledge your unhappy situation with shame and sorrow, for if you carry on like this I shall be forced to lay aside my gentleness and be a severe father with you.' But this threat has more weight than the freedom of choice he gives them in it, for he declares that it does not depend on him whether he will be mild and gentle with them, but that he is being driven to severity by their own fault. He says: 'It is for you to choose what you want me to be like. As for me, I am prepared to be gentle. But if you carry on as you have been doing I shall have to take up the rod.' Thus he puts himself in a stronger position after he claimed the authority of a father for himself; for it would have been ridiculous to begin with a warning like this, if he had not first prepared the way for himself by what he said, and given them grounds for apprehension.

He means by 'the rod' that strictness with which a pastor ought to correct his people's faults. Over against this he sets love (*caritatem*) and a spirit of meekness, not because the father hates the sons whom he reproves (for, on the contrary, the correction springs from love) but because by a sad expression and hard words he gives the appearance of being angry with his son. To express myself more clearly and in a word: no matter what expression he wears a father always loves his son, but he shows that love in teaching him in a quiet and loving way; but when he is upset by his sins and corrects him in rather stern words or even with the *rod*, he assumes the role of an angry person. Therefore since love is hidden when severe discipline is used, Paul is quite right in connecting love with a spirit of meekness.

Some interpreters take 'rod' here to mean excommunication. As far as I am concerned, although I grant them that excommunication is part of that severity with which Paul threatens the Corinthians, nevertheless I give it a wider application to include all reproofs of a sterner nature.

Notice here what pattern of behaviour a good pastor must follow, for he ought to be spontaneously disposed to gentleness in order to draw men to Christ, rather than drag them forcibly. He ought to maintain this gentleness, as far as he possibly can, and not descend to severity unless he is forced to do so. But when there is need of it, he must not spare the rod, for, while those who are teachable and willing must be treated gently, there is a need for hardness in dealing with the obstinate and insolent. And we see that the Word of God does not contain doctrine and nothing else, but also sharp reproofs which are scattered through it, in order to supply pastors with a rod. For it often comes about, through the obstinacy of the people, that pastors, who are naturally very gentle, are forced to assume another role as it were, by acting rigorously and sternly.

CHAPTER FIVE

It is actually reported that there is fornication among you, and such fornication as is not even among the Gentiles, that one of you hath his father's wife. And ye are puffed up, and did not rather mourn, that he that had done this deed might be taken away from among you. For I verily, being absent in body but present in spirit, have already, as though I were present, judged him that hath so wrought this thing, in the name of our Lord Jesus, ye being gathered together, and my spirit, with the power of our Lord Jesus, to deliver such a one unto Satan for the destruction of the flesh, that the spirit may be saved in the day of the Lord Jesus. (1-5)

1. *It is generally reported that there is fornication.* Since their disputes were arising from pride and excessive self-confidence, as we have already said, Paul moves on, appropriately enough, to the mention of their vices (*morbos*), the recognition of which ought to have been humbling them.

First of all he warns them that it is a very disgraceful thing that one of their flock should be allowed to have a wrong relation with his step-mother. It is not certain whether he seduced her from his father, as a prostitute, or kept her under the pretence of marriage. But that dubiety does not matter very much, for while the former would have been an extremely wicked and detestable fornication, on the other hand the latter would have meant an incestuous union foreign to natural respectability and seemliness. Now, so that he might not appear to be making a charge against them based on the uncertainty of suspicion, he says that he is bringing forward something that is a matter of common knowledge. For I take the word ὅλως (generally) as bringing out that it was not a doubtful rumour, but an obvious fact, news of which was broadcast everywhere, causing a great deal of offence.

Because Paul says that it was fornication of such a kind as is not named even among the Gentiles, some think that he refers to the incest of Reuben, who also committed incest with his mother-in-law. They think that Paul made no mention of Israel, because they had the blemish of such a shameful thing in their history, as if, indeed, the stories of the Gentiles did not refer to many cases of incest of the same kind! Therefore that fictitious notion is completely foreign to what Paul had in mind, for his reason for mentioning the Gentiles rather than the

Jews is that he wished to underline the ugliness of the crime all the more. He says: 'You allow this disgraceful thing, as if it were legitimate, something which would not be tolerated even among the Gentiles; no, and more than that, something which they have always looked upon with horror, indeed in the same light as a monster.' Therefore, when he asserts that this is not heard of among the Gentiles, he does not mean that no such thing ever took place among them, or is not mentioned in their literature, for tragedies have certainly been written about it; but that it is abominable to the Gentiles, in the same way as a loathsome and horrible monstrosity, for it is a bestial lust, which destroys even natural modesty itself.

If anyone should ask if it is fair that one man's sin should be made a matter for reproaching them all, I answer that the Corinthians are not blamed because one of their number had sinned, but because, as we shall see later, by closing their eyes to a shameful act, which deserved the severest punishment, they were giving encouragement to it.

2. *And you are puffed up.* He says: 'Are you not ashamed of yourselves for taking pride in something which ought to be filling you with humiliation?' Paul had previously asserted that even the highest possible qualities can give no cause for boasting, because men have nothing of their own, but in fact they have those same fine qualities by the grace of God and nothing else. But now he attacks them in a different way. He says: 'Seeing that you are covered with disgrace, what room have you, therefore, for pride and elation? For you are amazingly blind, in boasting when you are surrounded by shameful things, for this, as it were, goes against the grain with angels and men.'

When he says *and you have not rather mourned* he is arguing by contrast; for where there is mourning, there is no more boasting. It may be asked why they ought to have mourned over another's sin. I can give two reasons. (1) Because of the fellowship which exists between members of the Church, it was only right that they should all be affected by such a fatal lapse on the part of one of them. (2) When such a shameful act is committed in any church the guilt is not confined to the person responsible for it, but the whole company is to some extent contaminated. For example God humbles a father in the disgrace of his wife or children; and a whole family in the shame of one of its members. Each Church ought to ponder this, that it is stained with the mark of disgrace, whenever some infamous crime is committed in it. More than that, let us note that the wrath of God was kindled against the whole of Israel because of the sacrilege of one man, Achan (Josh. 7.1). It is not a case of God being so cruel that He vents His rage on the innocent because of somebody else's crime. But since there is already some evidence of His wrath, whenever a thing like that happens among a people, so by punishing all for the offence of one person, He makes it plain that the whole body is infected and defiled through contamination by the wrong. It can easily be inferred from this, that it is the duty of each Church to mourn over the sins of its individual members, as if they were family misfortunes involving the whole body. And there is no doubt that a godly and just amendment begins when we are set on fire with a zeal for holiness through dissatisfaction with the wrong, because otherwise severity will be full of bitterness.

That he . . . might be taken away from among you. Paul now makes clearer what charge he makes against the Corinthians, viz. their indifference, in closing their eyes to so great an abomination. From which it also appears that churches are provided with this power, that they can correct or remove by strict discipline any fault that there may be in them; and those which are not vigilant about clearing away filth, cannot be excused. For Paul condemns the Corinthians here. Why? Because they had been quite unconcerned about punishing one man for his crime. But his charge against them would have been unjust, if they did not possess this power. Therefore the power of excommunication is established by this passage. On the other hand, since this means of punishment has been given to the churches, Paul shows that those which do not use it, when circumstances require it, are sinning. For otherwise Paul would be unfair to the Corinthians, in charging them with this fault.

3. *For I certainly.* In view of the fact that the Corinthians were failing in their duty, and after he has condemned their negligence, Paul now shows what must be done. In order that this stain may be obliterated, the incestuous person must be put out of the society of the faithful. Thus he lays down that excommunication is the cure for the trouble; but for so long they had been putting that off, and in that they had been in the wrong. When he says that he had already come to that decision while 'absent in the body', in that way he makes his complaint against the carelessness of the Corinthians all the more serious, for an implied contrast underlies it. It is as if he said: 'You, who are on the spot, ought to have found a remedy for this disease long ago, since it is constantly before your eyes, while even I, who am far away, cannot put up with it.'

In case anyone should make loud protest, however, that, when he is so far away, he is forming a rash judgement on the strength of rumours, Paul insists that he is 'present in spirit', and by that he means that his path of duty was as plain to him as if he were personally alongside them, and saw the thing with his own eyes. Now it is worth while to see what he teaches about the method of excommunication.

4. *Ye being gathered together, and my spirit,* i.e. 'gathered along with me', but in spirit, since it was not physically possible for them to meet together. But he asserts that they will be together just as if he were personally present. It must be observed that Paul, apostle though he is, does not excommunicate by himself, to suit his own pleasure, but takes the church into consultation so that the matter might be dealt with by their joint decision. Indeed he goes ahead and shows the way, but when he associates others with himself, he means quite plainly that the power does not rest with one individual. But since the crowd never does anything with moderation or dignity unless they are guided by advice, a Presbytery was appointed in the ancient Church, i.e. a college of elders (*collegium seniorum*), who, by common consent, were entrusted with the first inquiry into a case. From them, the case, already prejudged of course, was brought down to the people. No matter what the case may be, it is quite out of keeping with the institution of Christ and the apostles, with the order of the Church, and in fact with fairness itself, that there should be put in the hands of one man the right to excommunicate, on his own authority, any person he wants. Let us therefore take note that when it is a question of excommunication this regular arrangement must be maintained, that this particular discipline must be exercised by the elders consulting together, and with the consent of the people. And let us also note that this is a remedy for the prevention of tyranny. For there is nothing in greater opposition to the discipline of Christ (*Christi disciplinae*) than tyranny; and the door is wide open to it, if all the power is surrendered to one man.

In the name of Our Lord. It is not enough for us to meet together, if it is not done in the name of Christ; for even the wicked meet together to hatch their evil, unlawful plots. Moreover, in order that a meeting may be held in Christ's name, two things are required: (1) it should begin with calling upon His name; and (2) nothing should be undertaken if it is not in accordance with His Word. Therefore, men make a promising start with anything they undertake to do, only when they call upon the Lord from their hearts, asking to be guided by His Spirit, and that all their plans may, by His grace, be directed to a successful outcome. To make a good start they must also 'ask at His mouth', as the prophet says (Isaiah 30.2); in other words, after consulting His oracles they must yield themselves and all their plans in complete obedience to His will. If this should be the procedure even with our least important actions, how much more must it be followed in weighty and serious affairs, but especially when we are involved in God's concerns rather than our own! For instance, excommunication is an ordinance of God Himself, and not of men; therefore whenever we have to use it, where shall we begin but with God? In short, when

Paul urges the Corinthians to meet in the name of Christ, he asks them, not so much to use Christ's name or confess Him with their lips (for the wicked can also do that), but to seek Him genuinely and from the heart. Further, in saying so, he indicates the seriousness and importance of what they are doing.

He adds, *with the power of Our Lord*. For, if the promise is true 'where two or three are gathered together in my name, there am I in the midst of them' (Matt. 18.20), it follows that whatever is done in such a gathering is Christ's work. We infer from this how important legitimate excommunication is in the sight of God, since it depends upon the power of God. For this word must also be implemented: 'What things soever ye shall bind on earth shall be bound in heaven' (Matt. 18.18). But since this statement ought to strike no ordinary terror into the hearts of those who despise God, so, for their part, faithful pastors, as well as all the churches, are warned by what Paul says here, how reverently they ought to proceed in such a serious matter. For it is certain that the power of Christ is not tied to the will or opinions of men, but is bound up with His eternal truth.

5. *To deliver to Satan for the destruction of the flesh*. Since, among other powers, the apostles were endowed with that of giving over the wicked and the obstinate to Satan, and using him as a scourge for correcting them, Chrysostom and those who follow him, take these words of Paul as referring to punishment of that sort. And this is in accordance with the exposition usually given of another passage, I Tim. 1.20, concerning Alexander and Hymenaeus. Thus they think that 'delivering to Satan' is nothing else but the infliction of some severe physical punishment. For myself, when I look more closely at the whole context, and at the same time compare what is said in the next epistle, I turn that interpretation down as forced and not in line with what Paul means, and take it to mean simply excommunication. For 'to deliver to Satan' is a fitting way to describe excommunication; because, while Christ reigns within, so Satan reigns outside, the Church. Augustine also has a similar comment in his 68th Sermon on the words of the apostle, where he is expounding this passage. Therefore, because we are received into the fellowship of the Church and remain in it on condition that we be under the protection and charge of Christ, I say that the person who is put out of the Church is, in a way, handed over to the power of Satan, because he is alienated and cut off from the rule of Christ.

The phrase which follows, *for the destruction of the flesh*, is added by way of alleviation. For Paul does not mean that the person being corrected is to be given up to Satan for complete destruction, or to be a slave to him for ever, but that his sentence is temporary, and more than that, one that will be for his good. Since, as far as the spirit is concerned, both its salvation and its damnation are eternal, he takes condemnation of the flesh to be temporary. He might have said: 'We will condemn him for a period of time in this world, in order that the Lord may keep him in His Kingdom.' Thus the objection, by which some try to disprove this explanation, is removed. For in view of the fact that the sentence of excommunication is directed against the soul rather than the body, they ask how it can properly be called the destruction of the flesh. I reply, as I have already suggested, that the destruction of the flesh is quite a different matter from the salvation of the spirit on this ground alone, that the former is temporal, while the latter is eternal. It is in this sense that the apostle speaks of 'the days of His flesh', with reference to Christ, in Heb. 5.7, meaning the period of His mortal life. But the reason why the Church severely punishes sinners and does not let them off in this world, is that God may spare them. If anyone wants to learn more about the discipline of excommunication, its causes, necessity, purposes, and moderation in its use, he may find it in my *Institutes* (4.12).

Your glorying is not good. Know ye not that a little leaven leaveneth the whole lump? Purge out the old leaven, that ye may be a new lump, even as ye are unleavened. For our passover also hath been sacrificed, even Christ: wherefore let us keep the feast, not with old leaven, neither with the leaven of malice and wickedness, but with the unleavened bread of sincerity and truth. (6–8)

6. *Your glorifying is not good.* He condemns their boasting, not only because they were putting themselves on a far higher level than men are entitled to do, but because they were taking a delight in their faults. Earlier he stripped men of all glory; for he has shown that, since they have nothing of their own, no matter how outstanding they may be, they owe everything to God alone. Indeed, what he is dealing with here is not that God is cheated of His right when mortal men claim the credit for themselves for their own virtues, but that the Corinthians were being extremely foolish in preening their feathers without any grounds for doing so. For they were as proud as if they were living in the conditions of a Golden Age, when in reality they were surrounded by many shameful and unseemly things.

Do you not know? So that they might not think it a matter of little or no importance to encourage such a great evil, Paul shows how damaging an easy-going and careless attitude is in a case like this. But he makes use of a proverbial saying to the effect that a whole society is infected by one person's disease. For in this context this proverb has the same meaning as these words of Juvenal (*Sat.* II.79 ff): 'A whole herd in the fields is laid low by the mange in one pig; and one choice grape becomes tainted by another.' I said, 'in this context', because elsewhere Paul uses it in a very different (i.e. good) sense, as we shall see (Gal. 5.9).

7. *Purge out therefore.* Having adopted the metaphor of the *leaven*, Paul continues to use it, although he makes a transition from a particular instance to more general teaching. For he is no longer speaking about the case of incest, but making an appeal to them for over-all purity of life, because we cannot remain in Christ if we are not cleansed continually. It is quite usual for him to do this: when he has said something about a particular matter, he takes the opportunity to pass on from that to words of general encouragement. He had mentioned the leaven in another connexion, as we have seen, but since this same metaphor suited the general teaching he is about to give, he makes further use of it.

Our Passover (pascha) has been sacrificed. Before I deal with the content, I shall say a little about the words themselves. The 'old leaven' is given that description on the same principle as the 'old man'; for corruption of nature is our earlier condition before we are born again in Christ. Therefore what we take with us from the womb is said to be 'old', and it must die when we are renewed by the grace of the Spirit.

The verb 'was sacrificed' (ἐτύθη), since it is between the name of Christ and the word for sacrifice (πάσχα), can be taken as referring to either. I have taken it to refer to sacrifice; however this does not matter very much because the meaning is not affected.

In v. 8, *Let us keep the feast*, the word ἑορτάζωμεν which Erasmus rendered by 'let us celebrate the feast' (*festum celebremus*) also means to share in the solemn feast after the sacrifice had been offered. This meaning seemed to suit the present context better. Therefore I have followed the Vulgate (*epulemur*) rather than Erasmus, because this rendering is far more in keeping with the mystery with which Paul is dealing.

Let us turn to the content. Since Paul wants the Corinthians to be encouraged towards holiness, he suggests that what had long ago been represented in the passover, ought now to be made a reality in us; and he explains what the relation between the figure and the reality is. In the first place, since the passover had two parts, the sacrifice and the sacred feast, he mentions both. For although some do not think that the passover lamb was a sacrifice, nevertheless reason succeeds in proving that it was a proper sacrifice, for in this rite the people were reconciled to God by the sprinkling of blood. But there is no reconciliation without a sacrifice. The apostle immediately and plainly confirms that; for he uses the verb θύεσθαι (to sacrifice), which is the appropriate word for sacrifices, and would otherwise be out of place in this context. The lamb, then, was sacrificed every year, and the feast used to follow immediately after, and last for seven successive days. 'Christ', Paul says, 'is our Passover'. He has been sacrificed once for all, and on this condition, that the effect of His unique sacrifice may be for ever. In the meantime what we must do is to eat, and that not once a year, but continually.

In the celebration of this sacred feast we must certainly abstain from leaven, as God ordered the fathers to abstain; but from what kind of leaven? Just as the rite of the passover represented the true passover to them, so its elements (*accessiones*) also pre-figured that reality which we possess today. Therefore if we want to feed on the flesh and blood of Christ, let us bring sincerity and truth to this feast, letting them be our unleavened bread. Let there be an end to all malice and wickedness since it is against God's will to introduce leaven into the passover. In short, he asserts that we will be members of Christ only when we give up malice and deceitfulness. However, this passage requires our careful attention, for it makes it plain that the old passover was not only μνημόσυνον, i.e. the memorial of a blessing in the past, but also a sacrament of the Christ who was to come, who is the means of our passing from death to life. Otherwise it would not hold good, that in Christ is the substance of the shadows of the law (Col. 2.17). This passage will also be effective for showing the sacrilege of the Papal mass to be false. For Paul does not teach that Christ is offered every day, but that the sacrifice having been effected once for all, what we have to do is to celebrate the spiritual feast all our lives long.

I wrote unto you in my epistle to have no company with fornicators; not altogether with the fornicators of this world, or with the covetous and extortioners, or with idolaters; for then must ye needs go out of the world: but now I write unto you not to keep company if any man that is named a brother be a fornicator, or covetous, or an idolator, or a reviler, or a drunkard, or an extortioner; with such a one no, not to eat. For what have I to do with judging them that are without? Do not ye judge them that are within, whereas them that are without God judgeth? Put away the wicked man from among yourselves. (9-13)

9. *I have written to you in a letter.* That letter, to which he refers, does not exist today. There is no doubt that many others are lost. But we can rest content that the Lord saw to it that sufficient survive to meet our needs. But because of its obscurity this passage is twisted to give different meanings. I think that we ought not to waste time in refuting these, but that I should simply state what seems to me to be the true meaning. He reminds the Corinthians of what he has already

advised them: to refrain from having any relations with the wicked. For the meaning of the word translated 'to have no company with' is to live on friendly terms with someone, and to be intimately involved with him. Moreover, his reminder has the effect of showing up their dilatoriness, because, despite his warning, they had done nothing.

He adds an exceptive clause, so that they might understand better that what he says refers, strictly speaking, to those within the Church, for they had no need to be warned about avoiding people outside, in the world. Briefly, then, he forbids the Corinthians to have social intercourse with those who, professing to be believers, are nevertheless living in a way that is disgraceful, and insulting to God. He might have said: 'Let all who wish to be considered brethren, either lead holy and worthy lives, or be excommunicated from the fellowship of the faithful; and let all the righteous keep from dealings and social relations with them. It would be superfluous to mention those who make no pretence about their ungodly lives for you ought to avoid them of your own accord, without any warning from me.' But this exception only makes the charge of neglect all the more serious, because in the very bosom of the Church they gave encouragement to an infamous man. For it is a more shameful matter to neglect those of one's own family than those outside.

10. *For then you would have had to go out of the world.* It is about this phrase especially that interpreters differ. For some say: 'You must rather emigrate from Greece.' But Ambrose says: 'You must rather die.' Erasmus puts it into the optative, as if Paul should say: 'Indeed I wish that it was permissible for you to leave the world altogether; but because you cannot do that, you may at least give up relations with those who falsely call themselves Christians, and whose lives, at the same time, give very bad examples.' Chrysostom's explanation comes somewhat nearer the truth. According to him the meaning is this: 'When I tell you to avoid fornicators, I do not mean all in that category, otherwise you would need to seek another world. For we are required to live among thorns so long as we are sojourners on the earth. The only stipulation I make is that you do not mix with fornicators who wish to be regarded as brethren, in case, by tolerating their wickedness, you may give the impression of approving it.' Thus the word 'world' here must be taken to mean this present life, as in John 17.15, 'I pray not, Father, that thou shouldest take them out of the world, but that thou shouldest keep them from the evil one.'

This objection can be made against this exposition: 'Since Paul has been speaking here about the time when Christians were still intermingled with and scattered among the ungodly, what is to be done now, when everyone has enlisted under Christ's banner? For there must be a departure from the world in our day also, if we want to avoid the company of the wicked; and there are no outsiders when all acknowledge the name of Christ, and are consecrated to Him in baptism.' If anyone is willing to follow Chrysostom, it will not be difficult for him to answer to this effect: that Paul has taken for granted the truth that, where the right of excommunication exists, it is a simple remedy for separating the evil from the good—if the churches do their duty. The Christians in Corinth had no jurisdiction over those outside, and they had no power to control their dissolute lives. Therefore it was necessary for them to leave the world, if they wanted to avoid the wicked, whose vices they could not cure.

I myself do not find it easy to accept interpretations which can only be made to fit in with the words if the words are twisted to suit them, and so I favour one that is rather different from all these. I take 'to go out' to mean 'to be separated'; and 'world' to mean 'the filthy things of the world'. It is as if Paul said: 'What need is there to warn you about the sons of this world, for, seeing that you have once and for all renounced the world, you ought to be keeping away from their company; for "the whole world is in the power of the evil one" (I John 5.19).' If anyone is not satisfied with that explanation, this is another probable one: 'I do not write to make a general appeal to you to avoid the company of the fornicators of this world; nevertheless you ought to be doing that on your own initiative, without any warning from me.' However I myself prefer the one I have given above. Indeed I am not the first to think of it, but what others have suggested before, I have brought more into line with Paul's argument, if I am not mistaken. Therefore it looks like an intentional omission here, when he says that he is not making reference to those outside, since the Corinthians ought to have been separated from them already, so that they may know that this practice of avoiding the wicked must be observed among themselves as well.

11. *If any man that is named a brother.* In the Greek there is a participle, and no finite verb.[1] Those who take this as referring to what follows introduce a meaning that is forced and different from Paul's intention. I admit, indeed, that the viewpoint is correct and worth noticing, viz. that no-one can be punished by the judgement of the Church unless his sin is known. But these words of Paul cannot be made to yield that meaning. Therefore, his meaning is: 'If anyone, whom you look upon as a brother, leads a life that is disgraceful and unworthy of a Christian, then have nothing to do with him.' In short, the description of

---

[1] Calvin refers to the reading in many Greek MSS—ἐάν τις ἀδελφὸς ὀνομαζόμενος, ἢ πόρνος, ἢ πλεονέκτης κ.τ.λ. But others, and Souter (Revisers' Text) read ἐὰν τις, ἀδελφὸς ὀνομαζόμενος, ᾖ (is).

'brother' here refers to a false profession, to which there is no corresponding reality. Moreover Paul does not give a complete list of sins
here, but mentions five or six by way of example. Finally, he gathers
up the remainder in the word 'such a one'; and those which he does
mention are those of which men are aware. For ungodliness of the
inner life, and anything secret, do not come under the Church's
judgement.

But it is not clear what Paul means by an 'idolator'. For how can
he, who has come under the command of Christ, be devoted to idols?
Some think that among the Corinthians at that time there were those
who were only half embracing Christ, and who were nevertheless
entangled at the same time in misguided superstitions. So it was with
first the Israelites and then the Samaritans long ago; no matter what
kind of worship of God they had, they used to spoil it with evil superstitions. But my own view is that it refers to those who, while they
despised idols, were making a show of worshipping them nevertheless,
in order to please the ungodly. Paul says that the Christian fellowship
must not put up with people like that; and this is justifiable in view of
the fact that they were so easily making a mockery of the glory of God.

But we must pay attention to the circumstances here, because, while
they had the church there, in which they could give pure worship to
God, and rightfully enjoy the benefit of the sacraments, nevertheless
they were coming into the church in such a way as not to give up the
unclean fellowship of the ungodly. I say this in case anyone may think
that we should be just as severe with those who in our day are away
from us under the tyranny of the Pope, and who defile themselves with
many erroneous rites. Indeed I say that they sin seriously in this respect,
and I admit that they should be sternly refuted, and be put under
constant pressure, so that one day they may learn to dedicate themselves
completely to Christ. But I am not so bold as to go so far as to think
that they should be excommunicated, for their circumstances are not
the same as those of the Corinthians.

With such a one you may not even eat. We must know, in the first
place, whether Paul is addressing the whole Church or individuals here.
To this I would reply that it certainly refers to individuals, but nevertheless it depends on the discipline of the fellowship. For the power of
excommunication is not granted to each member, but to the whole
body. The point is that no believer ought to enter into friendly relations with anyone whom the Church has excommunicated. Besides,
the authority of the Church would count for nothing, if individuals
were allowed to invite to their own tables those who have been debarred from the Lord's table. By the sharing of food is meant either
keeping house together, or the friendly intimacy of meals. For if I

enter an inn and see somebody who has been excommunicated sitting there, there is nothing to prevent me from eating along with him, for I have no power to put him out. But Paul means that, as far as it lies in our hands, we must avoid relations with those whom the Church has cut off from its fellowship.

Not content with this severity, the Roman Antichrist has continually broken out into interdicts, against helping anyone who is excommunicated, with food, fuel, drink, or other necessities of life. Now, that is not strictness of discipline but arbitrary and savage cruelty, which is in violent conflict with Paul's intention. Because we inflict this mark of public disgrace upon a man, in order that he may be filled with shame and come to his senses, Paul means that such a person should be regarded 'not as an enemy, but as a brother' (II Thess. 3.15). And, please God, even upon the innocent do they vent their rage with such extreme cruelty! Finally, even if there are sometimes those who are not undeserving of this punishment, I say that this kind of interdict is thoroughly unsuitable for a Church court.

12. *For what have I to do with judging them that are without?* There is nothing to hinder us from judging them also, and, more than that, even the devils are not exempt from judgement by the Word with which we are entrusted. But in this context Paul is speaking about the special jurisdiction of the Church. It is as though he said: 'The Lord has equipped us with this power to employ it against those who belong to His household. For this punishment is part of the discipline which is confined to the Church, and does not embrace those outside. Therefore we do not pass His sentence upon them, because the Lord has not made them subject to our inquiry and tribunal, for these are concerned with that particular judgement and punishment. We are therefore bound to leave them to the judgement of God.' The reason why Paul says that God will be their Judge is that He allows them to wander about unbridled like wild beasts, because there is no-one who can control their wilfulness.

13. *Put away the wicked man* (eiicete scelestum, ἐξάρατε τὸν πονηρόν). The usual explanation of this is that it refers to the man who committed incest with his mother-in-law. For those who take the badness to mean evil or an evil thing (*malum*) are refuted by Paul's Greek, where the article is masculine. But what if you prefer to make it apply to the devil? There is no doubt that one wicked and evil-living person gives him every encouragement to establish his throne in our midst. For ὁ πονηρός (the evil one), by itself, without any addition, denotes the prince of all crimes rather than any particular bad man. If this meaning is acceptable, Paul gives warning of how very important it is that the wicked should not be tolerated, because, if they are not, Satan is driven

out of his kingdom. But he maintains it in our midst when evil men are allowed to do what they like. However I do not challenge anyone who prefers to take this as referring to the man. Again, Chrysostom compares the strictness of the Law with the clemency of the Gospel, because Paul was content that the crime be dealt with by excommunication, whereas the Law demanded the death penalty for it; but there is no justification for that view. For here, Paul is not speaking to judges armed with the sword, but to a company unarmed, allowed to use only brotherly reproof.

CHAPTER SIX

Dare any of you, having a matter against his neighbour, go to law before the unrighteous, and not before the saints? Or know ye not that the saints shall judge the world? and if the world is judged by you, are ye unworthy to judge the smallest matters? Know ye not that we shall judge angels? how much more, things that pertain to this life? If then ye have to judge things pertaining to this life, do ye set them to judge who are of no account in the church? I say this to move you to shame. Is it so, that there cannot be found among you one wise man, who shall be able to decide between his brethren, but brother goeth to law with brother, and that before unbelievers? Nay, already it is altogether a defect in you, that ye have lawsuits one with another. Why not rather take wrong? why not rather be defrauded? Nay, but ye yourselves do wrong, and defraud, and that your brethren. (1-8)

Paul now begins to censure another fault of the Corinthians: an excessive eagerness for litigation, and this arose out of greed. But this reproof has two parts to it. The first is that, in pursuing their quarrels before the courts of the unbelievers, they were giving a bad name to the Gospel, and reducing it to a public laughing stock. The second is that, while Christians ought to suffer injuries, they were causing harm to others, rather than put up with their being involved in trouble of any kind. So the first part is particular, the second, general.

1. *Dare any of you.* This is the first part of the reproof. If anyone has a dispute with a brother, it ought to be resolved before believing judges, and not before unbelievers. Should anyone want to know why, I have already said that this is because the Gospel is discredited, and the name of Christ is exposed, as it were, to the derision of the godless. For the ungodly, prompted by Satan, are always on the alert, eager for opportunities to find something in the teaching of religion, which they may misrepresent. But when believers disclose the details of their quarrels to them, they seem to be offering them, almost on purpose, a golden opportunity for calumny. A second reason can be given: we are slighting our brothers, when we are willing to subject them to the judgement of unbelievers.

But this objection can be made: 'Since it is the magistrate's responsibility and his proper function to give legal decisions for everybody, and to inquire into disputes, why may unbelievers who hold the office of magistrate, not also have this authority? And if they do have it why are we prevented from protecting our rights in their courts?' I reply that Paul does not condemn here those who, by force of circumstances, must enter into legal proceedings before unbelieving judges, for instance anyone who is summoned to court; but he finds fault with those who, on their own responsibility, bring their brothers there, and do them injury, as it were, at the hands of unbelievers, when another remedy is available to them. It is therefore wrong to take the initiative in instituting proceedings against brothers in an unbelievers' court. It is in order, however, to come into court and conduct your case, if a charge is made against you.

2. *Do you not know that the saints etc.* This is an argument from less to greater. For Paul wishes to show that damage is done to the Church of God, when decisions, in disputes over earthly matters, are put in the hands of unbelievers, as if there was no-one in the fellowship of the godly fit for judging. So he argues: 'Since God has counted the saints fit for the great honour of appointing them judges of the whole world, it is intolerable that they should be debarred from judging in trivial matters, as if they were not capable.' It follows from this that the Corinthians harm themselves in transferring to unbelievers the honour which God has given them.

What is said here about judging the world ought to be traced back to that Word of Christ: 'When the Son of man shall sit on the throne of his glory, ye also shall sit upon twelve thrones judging the twelve tribes of Israel' (Matt. 19.28). For all power of judging has been handed over to the Son in such a way that He will associate His saints with Himself in this honour, as assessors. Besides, they will judge the world, as indeed they are already beginning to do, because their godliness, faith, fear of the Lord, clear conscience and integrity of life will leave the godless without excuse; just as it is said about Noah (Heb. 11.7), that by his faith he condemned all the men of his time. But the first interpretation suits the apostle's purpose better, for if you do not take the judging, mentioned here, in the proper sense, the argument will break down.

But even taking it like that, it does not seem to have much weight, for it is as if someone said: 'The saints are endowed with heavenly wisdom, which immeasurably surpasses all branches of human knowledge. Therefore they can reach conclusions about the stars better than astronomers.' But no-one would agree to that, and the reason for dismissing it is obvious: piety and spiritual doctrine do not supply us with knowledge of the human sciences. My answer here is that between the other sciences and skill in judging there is this distinction; while the former are acquired by keenness of intellect, by studying and by learning from authorities, the latter depend rather upon fairness and a sound knowledge of right and wrong.

But someone will say: 'Lawyers will judge better and more accurately than any ignorant believer; otherwise there is no need for knowledge of the law.' To this I reply: their advice is not absolutely debarred here; for if a decision on any obscure question must be sought from a knowledge of the laws, the apostle does not prohibit Christians from consulting lawyers. But the only thing he finds fault with the Corinthians for is their referring their disputes to the judgement of unbelievers, as if there were no suitable judges in the Church. And he reminds them how greatly superior is the judgement to which God has appointed his believing people.

The words *in vobis*, 'in you' [RV *by you*] I think stand for *inter vos*, 'among you'. For as often as the faithful meet together in the name of Christ there is already in their assembly a certain reflection of the future judgement, which will be brought completely to view on the last day. Therefore Paul says that the world is judged in the Church, where there is set up the judgement seat of Christ, from which He exercises His jurisdiction.

3. *Do you not know that we shall judge angels?* This passage is taken in different ways. Chrysostom reports that some understand it as referring to priests, but this is very forced indeed. Others explain it as the heavenly angels, in this sense, that angels are subject to judgement by the Word of God, and, if need be, they can be judged by us through that Word. Galatians 1.8 can be read in that light: 'If an angel from heaven were to bring any other gospel let him be accursed.' At first glance this explanation does not appear to be out of line with Paul's argument. For if all whom God has enlightened by His Word are possessed of so much authority that, by means of that Word, they judge not only men but also angels, are they not all the more eligible to judge concerning trivial and paltry matters? But as Paul uses the future tense here, referring to the last day, and as the words carry the suggestion of an actual judgement (as the saying goes), it would certainly seem better to me to understand what he says as referring to the apostate angels. For the argument will be none the less conclusive if taken like this: 'We shall judge the devils who began in such an excellent way, and even now, after falling from their high position, are still immortal creatures, and superior to this world of corruption. What then? Shall those things which are subservient to the belly, be exempt from our judgement?'

4. *If then you have to judge things pertaining to this life?* We must always take particular note of the kind of cases he is dealing with. For public trials are not within our province and ought not to be brought

under our control. But it is quite in order to settle private matters without the magistrate's investigation. Therefore, since we do not detract from the authority of the magistrate in reaching a decision ourselves, the apostle rightly tells Christians to keep away from the ordinary court, i.e. that of unbelievers. And in case they might plead that they were being deprived of a better remedy, he tells them to choose judges from the church, to settle the cases peacefully and fairly. In case they should say that they have no suitable men for this, he says that even the person of the lowest standing can do what is required. Therefore the authority of the magistrate is not impaired here, when he directs that their function should be handed over to people who are looked down upon. For (as I have already said) this is stated by way of anticipation, as if he said: 'Even the humblest and least significant among you will carry out this task better than the unbelieving judges to whom you are running, when there is absolutely no need for you to do so.'

Chrysostom very nearly agrees with this interpretation, although he adds something to it. For he thinks that the apostle meant to say that even if the Corinthians could find nobody among them with enough wisdom for judging, they must however choose some, no matter what they were like. Ambrose touches neither heaven nor earth, as they say. I think that I myself have faithfully expressed what the apostle had in mind: that he preferred the meanest among believers to unbelievers, when it was a question of ability to judge.

Some work out quite a different meaning. For they take the verb καθίζετε in the present, i.e. 'you are setting them to judge'; and those 'who are of no account in the Church' they interpret as unbelievers. But this is clever rather than sound, for that would be a poor description of unbelievers. Finally, the phrase 'if you have' would not go very well with a rebuke, for that condition weakens it; rather, 'while you have' would have to be used. Accordingly I am rather inclined to the view that a remedy for the evil is prescribed here.

However it appears from a certain passage in Augustine that this sentence was incorrectly understood by the men of long ago. For in his book, On the Work of Monks, where he mentions his occupations, he asserts that certainly the most irksome of all his duties was his being compelled to devote a part of the day to worldly affairs, but that he endured it patiently, because the apostle had imposed this necessity upon him. It appears from this passage and from a certain letter that the bishops were accustomed to sit at specified times to settle disputes; as if the apostle is referring to them in particular in this passage. But as things always grow worse, from that error there afterwards developed the jurisdiction which the officials of the bishops appropriate for themselves in money matters. In that ancient custom there are two things with which fault should be found; (1) that the bishops were involved in affairs that had nothing to do with their office; and (2) that they were doing God an injustice in pretending that they departed from their proper calling by His authority and command. The wrong was perhaps to some extent excusable. However it would be the height of audacity to excuse or defend this worldly custom, which has been prevailing in the Papacy.

5. *I speak to shame you.* The meaning is: if other considerations leave you cold, then at least turn this over in your minds, how disgraceful it is that there is not even one of your number, who can, in a friendly way, settle some matter that has arisen between brothers, for you concede this honour to unbelievers. Now this passage is not inconsistent with the assertion which we came across earlier: that he did not make reference to their faults in order to make them ashamed; for here, by reproaching them in the way he does, he is rather recalling them from disgrace, and shows that he is really concerned about their honour. He does not want them to think so poorly of their fellowship, that they take away this privilege from all their brethren and surrender it to unbelievers.

7. *Nay already it is altogether a defect in you.* We now come to the second part of the reproof, containing general teaching. For now he is finding fault with them, not on the ground that they were exposing the Gospel to mockery and a bad name, but because they were taking legal proceedings against each other. Paul says that this is a fault or failing. We must take note of the suitableness of the word he uses. For ἥττημα means 'weakness of mind', for instance when it goes to pieces under the pressure of injuries, and it is not strong enough to stand up against anything. Later it was used for faults of any kind, as they all spring from weakness and lack of resolution. Therefore what Paul is condemning in the Corinthians is their making trouble for each other by going to law. He tells them that this is because they are incapable of suffering injuries patiently. In light of the Lord's instruction to us not to be overcome by evil things, but rather to get the better of injuries by acts of kindness (Matt. 5.44; Rom. 12.21), it is quite certain that those, who cannot keep control of themselves so as to stand up against injuries, sin by their lack of endurance. If this lack of endurance reveals itself in legal disputes among believers, the conclusion is that these disputes are bad.

But in this way Paul seems to do away altogether with legal judgements on behalf of individuals. 'Those who go to law are completely in the wrong, therefore it will be wrong for anybody to protect his rights before a magistrate.' Some answer this objection in this way: that the apostle declares that where there are law-suits the whole situation is wrong just because one or the other of the parties necessarily has a bad case. But they do not get out of it with this sophistry, because he says that they go wrong not only when they inflict injury, but also when they do not bear it patiently. For myself I answer simply like this: since he has just given permission to have judges, he has thereby given enough indication that it is not out of order for Christians to pursue their rights with moderation, so long as no damage is done to love. From this it is easily inferred that he was so severe because of his knowledge of the circumstances at issue. Indeed wherever law-suits occur frequently, or the parties are obstinate in joining issue with each other with the utmost rigour of the law, it is perfectly obvious that their minds are inflamed far too much by wrongful, greedy desires, and that they are not prepared for calmness of mind and endurance of wrongs, according to the commandment of Christ.

Let me speak more plainly. Paul disapproves of law-suits for this reason, that we ought to endure injuries quietly. Let us now see if it is possible for anyone to take legal proceedings without becoming impatient. For if that is so, it will not be wrong to take legal proceedings in every case, but $\epsilon\pi\grave{\iota}\ \tau\grave{o}\ \pi o\lambda\acute{v}$, i.e. generally speaking. But I acknowledge that, as men's manners are corrupted, impatience or lack of endurance (as they say) is the inevitable accompaniment of almost all law-suits. But this does not however prevent our distinguishing between the thing itself and its bad accompaniment. Let us therefore remember that Paul does not disapprove of law-suits on the ground that it is wrong in itself to uphold a good case by having recourse to a magistrate, but because they are nearly always bound up with improper attitudes of mind, such as lack of self-control, desire for revenge, hostility, obstinacy and so on.

It is strange that this question has not been more carefully investigated by ecclesiastical writers. Augustine has given more attention to it than the others, and comes nearer the mark; but even he is not free from obscurity, whatever truth there may be in what he teaches. Those who wish to be more explicit in their teaching advise us that a distinction must be made between public and private retribution. For since retribution belongs to the magistrate by God's appointment, those who seek its aid are not irresponsibly taking vengeance into their own hands, but are having recourse to God as avenger. All that is wisely and rightly said; but we must go further. For if we are forbidden to seek vengeance, even from God; in the same way we would be debarred from having recourse to the magistrate for retribution.

Therefore I acknowledge that all revenge is ruled out for the Christian, and he must not practise it either by himself or through the medium of the magistrate; no, and he must not even desire it! If a Christian therefore wants to prosecute his rights in a court of law, without going against God, he must take special care not to come into court with any desire for revenge, any bad feeling, any anger, or in a word any poisonous thing. In all this love will be the best guide.

If someone points out that it is a very rare thing for anyone to go to law free from and innocent of every unworthy attitude of mind, I indeed admit as much, and at the same time say that it is rare to get an example of a good litigant. Indeed for many reasons it is worth while showing that the thing is not evil in itself but is spoiled by abuse. The *first* is that the impression may not be given that God was wasting His time in establishing law-courts. The *second* reason is in order that believers may know exactly what they are allowed to do, so that they may not undertake anything that would be against their conscience. That is why many rush into open contempt of God; once they have begun to reach beyond those limits imposed on them. The *third* reason is that they may be warned that restraint must always be observed, so as not to spoil, by their own misbehaviour, the remedy which God has entrusted to them. The *final* reason is that the boldness of the wicked may be checked by an unspoiled and genuine zeal; and this could only be done if we were allowed to subject them to legal punishments.

8. *Nay but you yourselves do wrong.* It is clear from this verse why he has inveighed against them with so much severity; because an improper lust for possessions had them in such a grip that they could not refrain from hurting each other. In order to bring out the extent of the evil he has just said that people who do not know how to suffer wrongs against them are not Christians. Here therefore there is an amplification taken from a comparison; because, if it is wrong not to bear wrongs patiently, how much worse is it to inflict them?

And that your brethren. This makes the evil all the worse. Because, if those who defraud strangers are doubly in the wrong, it is a monstrous thing for a brother to cheat or rob his brother. Now we are all brothers who name the one Father in heaven. However, if anyone deals with strangers in bad faith Paul does not treat the offence lightly; but he does show that the Corinthians were totally blind when they could think of consecrated brotherhood as something of no importance.

Or know ye not that the unrighteous shall not inherit the kingdom of God? Be not deceived: neither fornicators, nor idolaters, nor adulterers, nor effeminate, nor abusers of themselves with men, nor thieves, nor covetous, nor drunkards, nor revilers, nor extortioners, shall inherit the kingdom of God. And such were some of you: but ye were washed, but ye were sanctified, but ye were justified in the name of the Lord Jesus Christ, and in the Spirit of our God. (9-11)

9. *Do you not know etc.* By unrighteousness we are to understand

what is opposed to strict morality. So it is that those who cause injury to their brothers, who cheat and defraud others, who, in a word, trample on others in the pursuit of their own interests, are the unrighteous who will not enter into possession of the Kingdom of God. It is too obvious for words that here when Paul gives instances of unrighteous people, such as adulterers, thieves, covetous and revilers, he means those who do not repent of their sins, but obstinately persist in them. The apostle himself brings that out a little later in his own words, when he says that the Corinthians had once been like that. The wicked do indeed inherit the Kingdom of God, but only after they have been turned to the Lord in true penitence and justified after their conversion, and so ceased to be wicked. For although conversion is not the ground of forgiveness, nevertheless we know that it is only those who repent who are reconciled to God. But the use of the question makes for emphasis, for he makes it plain that he is speaking about something with which they are quite familiar, and which is a commonplace among all the godly.

Be not deceived. Having had occasion to deal with one sin, he goes on to speak of many. But I think that he has particularly noted those vices with which the Corinthians were afflicted. He uses three different terms in his censure of the sexual lusts, which, according to all the historical evidence, held sway, indeed ran riot, there. For Corinth abounded in riches. It was a famous centre of commerce, frequented by merchants of many nations. Luxury goes along with wealth, and it gives birth to lewdness and licentiousness of every kind. Besides, a nation already naturally prone to lust was being stimulated by many other corrupt things.

The difference between fornicators and adulterers is well enough known. By effeminate I understand those who, while they may not openly become prostitutes, nevertheless show how unchaste they are by the use of pandering words, by effeminate bearing and dress, and other means of attracting attention. The fourth term in this category is the most serious of all, viz. that unnatural and filthy thing which was far too common in Greece.

He illustrates his condemnation of injustice and wrongs by the use of three particular examples. He calls thieves those who deceive their brothers by any sort of fraud or camouflaged cunning. By extortioners he means those who lay violent hold of the goods of others, or like harpies drag them to themselves from all sides and devour them. But so that his idea might be stretched over a wide field he afterwards adds all covetous people also. By drunkards we must also understand those who indulge in excessive eating. He makes particular mention of revilers because it is very likely that that city was full of facetious and disparaging gossip. In short, Paul makes particular mention of those vices, which, as he saw, had a grip on the city.

But in order that his warning may carry more weight he says, *be not deceived*. With these words he advises them not to lull themselves with wishful thinking, in the same way as men are accustomed to make light of their sins, and so condition themselves to treating God with scorn. Therefore no poison is more dangerous than those attractive things which encourage us in our sins. Let us therefore avoid, not as the songs of the Sirens, but as the fatal stings of Satan, the words of godless men, who make a joke of the judgement of God and the condemnation of sins. Lastly, the appositeness of the verb κληρονομεῖν (to inherit) should be observed. For it shows that the Kingdom of heaven is the inheritance of sons, and therefore comes to us by the favour of adoption.

11. *And you were like that*. Some make this refer to a part only: 'some of you were like that', because in the Greek the word τινές (some) is added. But I think that it is more likely that the apostle is speaking of them all. Indeed I am of the opinion that that word is superfluous, in view of the usual practice of the Greeks, who often make use of it for the sake of ornament, but not as a term of limitation. However we must not understand him to mean that all are wrapped up in the same bundle as if he attributes all these vices to each one of them. But he only wishes to point out that no-one is free from these evil things until he has been born again by the Spirit. For we must hold that human nature, speaking universally, contains the seed of all evils, but that some vices predominate and make themselves evident in some men, as the Lord brings the depravity of the flesh to view by its fruits.

Thus in the first chapter of Romans Paul lists many kinds of vices and crimes, which spring from ignorance of God, and that ingratitude, of which he had shown all unbelievers to be guilty; not that every single unbeliever is tainted with all those vices, but because all are exposed to them, and no-one is free of every one of them. For a man who is not an adulterer sins in some other way. So also in the third chapter he makes these texts refer to all the sons of Adam: 'their throat is an open sepulchre; their feet are swift to shed blood; their tongue is deceitful and poisonous.' It is not the case that all are blood-thirsty and cruel, that all are treacherous or abusive in speech; rather, before they are made new men by God, one has a tendency to cruelty, another to treachery, this one to lust and that one to deceitfulness. The upshot is that there is no-one in whom there is not some evidence of the corruption common to all. Indeed all of us, to a man, are, by an inward, secret bias of the mind, subject to all vices, except in so far as the Lord puts a curb on them within us, so that they do not issue into the world in action. The meaning therefore is simply this: before they had received the grace of regeneration some of the Corinthians were covetous, others adulterers, others extortioners, others effeminate, others revilers; but now having truly been set free by Christ, they were like that no longer.

However the apostle's intention is to humble them by reminding them of what they were like before, then to awaken them to realization of the grace of God towards them. For the more we recognize the wretchedness of the condition from which the kindness of the Lord has rescued us, the more clearly do we see the rich fullness of His grace. Now the extolling of grace is a source of encouragement; because we ought to take great pains not to make the kindness of God worthless, when it should be held in such high esteem. It is as if he said: 'It is enough that God has pulled you out of that mud in which you had once been immersed.' Peter speaks in similar terms: 'The time that is past suffices for doing what the Gentiles like to do' (I Pet. 4.3).

But you have been washed. Paul uses three expressions to convey the one idea, so as to be more effective in preventing them from falling back again into the condition from which they had extricated themselves. Although these three phrases all refer, therefore, to the same thing, their very variety, nevertheless, gives a great deal of force to what he says. For there are implied contrasts between washing and unclean things; sanctification and contamination; justification and guilt. His point is that once they have been justified they must not bring themselves into a new state of guilt; having been sanctified they must not make themselves unclean again; having been washed they must not sully themselves with fresh filth. Rather they are to strive after purity, to continue in true holiness, to detest the filthy things of their former life. And from this we infer the purpose for which God reconciles us to Himself by the free remission of sins.

Although I have said that one thing is expressed by the use of three terms that does not imply that, in my view, there is no difference between them. For, strictly speaking, God justifies us when He clears us of our guilt by not laying our sins to our charge; He cleanses us when He wipes out the remembrance of our sins. So the only difference between these two is that the one is straightforward while the other is metaphorical. The metaphor is washing, for the blood of Christ is thought of as water. On the other hand He sanctifies by reforming our corrupt nature by His Spirit, and so sanctification has to do with regeneration. But in this passage the apostle's only purpose was to express himself in more than one way in magnifying the grace of God, which has delivered us from the bondage of sin, so that we may learn

from this how much we ought to shrink from everything that stirs up
the anger and vengeance of God against us.

In the name of the Lord Jesus etc. Paul makes a proper and judicious
distinction between functions. For the blood of Christ is the cause of
our cleansing; from His death and resurrection we obtain righteousness
and sanctification. But since the cleansing which Christ has carried out
and the obtaining of righteousness are of no benefit to any except those
who have been made to share in those blessings by the power of the
Holy Spirit, Paul is quite right in speaking of the Spirit along with
Christ. Christ, therefore, is the source of every blessing to us; it is
from Him that we obtain everything. But Christ Himself, with all
His blessings, is communicated to us by the Spirit. For we receive
Christ by faith; and it is by faith that His benefits (*gratiae*) are applied
to us. The author of faith is the Spirit.

*All things are lawful for me; but not all things are expedient. All things
are lawful for me; but I will not be brought under the power of any.
Meats for the belly, and the belly for meats; but God shall bring to nought
both it and them. But the body is not for fornication, but for the Lord;
and the Lord for the body: and God both raised the Lord, and will raise
up us through his power. Know ye not that your bodies are members of
Christ? shall I then take away the members of Christ, and make them
members of a harlot? God forbid. Or know ye not that he that is joined
to a harlot is one body? for, The twain, saith he, shall become one flesh.
But he that is joined unto the Lord is one spirit. Flee fornication. Every
sin that a man doeth is without the body; but he that committeth fornication sinneth against his own body. Or know ye not that your body is a
temple of the Holy Ghost which is in you, which ye have from God?
and ye are not your own; for ye were bought with a price: glorify God
therefore in your body.* (12–20)

12. *All things are lawful for me.* Interpreters make great efforts to
determine what connexion these verses have with what goes before,
since they appear to be inconsistent with the apostle's line of argument.
I shall omit the numerous explanations, and shall state what, in my
view, is the most appropriate. It is very likely that the Corinthians
retained, even up to that time, a great deal of their old licentiousness,
and smacked of the morals of the city. But where vices run riot with
impunity people take custom for law. Then they seek worthless pre-
texts to cover themselves up. That was happening here, where they
were turning to the pretext of Christian liberty to allow them to do
almost anything at all. They abandoned themselves to an extravagance
of luxury, and, as usual, a great deal of pride was mixed up with it.
Since it was a matter of external actions, they did not consider that they

were sinning. No! and it appears from what Paul says that they abused their liberty to such an extent that they stretched it to include fornication. Therefore, after he has spoken about their vices, it is very appropriate that he should now pass to criticism of those deceitful excuses, which they made use of to delude themselves about outward sins.

It is indeed certain that he is dealing with outward things which God has left to the discretion of believers. But by speaking in general terms he either censures their excessive licentiousness in an indirect way, or praises the boundless generosity of God, which is the best means of keeping our passions in check. For you can take it as a mark of intemperance when people, who are surrounded by such a variety of riches, do not hold themselves in check by their own efforts, and impose limits on themselves. First of all, indeed, he qualifies the liberty with two exceptions. Then he warns them that it does not extend to fornication at all. These words, 'all things are lawful to me', ought to be taken as if he were both anticipating (κατ' ἀνθυποφοράν) what the Corinthians might say, and speaking for them. It is as if he said: 'I am aware of the kind of retort you usually make when you want to avoid a reprimand for vices that affect others. You of course imagine that all things are lawful for you, without any distinction or qualification.'

But all things are not expedient. This is the first exception by which he puts a check on the use of liberty; they may not abandon themselves to unrestricted licence, because they must not lose sight of the need for edifying each other. The meaning is: 'It is not enough that this or that is allowed us, to be used as we like, for we must pay attention to what is for the good of our brothers, whose well-being we are bound to consider.' For, as he will afterwards bring out more fully and as he has shown in Romans 14.13 ff, in the sight of God each one has freedom within himself, on this condition, that all ought to limit the use of their liberty in the interests of each other's well-being.

I will not be brought under the power of anything. This is the second restriction on liberty. We are appointed lords over everything, but yet in such a way that we ought not to put ourselves under bondage to anything. That is what is done by those who cannot control their own desires. For I take the word τινός (any) to be neuter, and as referring not to persons but to the things themselves. Thus the meaning is: 'We are lords of all things, only let us not misuse this lordship so as to undergo a most wretched bondage; so that, because of passions that are excessive and uncontrolled, we are under the control of those outward things, which ought to be under our control. Indeed, when people are unduly peevish, because they are annoyed at having to give up anything for the sake of their brothers, the result is that they inevitably and stupidly put themselves in chains.'

13. *Meats for the belly and the belly for meats.* Paul shows here how material things should be used: to meet the needs of this present life, which fades away quickly, like a shadow. This agrees with what he says in chapter 7.31, 'We must use this world as if we were not making use of it to the full.' And we also gather from this how the Christian should have nothing to do with the eager pursuit of material things. Therefore, when there is some dispute about corruptible things, a believer will not let his thoughts dwell with anxiety on them. For liberty is one thing; the wrongful use of it another. Another sentence echoes this one: 'the Kingdom of God is not meat and drink' (Rom. 14.17).

But the body is not for fornication. Having disposed of the exceptions Paul now also adds that our liberty should not by any means be extended to include fornication. For at that time it was such a prevalent evil that it almost seemed as if it were permitted. That can also be seen from the decree of the apostles (Acts 15.20), where they prohibit the Gentiles from fornication, and include it among neutral things. For there is no doubt that that was done because generally they regarded it as lawful. Therefore Paul now says that fornication and food are on a different footing, for God has not intended the body for fornication, as he intended the belly for food. Paul confirms this by things which are opposites or incompatible, because the body is consecrated to Christ. But it is impossible for Christ to be bound up with fornication. His addition, 'and the Lord for the body', carries a good deal of weight, for since God the Father has united us to His Son, what a disgraceful thing it would be to tear our bodies away from that sacred union, and give them over to things quite unworthy of Christ.

14. *Besides, God both raised the Lord and will raise us up etc.* By looking at the position of Christ Paul shows how foreign fornication is to a Christian. For since Christ has been received into the glory of heaven, what has He in common with the filthy things of this world? However two aspects are included in these words. The first is: it is shameful and sinful that our body, which has been dedicated to Christ, should be desecrated by fornication, in view of the fact that Christ Himself has been raised from the dead, in order that He might enter on the possession of heavenly glory. The second aspect is that it is a disgraceful thing to prostitute our body to the filth of the earth, when we will be sharers in blessed immortality and heavenly glory along with Christ. There is a similar thought in Colossians 3.1: 'If then ye were raised together with Christ' etc. There is this difference, however, that here he is speaking about the final resurrection only, while in that passage he also speaks of the first resurrection, in other words, of the grace of the Holy Spirit, by which we are transformed into a new life. But

because the human understanding finds the resurrection almost incredible, the scripture, in the passages referring to it, reminds us of the power of God, in order to confirm our faith in it.

15. *Do you not know that your bodies are members of Christ?* This is an explanation, or if you prefer, a clarification of the previous sentence. For, on account of its succinctness, the phrase, 'the body is for the Lord' could be somewhat obscure. So, as if explaining it, he says that Christ is so joined to us, and we to Him, that we are united in one body with Him. It follows that if I join myself to a harlot I tear Christ apart, limb from limb, so far as it is in my power to do so; because it is an impossibility for me to drag Him into association with such uncleanness. Now since that must be absolutely detested Paul uses the phrase with which he usually dismisses anything unthinkable: *God forbid.*

We should note that the spiritual union which we have with Christ is not a matter of the soul alone, but of the body also, so that we are flesh of His flesh etc. (Eph. 5.30). The hope of the resurrection would be faint, if our union with Him were not complete and total like that.

16. *Or do you not know that he who is joined to a harlot.* He makes it plainer how seriously Christ is harmed by the man who has intercourse with a harlot. For one body is formed, and so he tears a member away from the body of Christ.

Paul adds a quotation from Genesis 2.24, but it is not clear what connexion he means it to have with his theme. For if he quotes it in order to prove that two people who commit fornication with each other become one flesh, he is distorting the meaning, from the true one to one quite alien to it. For Moses is not speaking there of the scandalous and forbidden cohabitation of a man and woman, but of the marriage union which God blesses. For he teaches that that bond is so close and indissoluble that it surpasses the intimacy which exists between a father and son; and that certainly cannot be said about fornication. This consideration sometimes makes me think that this quotation is not introduced in confirmation of the phrase immediately preceding, but the earlier one, as follows: 'Moses says that husband and wife come together as one flesh in the marriage bond, but he who is joined to the Lord becomes not only one flesh, but also one spirit with Him.' And so this whole section aims at making clearer the effect and dignity of the spiritual union (*coniugium*) existing between us and Christ.

But if someone finds that this explanation is not entirely satisfactory because it seems forced, I will bring forward another. Since fornication is a corruption of a divine institution it bears some resemblance to it. And what is said about marriage can to some extent be applied to fornication, not in order to bestow the same esteem upon it, but in order to reveal all the more clearly the seriousness of the sin. The words, 'the two shall become one flesh', refer, strictly and properly speaking, only to those who are married. But they are applied to fornicators who come together in a corrupt and unclean union, so that the contamination passes from the one to the other. For there is nothing absurd about saying that fornication has some resemblance to the sacredness of marriage, since it is a corruption of it, as I have said. But fornication is under God's curse, marriage under God's blessing. That is the nature of the similarity between things which are set over against each other in contrast. However, I would prefer to take these words as referring primarily to marriage, and then as improperly applied to fornication. I would put it like this: 'God pronounces husband and wife to be one flesh, in order that neither of them may cleave to the flesh of another; so that the adulterer and the adulteress do indeed become one flesh, and involve themselves in a union, but one that is under a curse.' And this is certainly more simple and more in agreement with the context.

17. *He that is joined to the Lord is one spirit.* Paul has added this in order to show that the union (*coniunctionem*) of Christ with us is closer than that of husband and wife; and that the former is much to be preferred to the latter, so that it must be cultivated by means of the strictest purity and fidelity. For if a man who is joined to a wife in marriage ought not to have union with a prostitute, it is a far more serious sin in the case of believers, who are not only one flesh with Christ, but also one Spirit. Here, then, there is a comparison between greater and less.

18. *Flee fornication. Every sin etc.* Having dealt with uprightness of conduct, Paul now shows how we ought to look on fornication with the utmost horror, keeping in mind how very shameful and filthy it is. He enlarges upon this by comparing it with all other sins: because, of all sins, this is the one which brands the body with the mark of disgrace. Indeed the body is also defiled by theft, murder, and drunkenness, in accordance with these and similar texts: 'Your hands are defiled with blood' (Isa. 1.15); 'You have offered your members instruments of iniquity unto sin' (Rom. 6.19). Because of this, and in order to avoid this confusion, some understand the words 'his own body' as referring to us who are united to Christ. But to me that seems clever rather than sound. Besides they do not get away with it even in that way, because the same thing can be asserted about idolatry as much as fornication. For the man who prostrates himself before an idol sins against union with Christ. Therefore, my explanation is that he does not completely deny that there are other sins, which also bring dishonour and disgrace upon our bodies, but that he is simply saying that those other sins do not leave anything like the same filthy stain on our bodies as forni-

cation does. Of course my hand is stained by theft or murder, my tongue by slander or perjury, my whole body by drunkenness; but fornication leaves such a mark impressed upon the body, as no other sin can do. In accordance with this comparison, or rather on the basis of a greater and less degree, other sins are said to be outside the body; but that does not mean, taking each one by itself, that it is because they do not touch the body at all.

19. *Do you not know that your body.* Paul uses two further arguments to keep us away from this filthiness. The first is that 'our bodies are temples of the Spirit'; and the second that we are not under our own jurisdiction because the Lord has acquired us for Himself as His own private property. There is a suggestion of emphasis in the use of the word temple, for, since the Spirit of God cannot stay in a place that is unclean, we make ourselves His dwelling-place only by consecrating ourselves as His temples. What a great honour God bestows upon us in wishing to dwell in us! So we should be all the more afraid lest we should drive Him away and He should abandon us, angered by our sacrilegious acts.

And you are not your own. This is the second argument, viz. that we are not under our own authority to live as we want. The reason he gives for that is that the Lord has paid the price for our redemption, and acquired us for Himself. Paul speaks in similar terms in Rom. 14.9: 'For Christ died and rose, in order that He might be Lord of the living and the dead.'

Then the word 'price' can be taken in two ways. We can understand it in a straightforward sense, as when we normally speak of something as having 'cost a price', because we wish to make it plain that we did not get it for nothing. The other meaning is that it is substituted for the adverb $\tau\iota\mu\acute{\iota}\omega\varsigma$, 'at a high price', 'dear', as we usually describe things which have cost us a lot. There is no doubt in my mind that the second is more satisfactory. Peter writes in similar terms: 'You have not been redeemed with gold and silver, but with the precious blood of a lamb without blemish' (I Pet. 1.18, 19). What it comes to is this: that redemption must hold us bound, and hold the licentiousness of our flesh in check with the bridle of obedience.

20. *Glorify God.* From this conclusion it is plain that the Corinthians assumed that they could do what they pleased in regard to external matters, and that had to be checked and bridled. Paul therefore supplies the means of correction here, where he warns them that the body, just as much as the soul, is subject to God, and therefore it is only right that both should serve His glory. It is as if he said: 'Indeed the mind of a believer must be pure before God, but also the outward conduct, which men see, must be in conformity, seeing that authority

over both belongs to God, who has redeemed both.' With the same
end in view he asserted in verse 19 that not only our souls, but also
our bodies are temples of the Holy Spirit, so that we may be under
no delusion about acquitting ourselves well towards Him, for we can
only do that when we yield ourselves to His service, wholly and
completely, so that He may also direct the outward actions of our
lives by His Word.

CHAPTER SEVEN

Now concerning the things whereof ye wrote: It is good for a man not to touch a woman. But, because of fornications, let each man have his own wife, and let each woman have her own husband. (1-2)

Since Paul has been speaking about fornication, he now makes a suitable transition to the subject of marriage, which is the remedy for avoiding fornication. Now it appears that, despite the great cleavages in the church at Corinth, some regard for Paul nevertheless remained, for when they were in doubt about something they asked his advice. We do not know what exactly their questions were, except what we can conjecture from his reply. But this much is well known, that as soon as the church was founded, a wrong belief crept into it by the trickery of Satan. What it meant was that a large proportion, holding a silly admiration for the unmarried state, looked down their noses at the sacred state of marriage; many of them indeed would have nothing to do with what they regarded as an unclean thing. Perhaps this infection had attacked the Corinthians also; or at least there were some extremely idle spirits, who, by making far too much of celibacy, were taking pains to turn the minds of believers away from marriage. However, in view of the fact that the apostle gives his teaching on numerous other matters, he reveals that he had been consulted about many of them. It is important that we should attend to his teaching on each one of them.

1. *It is good for a man etc.* Paul's reply consists of two parts. He teaches first of all that it would be 'good' if every man kept away from a woman, provided that he has the power to do so. In the second place he modifies this, as follows: since the weakness of the flesh does not make this possible for many people, they must not be indifferent to the remedy, which the Lord has supplied for them, and which they actually possess. Further, we must note what he means by the word 'good', when he asserts that it is good to keep away from marriage, lest we may reach the conclusion, opposite to what is intended, that the marriage bond is therefore bad. That is what happened in the case of Jerome, not so much because of ignorance, but, in my view, more through the heat of controversy. For although that famous man was endowed with outstanding virtues, yet he was handicapped by one serious defect, for in debate he was swept off his feet by excessive zeal, and so he was not always concerned about sticking to the truth. Thus

his inference here is as follows: 'It is good not to touch a woman, therefore it is wrong to touch her.' Paul certainly does not use 'good' in that sense here, so that it is set over against what is evil or full of vice. He only shows what is to one's advantage in view of all the troubles, annoyances and responsibilities, which beset those who are married. Then we must always pay heed to the modification which he adds. Therefore Paul's words can be made to yield no more than this, that it is indeed advantageous and suitable for a man not to be bound to a wife, so long as he is able to do without one. Let us explain that by an analogy (*similitudine*). Should anyone say: 'It would be good for a man not to eat, not to drink, not to sleep,' he would not be dismissing food, drink or sleep as evils. Rather, because whatever time is given to those things means so much less to spiritual things, he would mean that we would be the more blessed, if we could be free from those diversions, and devote ourselves entirely to meditation on heavenly things. Therefore, since there are many hindrances in married life, which interfere with a man's freedom, it would be good, for that reason, not to be involved in marriage.

But another question presents itself here; for these words of Paul seem to be inconsistent with the words of the Lord, in Gen. 2.18, that 'it is not good for the man to be without a wife'. The condition, which the Lord says, in that passage, is evil, Paul teaches here to be good. I answer that where the wife is a help to her husband, making his life happy, then that is in accordance with God's intention. For God so ordered it in the beginning that the man without a wife was half a man, as it were (*quasi dimidius homo*), and felt himself lacking in help which he particularly needed; and the wife was, as it were, the completion of the man (*quasi viri complementum*). Afterwards, sin made its attack and spoiled that institution of God, for in place of so great a blessing grievous affliction (*poena*) has entered in, so that marriage is the source and means of many troubles. Therefore whatever evil or trouble there is in marriage springs from the corruption of God's institution. Although there is still something left of the original blessing, so that the life of a single person is often much more miserable than that of a married person, yet, in view of the fact that married people are involved in many misfortunes, Paul is justified in advising that it would be good for a man to keep from it. In this way those difficulties which are attendant upon marriage are not glossed over. And yet, at the same time, no room is allowed for the vulgar jokes, which are generally made in order to discredit marriage, such as, 'a wife is a necessary evil', and 'a woman is one of the greatest of evils'. For sayings like that have come from Satan's laboratory; and their objective is nothing less than the branding of God's holy institution as dishonourable, so that, as a consequence, men may shrink from marriage, as though from the gallows (*a capitali noxa*) and plague.

What it amounts to is this, that we must remember to distinguish between the unblemished ordinance of God, and the punishments of sin, which came on the scene afterwards. For, according to this distinction, in the beginning it was good for a man to be joined to a wife, without anything to spoil it; and even now it is good but only to a degree, because the bitter is mixed with the sweet, on account of the curse of God. However for those who do not have the gift of continence marriage is a remedy, which is necessary and makes for health, as we shall see in what follows.

2. *But because of fornication.* Paul now requires that those who are subject to the vice of incontinency should have recourse to this remedy. For, although this sentence seems to be of general application, it ought to be restricted, however, to those who feel themselves driven by necessity. Each person must be the judge as to whether this applies to himself. Therefore, no matter what difficulty marriage is seen to have, all those who cannot stand up to the promptings of the flesh should know that this commandment has been laid upon them by the Lord.

But someone may ask: 'Is the cure of incontinency the only reason for contracting a marriage?' My reply is that that is not what Paul means. For to those who have the gift of being able to withhold from marriage, he allows liberty to marry or not to marry. But he commands others to have regard for their weakness by marrying. What it comes to is this: what is at question here is not the reasons for which marriage has been instituted, but the persons for whom it is necessary. For, if we look at the first marriage, we see that it could not be a remedy for a malady, which did not yet exist, but that it was set up for the procreation of children. It is true that after the Fall this other purpose was added.

This passage is also opposed to polygamy. For the apostle means that every woman should have her own husband and he maintains that there is a mutual obligation. Therefore once a man has pledged himself to faithfulness to his wife, he ought not to separate himself from her, and that is clearly done by a second union.

Let the husband render unto the wife her due: and likewise also the wife unto the husband. The wife hath not power over her own body, but the husband: and likewise also the husband hath not power over his own body, but the wife. Defraud ye not one the other, except it be by consent for a season, that ye may give yourselves unto prayer, and may be together again, that Satan tempt you not because of your incontinency.
(3–5)

3. *The husband to the wife.* Paul now lays down the rules for married life; or he teaches the nature of the duty of husband and wife. Indeed in the first place he lays down a general principle about mutual good-will: that the husband love his wife, and the wife her husband.

Others interpret the words 'due benevolence' (*debitam benevolentiam*) as 'the obligation of marriage', i.e. conjugal rights. Perhaps that is right. What prompts them to this view is that there immediately follows, 'the husband hath not power over his own body' etc. But it would be better were we to say that that is a conclusion from the preceding sentence. Husband and wife are, therefore, bound to mutual goodwill, and from that it follows that neither he nor she has power over his or her own body.

But it may be asked why the apostle places them on an equal footing, and does not demand obedience and subjection from the wife. My answer is that he did not intend to discuss all their duties, but only the mutual obligation which is concerned with intercourse. Husband and wife, therefore, have different rights and duties in other things, but in the preservation of married faithfulness they are on an equal footing. For the same reason polygamy is again condemned, for if it is a constant condition of marriage that the man renounces his power over his own body, and surrenders it to his wife, how can he afterwards act as if he were free, and join himself to somebody else?

5. *Do not deprive each other.* Profane people might think that Paul is not modest enough in dealing like this with the intimacies of husband and wife; indeed that it is not worthy of the dignity of an apostle. But if we consider the reasons which prompted him, we shall discover that he was forced to speak of those matters. First of all he was aware how powerfully a counterfeit show of purity deceives the godly, as we ourselves know from experience. For Satan hypnotizes us with what seems to be the right thing to do, so that we come to think of inter-course with our wives as making us unclean, and consider giving up our calling and assuming another state of life. Again, Paul knew how everyone is inclined to self-love, and eager to gratify his own pleasure. That is the reason why a husband, having satisfied his passion, not only neglects his wife but even despises her. And there are few who are not sometimes waylaid by this feeling of distaste for their wives. It is for those reasons that Paul deals so anxiously with the mutual obliga-tion of marriage. It is as though he said: 'If it ever enters the thoughts of those who are married to long for the single life, because it is holier, or because they are urged on by promiscuous desires, let them remem-ber that they are held fast by a mutual obligation. The man is only the half of his body, and it is the same with the woman. They do not have freedom of choice therefore, but, on the contrary, they must keep

themselves in check with these thoughts: since one needed the support of the other, the Lord has joined us together, so that we may help each other. Let each one help the other in his need; and let neither act as if he could do what he likes.'

Unless by mutual consent. Paul demands 'mutual consent', first of all because it is not simply a question of the continency of one of the parties, but of both. Immediately he also adds two other exceptions. The first is that it should only be done temporarily, since continuous continency is not in their power. Otherwise they might make an effort to undertake more than they are fit for, and fall under the wiles of Satan. The second exception is that they must not abstain from intercourse as if that abstinence were in itself a good and holy work, or as if it were a means of worshipping God; but in order that they may be able to have time for practices that are more worth while.

But though Paul had made such careful provision in this connexion Satan had the upper hand, however, so that he was urging many to unlawful divorce by means of an improper desire for an unmarried life. Having abandoned their wives, men fled into a life of solitude to please God better by living as monks. Against their husbands' will, wives took the veil, the badge of celibacy. They did not for a moment consider that by violating the faithfulness pledged to their partners, they were breaking the covenant of the Lord, and that by breaking the bond of marriage, they were shaking off the Lord's yoke.

Indeed this vice was corrected to some extent by the old Canons. For they forbade a husband to leave his wife against her will on the pretext of continency, similarly a wife to deny her body to her husband. But they went wrong in that they allowed both to live together in constant celibacy, as if men had every right to lay down something which is opposed to the Spirit of God. Paul expressly directs that those who are married should only deprive each other temporarily. The bishops allowed them to give up intercourse for ever. Is there anybody who does not see how this is plainly conflicting? Therefore no-one should be surprised at our open disagreement in this matter with the men of old, who certainly deviated from the clear expression of the Word of God.

That you may have leisure for fasting and prayer. We should note that Paul is not referring here to fasting and prayer in general and without distinction. The moderation which ought to be a constant, everyday feature of the lives of Christians, is one kind of fasting. Prayer, in its turn, ought to be made not only daily but also continually. But Paul is speaking of that kind of fasting, which is a solemn evidence of penitence, and seeks to ward off the wrath of God; or by which believers prepare themselves for prayer before undertaking some serious affair. Similarly he means the kind of prayer which requires a greater and more concentrated mental effort. For it is sometimes necessary for us to drop everything else in order to fast and pray: for example, when some disaster is threatening us, which appears to be a sign of God's wrath; or when we are struggling with some difficulty; or when something very important has to be carried out, such as the appointing of pastors. Now the apostle is justified in linking these two together, for fasting is a preparation for prayer; and Christ also brings them together, in saying: 'This kind of devil is not cast out except by fasting and prayer' (Matt. 17.21).

Therefore, when Paul says *that you may have leisure*, he means, that, having freed yourselves of all distractions, you may give your attention to this one thing. Now, if anyone objects that intercourse is a bad thing, because it comes in the way of prayer, the answer is easy: that does not make it worse than food and drink which hinder fasting. But believers must use discretion in deciding when it is time for eating and drinking, and when for fasting. It is also a matter of the same discretion to know when it is a proper time for having intercourse with their wives, and when they should let it give way to something else, which claims their attention.

And come together again, that Satan tempt you not etc. Paul now gives the reason, through ignorance of which the men of long ago made their mistake, of giving ill-considered and rash approval of a vow of life-long continency. For they reasoned in this way: 'If it is good for married people to agree sometimes not to have intercourse for a certain time, then it would be all the better were they to abstain permanently.' But they did not consider how dangerous this was, for Satan is given the chance to overwhelm us, when we attempt something beyond the limit of our feeble strength. 'But Satan must be resisted,' someone will say. What if there are no weapons and no shield? 'We must ask the Lord for them,' they say. But we shall ask the Lord in vain to come to our defence in a foolhardy fight. For that reason we ought to pay particular attention to the phrase 'because of your incontinency', for the weakness of our flesh exposes us to the temptations of Satan. If we want to drive them out and keep them out our proper course of action is to apply the remedy, which the Lord has given for our protection. Therefore, those who give up intercourse are acting thoughtlessly, indeed as if they had made an arrangement with God for perpetual power of resistance.

But this I say by way of permission, not of commandment. Yet I would that all men were even as I myself. Howbeit each man hath his own gift from God, one after this manner, and another after that. But I say to the unmarried and to widows, It is good for them if they abide even as I. But if they have not continency, let them marry: for it is better to marry than to burn. (6-9)

6. *By way of permission.* So that they might not take advantage of a rule such as he had laid down, and give the reins to lust, Paul adds a restraining note. He says that he has written these things in light of their weakness, so that they may remember that marriage is a remedy for sexual laxity. He also wants to prevent their making wrong and unrestrained use of the benefit it brings, in order to satisfy their passions anyhow, indeed without limit or sense of shame. At the same time he seeks to meet the jibes of unbelievers, so that no-one can raise the objection: 'So! are you afraid that husbands and wives do not have enough inclination for passionate indulgence in themselves, when you are giving encouragement to them.' For the Papists, those little saints, are also upset by this line of teaching, and would gladly cross swords with Paul, because he holds that married people should remain living together, and does not allow them to make a quick change to a life of celibacy. Paul therefore gives the reason for teaching as he does, and asserts that he has not recommended intercourse to those who are married, in order to entice them to find delight, or because he found pleasure in advising it, but that he had regard for what was called for by the weakness of the people, to whom he is speaking.

Unthinking fanatical supporters of celibacy make wrong use of both parts of this verse. Because Paul says that he speaks 'by way of permission' (*secundum veniam*) they infer from that, that intercourse in marriage is therefore sinful; for where there is need of forgiveness (*venia*) sin is present. On the other hand from his saying 'not by way of commandment' they infer that it is therefore a sign of greater sanctity to give up the married state and revert to celibacy.

To the first I reply: since I acknowledge that all human affections can get very much out of hand, I do not deny that there may also be in this connexion a lack of discipline (ἀταξία), which, I will allow, is sinful. And, more than that, this feeling, I grant you, is more violent than others, and almost bestial. But against that I also maintain, that whatever vice or disgrace there is about it, is so covered over by the honourableness of marriage, that it ceases to be a vice, or at least ceases to be thought of as such by God. That is how Augustine deals with the matter, and very well too, in his book *On the Advantage of Marriage* and often elsewhere. You may sum it up like this: the intercourse of husband and wife is a pure thing, it is proper and holy; for it is the institution of God. The uncontrolled passion with which men are aflame is a vice springing from the corruption of human nature; but for believers marriage is a veil which covers over that fault, so that God sees it no longer.

To the second misrepresentation of this verse I reply that since the name 'commandment' is properly given to matters affecting the duties of righteousness, and things pleasing to God in themselves, Paul accordingly denies that he is speaking 'by way of commandment'. Indeed he has already made it clear enough that we must, out of necessity, use that remedy which he had enjoined.

7. *For my wish would be that all men*. This is part of the exposition of the previous sentence. For Paul does not make any secret about which way is more fitting for a Christian; but he wishes everyone to think carefully about what God wants him to be. Why, then, has Paul not said, in the previous verse, 'by way of commandment'? The answer is because he has no desire to force them into marriage; but he would prefer if they could feel no need of it. But since that is not possible for everyone, he takes their inability into account. Moreover, if this passage had been properly weighed up, that false superstition in striving after celibacy, which has been the root and cause of tremendous evils, would never have made headway in the world. Paul makes it quite plain here that everyone does not have a free choice in this connexion, because virginity is a special gift, which is not bestowed indiscriminately on all. And Paul is not saying anything different from Christ Himself, when He says 'all men cannot receive this saying' (Matt. 19.11). Paul is therefore an interpreter of our Lord's words here, in saying that this ability of living without marriage is not given to everyone.

And what has been happening all along? Everyone, with no thought as to his ability, has been pleasing himself, and making a vow of perpetual continency. And it has not only been the common people and the uneducated who have gone wrong in this connexion. For there have been distinguished teachers, who, giving wholehearted approval to virginity, and at the same time, forgetting the weakness of human nature, have disregarded this warning of Paul, indeed of Christ Himself. In fact, Jerome, blinded by a zeal which defies description, does not merely slip, but rushes headlong, into false views. Virginity, I agree, is an admirable gift, but do not forget that it is a *gift*. Listen also to what Christ and Paul say, that everybody does not receive it, but only a few. Do not therefore take a rash vow about something that is outwith your control, and which you will not obtain as a gift, if you pay no regard to your vocation, and reach beyond the limits imposed on you.

Nevertheless the men of old were also wrong in the significance they gave to virginity, for they praise it as if it were the greatest of all the virtues, and they wish it to be thought of as a means of giving service to God. Even in that there is a dangerous error; and now another appears, because, after celibacy began to be thought of so highly, many tried to surpass others in making rash vows of perpetual continency, when scarcely one per cent of them had the ability and gift for it. A third error developed from that: the ministers of the Church were forbidden to marry, for marriage did not seem to be a way of life in keeping with the holiness of their order. God punished the presumption of those who despised marriage and made rash vows of everlasting continency, first by the secret fires of lust, and then with horrible and filthy practices. But because ministers of the Church were debarred from lawful marriage, the result of this arbitrariness has been that the Church has been deprived of many good and faithful ministers; for honest and wise men would not put themselves in a trap. At last, after a long period of time, lusts, which until then had been repressed, gave off their stench. It was not enough that those, in whose case it was a capital offence to have a wife, maintained mistresses, otherwise prostitutes, with impunity, but no home was safe because of the lustfulness of the priests. Even that was put in the shade, for unnatural and outrageous things came into the open, things which it is better to bury in everlasting oblivion, than to mention even by way of example.

8. *But I say to the unmarried.* This depends on what goes before, and is in a sense a deduction from it. For he had said that the gifts of God are distributed in different ways, that everybody does not have the gift of continency, and that those who do not have it ought to have recourse to the remedy of marriage. Now he turns to address the virgins, all who are unmarried, and widows, and concedes that they should have a desire for celibacy, if they are capable of it; but that each individual must know what he is able to do. It amounts to this: that the single state has many advantages, and these must not be overlooked, provided that each one is content with his own condition. Therefore, even if virginity is exalted to the third heaven, it still remains true, nevertheless, that it is not suitable for everybody, but only for those who have the special gift from God.

The Papists make the objection that when we are baptized we also make a promise to God that we will lead a pure life, a promise which we do not have power to keep. They are easily answered: we promise in that case no more than what God requires from all His people, but continency is indeed a special gift, which God has withheld from many. Therefore those who make a vow of continency act just like any uneducated, ignorant fellow who professes to be a prophet, or teacher, or interpreter of languages.

We must also note the word 'abide'. For it is possible for a person to lead an unblemished celibate life for a time, but there must be no thought that it must be like that for ever. Isaac was single until he was thirty, and was chaste throughout those years, in which the heat of passion is most active; afterwards however he is called into the married state. Jacob is an even more famous example. Therefore the apostle would wish those who are now cultivating chastity to continue and persevere in it. But because they have no certainty that it is a gift for all time, he tells them all to ponder what their gift is.

Finally, this passage shows that the apostle was unmarried at that time. Erasmus' inference that he was married, because he mentions himself along with married people, is capricious and pointless, because it could be inferred, by similar reasoning, that he was a widower because he speaks of himself along with widows. But the whole tenor of the words is to the effect that he was then unmarried, for I do not accept that conjecture that he had got rid of his wife somewhere, and had voluntarily given up the intimacies of marriage. For what right then would he have to say to married people: come together at once? It would certainly be incongruous were he not to obey his own directions, and observe the law which he imposed on others. But Paul is a remarkable instance of modesty; for while he himself is endowed with the gift of continency, he does not force others to do as he does, but he allows them the remedy for weakness, which he himself does without. Let him be a warning to us, so that, if we are powerfully blessed with some particular gift, we may not be over-exacting in requiring it of others, who have not yet reached that level.

9. *But if they have not continency.* Although Paul advises them to abstain from marriage, he always speaks conditionally: 'if it is possible', 'if they are capable of it'. But when the weakness of the flesh stands in the way of that freedom, he plainly directs them to marry, as if it were a matter about which there was no doubt at all. For this is said 'by way of commandment', so that no-one may think it is merely advice; and he is not only putting restraint on fornicators, but on those who are completely defiled, in God's sight, by inward passion. For there is no doubt that the person who is not continent tempts God, by neglecting the remedy of marriage. This is a situation which needs, not advice, but strict prohibition.

For it is better. This is not a true comparison, since lawful marriage is honourable in all, whereas burning is very bad. However the apostle has followed the normal mode of speaking, inaccurate though it may be. We do the same sort of thing in saying: 'It is better to renounce this world, so that we may obtain the inheritance of the Kingdom of heaven along with Christ, than to perish miserably in the pleasures of the flesh.' I mention this because Jerome constructs a puerile fallacy out of this passage: marriage is good, because it is a lesser evil than burning. I would say that if it was a laughing matter he does not make a very good joke; but since it is such an important and serious matter, it is a mean jibe, and not what you would expect from a man of good judgement. It must therefore be understood that the remedy of marriage is good and makes for well-being, since burning is something most loathsome and detestable in God's sight.

However, 'burning' must be defined, for many are troubled with the desires of the flesh, who do not need to have immediate recourse to marriage. And, to retain Paul's metaphor, it is one thing to burn, another to feel heat. Accordingly, what Paul calls burning here, is not merely a slight sensation, but being so aflame with passion that you cannot stand up against it. But since some delude themselves in vain, in thinking that they are absolved from all blame if they do not give in to lust, we should note that there are three degrees of temptation.

(1) Sometimes the assaults of lust are so strong that the will is overcome; for the worst kind of burning is when the heart is aflame with passion.

(2) Sometimes we are so molested by the darts of the flesh, that we fight back vigorously, and do not allow the true love of chastity to be driven away from us, but rather loathe all unseemly and filthy desires. Therefore all must be warned, and especially young people, that as often as they are assailed by sexual passion they should oppose such temptation with the fear of God, offer no opportunity to unchaste thoughts, ask the Lord to give them firmness to resist, and exert themselves with all their might to put out the flames of lust. If they make progress in this struggle, let them give thanks to God. For how many men will you find whose flesh has not caused them trouble to some extent? But if we check the full force of its attack before it can triumph over us, we do well; for then we are not burning, even if we are disturbed by heat. It is not that there is nothing wrong in the sensation of heat, but when we acknowledge our weakness before the Lord with humility and penitence, we may, all the same, be of good courage for the time being. To put it briefly: so long as, by the grace of the Lord, we are having the advantage in the struggle, and Satan's darts are not penetrating within, but are being vigorously warded off by us, let us not grow weary of the conflict.

(3) Between these two there is an intermediate kind of temptation: when a man even has his mind fully set against giving entry to passion, yet is inflamed by a blind passion, and is so disturbed that he cannot call on God with peace of conscience. Therefore such temptation, which prevents prayer being made freely to God, and disturbs peace of conscience, is burning which can only be extinguished by marriage. We now see that in considering all this, it is not merely a question of

whether a man can keep his body undefiled, but attention must also be given to the mind, as we shall see a little later on.

But unto the married I give charge, yea not I, but the Lord, That the wife depart not from her husband (but and if she depart, let her remain unmarried, or else be reconciled to her husband); and that the husband leave not his wife. But to the rest say I, not the Lord: If any brother hath an unbelieving wife, and she is content to dwell with him, let him not leave her. And the woman which hath an unbelieving husband, and he is content to dwell with her, let her not leave her husband. For the unbelieving husband is sanctified in the wife, and the unbelieving wife is sanctified in the brother: else were your children unclean; but now are they holy. Yet if the unbelieving departeth, let him depart: the brother or the sister is not under bondage in such cases: but God hath called us in peace. For how knowest thou, O wife, whether thou shalt save thy husband? or how knowest thou, O husband, whether thou shalt save thy wife? Only, as the Lord hath distributed to each man, as God hath called each, so let him walk. And so ordain I in all the churches. (10-17)

10. *To the married I command.* Paul now deals with another principle of marriage: that it is an indissoluble bond. Therefore he condemns all the divorces, which were an everyday occurrence among the heathen and, as far as the Jews were concerned were not punished by the Law of Moses. He says: 'Let the husband not send away his wife, and let the wife not depart from her husband.' Why? Because they are tied together in an inseparable bond (*individuo nexo coniuncti*). But it is strange that he does not make an exception in the case of adultery at least, for it is unlikely that he meant to tighten up on the teaching of Christ in any way. But I am quite sure that he makes no mention of this point, because he is referring to these matters in passing, and he preferred to send the Corinthians back to what the Lord allows or forbids, rather than go over everything, point by point. For when teachers intend to deal with something briefly, they teach in a general way, and exceptions are dealt with in detailed, as well as more inclusive and yet precise discussion.

But in interposing, 'not I, but the Lord', he corrects himself, and means that what he teaches here is taken from the Law of God. No doubt he also received the other things he was teaching, by the revelation of the Spirit, but he states that God is the source of this, in view of the fact that it is derived from the Law of God. If you want a particular passage, you will not find it anywhere in so many words. But since Moses declares at the beginning that the union of husband and wife is so holy, that because of it a man ought to leave his father and his mother (Gen. 2.24), we can easily deduce from this, that it may not be tampered with (*inviolabilis*). For a son is naturally duty bound to his father and mother, and cannot rid himself of that yoke. Since the marriage tie is given precedence over that bond, there is all the less justification for severing it.

11. *But if she does depart.* This must not be taken as referring to those who have been put away for adultery. That is clear from the punishment which it incurred in those days. For even under Roman law it was a capital offence,[1] and likewise under the common 'law of nations' (*ius gentium*). But since husbands often divorced their wives, either because their ways did not suit them, or because their personal appearance displeased them, or for any offence at all; and since wives sometimes left their husbands on account of cruelty or too much rough and inconsiderate treatment, Paul denies that marriage is broken off by divorces or differences of that sort. For it is a covenant consecrated in the name of God, which does not stand or fall according to the whim of man, so as to be made invalid at our pleasure. The point is this: since other agreements depend merely on the consent of men, they can similarly be dissolved by their consent. But, if those who have been bound together in marriage, now regret what they have done, they are no longer free to 'break the bond' (as the saying goes[2]) and go their own ways in search of a new arrangement with someone else. For if natural rights cannot be destroyed, much less can this, which, as we have already said, takes precedence over the principal natural bond that there is.

But in commanding the wife, who is separated from her husband, to remain unmarried, he does not imply that separation is acceptable, nor does he permit the wife to live apart from her husband. But if she has been put out of the house, or if she has been rejected, she must not think that even in those circumstances she is free from his power; for

---

[1] Aulus Gallius (*Attic Nights*, 10.23.5) quotes M. Cato (234–149 B.C.) as saying that a man has the right to kill a wife taken in adultery, and her companion also; but she could do nothing to her husband if he committed adultery. A domestic tribunal could also condemn a wife to death. This was superseded by the *Lex Julia de adulteriis* (18–16 B.C.), which created a standing court to deal with this and other sexual offences. It put an end to killing of the wife taken in adultery; but not to the killing of certain classes of *adulter*, such as slaves and *infames*. In the time of Constantine if not earlier, the woman and her paramour were sentenced to death. Justinian enacted (*Nov.* 123 c. 10) that while the supreme punishment should continue to be meted out to the *adulter*, the woman should be let off with a scourging and inclusion in a nunnery. She might be taken back by a forgiving husband at any time, failing that she must take the veil. Tr.

[2] *tesseram frangant*—a reference to the *tessera hospitalis*, a token of wood divided between two friends, in order that, by means of it, they or their descendants might always recognize each other. Tr.

a husband has no power to render a marriage invalid. Therefore, Paul is not here giving permission to wives to separate from their husbands of their own free will, or to live away from their common home, as if they were widows. But he declares that even those who are not taken back by their husbands remain bound, so that they cannot go to other husbands.

But what if the wife is lascivious, or in some other way unable to control herself? Is it not inhuman to deny her the remedy of marriage, when she is constantly burning with desire? To that I would reply that when we are harassed by the weakness of our flesh, we must seek the remedy. Thereafter it is the Lord Himself who must bridle and restrain us by His Spirit, even if things do not go as well as we should like. For if a wife falls into a long, drawn-out illness, nevertheless that does not give the husband justification for seeking another wife. Similarly, if after their marriage, the husband begins to suffer from some disease, the wife cannot, on those grounds, however, make a quick transition to another state. In brief: since God has appointed lawful marriage as the remedy for our incontinency, let us make use of it, so that we may not tempt Him, and suffer the penalty of our indiscretion. Having entered on marriage, let us hope that He will help us, if, contrary to our expectations, things go wrong.

12. *But I say to the rest.* He means by 'the rest' those who are exceptions to the general principle, which covers others. For an incompatible marriage is a different consideration altogether, when the parties to the marriage do not have the same religion. He deals with this question in two parts. The first is that the believer ought not to separate from the unbeliever, and ought not to seek divorce, unless he or she is put away (*repudietur*). The second is that if the unbeliever puts away his or her partner, because of the question of religion, then the brother or sister is freed from the marriage bond by such rejection. But why is it that Paul makes himself the source of these rules when they seem to conflict to some extent with those which he had just given above as from the Lord? He does not mean that they come from himself in such a way that the Spirit of God has nothing to do with them. But, since there was no clear and explicit statement on this subject in any part of the Law and the prophets, in this way he sought to prevent the ungodly from making false accusations about him, by taking personal responsibility for what he was about to say. Yet, so that it might not all be airily dismissed as the product of a human brain, he will afterwards say that his statements are not his mere subjective fancies. But there is nothing inconsistent with what was written above for since the sanctity of the marriage vow (*sanctitas fidei coniugalis*) depends upon God, what further need is there for a believing wife to

remain with an unbelieving husband, after she has been put out by him because of his hatred of God?

14. *For the unbelieving husband is sanctified in the wife.* Paul meets a difficulty which could make believers uneasy. The intimacy of marriage is unique, for the wife is the half of the man, and the two become one flesh; and the husband is the head of the wife, and she is her husband's companion in every way. Thus it seems to be an impossibility for a believing man to live with an unbelieving wife, or conversely, not to be defiled by so intimate a relation. Paul therefore declares here, that such a marriage is none the less holy and pure, and there must be no fear of defilement, as if the wife would contaminate the husband. Besides, let us recall that he is speaking here, not about the contracting of marriages, but about maintaining those which have already been entered into. For where it is a question of whether a man should marry an unbelieving woman, or a woman an unbelieving man, then this advice is relevant: 'Do not be yoked together with unbelievers, for there is no agreement between Christ and Belial' (II Cor. 6.14, 15). But the man who is already bound has freedom of choice no more; for that reason, the advice which is given is different.

Though people interpret the 'sanctification' referred to here, in different ways, I take it to apply simply to marriage. My view is as follows. By all appearances a believing wife might seem to become unclean from contact with an unbelieving husband, so that the partnership is unlawful. Yet it turns out differently. For the godliness of the one does more to 'sanctify' the marriage than the ungodliness of the other to make it unclean. Accordingly a believer can live with an unbeliever with a clear conscience, for, as far as sexual intercourse and ordinary everyday relations are concerned, the unbeliever is sanctified, so that he or she does not contaminate the believer with his or her uncleanness. In the meantime this sanctification is of no personal benefit to the unbelieving partner. Its only value is that the believer is not contaminated by intercourse with him or her, and the marriage itself is not profaned.

But a question arises from that. If the faith of a Christian husband or wife sanctifies a marriage, it follows that all the marriages of unbelievers are unclean, and are in the same position as fornication. To that I answer: to the unbelieving nothing is pure because they spoil, by their impurity, even the finest and loveliest of God's creations. So it comes about that they also make marriage unclean, because they do not recognize God as the source of it, and for that reason they are not the least capable of genuine sanctification, and with their guilty consciences they abuse marriage. It would be naïve to infer from that, that marriage in their case is in the same class as fornication, because, no matter how unclean it is to them, it is nevertheless pure in itself, seeing that it has been ordained by God. It fulfils the functions of preserving respectability in society, and checking promiscuous desires. And so, because of those purposes, it is approved by God, like the other parts of the social order (*ordinis politici*). A distinction must always therefore be made between the nature of a thing and its abuse.

Else were your children unclean. This is an argument based on the effect: 'If your marriage was unclean, then the children born of it would be unclean; but they are holy, therefore your marriage also is holy. Therefore, just as the ungodliness of one of the parents does not prevent the children from being born holy, so it does not stand in the way of the marriage itself being undefiled.' Some interpreters explain this passage in terms of proper status from the point of view of the law of the land (*de sanctitate civili*), i.e. the children are considered legitimate. But exactly the same thing can be said about the children of unbelievers. Therefore that explanation falls to the ground. Moreover, it is certain that Paul wished here to ease troubled consciences, so that no-one may think that he has contracted uncleanness, as I have already said. Therefore this passage is a noteworthy one, and based on the profoundest theology. For it shows that the children of believers are set apart from others by a certain special privilege, so that they are regarded as holy in the Church.

But how does this sentence harmonize with what Paul teaches in Ephesians 2.3, that we are 'all by nature children of wrath'; and also with David's cry, 'Behold I was conceived in sin etc.' (Ps. 51.5)? To that I answer that there is a universal propagation both of sin and condemnation in the seed of Adam. All, therefore, to a man, are included in this curse, whether they spring from believers or the ungodly, for not even believers beget children according to the flesh so that they are regenerated by the Spirit. Accordingly all are in the same natural condition, so that they are subject not only to sin but also to eternal death. But the fact that the apostle ascribes a special privilege to the children of believers here has its source in the blessing of the covenant, by whose intervention the curse of nature is destroyed, and also those who were by nature unclean are consecrated to God by His grace. So Paul argues in Rom. 11.16 that all Abraham's descendants are holy, because God had concluded a covenant of life with him. 'If the root is holy so are the branches,' he says. And God calls all who are descended from Israel His sons. Now that the dividing wall has been broken down, the same covenant of salvation which had its beginning with the seed of Abraham is extended to us. In view of the fact that the children of believers are made exempt from the common condition of mankind, in order to be set apart for the Lord, why should we keep them back from the sign [of the covenant]? If the Lord admits them to His Church by His Word, why should we deny them the sign? But exactly how the children of believers are holy, and how many of them nevertheless fall away, you will find explained in the tenth and eleventh chapters of Romans, and I have dealt with this in the commentary on those chapters.

15. *Yet if the unbeliever departs.* We come now to the second part of his handling of the question of a mixed marriage. In this verse Paul frees a faithful husband, who is himself prepared to live with a wife who is an unbeliever, but is rejected by her; and similarly frees a wife, who is put away by her husband, although there is no fault on her side. For in those circumstances the unbeliever makes a breach with God rather than with his or her partner. Here there is a special reason, because the primary and principal bond (*vinculum*) is not merely untied, but violently torn apart. Although some think that we today stand in an almost similar relation to the Papists, we must however carefully consider what the difference is between the two situations, so that we may not attempt anything rash.

In peace. Interpreters differ here too. For some take it in this way: 'We are called in peace, therefore let us avoid everything that makes for quarrels.' I take it more simply: 'As far as we can let us cultivate peace with all, for to that we have been called. We must not therefore separate from unbelievers in a high-handed way, but only if they themselves take the initiative and make the break. God has therefore called us in peace, in order that we may cultivate peaceful relations with all, by treating each individual well.' So this belongs to the first part of his treatment of the problem—that believers ought to remain with unbelievers, if the latter are agreeable etc.; for a desire for divorce is inconsistent with our Christian profession.

16. *For how do you know, O woman.* Those who think that this sentence confirms the second part explain it in this way: 'The uncertainty of hope ought not to keep you back, for how do you know etc.' But, in my view, the benefit to be gained inspires this word of encouragement, for it is a great and wonderful blessing if a wife wins over her husband. Indeed, unbelievers are not in so hopeless a plight that they cannot be moved to believe. They are certainly dead, but God can even raise the dead. Therefore when the believing wife has some hope of being effective, and cannot tell but that she may, by her goodness of life lead her husband back to the way, she ought to try every means before leaving him. For, as long as there is doubt about a man's salvation, we ought to be all the more ready to hope for the best.

But his statement that 'a husband can be saved by his wife', is really not strictly correct, for Paul makes man do what only God can do.

Yet there is nothing incongruous about it. For since God acts to good purpose by using His instruments, He imparts His power to them to some extent, or, at least, links it with their service in such a way that He says, what He does, is done by them. And so He has sometimes ascribed to them the honour which is due to Himself alone. Let us remember however that we are not able to do anything on our own, but only in so far as we are directed by Him, as instruments.

17. *Only, let each man so walk, as God has dispensed His grace to him, and each man as God has called him.* That keeps to the text. However, I have used the nominative (each man) so that the sense may run on more smoothly. The meaning is: 'The only solution is for each one to lead a life according to the grace given to him, and appropriate to his calling. Let every one, therefore, take pains about this, and try with all his might to serve his neighbours, especially so, when he ought to be urged on to such action by the particular function to which he has been called.' Paul mentions two things: 'calling', and 'measure of grace', and he charges us to pay attention to them in considering this matter. For it ought to be a great stimulus to us, spurring us on to service, that God counts us worthy of being appointed servants of His grace for the salvation of our brothers; on the other hand, our calling ought to keep us, as it were, under God's yoke, even if a man finds himself in rather unpleasant circumstances.

And so in all the churches. I think that Paul added this in order to meet the misrepresentations of some, who were alleging that he assumed more authority for himself over the Corinthians, than he had the courage to do over others. Yet he could have had another purpose in mind also, viz. that this teaching might carry more weight when the Corinthians understood that it had already been disseminated in all the churches. For we find it easier to accept what we are told we share with all believers. However, it would have annoyed the Corinthians to be held on a tighter rein than others.

Was any man called being circumcised? let him not become uncircumcised. Hath any been called in uncircumcision? let him not be circumcised. Circumcision is nothing, and uncircumcision is nothing; but the keeping of the commandments of God. Let each man abide in that calling wherein he was called. Wast thou called being a bondservant? care not for it: but if thou canst become free, use it rather. For he that was called in the Lord, being a bondservant, is the Lord's freedman: likewise he that was called, being free, is Christ's bondservant. Ye were bought with a price; become not bondservants of men. Brethren, let each man, wherein he was called, therein abide with God. (18-24)

18. *Was any one circumcised when he was called?* Since he had been

referring to 'calling', Paul takes the opportunity, as he often does, to make a short digression from a particular aspect, to a general exhortation about 'calling'. At the same time he confirms, with different examples, what he had said about marriage. What it comes to is this: once you have entered on your calling by God's will, you must not rashly withdraw from it because of external circumstances. He begins with circumcision, for it was a subject of dispute with many at that time. But he says that it makes no difference to God whether you are Gentile or Jew; and so he urges each person to be content with his own lot. We must always remember that Paul is dealing only with legitimate ways of life, which God has instituted and controls.

19. *Circumcision is nothing.* Apart from the fact that this comparison was suitable for the subject under consideration, Paul seems to have used it, however, on purpose, in order to criticize, in passing, the Jewish scrupulosity (*superstitionem*) and the arrogance that went with it. For, since the Jews took a great pride in circumcision, it was possible that many felt uneasy because they themselves were uncircumcised, imagining that that gave them a poorer standing. Paul therefore puts both conditions on the same level, in case aversion to the one might lead to an unreasonable longing for the other. But what he says must be understood as referring to the time when circumcision had already been done away with; for if God's covenant and commandment had been in his mind, he would undoubtedly have given greater value to circumcision. Indeed, in Romans 2.27-29 he belittles circumcision according to the letter of the law, and asserts that it counts for nothing with God. But in this place, where he simply places circumcision and uncircumcision in contrast, and then puts them both on the same level, it is quite clear that he speaks of it as a matter of indifference and of no importance. For its abrogation means that the mystery (*mysterium*) which was previously conveyed under it now ceases to belong to it; yes, and more than that, it means that it is a sign no longer, but a thing without any use. For on this principle baptism has taken the place of the legal symbol so that it is sufficient if we are circumcised by the Spirit of Christ, while our old man is buried with Christ.

But the keeping of the commandments. Since this was one of the commandments so long as the Church was bound fast to the ceremonies of the Law, we see that it is taken for granted that circumcision has been abolished by the coming of Christ, so that, while the ignorant and weak were permitted to make use of it, yet it brought them no benefit whatever. For Paul speaks of it here as something insignificant. It is as if he said: 'Since these are mere outward things, do not waste your time on them; but rather give your attention to godliness, and the duties which God requires, and which are the only things valuable in His sight.'

But it is childish of the Papists to cite this verse for demolishing the doctrine of justification by faith; for here Paul is not discussing the source of righteousness, or how we obtain it. All he is concerned with is that believers should direct their efforts in the right direction. It is as if he said: 'Do not waste your energy on futile things, but, on the contrary, occupy yourselves with the services which are pleasing to God.'

20. *Let each one abide in that calling.* This is the principle from which other things follow: each should be content with his calling, and persist in it, and not be eager to change to something else. In the Scriptures 'calling' is a lawful way of life, for it is connected with God, who actually calls us. That is pointed out to prevent anyone from misinterpreting this verse to give support to ways of life, which are clearly worldly and sinful.

But at this point someone is asking if Paul wishes to impose something binding on people, for what he says may seem to suggest that each one is tied to his calling, and must not give it up. But it would be asking far too much, if a tailor were not permitted to learn another trade, or a merchant to change to farming. To that I would reply that that is not the apostle's intention, for he only wishes to correct the thoughtless eagerness which impels some to change their situation without any proper reason, for perhaps they are moved by a wrong belief, or some other influence. In the next verse Paul brings this rule before everyone also: that they bear in mind what is more appropriate for their calling. Therefore, he does not lay it down, that each person must remain in a certain way of life, once he has adopted it; but, on the other hand, he condemns the restlessness which prevents individuals from remaining contentedly as they are, and his advice is: 'let the shoemaker stick to his last', as the old proverb has it.[1]

21. *Were you a slave when you were called?* We see here that Paul is aiming at quietening their consciences, for he urges slaves to be cheerful, and not to be upset, imagining that slavery would prevent their serving God. Therefore he says, 'care not for it'; in other words, 'do not be full of anxiety about how you may shake off the yoke, as if it were not a suitable condition for Christians to be in, but let your mind be at rest.' And from that we infer, not only that there are, by the providence of God, distinct stations and classes in society, but also that His Word directs us not to ignore them.

But if even you can become free. In my view the word 'even' carries

---

[1] The Latin proverb is *quam quisque Spartam nactus est, eam colat*: 'As Sparta is your inheritance, look after it.'

no more emphasis than is evident here: 'If, instead of being a slave, you could become even free, it would be more suitable for you.' But it is doubtful whether he is still speaking to slaves, or is now turning to address those who are free. In the latter case 'become' (γενέσθαι) would simply have been used for the verb 'to be' here. Either meaning fits in quite well, and both come to the same thing. Paul means to show not only that freedom is good, but also that it gives more opportunity than slavery. If he is speaking to slaves his meaning will be: 'When I tell you to be free from anxiety, I do not debar you from even enjoying liberty, if it comes your way.' If he is speaking to those who are free, it will be by way of concession, in words something like these: 'My advice to slaves is to be cheerful, even if being free is better and more desirable, should a person have the choice between them.'

22. *For he who has been called in the Lord as a slave.* To be called in the Lord when a slave, means to be chosen out of the slave class, and become a sharer in the grace of Christ. Now, this sentence has been put in to encourage slaves, and, at the same time, to curb the pride of the free-born. Since slaves find their condition humiliating, for in the eyes of the world they are worthless and contemptible, it is a precious thing to them that the bitterness of their bondage is alleviated by some comfort. Freemen, on the other hand, need to be held in check, so that they may not think too highly of themselves, and be swept off their feet with pride, because of their more honoured position. The apostle does both these things. For, since the liberty of the spirit is far preferable to the liberty of the body, he suggests that slaves ought to be able to put up with the bitterness of their situation, if only they would reflect upon that inestimable gift which has been bestowed upon them. He also says that the freemen ought not to be carried away, because they are on an equal footing with slaves in the thing that matters most. Indeed, we must not jump to the conclusion from this, that freemen are put on a lower level than slaves, or that the social order (*politicum ordinem*) is turned upside down. The apostle was aware of what both needed. The freemen had to be held back, as I have said, so that they might not lose control of themselves and be insulting towards slaves. Some encouragement really had to be given to the slaves, so that they might not be disheartened. Both these things rather make for the stability of the social order, while he teaches that physical disadvantage is compensated by a spiritual benefit.

23. *You have been bought with a price.* We had these words in the last chapter but for a different purpose. There I gave my explanation of the word 'price'. In this verse his point is that he certainly will not have it that slaves be anxious about their situation, but rather he wishes them to take care not to give themselves up to the ungodly or vicious

desires of their masters. 'For we are consecrated to the Lord, because He has redeemed us; therefore let us not make ourselves unclean to please men, and that is what we are doing when we submit to the evil things which they demand.' This warning was greatly needed at that time, when slaves were forced, by threats and floggings, even by the fear of death, to submit to all sorts of commands, without any choice or exception, so that men considered the procuring of prostitutes and other disgraceful practices of that sort, to be the duties of slaves, just as much as honest work. Therefore Paul is justified in making this exception, that they are not to obey and give themselves up to shameful and wicked practices. I wish that everybody had a thorough and complete grasp of this in his mind, then not so many would prostitute themselves to the inclinations of men, as if they were for sale. But for ourselves, let us remember that we belong to Him, who has bought us back.

24. *Let him abide with God.* I have already suggested that in this passage men are not bound by a principle which applies for ever, so that they may never be allowed to change their situation, even if at any time there may be good grounds for doing so. Paul is only seeking to check those impulses, uncontrolled by reason, which drive many hither and thither, so that they are confused by their constant restlessness. Paul therefore says that it makes no difference to God what a person's means of livelihood is in this world, since differences in this respect do not destroy harmony in religion.

Now concerning virgins I have no commandment of the Lord: but I give my judgement, as one that hath obtained mercy of the Lord to be faithful. I think therefore that this is good by reason of the present distress, namely that it is good for a man to be as he is. Art thou bound unto a wife? seek not to be loosed. Art thou loosed from a wife? seek not a wife. But and if thou marry, thou hast not sinned; and if a virgin marry, she hath not sinned. Yet such shall have tribulation in the flesh: and I would spare you. (25-28)

25. *Concerning virgins.* Paul now returns to the discussion of marriage with which he had already been dealing in the first part of the chapter. Now he had already referred to the subject which he is about to introduce, but briefly and not very explicitly. Therefore he comes to give a clearer explanation of what he thinks about virginity. But because this subject is full of dangers and difficulties, Paul always speaks conditionally, as we shall see. I take 'virgins', here, to mean the state of virginity itself. Paul says that he has 'no commandment of the Lord' about this, because nowhere in the Scriptures does God say who exactly should always remain unmarried. On the other hand, however,

L

since the Scripture says that male and female were created at the same time (Gen. 2.21), it seems to call all on equal terms and without exception to marriage. At any rate celibacy is never laid down or commended for anyone.

Paul says that he is giving advice, and he does not mean that it is problematic, with little or no certainty about it, but that it is definite and should be adhered to without any question. And the word he uses, γνώμη, means not only advice but also judgement or decision or opinion. Further, the Papists infer wrongly from this that it is permissible to go beyond the limits of the Word of God, whereas Paul had no thought at all of leaping over the boundaries of God's Word. For if anyone would look closer he will see that Paul introduces nothing here which Christ has not included in His words in Matthew 5.32 and 19.5 ff. But Paul acknowledges, by way of anticipating an objection, that he does not have a definite commandment of the Lord from the Law, making it clear who ought to enter upon marriage, and who ought not.

Having obtained mercy in order that I may be faithful. Paul produces authority for his judgement, in case anyone might think he could turn it down if he liked. For Paul maintains that he is not speaking as a mere man, but as a faithful teacher of the Church and an apostle of Christ. He acknowledges, as he usually does, his indebtedness to the mercy of God for this, for it is no ordinary honour, this, but indeed surpasses all the favours of men. From this it is apparent that any things devised by men and introduced into the Church have no similarity at all to this advice of Paul. Moreover, 'faithful' here means one who is loyal to the truth, i.e. not only one who carries out the duties he has to do with conscientious devotion, but also one who is equipped with knowledge so that he teaches plainly and honestly. For it is not enough for a teacher to have goodwill, if he does not have wisdom and knowledge of the truth.

26. *I think therefore that this is good by reason of the present distress, namely, that it is good for a man to be as he is.* Although I translate this verse of Paul's differently from Erasmus and the Vulgate, my meaning is the same as theirs nevertheless. They divide Paul's words in such a way that the same thing is repeated twice. On the other hand, I make one sentence only, and I have authority for doing so, for I am following ancient and reliable manuscripts which make one sentence of it, with the division made by a colon only. The meaning is this: 'In view of the 'difficulties' (*propter necessitatem*) which always press hard upon the saints in this life, I think that the best solution is for all to enjoy the freedom and independence of celibacy, for it would be a real benefit to them.' However some take the 'difficulties' (*necessitatem*) to apply

specifically to the apostle's own day and generation, in which believers were undoubtedly involved in a great deal of distress; but it seems to me that he rather meant the upsetting things, which believers constantly run up against in this present life. Therefore I extend them to cover all generations, and take this to be the meaning: in the world the saints are often driven about, this way and that, and are exposed to many different kinds of storms, so that they seem to be most unfavourably placed for marriage.

The phrase 'to be so' (*sic esse*) means 'to remain unmarried', or 'to refrain from marrying'.

27. *Art thou bound unto a wife?* Having stated what would be the best arrangement, Paul adds, however, that we ought not to be so influenced by the advantages of celibacy, that people who are united by the marriage bond should break free from it. This modifies the previous sentence, therefore, so that anyone who is impressed by Paul's recommendation may not consider celibacy seriously, and be contemptuous of marriage, without giving a thought to his own need and calling. Besides, not only does he forbid the breaking of the marriage bond by these words, but he seeks to put a stop to those aversions which usually creep in to a marriage, so that everyone may continue to lead a happy and peaceful life with his wife.

Art thou loosed from a wife? From the whole context is it evident that this, the second part of this verse, ought to be read in the light of individual circumstances. Accordingly he does not grant to everybody the choice of life-long celibacy, but only to those to whom it is given. Therefore, if a man is free from any compelling need, he should not be so rash as to put himself in chains; for freedom ought not to be lightly thrown away.

28. *But even if you do marry.* Since there was a danger lest anyone might take the last sentence to mean that he would be tempting God, if he were to bind himself to a wife, knowingly and wittingly (for that would mean his giving up his freedom), Paul removes this doubt; for he allows widowers (*viduis*) freedom to marry, and says that those who marry are not sinning.

The word *even* seems to be emphatic, for it brings out that, although no troublesome need makes it imperative, those who are single are not debarred from marrying, whenever they like.

And if a virgin marry. Whether this adds to what he has said, or is simply an example, we can say straight away that there is no shadow of doubt that Paul meant to extend the freedom to marry to everybody. Those who think it is an addition are led to think so because it seems more like an offence, more blameworthy, or at least giving more ground for shame, to lose the virgin's girdle (as the men of old used to

157

say), than to enter upon a second marriage after the death of one's husband. The argument would therefore be: 'If it is lawful for a virgin to marry, widows have a far better case.' I myself am rather inclined to think that he puts them both on the same footing, as follows: 'A virgin is allowed to marry, so also is a widow.' For some stigma of disgrace was associated with a second marriage in that ancient society, in view of the fact that they also used to bestow a garland of chastity upon matrons, who had been content with one marriage in their lives; and that honour had the effect of putting those, who married more than once, in a bad light. Further, there is that well-known saying of Valerius: 'It is a sign of legalized lack of self-control (*intemperantia*), when there is a strong desire for a second marriage.' Accordingly the apostle makes no difference between virgins and widows as far as freedom to marry is concerned.

Yet such shall have tribulation in the flesh. Paul frequently repeats the reason why he tends to favour celibacy in his exhortations, so that it may be clear that he prefers the one state to the other, not for its own sake, but rather for what it leads to. He says that many troubles are inseparable from married life, and for that reason he wishes all, who wish to avoid troubles, to keep away from marriage. When he says that they will have 'trouble (*tribulationem*) of the flesh', or 'in the flesh', he means, that the responsibilities and difficulties, in which married people are involved, spring from the affairs of the world. Therefore 'the flesh' means here man in his relations with others (*homo externus*). 'Spare' means 'to be considerate of them' or to wish that they be lifted above the troubles, which go along with marriage. It is as though he said: 'I wish to give due regard to your weakness, and do not want your lives ruined by troubles. But marriage brings many troubles along with it. The reason why I wish you not to long for marriage, is that you may be untouched by all its evils.' But we should not infer from this that Paul thinks of marriage as a necessary evil; for those troubles, of which he is speaking, do not spring so much from marriage in itself, as from its corruption; for they are the fruits of original sin.

But this I say, brethren, the time is shortened, that henceforth both those that have wives may be as though they had none; and those that weep, as though they wept not; and those that rejoice, as though they rejoiced not; and those that buy, as though they possessed not; and those that use the world, as not abusing it: for the fashion of this world passeth away. But I would have you to be free from cares. He that is unmarried is careful for the things of the Lord, how he may please the Lord: but he that is married is careful for the things of the world, how he may please his wife. And there is a difference also between the wife and the virgin.

She that is unmarried is careful for the things of the Lord, that she may be holy both in body and in spirit: but she that is married is careful for the things of the world, how she may please her husband. And this I say for your own profit; not that I may cast a snare upon you, but for that which is seemly, and that ye may attend upon the Lord without distraction. (29-35)

29. *Because the time is shortened.*[1] Once again Paul discusses the treatment of marriage as something sacred, in order to restrain the lustful passion of those, who, when they are married, think of nothing but physical satisfaction; and give no thought to God at all. Therefore Paul urges believers not to give the reins to passion so that marriage rushes them into worldly ways. Marriage is the remedy for incontinency. That is true, so long as use of it is governed by self-control. Therefore he tells those who are married to live together chastely, in the fear of the Lord. This can be done if they make use of marriage in the same way as they use other things which are of assistance to this earthly life, and lift up their hearts in contemplation of the life of heaven.

Now, he bases his argument on the shortness of human life. He says: 'The life we lead here is brief and transitory; therefore do not let it become an obsession with us. So let those *who have wives be as though they had none.*' Everyone, indeed, has this piece of wisdom on his lips; few have it truly and in earnest engraved on their hearts. In my first translation I followed a manuscript in Paris which, as I afterwards discovered, found no support at all in the many I consulted. (Erasmus joins the phrase τὸ λοιπόν to what follows. But that reading is more authentic.) I therefore thought it right to insert 'because' (*quia*) to make the meaning clearer, and this agrees with the reading in some of the old manuscripts. In view of the fact that when we give serious thought to anything we turn our attention to the future rather than the past, Paul warns us about the shortness of the time to come.

As though they had none. All the things which make for the enriching of this present life are sacred gifts of God, but we spoil them by our misuse of them. If we want to know the reason why, it is because we are always entertaining the delusion that we will go on for ever in this world. The result is that the very things which ought to be of assistance to us in our pilgrimage through life, become chains which bind us. In order to shake us out of our stupor the apostle quite rightly calls us back to think about the shortness of this life. From this he infers that the way in which we ought to make use of (*uti*) all the things of this world, is, as if we do not possess (*utamur*) them. For the man who

---

[1] Greek: ὁ καιρὸς συνεσταλμένος ἐστί, τὸ λοιπὸν ἵνα κ.τ.λ. Calvin: *quia tempus contractum est, reliquum est ut etc.* Vulgate: *tempus breve est; reliquum est ut etc.*

thinks of himself as an alien sojourner in the world, uses the things of the world as if they belonged to someone else; in other words, as things which are lent for the day only. The point is that the mind of a Christian ought not to be filled with thoughts of earthly things, or find satisfaction in them, for we ought to be living as if we might have to leave this world at any moment.

By 'weeping' Paul means when things are going badly; and by 'rejoicing' when they are going well; for it is quite usual to describe causes by their effects.

Finally, the apostle is not advising Christians, here, to get rid of their possessions. All that he asks for is that they do not find them completely engrossing.

31. *And those who use this world, as not using it to the full.* The participle χρώμενοι (using) is used in the first phrase, while the compound καταχρώμενοι (making full use of) is used in the second. But the preposition κατά generally imports a bad sense, or at least indicates intensity. Paul therefore suggests using things in a moderate and disciplined way, such as will not hinder or delay us on our journey, but enable us to keep pressing on to the goal.

For the fashion of this world passeth away. Paul gives a fitting description of the futility of the world with these words. He says: 'There is nothing stable or solid, for it is only a façade, or outward appearance, as men say.' But he seems to have been making an allusion to the stage in the theatre, for, on the instant that the curtains fall, their appearance intervenes, and what held the gaze of the audience is immediately swept from their sight. I do not see why Erasmus preferred the word 'condition' (*habitus*). In my view he is definitely obscuring the teaching of Paul; for *fashion* (*figura*) stands in tacit contrast to substance (*substantia*).

32. *But I would have you to be free from cares.* He returns to the advice which he had already given, but had not yet fully explained; and, as usual, he begins by recommending celibacy, and then allows individuals the freedom to choose what they think is suitable for them. Besides, he had good reason for reiterating the recommendation of celibacy, for he saw that the responsibilities of marriage are far from light. If a man can keep free of them, he ought not to throw away a benefit like that. And it is a great advantage to those who are intending to be married that they be warned in advance about those troubles, so that, if they unexpectedly run up against them afterwards, they may not fall into despair. We see that happening to a great many. They promised themselves pure honey, but when that hope does not materialize in practice, the slightest mishap is enough to depress them. Therefore, let them know in good time what they should expect, so that they

may be prepared to put up with everything. The meaning is: 'Marriage brings many distractions along with it. I should like you to be free from them, and to have nothing to do with them.'

But because he spoke of *trouble* and now mentions *cares* or anxieties, it may well be asked whether there is any difference between them or not. My view is that trouble has its source in sad occasions or circumstances, such as the death of children or partner; quarrels and little differences (as the lawyers call them) which result from being too fastidious; children's wrong-doing; the difficulty of bringing up a family; and similar things. Anxieties, I think, are connected with joyful circumstances, such as the frivolities at a wedding reception, joking, and other things to which married people give their attention.

He who is unmarried, is concerned about the things of the Lord. This makes it plain that Paul wishes Christians to be free from anxieties so that they may devote all their thoughts and efforts to the Lord. He says that celibacy allows of that; and so he desires all to enjoy that freedom. All the same he does not mean that unmarried people are always like that; for we ourselves know from experience that the cases of priests, monks and nuns present something very different, for one can think of nothing less connected with God than their celibacy. Add to that also our knowledge of so many disgusting fornicators who keep away from marriage in order that they might indulge in lustful practices as much as they like, and in order to keep their vice hidden. Where there is burning there can be no devotion to God. But what Paul is bringing out here is that the unmarried person is free, and nothing stands in the way of his thinking about the things of God. Believers make use of this freedom; others make everything serve their own ruin.

33. *He that is married is concerned about the things of the world.* 'The things of the world' we must understand as 'the things that belong to this present life', for, here, the world is taken to mean the circumstances of this earthly life. But someone will assume from this that all married people are outside the Kingdom of God, seeing that they think only about this world. To that I reply that the apostle is speaking about a part of their thinking. He might have put it: 'It is as though they are looking at God with one eye, but managing, at the same time, to look at their wives with the other. Again, marriage is like a burden, which so weighs on a believer's mind, that he does not step out so easily on his way to God.' But let us always bear in mind that these evils do not belong to marriage in itself, but come from the sin of men. That is why the misrepresentations of Jerome fall to the ground. For he collects all these things in order to put marriage in a bad light. For should anyone condemn farming, commerce, and other means of

livelihood, because not one of them is free from some evils, although they are surrounded by so many of the corruptions of this world, anyone would dismiss his nonsense with a laugh! We should note, therefore, that whatever evil there is in marriage, comes to it from another source. For at the present day a man would not be turned away from God through living with his wife, had he remained in a state of purity and had not spoiled the sacred institution of God; and the wife would be his helper in everything that is good, as indeed that was the purpose for which she was created.

But someone will say: 'If anxieties, which are condemned as sinful, are the constant accompaniment of marriage, however can those who are married call upon God and serve Him with a clear conscience?' My answer to that is that there are three kinds of anxieties. (1) There are some which are evil and ungodly in themselves, because they are born of lack of trust. Christ speaks about them in Matthew 6.25. (2) There are some which are necessary and do not cause God displeasure, e.g. the head of a family must be solicitous for his wife and children. And God does not want us to be logs of wood, incapable of having any thought for ourselves. (3) The third kind is a combination of the other two; that is to say, when we are concerned about those things, which really call for our concern, but we carry it too far, because of our natural tendency to go beyond the limits of anything. Therefore such anxieties are not at all evil in themselves, but they are bad because of ἀταξία, that is, undisciplined excess. Not only does the apostle want to find fault here with those sins which make us guilty in the sight of God; but on the whole he desires that we be free from every distraction, so that we may give our whole attention to God.

And is divided. It is astonishing that such differing views have arisen about these words. For the usual Greek reading has no similarity whatsoever to that of the Vulgate, so that the difference could not be put down to a mistake or carelessness, which often accounts for divergence in one letter or one word. For the Greek readings generally take it literally, as follows: 'The married man has his mind on the things of this world, and how he may please his wife. A married woman and a virgin are 'divided'. She who is unmarried thinks about the things of the Lord, etc.' And they take 'being divided' to mean 'differing', as though it had been put like this: 'There is a great difference between a married woman and a virgin. The one is free to attend to the things of God alone, while the other is definitely drawn this way and that by many different things.' But since this interpretation does not agree very well with the straightforward meaning of the word, I am not at all satisfied with it, all the more so because the meaning of the other reading is more suitable and less forced (and that reading is also to be found in some Greek manuscripts[1]). We may therefore understand it like this: a married man is divided in his interests, because he must give himself partly to God, and partly to his wife, and does not belong to God exclusively and completely.

34. *And the unmarried woman and the virgin.*[2] What he taught about men, he now repeats about women: viz. that virgins and widows are not prevented by the affairs of this world from giving their whole-hearted attention and efforts to God. Of course they do not all do so, but the opportunity is there, provided they set their minds to it. When he says 'that she may be holy in body and spirit' Paul makes it plain that the kind of chastity which is true and acceptable to God is where the mind is kept unstained for God. I wish that more attention were paid to that. As far as the body is concerned, we are aware of the brand of self-consecration which nuns, monks, and all the dregs of the Papist clergy, usually make to the Lord. Nothing more repulsive than their celibacy can be imagined! But, apart from chastity of the body altogether, there are those who are highly respected because of their reputation for chastity, yet how few of their number are not aflame with filthy, lustful passions! From this sentence of Paul's, we can conclude that chastity is only pleasing to God if it extends to the soul as well as the body. I wish that those who are always making a song about continency, would understand that it is God with whom they have to deal; for then they would not be so confident about crossing swords with us. However, at the present day the people who speak rather grandiloquently about continency are the very ones who openly and barefacedly make use of prostitutes. But even if they lead the most respectable of lives in men's eyes, that counts for absolutely nothing, if they do not keep their minds clean, and untouched by uncleanness of every kind.

35. *I say this for your benefit.* Take note of the apostle's moderation. Although he was well aware of the annoyances, troubles and difficulties of marriage, and, on the other hand, the advantages of celibacy, nevertheless he does not take it on himself to lay anything down. On the contrary, having commended celibacy, and being afraid that his readers might be impressed by his speaking so highly of it, and immediately say to themselves what the apostles said in answer to Christ (Matthew 19.10), 'It is good therefore to be like that,' without considering whether they were capable of it or not, Paul gives us clearly

---

[1] Westcott's and Hort's reading is the same as Calvin's. But good Greek MSS, including Codex Sinaiticus, support the reading he rejects. Tr.

[2] There is also a variant reading here. Calvin follows a reading adopted by Vulgate, Codex Vaticanus, and a few others. Tr.

to understand, that while he is pointing out what is most advantageous, he does not wish to make this binding on anyone.

There are two things worth noticing here. The first is the reason why we should aim at celibacy: not for its own sake, not because this state is on a higher level, but so that we may cleave to God, with nothing to separate us from Him. Now that is the one thing a Christian ought to be concerned about all through his life. The second thing is this—that no restraint ought to be put on people's consciences, with the result that someone may be kept back from marriage; but the freedom of each person must be respected. It is well known how many mistakes have been made in connexion with both these points. Certainly, as far as the second principle is concerned, those who had no hesitation about making a law about celibacy, prohibiting all the clergy from marrying, were more presumptuous than Paul. The same thing applies to those who swore vows of perpetual continency. Countless numbers of people have been dragged into eternal ruin by these chains. So, if the Holy Spirit has spoken through the mouth of Paul, the Papists cannot absolve themselves of the charge of fighting against God, when they bind men's consciences in regard to something about which He means them to be free. Of course, it may be that the Holy Spirit has formed a new plan since then, intending to bind with the very chains which He had previously rejected.

But if any man thinketh that he behaveth himself unseemly toward his virgin daughter, if she be past the flower of her age and if need so requireth, let him do what he will; he sinneth not; let them marry. But he that standeth stedfast in his heart, having no necessity, but hath power as touching his own will, and hath determined this in his own heart, to keep his own virgin daughter, shall do well. So then both he that giveth his own virgin daughter in marriage doeth well; and he that giveth her not in marriage shall do better. (36–38)

36. *If any man judges it unseemly for his virgin daughter, and if she passes the flower of her life, and it is necessary to do so; let him do what he wants; he does not sin; let them marry.* Paul now turns to address the parents, who had children under their control. For having heard the praises of celibacy being sung, and having also listened to the difficulties of marriage being related, they might be wondering if it was humane to allow their children to be involved in so much unhappiness, in case they might appear to be responsible for their troubles. For the fonder they are of their children, the more inclined they are to be anxious about them, and to be on their guard about what happens to them. So that he can rid them of this difficulty, Paul therefore teaches that it is their place to take care of their interests, in precisely the same way as one

who is answerable only to himself is bound to look after his own interests. But he maintains the distinction he has been making all along. On the one hand he recommends celibacy, but, on the other hand, he allows freedom to marry. More than that, he considers marriage as the remedy which incontinency requires, and which it would be wrong to deny to anyone.

In the first part of this section Paul speaks about giving daughters away in marriage. In it he asserts that fathers who come to the conclusion that the single life is not suitable for their daughters, do not sin in giving them away.

His use of the word ἀσχημονεῖν (to be unseemly) ought to be understood as referring to a personal quality of fitness, which is peculiar to each person's nature. For there is a general suitableness which philosophers look upon as an aspect of moderation, and everybody shares in that. There is also an individual suitableness, however, because what is suitable for one person may be quite unsuitable for another. Therefore, each individual ought to know (as Cicero says) what kind of character (*quam personam*) nature has given to him. Celibacy will suit one person, but he must not make himself the criterion for others. Again, others ought not to try to follow his example without asking if they have the ability for it; for that is behaving like apes, and we are certainly not meant to imitate them. Therefore, when a father has weighed up his daughter's temperament and decided that she is not fitted for a celibate life, he may give her in marriage.

Paul means by 'the flower of her age' a marriageable age. The lawyers define this as twelve to twenty. Paul points out, in passing, how understanding and sympathetic parents ought to be about making use of the remedy in those tender and dangerous years, when the power of the disease demands it.

And it is necessary to do so. I take this phrase to be an allusion to the girl's weakness, i.e. if she does not have the gift of continency; for under these circumstances she is forced to marry.

Jerome seizes upon the words, 'he sinneth not', as a chance to put marriage in a bad light, and depreciate it, as if it is not an honourable thing to give one's daughter away in marriage. But his views are childish. For Paul considers it enough to absolve the fathers of blame, so that they might not think it unkind to subject their daughters to the troubles of marriage.

37. *He who remains firm in his heart.* We come now to the second part of the section, and in it Paul deals with girls who possess the gift of abstaining from marriage. He therefore praises fathers who are concerned to see that the girls are not upset. But we must know what Paul requires here. His first stipulation is for strength of will: 'if anyone has

his mind fully made up about this.' However you must not take this to be the kind of resolution which monks made, viz. voluntarily binding oneself to life-long subjection. (For their vow is like that.) But Paul makes particular mention of this firm determination, because men often draw up plans far too hastily, and next day are sorry they made them. Because this is a serious matter he wants people to think well before making up their minds.

In the second place he describes the person as having no necessity; for, when they come to consider anything, many people are more obstinate than reasonable. And in the circumstances we are considering here, they renounce marriage without paying any attention to the question of their fitness to do so, but they think it enough to say, 'This is what I want'. Paul wants them to have the fitness, so that they may not make a decision hastily, but according to the measure of grace given to them. He explains this exclusion of necessity well in the phrase which follows, when he wants them to have 'power over their own will'. For it is as though he said: 'I do not want them to make up their minds before they are sure that they have been given the power to see it through; for it is a foolhardy, indeed a fatal, thing to fight against God's purpose.' But someone will say: 'According to this argument vows should not be condemned, so long as attention is paid to these stipulations.' To that I reply that we have no certainty about God's will for the future, and therefore, as far as the gift of continency is concerned, we ought not to make a decision which is binding all through our lives. Let us make use of the gift as long as we are allowed to have it. In the meantime let us commit ourselves to the Lord, ready to follow wherever He calls us.

And has decided in his own heart. Paul seems to have added this in order to make it clearer that fathers ought to weigh up every aspect well, before dismissing their worries and plans about giving away their daughters. For they often refuse to be married, because of either shame or lack of knowledge about themselves, yet they remain as sensual as ever, and as liable to be led astray. In this connexion fathers ought to consider what is best for their daughters, so that their own prudence may counteract their girls' inexperience or abnormal desire.

Now this passage helps to strengthen the authority of the father, which must be regarded as unassailable, since it owes its origin to the universal law of nature (*ex communi naturae iure*). If children are not allowed to do other things, things of far less importance, without their parents' approval, it would be obviously rather incongruous for them to be given freedom to contract their own marriages. And indeed careful provision to prevent that has been made by the civil law (*civili lege*), and above all by the Law of God (*Lege Dei*). That is why the dishonesty of the Pope is all the more detestable, for, ignoring respect for the law of God as well as the law of men, he has been so bold as to set children free from the yoke of subjection to their parents. But it is worth while noting the reason. He says: 'This is on account of the dignity of the sacrament.' (I ignore their ignorance in making a sacrament out of marriage!) But what sort of honourableness and dignity is there about it, I ask you, when, contrary both to the common standard of decency among all nations, and to God's eternal ordering, young people are given full scope for their lustful passions, so that they may run riot without any sense of shame, because they have the excuse that this is a sacrament. Let us therefore realize that, in connexion with the giving away of children in marriage, the authority of the parents is most important; provided that they do not abuse it by being domineering; for, to prevent that, the civil law also put restrictions on it. The apostle in requiring that there be no necessity was also of the opinion that parents' decisions ought to be influenced by what is best for the children. Let us therefore bear in mind that this proper balance between the parties is a fair guide: that children allow themselves to be directed by their parents, and that parents, on the other hand, do not drag their children into something against their will, but use their authority only for the purpose of seeking the children's advantage.

38. *Therefore he who gives in marriage does well, and he who does not give, does better.* This is the conclusion to both parts of the section. In a few words Paul absolves parents from any blame if they give their daughters in marriage; yet he asserts that they do better if they keep them at home, unmarried. Once again, however, do not take it that celibacy is preferred to marriage here. That is only so in the one exception put before us a little earlier. For where the girl is not capable of abstaining from marriage, the father who tries to keep her back from it is acting unadvisedly. Indeed he is no longer a father, but a cruel tyrant. The whole discussion amounts to this. (1) Celibacy is preferable to marriage, because it gives us freedom, and, in consequence better opportunity for the service of God. (2) Yet no compulsion should be used to prevent individuals from marrying, if they want to do so. (3) Moreover marriage itself is the remedy which God has provided for our weakness; and everybody who is not blessed with the gift of continency ought to make use of it. Every person of sound judgement will agree with me in saying that the whole of Paul's teaching on marriage is summed up in these three sentences.

A wife is bound for so long time as her husband liveth; but if the husband be dead, she is free to be married to whom she will; only in the Lord.

But she is happier if she abide as she is, after my judgement: and I think that I also have the Spirit of God. (39–40)

39. *A wife is bound (by the law).* What he had said before applied equally to men and women, but because wives might appear to have less freedom, because of the modesty of their sex, he needed to give some special guidance for them also. Therefore he now teaches that women are as free as men to enter on a second marriage, after the death of their first partner. We have already mentioned that those who were eager for second husbands were branded with the stigma of lack of self-control, and it was something of an insult to them, when those who had been content with one husband used to be given a 'garland of chastity'. More than that, this earlier outlook gained a good deal of ground among Christians at one time, for second marriages had no blessing pronounced on them, and some Councils did not allow ministers to take part in them. The apostle condemns arbitrariness of that sort here, and says that no barrier must be put in the way of widows' marrying, if they want to do so.

It makes no difference, and certainly not to the meaning, whether we say that the wife is bound 'to the law' or 'by the law'. For the law certainly affirms that the union of husband and wife is indissoluble. If you take the dative it will mean, however, the authority of the law, and her obligation to it. Now, Paul is arguing from antithesis; for if a wife is bound to her husband for the duration of his life, she is set free by his death. After she has been released, she 'may marry anyone she likes'.

When the verb to sleep is used for dying, the reference is not to the soul, but to the body. That is plain from the constant use of the word in Scripture. Certain hot-heads, therefore, are only showing their ignorance, when they quibble about this little word, in order to prove that after our souls are separated from our bodies, they are deprived of feeling or understanding, in other words, of their life.

Only in the Lord. People take it for granted that this is added to let Paul warn them, in passing, that they must not enter on the yoke of marriage with unbelievers, or be eager for their companionship. Although I acknowledge the truth of that, my opinion is that these words include more than that, viz. that they should enter on this second marriage reverently and in the fear of the Lord. For it is in that way that a favourable start is given to a marriage.

40. *But she is happier if she remains as she is.* Why? Is it because widowhood is a virtue in itself? No, but because it will mean fewer distractions, and more freedom from worldly cares.

In adding, 'according to my judgement', Paul does not mean, by that phrase, that there is some doubt about his opinion. But it is as though he said that that was what he had decided about the matter; for he immediately adds that he has the Spirit of God; and that gives complete and genuine authority enough. But he says 'I think', striking an ironical note. For since the false apostles were repeatedly speaking in boastful terms about the Spirit of God, in order to arrogate authority to themselves, and trying at the same time to belittle Paul, he says that it appears to him that he also possesses the Spirit, just as much as they.

CHAPTER EIGHT

Now concerning things sacrificed to idols: We know that we all have knowledge. Knowledge puffeth up, but love edifieth. If any man thinketh that he knoweth anything, he knoweth not yet as he ought to know; but if any man loveth God, the same is known of him. Concerning therefore the eating of things sacrificed to idols, we know that no idol is anything in the world, and that there is no God but one. For though there be that are called gods, whether in heaven or on earth; as there are gods many, and lords many; yet to us there is one God, the Father, of whom are all things, and we unto him; and one Lord, Jesus Christ, through whom are all things, and we through him. Howbeit in all men there is not that knowledge: but some, being used until now to the idol, eat as of a thing sacrificed to an idol; and their conscience being weak is defiled. (1-7)

Paul now moves on to another question, which he had merely touched on in chapter 6, without developing it further. For when he had spoken about the greed of the Corinthians, and had closed that part of his discussion in that chapter with the sentence: 'The covetous, extortioners, fornicators, etc. shall not inherit the Kingdom of God,' he had gone on from that to speak of Christian liberty, 'all things are lawful for me'. He had taken the opportunity to pass on from that to deal with fornication, and from that, to marriage. So, at last, he follows up the passing reference he had made to 'in-between' things, to bring out now, how our freedom ought to be modified in so far as the 'in-between' things are concerned. By 'in-between things' I mean things which are neither good nor bad in themselves, but neutral; and which God has given us power to use. Further, we ought to practise moderation in using them, so as to preserve the distinction between freedom and licence. He first of all picks out one particular kind in preference to the others, for in this the Corinthians were going seriously wrong. They were attending the religious feasts, which the idol-worshippers held in honour of their gods, and were eating indiscriminately of the meats, which were sacrificed to these gods. Since this caused many people to raise their hands in horror, the apostle teaches that they are wrong in taking advantage of the freedom, which the Lord has granted them.

1. *Concerning things sacrificed to idols.* Paul begins by freely granting them a concession, acknowledging whatever they were going to

question, or find fault with. He might have put it: 'I am aware of how you justify yourselves; you make the excuse of Christian freedom. You claim that you have knowledge, and that not one of your number is so misguided as to be unaware of the fact that there is but one God. I grant all that to be true, but what is the use of knowledge, which involves the brethren in shipwreck?' So he concedes to them what they themselves would assert, but at the same time he makes it plain that their excuses are futile and valueless.

Knowledge puffs up. He shows from the effects just how stupid it is to boast about knowledge, when love (*caritas*) is absent. He could have expressed himself like this: 'What is the use of knowledge, when all it does is to make us swollen-headed, and superior, whereas it is of the very essence of love to edify?' This passage, which would otherwise be obscure because of its conciseness, can easily be understood in this way: 'Anything which lacks even a suggestion of love, is worthless in God's sight, is in fact displeasing to Him—how much more so anything that openly joins battle with love? But this knowledge, about which you Corinthians boast, is definitely in the opposite camp to love, for it fills men with arrogance, and makes them look contemptuously on their brothers. *Love*, on the other hand, moves us to concern for our brothers, and encourages us to look to their upbuilding. No wonder I would say, accursed be that knowledge which produces arrogant men, and is untouched by a concern for other people's welfare!'

Paul, however, did not mean that this fault should be laid at the door of erudition, in the sense that learned people are very often not only smug and vain, but also contemptuous of others at the same time. Again, he did not mean that learning, by its very nature, breeds arrogance. He simply wanted to show the effect that knowledge has on men, when fear of God and love (*dilectio*) of the brethren are lacking. For unbelievers do take advantage of all the gifts of God in order to put themselves on a pedestal. Thus riches, honours, official positions, high birth, good looks and similar things go to people's heads; for they are carried away by a misplaced confidence in them, and become as arrogant as can be. Of course it is not always so, for we come across many people who are wealthy, good-looking, weighed down with honours, holding official positions, of noble birth, who remain humble people all the same, and have not a scrap of pride about them. But whenever that situation, which we have been describing, does come into being, we ought not to put the blame for it, however, on those things which, all agree, are the gifts of God. In the first place that would be unfair and stupid. Secondly in transferring the blame to things, which are in fact neutral, we would be letting off the very men, who alone are at fault. What I am saying is this: if it is the property of riches to make men proud, then if a rich man is proud no blame can be attached to him, for the evil comes from the riches.

Therefore it must be accepted that knowledge is good in itself, but because religion is the one and only basis for it, it becomes a futile, fading thing, so far as unbelievers are concerned, for love is its essential seasoning, and without that, it is ineffectual. Indeed where there is no sign of that serious knowledge of God, which humbles us and teaches us to be concerned about our brothers, what you discover is something which is imagined to be knowledge, rather than knowledge itself, and that even in those who are looked upon as the most learned. But knowledge must no more be blamed for this, than a sword for falling into the hands of a madman. This may be said, because of certain extremists who furiously protest against all the liberal arts and sciences, as if their only function was to encourage men's pride, and had no valuable contribution to make to our everyday life. But those very people who decry them like this are so vociferous in their pride, that they are living exemplars of the old proverb: 'Nothing is so arrogant as ignorance.'

2. *If any man thinks.* He who thinks that he knows something is a person who puts a high estimation on what knowledge he has, and, in a superior way, looks down his nose at others. For here Paul is condemning, not knowledge itself, but the self-seeking and arrogance which are its products in the case of unbelieving men. On the other hand he is not telling us to be sceptics, always uncertain and doubt-ridden. No more does he approve of a false, counterfeit modesty, when we make out that we are doing a fine thing in adopting the attitude of not understanding things we really do know. Therefore the man who thinks he knows something, or, in other words, who becomes swelled-headed, by his own estimation of what knowledge he has, so that he puts himself on a higher level than others, and is highly pleased with himself, knows nothing yet as he ought to know. For the foundation of true knowledge (*verae scientiae*) is personal knowledge (*cognitio*) of God, which makes us humble and obedient; and far from putting us on a pedestal it wholly abases us. But where there is pride, there is no knowledge of God. This is a beautiful passage, and my wish is that everybody would learn it by heart, so that they might keep to the rule of right knowledge (*rite sciendi regulam tenerent*).

3. *And if anyone loves God.* This is the culminating statement, and in it Paul shows that if we love God, it is the most praiseworthy thing in Christians, and indeed it makes knowledge and every other gift praiseworthy also. For, in that event, we shall also love our neighbours in Him. In this way all that we do will be done in moderation, and so

will be approved by God. Paul teaches, therefore, from the consequences, that no teaching can be approved which is not 'baptized' in the love of God (*amore Dei intincta*), for only that can ensure that such gifts as we have, meet with His approval. The way it is put in the Second Epistle (5.17) is this: 'If any man is in Christ, he is a new creature.' By that Paul means that, without the Spirit of regeneration, everything else, no matter how fine in appearance, is valueless. 'To be known by God' simply means to be held to possess a certain standing, or to be counted among His sons. So He removes all the proud from the book of life and from the list of the godly.

4. *Concerning, therefore, the eating of things sacrificed to idols.* Paul returns to the phrase with which he had begun the chapter, and speaks more explicitly about the excuse, which the Corinthians were pleading. For since the whole trouble had its origin in the fact that they were suiting themselves, and looking down upon others, Paul condemned, in general terms, the knowledge which is full of arrogance, and unappealing through the absence of love. Now he comes to the point, explaining the kind of knowledge, in which they were priding themselves. This is what they said: 'An idol is a mere figment of the human brain, and, for that reason, must be regarded as nothing. It follows that the consecration, which is made in the name of an idol, is silly, fanciful, and meaningless. Therefore a Christian, who has no respect for the idol, and eats of the food offered to it, is not made unclean.' That is how they were justifying themselves, and Paul does not dismiss what they say as false, for there is valuable teaching in it, but he rejects it because they were making wrong use of it, in allowing no room for love to operate.

As far as the words are concerned, Erasmus reads, 'an image has no existence' (*nullum est simulacrum*). I myself prefer 'nothing' (*nihil*) as the Vulgate puts it. For the reasoning is: an idol is nothing, because God is the only God. For the one thing follows inevitably from the other: if there is no other God besides our God, then an idol is an idle fancy and a mere nonentity. When Paul says: 'and there is no other God but one', I take the copula 'and' causally, to mean 'because'. For the reason that an idol is nothing is that it ought to be given a value according to what it represents. But the purpose it is meant to serve is the representing of God; one should rather say the representing of unreal gods, seeing that there is the one God who is invisible and incomprehensible. Careful attention must be given to the reason: 'an idol is nothing because there is no God but one,' for He is invisible and cannot be represented by a visible sign, and so that thing cannot be used for worshipping Him. Therefore whether idols are set up to represent the true God, or false gods, in every case it means the creation of something that is perverting. That is why Habakkuk calls idols 'teachers of lies' (2.18); for they deceive men, first, by portraying a figure or image of God, and then by the misleading name which they have. Therefore οὐδέν (nothing) does not refer to the idol's substance but to its quality, for, after all, an idol is made of some material, whether silver, wood or stone. But seeing that God does not wish to be represented in this way, the idol is futile and counts for nothing, so far as being of any significance or value is concerned.

5. *For even if there be that are called gods.* Paul says: 'They have a name, but there is no reality behind it.' For, here, 'to be named' means to be highly regarded by men. He has also made use of a general division, when he says, 'in heaven or on earth'. The gods described as in heaven are the heavenly hosts, as the Bible calls the sun, moon and the other stars. But Moses shows how far removed they are from being divine, by the fact that they were created to be of use to us. The sun is our servant, the moon our hand-maid. How silly then to worship them as gods! Again, I think that those described as gods on earth are, strictly speaking, the men and women for whom religious rites had been instituted. For, according to Pliny, those who had been of great service to the human race were immortalized by religious ceremonies, so that they were worshipped as gods. For example, Jupiter, Mars, Saturn, Mercury, Apollo were mortals, but after their death, they were translated to the company of the gods. In later times this happened to Hercules, Romulus, and finally the Caesars, as if men really had the power to make gods, as they pleased, when, in fact, they cannot bestow life or immortality on themselves! Indeed there are other gods of the earth, animals or inanimate things, such as the ox, serpent, cat, the onion and garlic among the Egyptians; and among the Romans the stone Terminus, and the stone Vesta. These, then, are gods in name only; but Paul says that he is not wasting time on deities of that sort.

6. *Yet to us there is one God, the Father.* Even if Paul says these things in anticipation of what they might say, nevertheless he makes reference to the excuse of the Corinthians in such a way as to be giving instruction at the same time. For, from what is the greatest characteristic of God, he proves that He is the only God: 'Whatever has its origin in someone or something else, outside itself, is not eternal, and therefore is not God. Everything has its origin from one Person, therefore only that Person is God.' Again: 'Only He indeed is God, who gives existence to everything, and from whom everything flows, as from the supreme source; but there is only One Person from whom all things flow; therefore there is but One God.'

When he adds *and we unto Him* (εἰς αὐτόν) Paul means that we continue to live in God, since it was He who once created us. This clause may seem to suggest something else, viz. that since we hold that we took our origin from Him, we therefore ought to give back our lives to Him, so that they may attain their true purpose. That is the meaning εἰς αὐτόν bears in Rom. 11.36. Here, however, it is used in the place of the ablative, ἐν αὐτῷ, which is common enough in the writings of the apostles. He therefore means that, in our present circumstances, we ought to be resting upon the power of God, seeing that we were once created by Him. That interpretation is supported by the statement he makes immediately afterwards about Christ: that we are 'through Him'. For Paul wished to ascribe a common activity to the Father and the Son, yet maintaining the distinction, which is appropriate to the Persons. Therefore he says that we subsist *in* the Father, and we do so *through* the Son; for the Father is indeed the source of all existence, but as we cleave to Him *through* the Son, so He pours out the power of being into us through Him alone.

One Lord. These are relative statements about Christ; in other words, they refer to the relation He bears to the Father. For everything which applies to God, properly applies to Christ, when no specific mention is made of Persons. But in this passage where the Person of the Father is considered along with the Person of the Son, the apostle is quite right in making a distinction between their particular functions.

Now the Son of God, after He had been manifested in the flesh, received from the Father Lordship and power over all things, so that He alone reigns in heaven and earth; and the Father exercises His power through Him. That is why our Lord is referred to as *One*. But the fact that Lordship is ascribed to Him alone does not result in the abolishing of all worldly ranks (*mundi ordines*). For Paul is referring to spiritual Lordship, whereas the authorities of this world are 'political' (*dominia mundi politica*). This corresponds to what he was saying a little before, 'there are many who are called lords', but he means by that, not kings, or others who enjoy superior rank and authority, but idols or demons, to whom stupid men, without any justification, ascribe pre-eminence and government. Therefore, although our religion acknowledges only One Lord, that does not prevent the State having many lords, to whom honour and respect are due in that One Lord.

7. *Howbeit in all men there is not that knowledge.* In a word he refutes all that he had previously introduced as from their lips, showing that it is not enough for them to know that what they are doing is right, if they are not concerned about their brothers as well. When he said before, 'We know that we all have knowledge,' he was referring

to those whom he was taking to task for abusing their freedom. On the other hand he is now pointing out that they are bound up with many weak and ignorant people, to whom they must adapt themselves. It is as though he said: 'In God's sight your view-point is perfectly correct, and if you were the only people in the world, you would be as free to eat meat offered to idols as any other foods. But be considerate of your brothers, to whom you owe something. You have knowledge; they are ignorant. What you do ought to be influenced not only by your knowledge, but also by their ignorance.' This reply deserves special attention: for there is nothing that each of us is more given to doing, than looking to his own interests, without giving a thought to others. For that reason we are only too glad to listen to our own point of view, and we do not give serious thought to the fact that, when it is a question of things we must do openly and publicly, it is not only our consciences which must be considered, but also those of our brothers.

But some with a conscience about the idol. Their ignorance lay in their being inhibited by some superstitious belief about an idol possessing some sort of power, or there being a certain virtue in their ungodly and idolatrous consecration (of meats). But Paul is not speaking about idol-worshippers, who were total strangers to the true religion, but of the ignorant people, who were not yet sufficiently informed to understand that an idol is nothing, and that, consequently, the consecration, which was made in the name of the idol, had no significance. They were thinking along these lines: 'Since an idol is a real thing, the consecration, which is made in its name, is not without meaning therefore. Further, those meats, once they were offered to idols, are no longer pure.' The result was that they felt that, if they ate of them, they were contracting some degree of uncleanness, and were, in some way, making themselves partakers along with the idol. When, by our example, we are encouraging our weak brethren to be bold, and undertake something that is against their conscience, we are raising the very stumbling-block for which Paul is condemning the Corinthians.

And their conscience being weak is defiled. God does not want us to set our hand to anything, without being quite sure that it is acceptable to Him. Therefore, anything a person does with a wavering conscience is, because of that very uncertainty, sinful in God's sight. That is precisely what Paul says in Rom. 14.23: 'Whatsoever is not of faith is sin.' Therefore, there is truth in the common saying that 'they build for hell, who build against their conscience'. Since the goodness of actions springs from fear of God and integrity of conscience, so, on the other hand, it does not matter how good an action may appear to be, if there is something wrong with the mental attitude behind it, then the action is vitiated. For anyone who boldly sets out on some-thing that is against his conscience, is showing a certain contempt for God. For when we respect God's will in everything, it is proof that we fear Him. So you will even be showing contempt in moving a finger, for example, if there is doubt in your mind as to whether that is in line with His will or not. There is also a further thing to be borne in mind about meats, for they are sanctified to us only *by the Word*. If that Word is lacking, uncleanness persists and it alone, not because the things which God has made are unclean, but because man uses them in an impure way. In a word, as men's hearts are purified by faith, so nothing is pure in God's sight apart from faith.

But meat will not commend us to God: neither, if we eat not, are we the worse; nor, if we eat, are we the better. But take heed lest by any means this liberty of yours become a stumblingblock to the weak. For if a man see thee which hast knowledge sitting at meat in an idol's temple, will not his conscience, if he is weak, be emboldened to eat things sacrificed to idols? For through thy knowledge he that is weak perisheth, the brother for whose sake Christ died. And thus, sinning against the brethren, and wounding their conscience when it is weak, ye sin against Christ. Wherefore, if meat maketh my brother to stumble, I will eat no flesh for evermore, that I make not my brother to stumble. (8-13)

8. *But meat does not commend us to God.* This was, or could have been another excuse for the Corinthians: that the worship of God does not depend upon foods. Indeed Paul teaches that very thing in Rom. 14.17: 'The kingdom of God is not eating and drinking.' Paul answers: 'We must take care, however, that the use of our freedom does not cause harm to our neighbours.' In this he tacitly acknowledges that in God's sight it does not matter what foods we eat, because He allows us to use them freely, without any conscientious issue; but this freedom must be controlled by love, when we are involved with other people. Therefore the Corinthians' argument was defective, for they were making a judgement on the whole situation by looking only at a part of it, for, when it comes to the practical affairs of life, love must receive proper consideration. There is no doubt, therefore, that meat does not commend us to God, and Paul agrees; but he modifies it by saying that love is recommended to us by God, and it would be sinful to neglect it.

Nor, if we eat, are we the better. He is not referring to well-satisfied stomachs, for the man who has had his meal has obviously a better filled stomach than the man who is hungry. But he means that we stand neither to gain nor lose, so far as righteousness is concerned, whether we eat or do not eat. Moreover, he is not speaking about every kind of abstinence, or every kind of eating, without discrimination. For over-indulgence and extravagance, in themselves, do not meet with God's approval, while sobriety and moderation please Him. But let us grasp that the Kingdom of God, which is spiritual, does not lie in these external practices, and therefore that neutral things (*res medias*) in themselves are of no value in God's sight. Although he puts that on the lips of others, when he anticipates their arguments, he is admitting, nevertheless, that it is true, for it is derived from his own teaching, which we referred to briefly in the last paragraph.

9. *Take heed lest this liberty of yours.* He leaves their freedom intact, but he puts a restriction on it, in so far as its use must not upset those who are weak. And he is quite explicit about his wish that consideration should be given to the weak, i.e. those who are not yet very well grounded in godliness. Since they are usually looked down upon by everybody, the Lord wishes, indeed commands, us to be concerned about them. At the same time he hints that tough giants, who want to play the tyrant, and put our freedom under their control, can be safely ignored; because one need not be afraid of offending people who are not led into sin by weakness, but who, at the same time, are eagerly on the look-out for something to find fault with. We shall soon see what Paul means by a stumbling-block.

10. *If anyone sees you, although you have knowledge.* In this sentence it is becoming clearer just how much freedom the Corinthians were allowing themselves, for when unbelievers were making some sort of sacred feast for the idols they had no hesitation about going and eating of the sacrifice along with them. Paul now shows the bad results to which this practice led.

In the first part of the sentence I have substituted 'although you have knowledge', for 'who have knowledge'. In the second part, where it reads 'who is weak', I have added 'nevertheless'. To me, that was necessary in order to clarify Paul's thought. For he makes a concession, as though to say: 'Granted that you have knowledge; but someone who sees you, though he is not equipped with knowledge, is encouraged by your example to venture on what you are doing, when, in fact, he would never have made a move had no lead been given him. But now, when he is trying to be like someone else, he thinks that that person's example provides him with a good enough excuse, whereas the truth is that all the time he has a bad conscience about what he is doing.' For here 'weakness' means ignorance, or a wavering conscience. I am well aware of the way in which others explain it. They take this 'stumbling-block' to mean that ignorant people, who are influenced by someone else's example, suppose that in this way they are offering some sort of service to God. But this notion is quite out of line with Paul's meaning. For he found fault with them (as I said), because they were inciting the ignorant to go against their conscience, and go headlong into something, which they themselves did not think was right for them to do.

'To be built up' means here 'to be encouraged'. But the building which is not founded on sound teaching is a ruinous one indeed.

11. *And your brother will perish.* We should note that to undertake something, when your conscience is in doubt about it, or against it, is a serious sin, even if men usually dismiss it lightly. What we should be striving to reach all through our lives is the will of God. Therefore our going against His will, is the one thing which vitiates all our actions. And we go against it not only with our external actions, but also with our thoughts, when we let ourselves do something which is against our conscience, even if the thing is not wrong in itself. Therefore let us remember that we are rushing headlong to disaster whenever we persist in our own way in opposition to our conscience.

Apart from that I read this sentence interrogatively: *will he perish through your knowledge?* It is as though he said: 'Is it reasonable that your knowledge should bring your brother to ruin? Have you knowledge of what is right simply in order to destroy someone else?' He used the word 'brother' so that he might condemn them for their pride and the cruel indifference to others which went with it. His meaning is: 'The person whom you despise is weak, without a doubt, but at the same time he is your brother, for God has adopted him. Therefore your heart is hard when you are giving no consideration to your brother.' But there is even more force in the subsequent statement that the ignorant or weak have also been redeemed by the blood of Christ. For one can imagine nothing more despicable than this, that while Christ did not hesitate to die so that the weak might not perish, we, on the other hand, do not care a straw for the salvation of the men and women who have been redeemed at such a price. This is a memorable saying, from which we learn how precious the salvation of our brothers ought to be to us, and not only that of all, but of each individual, in view of the fact that the blood of Christ was poured out for each one.

12. *And thus, sinning against the brethren etc.* If the soul of every weak person costs the price of the blood of Christ, anyone, who, for the sake of a little bit of meat, is responsible for the rapid return to death of a brother redeemed by Christ, shows just how little the blood of Christ means to him. Contempt like that is therefore an open insult to Christ. We have already said how a weak conscience may be injured, viz. when it is given encouragement to do something wrong, so that the person

179

is reckless and foolish enough to advance further, than he himself thinks right.

13. *Wherefore, if meat maketh my brother to stumble.* So that he might be more severe in his reproof of the pride which they take in their freedom, Paul asserts that we must not simply keep away from one particular feast, rather than offend a brother, but we must give up eating meats for life. Not only does he lay down what should be done, but he states that he himself will conform. He is using hyperbole, of course, because it is hardly possible for anyone to abstain from meat all his life long, if he continues to lead a normal life among others. Even so, he means that he would never avail himself of the freedom, which he possesses, rather than cause the weak to stumble. For that freedom should only be used if it is controlled by the rule of love. I wish that careful thought would be given to this by those who make everything turn to their own advantage, so that they cannot bear to give up even the smallest whit of their rights, for the sake of a brother. I also wish that they would attend not only to what Paul teaches, but to what he sets before us by his own example. How far ahead of us Paul is! Therefore, when he shows such willingness to discipline himself to this extent for the sake of his brothers, which of us would not submit to the same conditions?

But however hard it may be to put this teaching into practice, yet, so far as the meaning itself is concerned, there is no difficulty, except where it has been corrupted by some people with irrelevent glosses, and by others with bad distortions. Both go wrong over the word 'to offend'. For they take 'to offend' to mean 'to incur the hatred or displeasure of men', or what is nearly the same thing, 'to do what displeases them, or does not find much favour with them'. But the context makes it as plain as can be that what is meant is keeping a brother back from the right way by showing him a bad example, just like putting an obstacle in his path; or being responsible for his fall. Therefore Paul is not dealing here with keeping on the right side of men, but with encouraging the weak, to prevent their collapse, and with giving them wise guidance to save them from departing from the right way. But, as far as those who misunderstand are concerned, those of the first group are fatuous, as I have said; while the others are bad and impudent as well.

The 'fatuous people' are those who allow Christians hardly any use of neutral things in case they might 'offend' those who are superstitious. They say: 'In this passage Paul is debarring everything which gives rise to offence. But the eating of meat on Friday is a sure way of causing offence. Therefore we must refrain from doing so, not only when we are in the presence of weak people, but every single week, without exception, for you never know when they might find out about it, if we did eat meat.' I am ignoring the wrong way they understand the verb 'to cause to stumble' (*scandalizandi*). But they are on quite the wrong lines in not paying attention to the fact that here Paul is attacking those who make improper use of their knowledge at the very time they should not do so, in front of the weak, the very people whom they do not bother to instruct. Therefore the grounds for reproof will be removed if teaching has been given beforehand. Again, Paul is not telling us to make sure beforehand that what we do will not cause 'offence', except where there is immediate and obvious danger of doing so.

I come now to those of the other group. They are would-be imitators of Nicodemus, and make that an excuse for compromising themselves with unbelievers by sharing in their idol-worship. But, not being content with providing an excuse for the wrong they themselves are doing, they also want to force others into the position where they will need to do the same thing. The condemnation of their wicked hypocrisy could not be expressed more clearly than the way Paul does it here, for he shows that all, who by their example give encouragement to the weak to take part in the worship of idols, are doing serious harm both to God and men. However, they defend themselves by showing that erroneous beliefs must be encouraged in the hearts of the ignorant, and that the latter ought to be given a lead in the matter of idol-worship, in case an unreserved, frank condemnation of it might 'offend' them. In light of that I will not do them the honour of taking the trouble to refute their impudent suggestions! I would simply advise my readers to compare Paul's day with ours, and decide for themselves from this, if it is permissible to be present at masses and other abominations, which are such a stumbling-block to the weak.

CHAPTER NINE

Am I not free? am I not an apostle? have I not seen Jesus our Lord? are not ye my work in the Lord? If to others I am not an apostle, yet at least I am to you: for the seal of mine apostleship are ye in the Lord. My defence to them that examine me is this. Have we no right to eat and to drink? Have we no right to lead about a wife that is a believer, even as the rest of the apostles, and the brethren of the Lord, and Cephas? Or I only and Barnabus, have we not a right to forbear working? What soldier ever serveth at his own charges? who planteth a vineyard, and eateth not the fruit thereof? or who feedeth a flock, and eateth not of the milk of the flock? Do I speak these things after the manner of men? or saith not the law also the same? For it is written in the law of Moses, Thou shalt not muzzle the ox when he treadeth out the corn. Is it for the oxen that God careth, or saith he it altogether for our sake? Yea, for our sake it was written: because he that ploweth ought to plow in hope, and he that thresheth, to thresh in hope of partaking. If we sowed unto you spiritual things, is it a great matter if we shall reap your carnal things? If others partake of this right over you, do not we yet more? Nevertheless we did not use this right; but we bear all things, that we may cause no hindrance to the gospel of Christ. (1-12)

1. *Am I not free?* He confirms from actual fact what he had just been saying, that he would never taste meat all his life, rather than cause a brother to stumble. At the same time he makes it plain that he cannot demand anything from them which he himself had not put into practice. There is no doubt that natural justice requires that anybody who imposes some obligation on others, should observe it himself. But a Christian teacher, above all, should discipline himself in this way, so that men may always see his teaching backed up by the example of his life. We know from our own experience that what Paul was asking from the Corinthians is an exceedingly difficult thing, viz. for the sake of their brothers to refrain from using the freedom (*potestas*) granted to themselves. He would not have got very far with this, if he himself had not first of all given a lead. And indeed he had committed himself to doing so, but because all of them would not trust him on the strength of a mere promise about the future, he tells them what he has done already. He quotes a remarkable instance of his giving up the freedom, which he could otherwise have used, and doing so only to prevent the false apostles having a chance to criticize

him. It was when he preferred to earn his living by his own hands, rather than be supported at the expense of the Corinthians, whom he was providing with the Gospel.

He goes on to deal at length with the right, which belonged to the apostles, of receiving food and clothing. One reason for doing so was to give them more encouragement to follow his example, and give up many things for the sake of their brothers; for the fact was that they were unduly stubborn about standing on their rights. Another reason for Paul's dealing with this matter was that he might show up the unfairness of those who were putting him in a false light, for they seized on something, which was beyond criticism, as an excuse for disparaging him. He makes use of rhetorical questions to drive home his argument more forcibly. The question, 'Am I not free?' is a general one. When he adds, 'Am I not an apostle?' he narrows it to a particular kind of freedom; as though to say, 'If I am an apostle of Christ, why should my situation be worse than that of others?' So he proves his freedom on the grounds of his being an apostle.

Have I not seen Jesus Christ our Lord? He takes care to add this, so that he might not be regarded as in some way inferior to the rest of the apostles. For those who were hostile and jealous were loud-mouthed in their repeated assertions of this one thing: whatever Paul had of the Gospel he had received at the hands of men, for never had he cast eyes on Christ. There is no doubt that he had never been in Christ's company, when He was in the world; but Christ had appeared to him after His resurrection. But it is a greater privilege to have seen Christ in His immortal glory, rather than clothed in the humility of His mortal flesh. Paul refers to his vision in chapter 15.8 of this letter, and mentions it twice in Acts (22.6 ff, 26.13 ff). This particular question therefore seeks to put his call beyond dispute, because, even if he had not been nominated as one of the twelve, the decision, which Christ made known from heaven, was no less authoritative.

Are you not my work in the Lord? In the second place he now establishes his apostleship by the effect it had, viz. his winning the Corinthians for the Lord by the Gospel. Now, Paul is making a great claim for himself, in calling their conversion his work; for it involves a kind of new creation of the soul.

But how does this fit in with what he said in I Cor. 3.7, that 'he who plants is nothing, and he who waters is nothing'? My answer is that since God is the efficient cause, while man, with his preaching, is an instrument, which is futile by itself, we must always speak of the effectiveness of the ministry in such a way that all the praise for the work remains with God alone. But sometimes, when the ministry is being referred to, man is compared with God, and then it holds good that 'he who plants is nothing, and he who waters is nothing'. For what can be left to man if he is sharing in the work with God? So the Scripture reduces ministers to nothing, when it puts them alongside God; but when it is a matter of the ministry alone, and no comparison with God is being made, its effectiveness is praised in glowing terms, as is done here. For, in those circumstances, it is not a question of what man can do on his own without God, but rather that God Himself, who is the agent, is joined with the instrument, and the power of the Spirit is added to the labour of man. In other words it is not a question of what man himself carries out on his own resources, but what God does through him.

2. *If to others I am not an apostle*. The point of this sentence is that he wants to make it impossible for the Corinthians to question the authority of his apostleship. He says: 'If there are some who have doubts about my apostleship, that should not be so in your case, however, for, since I planted your church by my ministry, either you are not believers, or you are bound to recognise me as an apostle.' And, so that he may not give the impression of relying on words only, he reminds them that facts bear it out, for God had put His seal to his apostleship in the form of the faith of the Corinthians themselves. But if anyone objects that this applies also to the false apostles, who gather followers about them, I reply that pure teaching is the first essential, if anyone is to have his ministry confirmed by results in the sight of God. So, if impostors have been deceiving some of the ordinary people, and even nations and kingdoms as well, by their lies, there is nothing here to give them grounds for preening their feathers. But even if people who do not proclaim the Gospel 'in sincerity' (as it is put in Phil. 1.17) are sometimes the means of spreading the Kingdom of Christ, Paul is quite justified in inferring from the results of his work, that he has been sent by God; for the structure of the Corinthian Church was such that the blessing of God was plainly visible in it; and that ought to have had the effect of confirming Paul's office.

3. *My defence*. Besides the main subject, with which he is now dealing, he seems to have had the subsidiary purpose here of putting a stop to the misrepresentations of those who protested against his calling, as if he had been one of the ordinary run of ministers. He says, 'I am accustomed to making use of you as my shield, whenever anyone detracts from the honour of my apostleship'. The result of this is that the Corinthians are harming themselves and acting against their own interests, if they do not recognize him as an apostle. For if their faith was solemn evidence of Paul's apostleship, and his defence against slanderers, the one thing could not be overthrown without the other collapsing along with it.

While others read, 'those who interrogate me', I have rendered it, 'those who inquire into my situation'; for he means those who were making his apostleship a debatable issue. I agree that Latin writers speak of the accused being interrogated legally; but the meaning of the word ἀνακρίνειν, which Paul uses, seemed to me to be brought out better by my expression.

4. *Have we no right to eat and to drink?* From what he has already said he concludes that he had a right to receive food and clothing from them, for Paul was eating and drinking, but not at any cost to the Church. Therefore this was one way in which he was now surrendering his freedom; another was that he did not have a wife, whose maintenance was also a charge upon all of them. Eusebius infers from these words that Paul was married, but had left his wife in one particular place, so that she might not be a burden on the churches; but this is a false assumption, for this could as easily be said by a single person.

In calling a Christian wife 'sister', Paul shows, first of all, how strong and lovely (*amabilis*) the union between a believing husband and wife ought to be, for it is maintained by a double bond. In the second place he is suggesting that they ought to be very modest and considerate in their dealings with each other. It is also legitimate to infer from this that marriage is anything but unsuitable for ministers of the Church. I make no mention of the fact that the apostles made use of it, for we shall soon be referring to their example. But Paul is showing here, in a general way, what everybody is allowed to do.

5. *Even as the rest of the apostles.* In addition to the Lord's commission, he refers to what others are in the habit of doing. And, in order to put the giving up of his right in an even clearer light, he proceeds step by step. First of all he cites the example of the apostles. Then he adds, 'More than that, the very brothers of the Lord have no difficulty about having a wife; yes, and what is more, Peter himself, who, by common consent, is given the first place, allows himself the same right.'

By 'the brothers of the Lord' he means John and James, who 'were reputed to be pillars', as he reveals in Galatians 2.9. And, in line with the usual custom of the Scripture, he calls 'brothers' those who were related to Him by birth.

Anyone who wants to find support for the Papacy in this passage is simply making a fool of himself. We quite agree that Peter was indeed recognized as the first among the apostles, for in every company of people it is always necessary that there should be someone to take the lead over the others. And they themselves were ready to respect Peter, because of his wealth of outstanding gifts; for it is right that all who outshine others in the gifts of God's grace should be held in high regard and honour. But Peter's primacy was not lordship, indeed there was no comparison between it and the absolute authority of a lord (*dominatio*). For, although he stood out among the others, he was yet answerable to his colleagues. Besides, it is one thing to be first in the Church alone, it is quite another to claim for oneself sovereignty or pre-eminence over the whole world. Even if we agree to all this so far as Peter is concerned, what has that to do with the Pope? For as Matthias succeeded Judas, so some Judas could take Peter's place. Yes, and we now see, after a period of more than 900 years of his successors, or at least those who boast that they are his successors, that not one of them is a whit better than Judas. But this is not the place for discussing these things; see my *Institutes* (4.6).

We must notice one last point here, viz. that the apostles did not shrink from marriage, like the Papal clergy, who detest it so much, because it does not befit the sanctity of their order. But it was later than the apostles that men lit upon the remarkable piece of wisdom that the priests of the Lord are defiled if they have intercourse with their lawful wives. At last it went so far that Pope Syricius[1] had no hesitation about calling marriage 'an uncleanness of the flesh, in which no-one can please God'. What, then, will happen to the unfortunate apostles, who persisted in this impurity until their deaths? But here the Papists evade the issue by a fine piece of cunning reasoning, of their own devising. For they say that the apostles refrained from intercourse, but took their wives about with them, so that they might get the fruits of the Gospel, in other words their maintenance at other people's expense. As if, indeed, they could not be supported by the churches unless they wandered from place to place! And also as if one could believe that those wives ran all over the place of their own free will, and when there was no need to do so, simply in order to live in idleness at public expense! Ambrose's explanation that the reference is to other men's wives, who were eagerly following the apostles to hear what they had to teach, is far-fetched indeed.

7. *Who has served as a soldier at his own expense?* The present tense of the verb is used, bearing the sense, 'is in the habit of serving as a soldier'. However, I have put it in the perfect so as to tone down the harshness.

To move on, with the use of three comparisons, all of them drawn from men's everyday life at that, Paul now affirms that it was quite in order for him to live at the Church's expense, if he wanted to; and he does so, to show that he is claiming no more for himself than what ordinary human consideration (*humanitas*) requires. The first is taken from military law, for soldiers are usually issued with their rations at the public expense. The second is derived from vine-dressers, for the

[1] Held office A.D. 384–399.

grower plants a vine, not for amusement, but to gather fruit from it. The third is from cattle-rearing, for the herdsman does not work for nothing, but enjoys the milk of the flock, that is, the produce provides for his maintenance. When natural justice lays down this as the fairest way of doing, will anyone be so unjust as to deny the necessities of life to the pastors of the Church? But even if it were the case that some men serve as soldiers and provide for themselves, as, for instance, the Romans once did before the days of the levying of tribute and taxes, that does not conflict with what Paul is saying, for he is only arguing from the common and universally accepted custom.

8–9. *Do I speak these things after the manner of men?* In case anyone might refuse to be convinced, saying that it is quite a different matter in so far as the things of God are concerned, and therefore that Paul has been wasting his time in introducing so many similes, he now adds that the very same thing is laid down by the Lord. To speak after the manner of men sometimes means to speak according to the perverted understanding of the flesh, as in Romans 3.5. But here it means to deal only with those things with which men are familiar, and which are valid only in the human market (as they say). But the fact is that God Himself wished men to have wages as a reward for their labours. Paul proves that from God's prohibiting the muzzling of the mouth of the ox when it is treading out the corn; and, so as to make it apply to the circumstances with which he is dealing, he says that God was not concerned about the oxen, but rather was thinking about men.

First, it may be asked why Paul made particular choice of this proof-text, when far clearer illustrations were available for him in the law, for example Deut. 24.15, 'The wages of the hired servant shall not be with you all night'. But anyone who will pay closer attention to this, will realize that there is more force about this text, in which the Lord asks us to care for cattle, for from this it can be seen, by inferring from the less to the greater, that, when He wants the dumb animals to be treated well, He requires much greater equity to be shown by men in their dealings with each other. When he says that 'God does not care for the oxen', we must not misunderstand him, as if his intention is to put oxen outside the providence of God, since God does not neglect even the tiniest sparrow. Again, we must not make the mistake of thinking that Paul means to explain that commandment allegorically; for some empty-headed creatures make this an excuse for turning everything into allegory, so that they change dogs into men, trees into angels, and convert the whole of Scripture into an amusing game.

But what Paul actually means is quite simple: though the Lord commands consideration for the oxen, He does so, not for the sake of the oxen, but rather out of regard for men, for whose benefit even the very oxen were created. Therefore that humane treatment of oxen ought to be an incentive, moving us to treat each other with consideration and fairness; as Solomon puts it in Proverbs 12.10: 'A righteous man regardeth the life of his beast: But the tender mercies of the wicked are cruel.' You should understand, therefore, that God is not concerned about oxen, to the extent that oxen were the only creatures in His mind when He made the law, for He was thinking of men, and wanted to make them accustomed to being considerate in behaviour, so that they might not cheat the workman of his wages. For the ox does not take the leading part in ploughing and threshing, but man, and it is by man's efforts that the ox itself is set to work. Therefore, what he goes on to add, 'he that plougheth ought to plough in hope' etc., is an interpretation of the commandment, as though he said, that it is extended, in a general way, to cover any kind of reward for labour.

10. *Because he that plougheth ought to plough in hope.* There are two readings in this verse, even in the Greek manuscripts, but the one which I have adopted is more generally accepted: 'He that thresheth, in hope of sharing in his hope.' However, the reading which does not repeat *hope* twice in the second clause seems simpler and more natural. Therefore, were I free to choose, I would prefer to read it in this way: 'He who ploughs ought to plough in hope, and he who thresheth in hope of partaking.' However, because nearly all the Greek manuscripts agree in following the first reading, and the meaning is not affected, I have not presumed to depart from it.[1]

However, Paul is explaining the commandment quoted in verse 9, and in that connexion says that it is unfair that the farmer should put out his work on ploughing and threshing fruitlessly, but that the whole object of his labour is his hope of gathering the fruit. In that case, it is right to infer that that applies to oxen as well; but Paul's intention was to give it a wider bearing, and make it apply particularly to men. Now, the farmer is said 'to partake of his hope', when he enjoys the produce, which he has harvested, but for which he certainly hoped when ploughing.

11. *If we sowed unto you spiritual things.* One ground for hesitancy remained. For the objection could be made that all work relating to life in this world ought, quite definitely, to be rewarded with food and clothing; that ploughing and threshing produce returns, in which those who do the actual work come to share; but that the Gospel is in a different category altogether, for its fruit is spiritual; and that therefore the minister of the Word, if he wants to receive fruit which

---

[1] Of the Greek variants the one Calvin would have preferred is now known to be the best attested, whereas the reading he felt forced to adopt on the evidence then available is the least well attested on the evidence now available.

answers to his labour, ought not to demand anything material. So, in case anyone might prevaricate in this way, Paul argues from greater to less. He might have expressed himself like this: 'Although food and clothing are in a different category from the work the minister does, yet what loss do you suffer, if you pay for something which is beyond price, with something very cheap and trifling? For just as the soul is much superior in nature to the body, so is the Word of God in a higher class than material food, since it is the food of the soul.'

12. *If others make claim to this right over you, do not we still more?* Once again he gives support to his own right by referring to the example of others. For why should he alone be refused what others were claiming as their due? For since no-one had worked harder than he among the Corinthians, no-one deserved a reward more. However, he does not say what he has done, but what he would have done by virtue of his right, if he had not voluntarily refrained from using it.

Nevertheless we did not use this right. He now returns to the heart of the matter, that he had of his own free will given up that right, which no-one could deny to him; and that he preferred to endure anything rather than make use of his freedom in a way that would hinder the progress of the Gospel. Therefore he wishes the Corinthians to follow his example and keep this aim before them: not to place any obstacle in the way of the Gospel, or delay its progress; for they, on their part, had to do exactly the same thing as he declares he does. And here he confirms what he has said before, that we must take thought about what is to the best advantage.

Know ye not that they which minister about sacred things eat of the things of the temple, and they which wait upon the altar have their portion with the altar? Even so did the Lord ordain that they which proclaim the gospel should live of the gospel. But I have used none of these things: and I write not these things that it may be so done in my case: for it were good for me rather to die, than that any man should make my glorying void. For if I preach the gospel, I have nothing to glory of; for necessity is laid upon me; for woe is unto me, if I preach not the gospel. For if I do this of mine own will, I have a reward: but if not of mine own will, I have a stewardship intrusted to me. What then is my reward? That, when I preach the gospel, I may make the gospel without charge, so as not to use to the full my right in the gospel. For though I was free from all men, I brought myself under bondage to all, that I might gain the more. And to the Jews I became as a Jew, that I might gain Jews; to them that are under the law, as under the law, not being myself under the law, that I might gain them that are under the law; to them that are without law, as without law, not being without

law to God, but under law to Christ, that I might gain them that are
without law. To the weak I became weak, that I might gain the weak:
I am become all things to all men, that I may by all means save some.
(13–22)

13. *Do you not know?* Apart from the main subject which he is
discussing, Paul seems to have spent more time on the discussion of
this point, so as to upbraid the Corinthians indirectly for their mean
attitude in allowing the ministers of Christ to be wronged in connexion
with what they are properly entitled to receive. For if Paul had not
voluntarily refrained from making use of his freedom, there was a
danger of the way being barred to the Gospel. The false apostles would
never have achieved that, if ingratitude, to which the Corinthians were
already prone, had not cleared the way for their misrepresentations.
Of course the Corinthians ought to have rejected them vigorously, but
what they did was to reveal their extreme credulity, so that they would
have been ready to reject the Gospel if Paul had taken advantage of his
right. Such contempt of the Gospel, and such lack of consideration
for their apostle, deserved severer reproof than this, but Paul, having
found another chance to refer to it, does so tacitly and gently, in line
with his usual moderation in fact, so as to give them advice without
insulting them.

Now, he makes use of a different simile to prove that he had not
taken advantage of a right which the Lord gave him. And he borrows
examples from other sources no longer, but shows that the Lord
directed that the churches should supply their ministers with the means
of subsistence. There are some who think that there are actually two
comparisons in this verse, the first indeed being the priests of the Lord,
but the other those who offered sacrifices to heathen gods. But I am
inclined to think that Paul, as he usually does, has used different terms
to describe the same thing. An argument derived from the custom of
the heathen, would certainly have been a poor one, for the revenues
of the priests were not devoted to necessities like food and clothing,
but to costly furnishings, regal splendour and extravagant luxury.
These things would therefore have had no bearing whatsoever on the
matter. However I do not challenge the view that Paul was alluding
to different kinds of ministries, for there were priests of a higher order
(*maioris ordinis*), and afterwards there were the Levites, who were
inferior to them, as is well known. But that is hardly the point.

The point is this: the Levitical priests were the ministers of the
Church of Israel; and the Lord appointed that they should be provided
with the necessities of life from their own ministry. Therefore the
same fair principle should be observed today in the case of ministers of
the Christian Church; but the ministers of the Christian Church are

those who preach the Gospel. This verse is quoted by the Canonists, when they want to prove that those with empty stomachs must be filled, so that they may carry out their sacrifices; but I leave it even to the very children to decide how ridiculous that is. These men seize at once on anything that Scripture says about the means of subsistence which must be given to ministers, or about the respect in which they must be held, and twist it to suit themselves. All I do, therefore, is to urge my readers to pay attention to what Paul is actually saying. His argument is that pastors, whose work is the preaching of the Gospel, must be supported, because long ago the Lord prescribed certain necessities of life for the priests, in view of the fact that they gave their services to the Church. Accordingly we must maintain a distinction between the priesthood of ancient times and that of our own day. Under the Law priests were appointed to be in charge of the sacrifices, to serve the altar, and look after the tabernacle and temple; in our day they are appointed to proclaim the Word and dispense the sacraments. The Lord has not appointed any sacrifices for the holy ministers to busy themselves with; there are no altars at which they may stand to offer sacrifices.

Those who apply this analogy (*anagoge*), derived from sacrifices, to anything other than the preaching of the Gospel, are patently ridiculous. And more than that, it is easy to infer from this verse that all the Popish priests, from the chief one himself to the least important member, are temple robbers (*sacrilegos*), for they greedily devour the revenues meant for genuine ministers, without carrying out any of the appropriate duties whatever. For what ministers does the apostle tell them to support? They must support those who devote themselves to preaching the Gospel. What right have those Popish priests to claim the rewards of the priests for themselves? The answer is because they intone and offer sacrifices. Yet God has not asked them for any such things; so it is plain that they are appropriating the reward that belongs to others.

Finally, when Paul says that the Levitical priests were 'sharers in the altar', and 'ate of the things of the temple', he means, by metonymy, the offerings that were presented to God. For they claimed the sacred animal sacrifices entire for themselves; and in the case of less important sacrifices the right shoulder, kidneys and the tail; as well as tithes, offerings, and first-fruits. Therefore the second ἱερόν in this sentence is taken to mean the Temple.

15. *And I am not writing these things.* Since the impression might be given that Paul was eager for the Corinthians to pay him in the future, he removes any such suggestion, and asserts that, far from wanting any such thing, he would rather die than bring about the loss of what gives him cause for boasting, viz. that he had given his services to the

Corinthians for nothing. And there need be no surprise about his putting such value on this reason for boasting, for he was aware that the authority of the Gospel to some extent depended upon it. For he might have given the false apostles such an opportunity for scoffing at him, that there was a danger of the Corinthians treating him with contempt, and receiving them with loud approval. He preferred to have the chance to spread the Gospel, even more than his very life.

16. *For if I preach the gospel.* To show how very important it was that he should not be deprived of this cause for boasting, Paul points out what would have happened if he had done nothing more than discharge his ministry, viz. that he would then have done no more than what the Lord had imposed upon him with an unavoidable necessity. In making that clear, he is saying that he had, in that respect, no cause for boasting, since this was something he could not get out of.

But someone may ask what sort of boasting Paul means here, for in II Tim. 1.3 he takes pride in his carrying out his duties as a teacher 'with a clear conscience'. My reply is that he speaks of a cause for boasting with which he could challenge the false apostles, when they were on the look-out for an excuse to malign him, as will be seen more clearly in what follows.

However, this is a remarkable sentence. We learn from it, in the first place, the nature of the call which ministers receive, and how tightly they are bound to God; and, secondly, what the office of the pastor involves, and embraces within itself. Once a man has been called, then, let him get it into his head that he is no longer free to draw back, when it suits him, if, for example, frustrations take the heart out of him, or troubles overwhelm him; for he is dedicated to the Lord and to the Church, and held fast by a sacred bond, which it would be sinful for him to break.

As far as the second point is concerned, Paul says that the threat of a curse lies over his head, if he does not preach the Gospel. Why? It is because he has been called to do that, and for that very reason he is controlled by a compulsion which drives him on.

How then can anyone who takes up the same task after him avoid this constraint? What sort of 'apostolic succession' is there, then, in the case of the Pope and the mitred bishops, who take the view that there is nothing more incompatible with their role, than the duty of teaching?

17. *For if I do this.* The reward, to which he refers here, is what the Latins call *operae pretium*, 'the reward for trouble', and he spoke of that before as grounds for boasting. Others explain this in a different way: that a reward is offered to all who carry out their task faithfully and whole-heartedly. But I myself understand by 'the man who acts of

his own free will' one who is so enthusiastic and single-minded in his desire for instructing others, that he does not turn up his nose at anything that he knows will be of service to the Church. In the same way, he means by the 'unwilling', on the other hand, those who certainly do what necessity lays upon them, but they do it with a grudge because it conflicts with what they want themselves. For it is always the case that the man who enters into any task with zest is also willing to submit to anything, the neglect of which would mean hindering the completion of the work. So Paul, who did things willingly, was not in the habit of teaching in a merely formal way, but made use of everything which he realized was suitable for helping and furthering his teaching. This, therefore, was his 'reward for trouble', and his cause for boasting: that he readily gave up his right, for he was devoting himself to what he had to do with willingness and real earnestness.

But if not of my own will, I have been entrusted with a commission. However others may explain this, the true meaning, in my view, is that the service of a man, which is done grudgingly and, as it were, against his will, is quite unacceptable to God. Therefore, whenever God has demanded something from us, we are deceiving ourselves, if we imagine that we are fulfilling it properly, when we do it grudgingly. For the Lord expects his servants to be eager, so as to take pleasure in obeying Him, and demonstrate their cheerfulness by acting without any hesitation. In short, Paul means that the only way in which he would do justice to his calling, would be by doing his duty with willingness and unbounded eagerness.

18. *What then is my reward?* The conclusion he comes to from the preceding argument is that the reason for his boasting lies in his giving his services to the Corinthians for nothing; because that makes it plain that he is devoting himself to the task of teaching willingly; for he takes pains to overcome all the hindrances to the Gospel, and, not being content with the fact that he has done his teaching, and leaving it at that, he is anxious to increase its influence in every way. Therefore, this is a summary of what he says: 'I am forced to preach the Gospel. If I do not do it, a curse threatens me, because I am resisting the call of God. But it is not enough to preach, unless I do it willingly, for the person, who carries out the command of God unwillingly, is not measuring up to the requirements of his office as he should. Now, if I obey God willingly, then I do have a right to boast. Therefore, it was necessary for me to make the Gospel without charge, so that I could be justified in boasting.'

The Papists try to find support in this verse for works of supererogation, which they have invented. They say: 'Paul would have done all that was required of him by simply preaching the Gospel; but he adds something else as well; therefore he does something over and above what he is obliged to do; and, remember, he makes a distinction between what one does voluntarily, and what one must do.' My answer to all that is that Paul did indeed go beyond what was normally required of pastors in their calling, seeing that he did not take the pay, which the Lord allows pastors to take. But it was part of his duty to take steps against every possible cause of offence, which he saw would arise. Now, he was aware that there would be no further progress for the Gospel, if he were to take advantage of his right; but even if that was something unusual, I maintain, however, that he offered to God no more than he was bound to give. For I ask, 'Is it not the duty of a good pastor to do away with things which cause offence, so far as it lies in his power?' And again I ask, 'What else did Paul do but precisely that?' Therefore we have no right to imagine that he gave to God something which he did not owe Him, since he only did what the requirement of his office called for—even if it was an unusual exigency. Let us hear no more, then, about this wicked fantasy, that we make amends for our sins in God's sight by works of supererogation. And what is more, let there be an end to the use of the term itself, for it is bursting with devilish pride. There is no doubt that this verse is wrongly twisted in order to yield that interpretation.

Now, the error of the Papists is refuted in a general way, in what follows. It is wrong to call all works which fall under the heading of the Law 'works of supererogation', as is plain from the words of Christ: 'When ye shall have done all the things that are commanded you, say, we are unprofitable servants; we have done that which it was our duty to do' (Luke 17.10). Now, we agree that no work is good, or acceptable to God, that is not included in the law of God. I prove this second statement in the following way. There are two classes of good works, for they can all be classified under either the service of God, or love. But nothing belongs to the service of God, if it does not rest upon this fundamental principle: 'Thou shalt love the Lord with all thy heart, with all thy soul, with all thy strength.' There is also no duty of love, which is not covered by the precept: 'Thou shalt love thy neighbour as thyself' (Mark 12.30, 31). The Papists hold out that it is possible for someone to be acceptable to God if he pays the tenth part of his income; and from that they infer that if he does more, and gives as much as a fifth part, he is doing a work of supererogation. It is easy to destroy that sophistry. For the fact that the works of believers are accepted, is not because they are perfect by any means, but because their imperfection and inadequacies are not reckoned against them. Therefore, if they do a hundredfold more than what they are doing, even then they do not go beyond the limit of the service which they owe to God.

So as not to use to the full my right in the gospel. It is clear from this that taking advantage of our freedom so as to create a stumbling-block is irresponsible licence and a misuse of freedom. Therefore we must stick to the rule not to give any cause for offence. And this verse emphasizes what I have mentioned above, that Paul did not go beyond the requirements imposed by the nature of his office, because the freedom which God granted him should not have been abused in any way.

19-20. *For though I was free from all.* ἐκ πάντων, i.e. *from all*, can be taken either in the neuter or masculine; in the neuter referring to things, and in the masculine to persons. I prefer the masculine.

So far Paul had shown only in one particular instance how careful he had been to adapt himself to the weak. Now he adds a general closing statement, following it with particular examples. The general statement is that since nobody had authority over him, he yet lived as if everybody had power over him; and he voluntarily makes himself subject to the weak, to whom he was not bound in any way. The particular instances are that among the Gentiles he was like a Gentile, and among the Jews he behaved like a Jew. In other words, since he was careful about observing the religious ceremonies of the Jews, when he lived among the Jews, he was just as concerned not to upset the Gentiles by his keeping them.

He uses the word *as* to bring out that what he did, did not mean that he had less freedom, for no matter how he might accommodate himself to men, yet in God's eyes he still remained the same within himself. 'To become all things' means to adopt every sort of attitude as the situation demands, or to assume different roles in accordance with the way people differ. When he says that he became without the law and under the law, we must realize that he is referring only to the ceremonial law, for the moral law was common to both Gentiles and Jews; and Paul would not have been allowed to gratify men as far as it was concerned. For this principle only applies to neutral things, as we said before.

21. *Not being without law to God.* By this parenthesis he wishes to modify the harshness of the expression; for it might be harsh at first to hear that he had become 'without law'. Therefore, so that the wrong meaning might not be drawn from it, he adds, by way of correction, that he has always kept in mind one law, that he was subject *to Christ.* He also hints, in this addition, that bad feeling was being stirred up against him, wrongly and undeservedly, because he seemed to be inviting men to lead lives of unrestrained licence, in teaching exemption

from slavery to the Law of Moses. He describes it explicitly as indeed 'the Law of Christ', in order to eradicate the undeserved reproach with which the false apostles were branding the Gospel; for he is pointing out that everything which makes for a perfect law for right living is included in the teaching of Christ.

22. *To the weak I became as weak.* Here Paul makes another general statement, in which he describes the kind of men to whom he adapted himself, and for what purpose. He adopted the Jewish way of life in the company of Jews, but not before all of them; for many of them were obstinate, and under the influence of Pharisaism, pride, or ill-will they would have liked to see Christian freedom suppressed altogether. Paul would never have deferred to the same extent to people like that, for Christ does not want us to trouble ourselves about them. Our Lord says 'Let them alone, they are blind, and leaders of the blind' (Matt. 15.14). Therefore we must adapt ourselves to the weak, but not to the stubborn. His purpose was to bring them to Christ, not to further his own interests, or to retain their goodwill.

To these two points a third must be added, that except in regard to neutral things, which otherwise fall within our freedom, he did not act out of deference to the weak.

Now, if we consider how great a man Paul was, in condescending to such an extent, have we not cause to be ashamed, we who are next to nothing in comparison with him, if we are so absorbed in ourselves that we look down our noses at the weak, and do not deign to give way to them in anything? But, seeing it is right for us to put the apostle's command into action, and adapt ourselves to the weak, and to do so in connexion with neutral things, and out of consideration for the upbuilding of the weak, on the other hand; those people are in the wrong, whose main concern is to keep their lives free from trouble, and who, for that reason, take care not to give offence to people, to the wicked that is, rather than to the weak. Moreover, those who do not distinguish between things which are neutral, and things which are forbidden, are doubly in the wrong. Because they do not make that distinction they have no hesitation about undertaking things, which God has forbidden, in order to please men. But their crowning sin is their making wrong use of this sentence of Paul's, in order to make excuses for their own wicked hypocrisy. However, if anyone remembers these three points, which I have touched on briefly, he will be ready to refute those people.

We must also pay attention to the phrase which Paul uses at the close. For he shows that in trying to win everybody, he was aiming at their salvation. However, he ends, here, by modifying the general statement (unless you prefer the reading of the Vulgate, 'that I may save all', which is also found to this day in some Greek manuscripts); for in this passage he even retracts, 'that I may by all means save *some*'. But because the consideration for others, which Paul speaks about, is sometimes thrown away, so far as results are concerned, this modification is very suitable: viz. although he might not be of service to everybody, he had, nevertheless, not given up his concern for the welfare of at least a few.

And I do all things for the gospel's sake, that I may be a joint partaker thereof. Know ye not that they which run in a race run all, but one receiveth the prize? Even so run, that ye may attain. And every man that striveth in the games is temperate in all things. Now they do it to receive a corruptible crown; but we an incorruptible. I therefore so run, as not uncertainly; so fight I, as not beating the air: but I buffet my body, and bring it into bondage: lest by any means, after that I have preached to others, I myself should be rejected. (23–27)

23. *That I may be a joint partaker thereof.* Since the Corinthians might get it into their heads that what Paul did was something that applied to him alone, because of the office he held, he argues, in light of what the Gospel is aiming at, that all Christians share in this. For when he declares that he desired to 'become a sharer in the Gospel', he is hinting that those who do not do as he does are not fit for the fellowship of the Gospel. To become a partaker of the Gospel, is to receive its fruit.

24. *Know ye not that they which run in a race.* He has finished what he wanted to teach. Now, in order to impress it on the minds of the Corinthians, he adds an exhortation. In short, he says that what they had attained so far is nothing, unless they keep steadily on; because it is not enough that they once started off on the way of the Lord, if they do not make an effort to reach the goal. This corresponds to the word of Christ in Matt. 10.22: 'He that endureth to the end, the same shall be saved.'

And indeed he borrows a simile from the race-track. For just as many indeed go down into the arena, but only the man who reaches the goal first receives the crown, so anyone who has once set out on the race to which the Gospel summons us, has no reason for being pleased with himself, unless he keeps going on until death. But our struggle is not like theirs in this way: in their race only one man, the man who has outstripped all the others, is the winner, and obtains the prize; in our case, on the other hand, it is better than that, for many people may receive the crown at once. For all that God demands of us is that we keep pressing strenuously on all the way to the goal. So one person does not get in the way of another, but, on the contrary, those who run in the Christian race, do all they can to help each other.

Paul puts the same idea in a different way in II Tim. 2.5: 'An athlete is not crowned unless he competes according to the rules'.

So run. Here we have the application of the comparison. It is not enough that we have made a start, if we do not continue to 'run' all through our life. For our life is like the race-track. Therefore it will not do for us to grow tired after a little while, for example half-way, for nothing else but death marks the end of the race.

The particle *so* (οὕτω) can be taken in two ways. Chrysostom joins it to what goes before, as follows: 'As those runners do not stop running until they reach the goal, you must persevere, and must not stop running as long as you live.' But it will go quite well with what follows, as if Paul said: 'You must run, not in such a way that you fall out in the middle of the race, but in such a way that you obtain the prize.'

I have nothing to say about the word *stadium* (race-track) and about the different kinds of races, because information about them can be found in the lexicons; and it is common knowledge that some races were on horseback and others on foot. Further, there is not much need for these things in order to understand what Paul means.

25. *And every man that striveth in the games.* In view of the fact that he had been encouraging them to persevere, he had still to make it clear how they should persevere. He now does so by using the simile of boxers, not indeed in a thorough-going way, but only in so far as the problem with which he is dealing demanded, viz. the problem of how far they ought to give in to the weakness of their brothers. Paul confines himself to that. But he argues from less to greater, saying that we should be ashamed of ourselves if we are reluctant about giving up our right, when boxers eating a special food of their own, and little of it at that, certainly not to the point of over-eating, are willing to give up delicacies of every kind, so that they might be all the fitter for the fight. And they do this for the sake of a corruptible crown. But if they think so highly of a wreath of leaves, which withers almost at once, should we not put all the greater value on an everlasting crown? Do not let us make any difficulties, therefore, about giving up something of our right. It is so well known that athletes were content with the most frugal diet, that their way of life has become proverbial.

26. *I therefore so run.* Paul comes back to himself, so that, by pointing to his own example, he can give more weight to his teaching. Some think that what he says here refers to the full assurance of hope, as though he said: 'I do not run in vain, and I am not running the risk of being made a fool of, in so far as my work is concerned, because I have the promise of the Lord, and that never fails.' But I am inclined to think that he wishes to direct believers on their way, right to their

destination, so that they may not wander in uncertainty. He might have put it in this way: 'The Lord keeps us occupied here with "running" and "fighting", but He sets a goal before us at which we ought to aim; and He lays down reliable rules for "boxing", so that we may not tire ourselves out to no purpose.' For he combines both of the comparisons which he had used. He says, 'I know where I am running to, and I am anxious like an experienced prize-fighter not to miss my blow.' These things ought to stir the heart of a Christian, and give him encouragement to enter with greater enthusiasm into all the duties of the Christian faith; for it is a great thing not to be wandering about in diversions, which get one nowhere.

27. *But I buffet my body.* 'I bring my body under.' Budaeus reads: 'I keep a watchful eye on.' But I think that here the apostle uses the verb ὑπωπιάζειν in the sense 'to keep at work like a slave'. For he is telling us that he is not self-indulgent, but represses his desires. That cannot be done unless one gains the upper hand over the body, and keeps its desires under control, so that, like a wild and unbroken horse, it grows accustomed to obeying. The monks of long ago, wanting to comply with this direction, thought out many disciplinary exercises; for they used to sleep on benches; they forced themselves to keep unduly long night vigils; and, in their way of life, kept clear of all luxuries. But they missed the main point, and did not grasp the reason why the apostle tells us to do this, because they had another precept in mind, 'Make no provision for the flesh, to gratify its desires' (Rom. 13.14). For what Paul says in I Tim. 4.8 always holds good: that 'bodily exercise is profitable for little'. But let us treat our body as if it were a slave, so that it may not keep us back from the duties of religion by its lustfulness; and, let us do so for another reason, so that we may not cause trouble for, or offence to, others, by giving in to it.

That when I have preached to others. Some explain these words in this way: 'So that, having taught others faithfully and well, I may not incur the condemnation of God by leading an evil life.' But it will read better to take this phrase as referring to his relation with others, in this way: 'My life ought to provide some sort of example to others. Therefore I take pains to live in such a way that my character and conduct do not conflict with what I teach, and that I may not, therefore, neglect the very things which I demand of others, so involving myself in great disgrace and causing serious offence to my brothers.' The phrase can also be taken along with what he said in a preceding statement to this effect: lest I am defrauded of the Gospel, in which others come to share through my work.

CHAPTER TEN

For I would not, brethren, have you ignorant, how that our fathers were all under the cloud, and all passed through the sea; and were all baptized unto Moses in the cloud and in the sea; and did all eat the same spiritual meat; and did all drink the same spiritual drink: for they drank of a spiritual rock that followed them: and the rock was Christ. Howbeit with most of them God was not well pleased: for they were overthrown in the wilderness. (1-5)

Paul now uses examples in support of what he had been teaching by his twofold comparison. The Corinthians were doing just as they liked, and were boasting, as if they were veterans already, or at least had completed their course, when in fact they had hardly left the start-line. Paul describes this groundless exultation and confidence in this way: since I see that you are quite content to mark time on the very starting-point and not move on, I would not have you ignorant about what happened to the Israelites for doing the same thing, so that their example may make you wake up. When examples are used, any difference tends to destroy the force of the comparison; therefore Paul says, first of all, that there is no point of difference between the Israelites and us, which would put our whole situation in a different category from theirs. Therefore, because he intended to threaten the Corinthians with the same vengeance which befell the Israelites, he begins like this: do not take pride in some special privilege, as if your standing with God is better than theirs was. For they had the same benefits which we enjoy today. The Church of God was in their midst, as in ours today. They had the same sacraments, to be testimonies to them of the grace of God. But when they abused their gifts, they did not escape the judgement of God. Therefore, you should be afraid, because the same thing threatens you. Jude uses the same argument in his letter.

1. *They were all under the cloud.* The apostle intends to show that the Israelites were the people of God, just as much as we are, so that we may realize that we will not escape with impunity from the hand of God, which punished them so severely. For the point is this: if God did not spare them, He will not spare us, for our situation is the same as theirs. Paul proves this similarity from the fact that they had been furnished with the same signs of the grace of God. For the sacraments are tokens by which the Church of God is discerned. Paul deals first

with baptism, and he teaches that the cloud, which protected the Israelites from the heat of the sun in the desert, and directed them on their line of march, as well as their crossing of the sea, was indeed like baptism in their case. He says that in the manna and the water flowing out of the rock, there was a sacrament, which corresponded to the Holy Supper.

He says: they *were baptized into Moses*, in other words, under the ministry or leadership of Moses. For I take the preposition εἰς to have been adopted here in place of ἐν, because without a doubt we are baptized 'in the name of Christ', and not of any man at all, as Paul said in chapter 1.13. There are two reasons for that. The first reason is that in baptism we are initiated into the teaching of Christ alone, and the other is that only His name is invoked, since baptism rests solely upon His power. Therefore they were baptised 'in Moses', i.e. under his guidance and ministry, as I have already said. How? 'In the cloud and in the sea.' 'Therefore', someone will say, 'they were baptized twice.' To that I reply that two signs are referred to, but they effect one baptism, corresponding to ours.

But a more difficult question arises. For there is no doubt that these gifts, about which Paul tells us, produced temporal benefits. For the cloud sheltered them from the heat of the sun, and showed them their way, and these are physical benefits, concerned with this present life. In the same way the crossing of the sea meant their escape from the cruelty of Pharaoh and their deliverance from the immediate danger of death. But the benefit of our baptism is spiritual. Why then does Paul make sacraments out of earthly benefits, and seek some spiritual mystery in them? I answer that Paul had good cause for seeking something more than physical advantages in miracles of that sort. For even if God was willing to give help to His people relating to life in this world, His main purpose however was to bear witness to Himself, and reveal Himself, as their God, and eternal salvation is included under that.

Throughout the Scriptures the cloud is called the sign of His presence. Therefore when He declared, by the cloud, that He was present with them, as His own chosen people, there is no doubt that they had, in the cloud, not only an earthly blessing, but also a token of spiritual life. Thus the cloud had a double purpose; and it was the same with the crossing of the sea. For the way was opened up for them through the middle of the sea, so that they escaped from the hand of Pharaoh; but the only reason for that was the fact that the Lord, having once taken them under His care and protection, was determined to guard them in every way. Therefore they concluded from this that they were the objects of God's care, and that He was concerned about their salvation.

That is also why the Passover, which was instituted to keep the remembrance of their deliverance, was, nevertheless, at the same time, a sacrament of Christ. How is that so? Because God had shown Himself as their Saviour in something that was a benefit for them in this world. Anyone who will give proper attention to these things will find nothing absurd in what Paul says. More than that, he will see, both in spiritual substance and visible form, the closest agreement between the baptism of the Jews and ours.

Somebody makes the further objection, however, that not a word is said about all this in the Scriptures. I admit as much, but there is no doubt that, acting by His Spirit, God made good the lack of explicit reference. For example, we find that in the case of the brazen serpent, Christ Himself bears witness to the fact that it was a spiritual sacrament (John 3.14). Yet we do not find any mention of that aspect of it. But, in His own way, the Lord revealed the secret, which would otherwise have been unknown, to the believers of that time.

3. *The same spiritual meat.* Paul now mentions the other sacrament, which corresponds to the most Holy Supper of the Lord. He says: 'The manna and the water which flowed out of the rock, were not only of value as food for the body, but also as spiritual nourishment for the soul.' It is certainly true that both provided sustenance for the body, but that did not prevent them from serving another purpose as well. Therefore when the Lord met the needs of the body in this world, He provided for the eternal welfare of souls at the same time. These two aspects are easily reconciled, were it not for the difficulty raised by the words of Christ in John 6.31 ff, where he treats manna as corruptible food for our stomachs, and contrasts it with the true food of the soul. His words seem to differ a good deal from what Paul says here. This problem can be easily solved. When the writers of Scripture are dealing with the sacraments, or other things for that matter, sometimes their method is to be guided in what they say by the capacity of the people, with whom they are dealing. For example, Paul does not always speak about circumcision in the same way. When he examines it from the point of view of its being an institution of God, he says that it was 'a seal of the righteousness of faith'. On the other hand when he is contending with those who were boasting in the mere outward sign, and were wrongly putting their trust in it for salvation, he says that it is the sign of being under a curse, because by it men put themselves under obligation to keep the whole law. He is dealing only with what the false apostles thought about it, for he is not concerned to argue against the unadulterated institution of God, but against their perversion of the truth. Thus, when the carnal crowd preferred Moses to Christ, because he had fed the people in the desert for forty years,

and they thought of the manna only as food for the stomach, not looking for anything else indeed, Christ, in His reply to them, does not explain the significance of manna, but, ignoring everything else, makes what He has to say suit the minds of His listeners. He might have put it this way: 'You think very highly of Moses, to the point of wonder indeed, as a most outstanding prophet, because he filled the stomachs of your fathers in the desert. For you have this one objection against me, I count for nothing in your eyes because I do not supply you with an abundance of food for your stomachs. But if you consider corruptible food so valuable, what are you to think about bread which gives life, and nourishes our souls unto eternal life?' We see, therefore, that in that passage the Lord is not influenced in what He says by the nature of the manna, but rather by the understanding of His hearers. On the other hand Paul is dealing here with the ordinance of God, and not with the way unbelievers abuse it.

Further, when Paul says that the *fathers ate the same spiritual meat*, he first of all gives a hint of what the power and efficacy of the sacrament is; and secondly he shows that the old sacraments of the law had the same power as ours have today. For if manna was spiritual food, it follows that bare forms (*figuras nudas*) are not exhibited to us in the sacraments, but the reality figured is truly given at the same time (*rem figuratam simul vere dari*). For God is not so deceitful as to nourish us on empty appearances (*figmentis*). A sign (*signum*) is indeed a sign, and retains its own substance (*substantiam*). But just as the Papists, on the one hand, are ridiculously dreaming of some sort of transformations, so, on the other hand, we have no right to separate the reality and the figure (*veritatem et figuram*) which God has joined together. The Papists confound the reality and the sign (*rem et signum*); unbelievers such as Schwenkfeld and men like him separate the signs from the realities (*signa a rebus*). Let us preserve a middle position, that is, let us keep the union made by the Lord, but at the same time the distinction between them, so that we do not, in error, transfer what belongs to one to the other.

We have still to deal with the second point about the resemblance between the old signs and ours. It is a well-known dogma of the Schoolmen that 'the sacraments of the old Law merely figured (*figurasse*) grace, but that ours confer it (*conferre*)'. This passage is most suitable for refuting that error. For it proves that the reality of the sacrament (*rem sacramenti exhibitam*) was conveyed to the people of old just as much as to us. It is therefore wicked of the men of the Sorbonne to suppose that the holy fathers had the signs without the reality under the Law. I am quite ready to agree that the efficacy of the signs is at once richer and more abundant for us since the incarnation of Christ than it was for the fathers under the Law. So the difference between us and them is only one of degree, or, as the common saying goes, one of 'more or less', because what they had in small measure, we have more fully (*plenius*). But it is not the case that they had mere figures while we obtain the reality.

Some people explain these words as if the Israelites together ate the same bread among themselves, and they do not mean that they are to be compared with us. But these people do not pay attention to Paul's intention. For what he is driving at here is just this, that the ancient people were provided with the same benefits as we are, and shared in the same sacraments, so that we may not imagine that, by trusting in some special privilege, we will be exempt from the punishment which they had to undergo. However, I do not want to quarrel with anyone about this; I am simply stating my own point of view. Nevertheless I am well aware of the attractive case presented by those who take the opposite explanation, viz. that it agrees very well with the simile which had just been used; that the same race-track was laid out for all the Israelites; they all set out from the same starting-point; they all proceeded along the same course; they all shared in the same hope, but many of them were debarred from the prize. Yet when I examine everything closely, I am not induced by these reasons to give up my point of view, for the apostle has good reason for mentioning two sacraments only, and baptism in particular. Why did he do this but to contrast them with us? Certainly if he had kept his comparison within the limits of the body of the Israelites, he would have cited circumcision and other better known and more important sacraments instead. But he preferred to take those which were not so well-known, because they were more effective for bringing out the contrast between us and them. Otherwise the lesson which he adds would not be very apposite, viz. 'all these things happened to them to be an example (*in figuram*) to us, because we see the judgements of God that fell on them, and also threaten us, if we get involved in similar sins'.

4. *And the rock was Christ.* Some people are stupid enough to distort these words of Paul, as if he said that Christ was the spiritual rock, and as if he had nothing to say about that rock which was a visible symbol; for we know quite well that Paul is dealing with outward signs. Their objection, that the rock is actually described as spiritual, is a trifling one, because this epithet is only applied to it so that we may know that it was the symbol of a spiritual mystery. All the same, there is no doubt that Paul compares our sacraments with those of the Israelites.

Their second objection is more foolish and childish. They ask: 'How could a rock, which remained fixed in one spot, *follow* the Israelites?' They ask that, as if it were not as clear as can be, that the word rock denotes the stream of water, which never failed the people. For Paul is praising the grace of God, because He commanded the water, which was brought out of the rock, to flow along wherever the people journeyed, as if the rock itself accompanied them. Now, if Paul meant that Christ is the spiritual foundation of the Church, why did he use the past tense of the verb *was*? It is quite clear that he is referring to something which only affected the fathers. Let us hear no more, then, about this silly fiction, which gives a chance to quarrelsome men to show how impudent they are, rather than allow sacramental forms of speaking.

I have already said that in the old sacraments the reality was united with the signs and conveyed to the people. Therefore, since they were figures (*figurae*) of Christ, it follows that Christ was tied to them, not locally indeed, and not in a union of nature or substance, but sacramentally. That is why the apostle says that the rock was Christ, for metonymy is very commonly used when speaking about the sacraments. Therefore the name of the reality is transferred to the sign here, because it applies to it, not properly, but figuratively, because of that union about which I have already spoken. But since this will be dealt with more fully in chapter eleven, I am making only a slight reference to it here.

There is still another question. Since we now eat the body and drink the blood of Christ, how were the Jews partakers of the same spiritual meat and drink, when the flesh of Christ was not yet in existence for them to eat? To that I reply that although the flesh did not yet exist, it was food for them all the same. And that is not a piece of useless sophistry; for their salvation depended on the benefit of the death and resurrection, and for that reason on the flesh and blood, of Christ. Therefore it was necessary for them to receive the flesh and blood of Christ, so that they might share in the blessing of redemption. The receiving of it was the secret work of the Holy Spirit, who was active in such a way that the flesh of Christ, even if it was not yet created, might be efficacious in them. He means, however, that they ate in their own way, which was different from ours, and, as I have said already, that Christ is now conveyed to us more fully, because of the greater degree of revelation. For in our day the eating is substantial (*substantialis est manducatio*), something which was not yet possible in their time. In other words, Christ feeds us with His flesh, which was sacrificed for us, and which was appointed to be our food, and from this we draw our life.

5. *But many of them were not pleasing to God.* We now see the reason for the apostle beginning as he does, viz. so that we may not assume that we are in any way worthier than, or superior to them, but that

we may walk in humility and fear. For that is the only way to make sure that the light of truth and such a wealth of gracious favours have not been thrown away, as far as we are concerned. Paul says: 'God had chosen all of them as His people, but many of them fell from grace. Let us be on our guard, therefore, so that the same thing does not happen to us, when examples like theirs are there to warn us; for when God punished them so severely, He will not let us go unpunished for doing the same thing.'

Another objection is raised here. If it is true that hypocrites and ungodly men ate the spiritual food at that time, do unbelievers in our day receive the reality itself in the sacraments? Some are afraid that the unbelief of men might appear to take away from the truth of God, and so they teach that the reality is obtained by the ungodly along with the sign. But their fear is quite groundless, for the Lord offers what the sign represents (*figurat*) to worthy and unworthy alike, but everyone is not capable of enjoying it. At the same time the nature of the sacrament is not changed, nor is any of its efficacy lost. In the same way the manna, so far as God was concerned, was *spiritual* food even to unbelievers, but, because unbelievers had mouths that were purely *carnal*, they did not eat what was given to them. I postpone fuller treatment of this question to chapter 11.

For they were overthrown. Evidence is produced by way of proof that they did not please God, for God, in His wrath, dealt with them severely, and punished them for their ingratitude. Some take this as referring to the whole of the people, who perished in the desert, with the exception of two only, Caleb and Joshua. But I take the view however that he simply means those whom he is about to mention in their different categories.

> *Now these things were our examples, to the intent we should not lust after evil things, as they also lusted. Neither be ye idolaters, as were some of them; as it is written, The people sat down to eat and drink, and rose up to play. Neither let us commit fornication, as some of them committed, and fell in one day three and twenty thousand. Neither let us tempt the Lord, as some of them tempted, and perished by the serpents. Neither murmur ye, as some of them murmured, and perished by the destroyer. Now these things happened unto them by way of example; and they were written for our admonition, upon whom the ends of the ages are come. Wherefore let him that thinketh he standeth take heed lest he fall. (6-12)*

6. *Now these things were our examples.* He warns us in still clearer terms that the punishments, which were inflicted on them, provide a relevant lesson for us, so that we may not provoke the wrath of God

as they did. Paul says: 'In the way He punished them, God, as it were, presented us with a clear picture (*in tabula*) of His severity, so that we may take it to heart, and learn to fear.'

I shall be saying something about the word 'example' (*typus*) soon. In the meantime I would just like to point out to my readers that I have not departed from the readings of both the Vulgate and Erasmus (*in figura*) without due thought. For they obscure, or at least do not bring out clearly, Paul's meaning that in His dealings with that people, God has given us a picture which should teach us a lesson.

To the intent we should not lust after evil things. He now gives certain instances, or, better, definite examples, so that they may give him a chance to condemn a number of sins, which it was only right to bring forcibly to the notice of the Corinthians.

I think that the incident referred to here is that recounted in Numbers 11.4, even if others connect it with what we find in Numbers 26.64. When the people had been living on manna for some time, they finally took a dislike to it, and they began to long for other kinds of food, such as they had been accustomed to having in Egypt. Now, they were sinning in two ways; in rejecting something which was God's special gift; and in longing, open-mouthed, for a variety of foods and delicacies, contrary to the will of God. This greediness offended the Lord, and He inflicted on the people a severe plague. As a result the place was called 'the graves of lust' (Kibroth-hattaavah) because *they buried there* those who had been struck down by the Lord. By this example the Lord has revealed how much He hates those desires which spring from dislike of His gifts, and from our greed; for anything that goes beyond the limit imposed by God is rightly considered evil and unlawful.

7. *Neither be ye idolaters.* Paul is alluding to the story recorded in Exodus 32.7 ff. For when Moses delayed on the mountain longer than the inconsiderate people could endure in their fickleness, Aaron was forced to make a molten calf, and set it up for worship. It was not that the people wanted to change their God, but to have some visible sign of the presence of God, and this was in line with their carnal mind. In punishing them very severely at that time for this idolatry, God made it plain how greatly abhorrent idolatry is to Him.

As it is written, The people sat down etc. Few people give the proper explanation of this passage, for they think that it was a case of intemperance leading to lasciviousness; as the well-known saying has it, 'Dancing comes after a well-filled stomach.'[1]

But Moses is speaking about a sacred feast, one they were keeping in honour of the idol. Therefore the feasting and the playing were both

---

[1] French: 'après la panse, la danse'.

aspects of the idolatry. For it was as much the practice of God's people, as of those who were devoted to false gods, to combine feasting with the sacrifice, as part of their divine worship; and no unclean or worldly person was allowed to be present at this. The Gentiles also appointed sacred games in honour of their idols; and there is little doubt that on this occasion the Israelites were following their example in worshipping their calf. For men are so presumptuous by nature that, without any justification, they make God such that He will favour whatever they do. Therefore the Gentiles have become so foolish as to believe that their gods are pleased with, for example, the most unseemly spectacles, immodest dances, filthy language, and immorality of all sorts. So, following their example, the people of Israel carried through their religious feast, and then proceeded to keep the games, so that nothing might be omitted from the worship of their idol. This straightforward meaning is the true one.

But at this point the question is asked: Why does the apostle mention the feast and the games rather than the worship, for after all that is the central thing in idolatry, while the other two are only accessory features? Doubtless the apostle chose to deal with what suited the situation of the Corinthians best. For it is not likely that they were in the habit of attending the gatherings of unbelievers in order to prostrate themselves before the idols, but they used to share in the feasts, which the unbelievers held in honour of their gods, and did not keep away from the debased rites which were the marks of idolatry. Therefore it is not without good reason that the apostle declares that the way in which they are sinning is expressly condemned by God. In short, he means that we cannot have contact with any feature of idolatry, without being made unclean, and those who defile themselves by dealing with things which are the outward marks of idolatry will not escape punishment from the hand of God.

8. *Neither let us commit fornication.* Paul now turns to fornication. From historical records it is clear that the Corinthians indulged in this freely, and it is easy for us to gather from earlier chapters, that those who had given their allegiance to Christ were not yet free from this vice by any means. The punishment for this sin ought to make us afraid, and remind us how much God hates filthy and lustful passions, for in one day twenty-three thousand, or, according to Moses, twenty-four thousand, of them perished. But although they differ about the numbers, it is easy to reconcile their statements. For it is not unheard of, when there is no intention of making an exact count of individuals, to give an approximate number. For example, there were those whom the Romans called the *Centumviri*, The Hundred, when, in fact there were one hundred and two of them. Therefore, since about twenty-

four thousand were destroyed by the hand of the Lord, in other words, over twenty-three thousand, Moses gives the upper limit, Paul the lower, and so there is really no discrepancy. This story is to be found in Numbers 25.9.

There is one difficulty here, however. Why does Paul say that this slaughter was due to fornication, when Moses tells us that the wrath of God was roused because the people had allowed themselves to be initiated in the rites of Baal-peor? But the defection began with fornication; and the children of Israel had fallen into that disobedience, not so much because they were influenced by any devotion they had to the false religion, but rather because they were captivated by the blandishments of prostitutes. Therefore whatever resulted from the defection ought to be attributed to fornication. For Balaam had advised the Midianites to give their daughters as prostitutes to the Israelites, with the object of alienating them from the true worship of God. More than that, such great blindness as theirs, in allowing themselves to be led into disobedience by the alluring ways of prostitutes, was a punishment for their lust. Let us learn, therefore, that fornication is not a trivial sin, seeing that on that occasion God dealt with it so harshly and indeed in more ways than one.

9. *Neither let us tempt Christ.* This sentence refers to the story recorded in Numbers 21.6. For, when the people had grown tired of the length of time, they began to complain about their lot, and to speak against God, saying, 'Why has God made fools of us' etc. Paul describes this grumbling of the people as 'tempting' (*tentationem*) and not without justification, for 'tempting' is incompatible with endurance. The only reason why the people were rebelling against God at that time was that they were urged on by an overwhelming desire, and could not wait until the coming of the time appointed by the Lord. Let us take note, therefore, that the root of this evil, about which Paul warns us here, is the impatience which reveals itself when we want to anticipate God and do not put ourselves under His direction, but, on the contrary, expect Him to fall in with our decisions and demands. God punished the Israelites severely for this presumption. But He always remains the same—a righteous Judge. Therefore, unless we want to suffer the same punishment, do not let us put Him to the test.

This verse bears remarkable witness to the eternity of Christ. Erasmus' evasion carries no weight: 'let us not tempt Christ, as some of them tempted God', for it is forcing it too much to supply the name of God. It is not at all strange that Christ is called the Leader of the Israelites; for, just as God has never shown His graciousness to His people except through Him as Mediator, in the same way He has conferred no benefit except at His hand. Again, the angel who first appeared to Moses and then was always with the people on their journey is often called Jahweh (יהוה). We should conclude, then, that that angel was the Son of God, and that even then He was already the Guide of the Church, of which He was the Head.

Because the designation *Christ* has a meaning that is appropriate to His human nature, it could not yet be applied to the Son of God at that time; but it is given to Him here through communication of properties just as we read elsewhere that 'the Son of Man came from heaven' (John 3.13).

10. *Neither murmur ye.* Others think this refers to the grumbling which arose, when the twelve men who had been sent to spy out the land returned and shook the resolution of the people. But since that complaint was not immediately punished by some particular scourge from the Lord, the only punishment that was inflicted being the exclusion of them all from the possession of the land, this verse must be explained in some other way. It was certainly a very severe punishment to be denied entry to the land, but, in saying that they were killed by the destroyer, Paul means some other kind of retribution, obviously enough.

I therefore refer to the story which we have in Numbers 16. When God had punished the pride of Korah and Abiram, the people raised a tumult against Moses and Aaron, as if they were to blame for the plague which the Lord inflicted. God punished this uproar of the people with fire from heaven, which devoured more than fourteen thousand of them. So this provides a clear and memorable proof of the wrath of God operating against rebels and trouble-makers who raise their voices against Himself.

Of course they were complaining about Moses; but, since they had no grounds for insulting him, and the only reason they had for burning with anger against him was that he had faithfully carried out the task which God had laid upon him, they were in reality making an attack upon God by grumbling as they did. Let us then remember that it is God with whom we have to deal, not men, if we set ourselves against the faithful ministers of God. Let us also realize that this presumption will not go unpunished.

By the 'destroyer' should be understood the angel who carried out the judgement of God. Now, He sometimes uses the services of bad angels, sometimes of good, to punish men, as different passages of Scripture make clear. Since Paul makes no distinction between them here, the reader may take it as referring to whichever he likes.

11. *Now all these things happened as types.* He again repeats that all these things happened to the Israelites so that they may be 'types' to us, in other words examples by which God sets His judgements before our

eyes. I know very well that others make more ingenious theories about these words, but I think that I have grasped what was in the apostle's mind when I say that these examples bring home to us, as if they were pictures painted by an artist, what sort of judgement threatens idolaters, fornicators, and others who despise God; for these are living pictures revealing God to us in His anger with sins like those. This explanation, as well as being simple and realistic, also has the advantage of silencing certain madmen, who distort this passage in order to prove that the only things ever done among that ancient people were things which foreshadowed what was to come. They first of all take it for granted that that people prefigure (*esse figuram*) the Church. From that they conclude that all that God promised them or gave them, whether benefits or punishments, only prefigured what had to be brought to full reality with the coming of Christ. This is a most damaging piece of nonsense, because it does serious injury to the holy fathers, and still more serious injury to God. For those people foreshadowed the Christian Church in such a way that they were at the same time a genuine Church. Their circumstances so delineated ours that the essential features of a Church were nonetheless already present in those days. The promises given to it adumbrated the Gospel in such a way that it was included in them. Their sacraments served to prefigure ours but in such a way that they were still true sacraments with an efficacy applying to their day as well. To sum up, those who made a proper use of the Word (*doctrina*) and sacraments (*signis*) in those days were endowed with the same Spirit of faith as we are. These words of Paul, then, give no support to those fools, for these words do not mean that the events of that age were 'types' in the sense that they had no real significance for that time, but were a kind of empty show. But on the contrary, as I have explained, they plainly teach us that there, as in pictures, plain for us to see, are things which should be a warning to us.

And they were written for our admonition. This second clause draws out the first. For the fact that these things were committed to writing was no advantage to the Israelites, but only to us. However it does not follow from that that those retributions were not real punishments of God, which effectively disciplined them at that time; but God not only put His judgements into effect at that time, but also intended that there should be a perpetual record of them for our admonition. For what use would the account of them be to the dead? And what use would it be to the living, if they did not take warning from the examples of the other people, and come to their senses? But Paul takes for granted the principle, about which all believers should be in agreement, that nothing is recorded in the Scriptures, which is not to our advantage to know.

Upon whom the ends of the ages are come. The word *ends* (τέλη) some-times means *mysteries,* and perhaps that meaning would suit quite well in this verse. However I follow the accepted interpretation, for it is more straightforward.

Paul says, then, that the ends (*terminos*) of all the ages have come upon us, since the fullness of all things is congruous with this present age, seeing that we are already in the last times. For the Kingdom of Christ is the special goal to which the Law and all the Prophets look. Besides, this sentence of Paul's conflicts with the popular idea that God was more unyielding under the Old Covenant, and was always equipped and ready to punish offences, but that now He has begun to be easy to move, and much more willing to excuse us. And, in similar vein, they make out that we are under the law of grace, because we have a God who is much more easily appeased than the men of old found Him. But what is Paul actually saying? If God inflicted punishments on them, no more will He let us off with anything. No more, then, of the mistaken view, that God is now more lax about punishing sins! Indeed we must acknowledge that the goodness of God has been poured out on men much more gloriously and richly with the coming of Christ, but what bearing has that on letting sinners off with impunity, the very people who take undue advantage of His grace?

Only this point must be noted: that there is a different kind of punishment today, because, as God rewarded the faithful of long ago more with material blessings, in order to make His fatherly love plain to them, so He demonstrated His wrath more by physical punishments. On the other hand, in the fuller revelation which we now enjoy, He does not inflict outward punishments so often, and He does not so frequently make use of physical punishment in dealing with the wicked. You will find more about this subject in my *Institutes* (2.10.3).

12. *Wherefore let him that thinketh he standeth.* Paul concluded from the foregoing that we must not pride ourselves in the fact or way that we began, or in our progress, so that we become complacent and do nothing. For the Corinthians were so boastful about their own situa-tion that they forgot how weak they were, and fell into many shameful practices. Theirs was an unwarranted self-confidence, similar to what the prophets were always condemning in the people of Israel. But since the Papists twist this verse in order to establish their ungodly dogma that we must always be in a state of uncertainty so far as faith is concerned, let us take note that there are two kinds of assurance.

The one rests on the promises of God, so that the believer is con-vinced in his heart that God will never leave him, and relying on this unconquerable conviction he stands up to Satan and sin, cheerful and undaunted. At the same time, however, remembering his own weakness, he falls back on God in fear and humility, and in his anxiety willingly commits himself to Him. This kind of assurance is a holy thing, and cannot be separated from faith, as is apparent from many passages of Scripture, especially Romans 8.33.

The other kind of assurance has its roots in nonchalance, when men are bursting with pride because of the gifts they have, and are quite unconcerned about their own situation, but rather acquiesce in it, as if they were beyond the reach of danger; with the result that they are open to all the attacks of Satan. It is this kind of assurance that Paul wants the Corinthians to give up, because he saw that their self-satisfaction rested on a senseless belief. But he does not tell them to be in a state of anxiety and uncertainty about the will of God, or to be afraid that there is doubt about their salvation, in the way the Papists imagine.

To sum up, let us remember that Paul is speaking to men who were swollen-headed because of a misplaced confidence in men, and he is putting a stop to that weakness, which came from depending on men, and not on God. For after he praised the Colossians for their solidity or 'firmness of their faith' (Col. 2.5), he tells them to remain firmly rooted in Christ, and to be 'built up in Him, and established in the faith' (Col. 2.7).

There hath no temptation taken you but such as man can bear: but God is faithful, who will not suffer you to be tempted above that ye are able; but will with the temptation make also the way of escape, that ye may be able to endure it. Wherefore, my beloved, flee from idolatry. I speak as to wise men; judge ye what I say. The cup of blessing which we bless, is it not a communion of the blood of Christ? The bread which we break, is it not a communion of the body of Christ? seeing that we, who are many, are one bread, one body: for we all partake of the one bread. Behold Israel after the flesh: have not they which eat the sacrifices communion with the altar? (13-18)

13. *No temptation has taken you which is not human.* Others can be content with their own interpretations. I myself think that this was written to encourage them, so that, after hearing such dreadful examples of the wrath of God as Paul has just mentioned, they might not be disturbed and alarmed, and so lose heart. Accordingly, so that his exhortation might be to some effect, he adds that there is opportunity for repentance. He might have put it in this way: 'There is no need to despair, and I myself had no intention of giving you cause for losing heart. Indeed what has befallen you is no more than what usually happens to men.' Others are rather inclined to think that he is rebuking their faint-heartedness in giving in when slight temptation attacked them; and there is no doubt that the word *humanus*, translated *human*,

sometimes means 'moderate'. Therefore the meaning, according to them, is: 'Was it right for you to succumb to a slight temptation?' But since it suits the context better if we look upon this verse as consolation, for that reason I am rather inclined to that view.

But God is faithful. Just as he told them to be of good heart so far as the past was concerned, so as to move them to repentance, so he also encourages them with a definite hope for the future, for God 'will not allow them to be tempted beyond their strength'. But he warns them to look to the Lord, because, if we rely on our own resources, temptation, no matter how slight, will get the better of us at once, and it will be all up with us. He calls the Lord faithful. Paul means more than that He is true to His promises. He might have put his meaning in this way: 'The Lord is the proved Protector of His people, and in His keeping you are secure, for never does He leave His people on their own. Therefore, once He has taken you under His own faithfulness (*in suam fidem*), you have no need to be afraid, so long as you depend wholly on Him. For He would certainly be playing us false if He were to withdraw His support at the moment we needed it; or if, when He sees us in our weakness bow down under the load, He were to draw out our struggles (*tentationes*) still further.'

But God helps us in two ways, so that we may not be overwhelmed by temptation: He supplies us with the resources we need, and sets a limit to the temptation. The apostle speaks mostly about the second of these here. He does not ignore the first, however, viz. that God mitigates temptations to prevent their overpowering us by their weight. For He knows how far our ability can go, when He Himself has given it to us, and He adjusts our temptations to that degree of ability. I take the word 'temptation' here in a general way, for everything that is an enticement to us.

14. *Wherefore, my beloved, flee from idolatry.* Paul now returns to the main subject, from which he had digressed for a little, for, fearing that straightforward teaching might leave them cold, he inserted the general exhortations which we have been reading. But he now resumes the argument which he has already begun, viz. that a Christian may not become actively involved in the religious rites of unbelievers. That is why he says: 'Flee from idolatry.'

We must see, first of all, what he means by the word *idolatry*. He certainly did not suspect the Corinthians of being so ignorant or so foolish that he thought that they gave whole-hearted worship to the idols. But since they had no scruple about going frequently to the gatherings of unbelievers, and taking part along with them in certain rites, which were recognized as the way to honour the idols, he condemns this presumption of theirs, because it sets a very bad example.

Therefore when he mentions idolatry here there is no doubt that he is speaking about outward idolatry, or, if you like, the open profession of idol worship. For, just as God is said to be worshipped by kneeling and other signs of reverence, whereas the fundamental and true way to worship Him is in our hearts, so it is in the case of idols, the same principle applying to opposites. There are a great many people wasting their time today in seeking to excuse their outward practices by saying that there is no question of their heart being involved, when Paul in fact condemns those very actions, and quite rightly too! For, in view of the fact that God ought to have not only the inward love of our hearts, but also our outward devotion, the man who gives token outward worship to an idol is to that extent depriving God of His due. The man can protest as much as he likes that his heart is not in it, but he cannot hide the action itself, transferring to an idol the honour which is God's by right.

15. *I speak as to wise men.* Since Paul was going to base his argument on the mystery of the Supper, he uses this little preface to give them some encouragement, so that they might give better attention to the greatness of this mystery. He might have expressed himself in this way: 'I am speaking to no beginners! You are well aware of the power of the Holy Supper, for in it we are ingrafted into the body of the Lord. How shameful of you, then, to enter into the fellowship of unbelievers so as to become united in one body with them!' But he condemns their lack of thought in silence, for after being instructed in the school of Christ, they were stupidly involving themselves in what was sinful—and there was no denying that.

16. *The cup of blessing.* Although the most Holy Supper of Christ has two elements, bread and wine, Paul begins with the second. He calls it 'the cup of blessing', since it was intended to be a mystical blessing (*mysticam eulogiam*). For I do not agree with those who understand 'blessing' (*benedictio*) as 'thanksgiving', and explain the verb 'to bless' in the sense 'to give thanks'. Of course I grant that it is sometimes used with this meaning, but never in the construction which Paul adopts here. Erasmus' introduction of a preposition is very forced. But my own interpretation is easy and straightforward.

Therefore 'blessing the cup' means setting it apart for this one purpose, that it might be for us a sign of the blood of Christ. It becomes that by the Word of promise, when, in accordance with Christ's direction, believers meet together to keep the memorial of His death in this sacrament. On the other hand, in the case of the Papists, consecration is a kind of magic, that has its roots in heathendom, for it has no resemblance to the unadulterated rite which Christians follow. Of course everything that we eat is also sanctified by the Word of God,

as Paul himself tells us in I Tim. 4.5. But in that context the blessing
has a different purpose, viz. so that the use of the gifts of God may be
pure, and may serve the glory of their Giver and our own good. On
the other hand, the object of the 'mystical blessing' in the Supper is that
the wine may no longer be ordinary drink, but be set apart as the
spiritual food of our souls, when it becomes a pledge (tessera) of the
blood of Christ.

Paul says that the cup blessed in this way is κοινωνία, a communion
in the blood of Christ. 'What exactly does that mean?' someone asks.
Keep controversy out of it, and everything will be quite clear! It is
true that believers are bound together by the blood of Christ, so that
they become one Body. It is also true that a unity of that kind is
properly called a κοινωνία or communion. I would also say the same
thing about the bread. Moreover, I am paying attention to what Paul
adds immediately afterwards, as though by way of explanation, that
we 'are all made one body, because we share the same bread together.'
But, I would ask, what is the source of that κοινωνία or communion,
which exists among us, but the fact that we are united to Christ so
that 'we are flesh of His flesh and bone of His bones'? For it is necessary
for us to be incorporated, as it were, into Christ in order to be united
to each other. Besides, Paul is discussing here not a mere human
fellowship (non tantum de mutua inter homines communicatione), but the
spiritual union between Christ and believers (sed de spirituali Christi et
fidelium unione), in order to make it plain from that, that it is an
intolerable sacrilege for them to be contaminated by communion with
idols. Therefore from the context of this verse we can conclude that
κοινωνία or communion of the blood is the alliance (societatem) which we
have with the blood of Christ when He ingrafts all of us into His body,
so that He may live in us, and we in Him.

Now, of course I agree that the reference to the cup as a communion
is a figure of speech, but only so long as the truth which the figure
conveys is not destroyed; in other words, provided that the reality
itself is also present, and the soul receives the communion in the blood,
just as much as the mouth tastes the wine. But the Papists could not
say that the cup of blessing is a communion in the blood of Christ, in
their case, for they observe a mangled and mutilated form of the Supper
—if the name 'Supper' can even be used of that strange ceremony,
which is a mosaic of many human inventions, and retains scarcely the
slightest trace of what our Lord instituted. But even if everything else
conformed to the right use of the Supper, this one thing conflicts with
it, that the cup, which is half of the Sacrament, is denied to all the
people.

The bread which we break. It appears, from this, that in the early

Church it was the custom for each person to break a piece for himself from the one loaf, so that their union in the one body of Christ might be made quite plain to all the believers. It is also clear, from the evidence of men who were eminent in the Church in the three centuries after the apostles, that this practice was kept up for a long time. After that superstition carried the day, with the result that no-one dared touch the bread with his own hands, but the priest put it into his mouth.

17. *Seeing that we are one bread.* I have already pointed out above that it was not Paul's intention here to encourage us to love·one another, but he mentions this, in passing, so that the Corinthians may understand that we must also cultivate that unity, which is ours with Christ, in our public profession, in view of the fact that we all meet together to share the symbol of that sacred unity. In this, the second part of his reference to the Supper, Paul mentions only the other element in the Sacrament, and it is quite usual for Scripture to use synecdoche and describe the whole Supper as 'the breaking of bread'. My readers should take a warning from this, in passing, so that no inexperienced person may be worried by the obnoxious quibble of a few forceful tricksters, to the effect that since Paul mentions bread only, he intended to deprive the people of half the Sacrament.

18. *Behold Israel after the flesh.* Paul uses another example to prove that it is the nature of all religious rites to bind us in some sort of union (*societas*) with God. For the Law of Moses allowed no-one to the sacrificial feast, unless he prepared himself properly; and of course I am speaking not just about priests, but about the people who ate what was left over from the sacrifice. It follows from this that all who eat the flesh of the sacrificed animal share in the altar; i.e. in that sanctification, of which God thought His temple and all the rites carried out there, worthy.

The phrase 'according to the flesh' would appear to be inserted so that the Corinthians may compare the Israelite and Christian rites, and come to think all the more highly of the efficacy of our Supper. He might have put it this way: 'If there was so much power in the old signs (*figuris*), and in those rudiments of early training, we will discover that there is much more in our Supper, in which God reveals Himself much more fully.' However, I think that it is simpler to understand that, in using these words, Paul only meant to distinguish the Jews who were obedient to the Law, from those who had been converted to Christ.

One other contrast had still to be made, viz. if the sacrifices of God sanctify His worshippers, on the other hand the sacrifices offered to idols bring uncleanness. For it is God, and God alone, who sanctifies;

therefore all other gods make unclean. Again, if believers are brought by the mysteries into fellowship and union with God, then unbelievers are admitted by their superstitious practices into the fellowship of their idols. But before dealing with this, the apostle meets by anticipation (*per anthypophoram*) a question which could be raised in objection.

What say I then? that a thing sacrificed to idols is anything, or that an idol is anything? But I say, that the things which the Gentiles sacrifice, they sacrifice to devils, and not to God; and I would not that ye should have communion with devils. Ye cannot drink the cup of the Lord, and the cup of devils: ye cannot partake of the table of the Lord, and of the table of devils. Or do we provoke the Lord to jealousy? are we stronger than he? All things are lawful; but all things are not expedient. All things are lawful; but all things edify not. Let no man seek his own, but each his neighbour's good. (19-24)

19. *What do I say then?* At first glance it might appear that the apostle's argument is not true, or that he is making out that idols have some reality and some power. And exception could easily be taken on these lines: 'What sort of comparison is there between the living God and idols? God brings us into union with Himself by means of the sacraments. Agreed! But how does it come about that idols, which are nothing, are so powerful that they can do the same thing? Or do you think that idols are anything, or can do anything?' Paul replies that he is not thinking about idols in themselves, but rather about the attitude of mind of those who sacrifice to idols. For that was the source of the uncleanness which he had implicitly referred to. Therefore he does acknowledge that an idol is nothing. He also owns that the Gentiles are only deceiving themselves in indulging in solemn rites of dedication, and that God's creatures are not corrupted by such futile things. But because those rites are aiming at something which is full of superstition, and also condemned, and because the whole proceedings are wicked, he comes to the conclusion that all who actively associate themselves with them become polluted.

20. *But the things which the Gentiles sacrifice.* A negative needs to be supplied to help us understand his reply better, in this way: 'I do not say that an idol is anything, nor do I think that it has any power; but I am saying that what the Gentiles do sacrifice they sacrifice to the devil and not to God, and that is why I consider that what they do has its source in a perverse and ungodly superstition. For we must always pay attention to the motive behind anything. Therefore a man who connects himself with them, makes it clear to everyone that he is taking part in the same false religion as they do'. Paul is therefore continuing in the strain in which he had already begun: If it was only

God with whom we had to do, those things would be of no significance, but when we are involved with men they become sinful,
because everyone who sits down at an idol's feast, reveals himself as a
worshipper of the idol.

Some people take *demons* (*daemones*) to mean, in this context, the
imaginary gods of the Gentiles, since the latter usually speak of them
in this way. For when they used the term demons they meant the
lesser gods, such as heroes, and so the word bore a good sense for them.
Plato certainly uses it a great deal for genii or angels. That meaning
however would be quite out of line with what Paul has in mind, for
he means to show what a serious sin it is to take part in any proceedings,
which bear the obvious marks of being the worship of idols. Therefore
what he wanted to do was, not to minimize, but rather to make as
clear as possible, the disregard of God involved in it. How inappro-
priate it would have been, then, to use a term denoting honour to
cover a sin of the highest order! The prophet leaves us without any
doubt (Deut. 32.17) that those things which are sacrificed to idols are
sacrificed to devils (*diabolis*). In that verse from the writings of the
prophet, the Greek version, which was in common use in Paul's day,
has the word 'devils' (δαιμόνια, *daemonia*), and Scripture normally uses
the word in that sense. How much more likely, then, that Paul should
have borrowed his words from the prophet, in order to point out just
how serious the evil was, rather than that, echoing the language of the
heathen, he should have made light of the very thing he wanted to be
regarded with the utmost horror.

But all this might seem to conflict with what I said above that Paul
pays attention to what is in the mind of the idol-worshippers; for it is
not their intention to worship devils, but the imaginary gods of their
own invention. I reply that there is no incongruity between the two;
for when men become so futile in their thinking that they offer
worship to the creatures rather than to God alone, they are ripe for the
punishment of being servants of Satan. For they do not find that
intermediary position between God and Satan, for which they are on
the look-out, but, as soon as they turn their backs on the true God,
Satan immediately sets himself before them as an object of worship.

And I would not that you should have communion with devils. If the
term 'demon' stood for neutral beings, how pointless this sentence of
Paul's would be, when, in fact, it is heavily charged with severity
against idol-worshippers! He gives the reason for the wish he makes,
viz. because no-one can have communion with God and idols at the
same time. But people are given a promise of communion in all sacred
rites. Let us therefore realize that it is after we have said farewell to
everything sacrilegious, and only then, that Christ admits us to the

holy feast of His body and blood. For the man who wants to obtain the one must give up the other. Oh! thrice miserable is the lot of those who, because they are afraid of offending people, have no hesitation about corrupting themselves with forbidden superstitious rites! Since they behave in this way, they are responsible for cutting themselves off from communion with Christ, and for barring the way for their own approach to His table of salvation.

22. *Or do we provoke the Lord?* He has given his teaching; now he rouses himself to speak in more vehement terms, because he was aware that an offence against God, of the most atrocious kind, was being dismissed as nothing by them, or at least regarded as a mistake of the least consequence. The Corinthians were imagining that their presumption was excusable, just as not one of us can bear to be criticized, but seeks one subterfuge after another to shelter behind. But Paul is quite right in saying that in this way we wage war with God; for God requires this, and no more than this, from us, that we adhere to everything which He makes known in His Word. Therefore, is it not the case that those who evade the issue, thinking that they may disobey the commandment of God without suffering the consequences, are openly taking up arms against God? And that is why the prophet pronounces a curse on all those who call evil good, and darkness light (Isa. 5.20).

Are we stronger than He? Paul is warning how dangerous it is to provoke God, because no-one can do so except to his own destruction. When men are involved one cannot tell how the fortune of war will go, as they say; but anyone who fights with God is voluntarily inviting his own ruin, nothing less. Therefore, if we are afraid of having God for an enemy, we should have a greater fear of trying to make excuses for flagrant sins, i.e. anything that is in conflict with His word. We should also shudder at the thought of calling in question things which He has told us, because that is nothing else but climbing up to heaven as the giants did.

23. *All things are lawful; but all things edify not.* Once again Paul returns to the principle of Christian freedom, by which the Corinthians were defending themselves, and he rebuts their objection with the same explanation that he gave before. Being present at the feast, and eating of flesh that had been sacrificed, were physical or external things, and therefore, in themselves, quite permissible. Paul asserts that there is no question about that at all, but he meets their objection by saying that we must have regard to the upbuilding of other people. 'All things are lawful for me', he says, 'but all things are not beneficial', i.e. to our neighbours; for not one of us ought to be out for himself alone, as Paul adds in the next verse, but we must keep clear of anything which would be harmful to our brothers.

Paul then specifies the kind of help which should be given them, viz. everything that makes for their upbuilding; for, so far as helping is concerned, we have to look to more than benefiting them materially. 'What does that imply?' someone will ask. 'Do you mean that something which God, in other circumstances, allows, ceases to be permissible if it is not to the advantage of our neighbours? For if that is the case then our freedom would be in the control of men.' Give careful thought to what Paul is actually saying, and you will realize that, after all, your freedom is not impaired in the slightest, when you accommodate yourself to your neighbours, but, in fact, all that is restricted is the exercise of it. For Paul agrees that it is lawful, but he says that it must not be used, if it does not make for the upbuilding of people.

24. *Let no man seek his own but each man what belongs to another.* Paul writes on the same theme in Romans 14: 'Let nobody do what he likes, but let everybody make it his business to offer no offence to his brothers, for the sake of their upbuilding.' This injunction is very necessary, for our nature is so corrupt that each of us looks to his own interests to the neglect of those of his brothers. But just as the law of love wants us to love our neighbours as ourselves so it summons us to a concern for their welfare. Finally, the apostle does not explicitly say that individuals must not think about their own interests at all, but he does not want them to be so bound up in them, that they will not give up part of their right, whenever the welfare of their brothers demands it.

Whatsoever is sold in the shambles, eat, asking no question for conscience sake; for the earth is the Lord's, and the fulness thereof. If one of them that believe not biddeth you to a feast, and ye are disposed to go; whatsoever is set before you, eat, asking no question for conscience sake. But if any man say unto you, This hath been offered in sacrifice, eat not, for his sake that shewed it, and for conscience sake: conscience, I say, not thine own, but the other's; for why is my liberty judged by another conscience? If I by grace partake, why am I evil spoken of for that for which I give thanks? Whether therefore ye eat, or drink, or whatsoever ye do, do all to the glory of God. Give no occasion of stumbling, either to Jews, or to Greeks, or to the church of God: even as I also please all men in all things, not seeking mine own profit, but the profit of the many, that they may be saved. (25-33)

25. *Whatever is sold in the meat market.* Paul has spoken above about making a pretence of worshipping idols, or at any rate about those activities in which the Corinthians could not take part without making it obvious that they were associating themselves with the superstitious rites of unbelievers. Now, Paul demands of them, not only that they refrain from making any open profession of idol worship, but also that

they be careful to avoid anything that causes offence to others, for offence usually arises when things, neutral in themselves, are handled indiscriminately. For even if the sins, in which the Corinthians were indulging, belong to one general class, yet they vary in degree. Now, in so far as the eating of foods is concerned, he begins by laying down a general statement: we can eat anything we like with a clear conscience, because the Lord allows that. In the second place, he modifies this freedom when it comes to practice, to prevent damage being done to people of tender conscience. So this, the concluding part of the discussion, has two parts to it; the first has to do with the freedom and power we have in connexion with neutral things; and the second concerns the modification of that so that the exercise of freedom may be controlled by the rule of love.

Asking no question. ἀνακρίνεσθαι, the verb Paul uses here, means to consider two sides of anything, so that a man cannot make up his mind, leaning now this way, now that. Therefore, in so far as making any differentiation among meats is concerned, Paul frees our consciences from all uneasiness and uncertainty, because it is right that, when it is clear to us from the Word of the Lord that what we do meets with His approval, our minds should be at peace and free from anxiety.

For conscience sake. In other words, before the judgement seat of God. Paul might have put it this way: 'Since it is God with whom you have to do, there is no question of debating with yourself whether this is permissible or not. For I grant you that it is safe for you to eat what you like, because the Lord allows you to have everything, and there are no exceptions.'

26. *The earth is the Lord's.* Paul cites David as a witness, in confirmation of the freedom which he described. 'But', someone will say, 'what has this to do with it?' I answer: if the earth and its fulness belong to the Lord, there is nothing in the world which is not sacred and pure. We must always pay attention to the question with which the apostle is dealing. Doubt could be raised as to whether the creatutes of God were made unclean by being used as sacrifices by unbelievers. Paul denies that, because the lordship and possession of the whole earth remain in the hands of God. But, by His power, the Lord maintains the things which He has in His hands, and, because of that, He sanctifies them. Therefore everything that the sons of God use is clean, since they take it from the hand of God and no other source.

By the *fullness of the earth* the prophet means the wealth of good things with which the earth is provided and enriched by the Lord. For if the earth had no trees, plants, animals and other things, it would be like a house bare of furniture and utensils of every kind, even more, it would be a mutilated thing, and horrible to behold. A simple answer can be given to anyone raising the objection that the earth lies under a curse because of sin: Paul is thinking about its pure and unspoilt nature here, because he is dealing with believers, for whom everything is sanctified by Christ.

27. *If one of the unbelievers invites you.* Paul immediately introduces an exception, viz, if a believer has been warned that what is set before him has been offered in sacrifice to idols, and he realizes there is danger of causing offence, then he commits a sin against his brothers if he does not abstain. In a word, then, Paul teaches that we must not do injury to tender consciences.

When he says, 'and you are willing to go', he is tacitly hinting that he himself does not approve of this very much, and that it would be better if they declined. But since it is a neutral thing, he does not want to forbid it out and out. Certainly the best course would be to keep well away from traps such as these, not because those who accommodate themselves to men only so far as going to the sacrifices (*usque ad aras*) should be condemned out of hand, but because we ought to proceed with caution when we realize that there is a likelihood of falling.

29. *Conscience, I say, not thine own, but the other's.* Paul always takes great care not to reduce our freedom, or to appear to detract from it in the slightest degree. 'You ought to give way on this matter to the weak conscience of your brother, so as not to take advantage of your own right and cause him offence in the process; but, at the same time, your conscience remains as free as ever, since conscience itself is kept outwith his control. So, while I am imposing a restriction upon you so far as actual practical relations with others are concerned, let there be no question of that restriction bringing your conscience itself into subjection to someone else.'

We must observe that in this verse the word conscience is used in its strict sense, whereas in Romans 13.5 and I Tim. 1.5 it has a broader significance. Paul says there: 'We ought to obey rulers, not only on account of the wrath of God, but also for the sake of conscience', in other words not just because of the fear of punishment, but because the Lord commands us, and it is our duty, to do so. Is it not right that we should adapt ourselves to our weak brothers on the same grounds also, that is, because we are under obligation to them to do so, in God's sight? Again, the end of the charge is love that issues from a good conscience. Does not the attitude of love depend upon a good conscience? Thus, as I have already said, the meaning is a narrower one here, viz. since the soul of a believer looks only to the judgement seat of God, and not to any human authority, and rejoices in the blessing of freedom procured for it by Christ, it is under obligation to no individuals, or bound to no conditions of time or place.

Some manuscripts repeat 'the earth is the Lord's'. But probably a reader once wrote it in the margin, and it then crept into the text. However, it is an insignificant point.

For why is my liberty judged by another conscience? It is not clear whether Paul is speaking for himself, here, or whether he is putting this objection on the lips of the Corinthians. If we take it as his own statement it will be in corroboration of the preceding statement. He might have put it like this: 'Because you restrain yourself for the sake of another person's conscience, that does not mean that your freedom is put under his control.' If he is speaking on behalf of the Corinthians the meaning will be: 'You are imposing an unfair principle upon us, because you intend that our freedom should stand or fall according to the inclination of other people.' However, my own view is that Paul is saying this about himself, and I give a different explanation, for so far I have been giving the point of view of others. Accordingly, my interpretation is that the word 'judged' is used here for 'condemned', as usually happens in Scripture. But Paul gives serious warning that, if we use our freedom just as we like, and thereby cause offence to our neighbours, the result will be that they will condemn our freedom. Therefore, because of our fault and lack of consideration, the outcome will be that this matchless gift of God will be condemned. Unless we are on our guard about this danger, we are ruining our freedom by making wrong use of it. Therefore this argument is of immense value in supporting all that Paul has to say.

30. *Therefore if I by grace partake.* This argument is the same, or nearly the same, as the one we have just had. Since it is owing to God's favour that all things are lawful to me, why should what I do be interpreted as a sin on my part? Of course we cannot prevent wicked people from maligning us, and even the weak from being angry with us at times, but Paul takes to task, for their lack of self-control, those who wilfully give grounds for offence to others, and do damage to weak consciences, without any justification, and without any useful purpose being served. Thus Paul wants us to make proper use of our blessings so that, by not indulging in thoughtless licence, we may not give the weak any chance to malign us.

31. *Whether therefore ye eat.* So that they may not get the impression that, because this is such a trifling matter, there was therefore no need to be concerned about avoiding censure, Paul teaches that there is no part of our life or conduct, however insignificant, which should not be related to the glory of God, and that we must be concerned, in eating and drinking, to do all we can to promote it. This sentence agrees with the preceding one, for if we are zealous for the glory of God, as we ought to be, we will, as far as it lies in our power, prevent

His blessings becoming the subjects of abuse. It was well put in the ancient proverb: 'We must not live to eat, but we must eat to live.' So long as the main purpose of life is kept in mind at the same time, the consequence will be that our food will in a sense be consecrated to God, for it will be intended for His honour.

32. *Give no occasion of stumbling.* Here is the second thing which we ought to be aiming at—the rule of love. Thus, zeal for the glory of God takes the first place, concern for our neighbours the second. Paul mentions Jews and Gentiles, not only because the Church of God was made up of these two classes, but in order to show that we owe something to everyone, even to strangers, so that if at all possible we might *gain* them.

33. *Even as I also please all men in all things.* Because Paul is speaking in a general way, without making any exceptions, some people wrongly extend this to cover things, which are forbidden and against the word of God, as if we had every right, in the interests of our neighbours, to dare to do more than the Lord allows us. But in fact nothing could be more certain than that Paul only accommodated himself to men in connexion with things, which were neutral and, in themselves, quite permissible.

Finally, we must pay attention to the purpose for doing this: *that they may be saved.* Therefore no concession ought to be made to them in connexion with anything which works against their salvation, but discretion, and spiritual discretion at that, must be exercised.

CHAPTER ELEVEN

Be ye imitators of me, even as I also am of Christ. Now I praise you that ye remember me in all things, and hold fast the traditions, even as I delivered them to you. But I would have you know, that the head of every man is Christ; and the head of the woman is the man; and the head of Christ is God. Every man praying or prophesying, having his head covered, dishonoureth his head. But every woman praying or prophesying with her head unveiled dishonoureth her head: for it is one and the same thing as if she were shaven. For if a woman is not veiled, let her also be shorn: but if it is a shame to a woman to be shorn, or shaven, let her be veiled. For a man indeed ought not to have his head veiled, forasmuch as he is the image and glory of God: but the woman is the glory of the man: For the man is not of the woman; but the woman of the man: for neither was the man created for the woman; but the woman for the man: for this cause ought the woman to have a sign of authority on her head, because of the angels. Howbeit neither is the woman without the man, nor the man without the woman, in the Lord. For as the woman is of the man, so is the man also by the woman; but all things are of God. Judge ye in yourselves: is it seemly that a woman pray unto God unveiled? Doth not even nature itself teach you, that, if a man have long hair, it is a dishonour to him? But if a woman have long hair, it is a glory to her: for her hair is given her for a covering. But if any man seemeth to be contentious, we have no such custom, neither the churches of God. (1-16)

1. *Be imitators of me as I am of Christ.* This shows us how badly the chapters have been divided, because this sentence has been separated from the preceding sentences, to which it belongs by right, and joined to those which follow, to which it is quite irrelevent. Let us treat this sentence, then, as part of the last chapter. In it Paul had introduced his own example to support what he was teaching. Now he urges the Corinthians to imitate what he had done, even as he imitated Christ, so that they may grasp that this is exactly what they are required to do.

Two things are to be noted here: (1) that Paul does not tell others to do what he himself had not first put into practice; (2) he points himself and others back to Christ as the one exemplar of right action. For, just as it is of the essence of a good teacher not to give any directions in word which he is not prepared to carry out in action, so he ought not to be so exacting as to expect others to do whatever he does all the time. That is what over-scrupulous people usually do, for they want to force on other people everything that they themselves find delight in, and they want their own example to be looked upon as completely binding. And worldly people also have a natural tendency to follow the wrong sort of examples (κακοζηλίαν), and, ape-like, make an effort to do exactly what they see done by people who exercise great influence. Further, we are well aware of the number of evils brought into the Church by that preposterous eagerness for imitating everything done by the saints, without any exceptions. That is why we must be all the more careful about keeping to this teaching of Paul, to the effect that we are only to follow men, provided that they have Christ as their prototype (πρωτότυπον). As a result, the examples of the saints would have the effect, not of drawing us away from Christ, but rather of pointing us to Him.

2. *But I praise you.* Paul now passes on to a different theme. He is going to give the Corinthians instruction about the kind of seemliness they ought to maintain when they meet for worship. For in the same way as the clothes a man wears, or the attitude he adopts, sometimes spoil, sometimes enhance, his appearance, so seemliness brings a grace to all his actions, while unseemliness ruins them. Therefore a great deal depends on τὸ πρέπον, i.e. propriety, and not only for bringing grace and attractiveness to our actions, but also for letting our imaginations become accustomed to what is honourable. While, generally speaking, this holds good in everything, yet it is particularly true of sacred things. For if we do not maintain dignity in the Church by conducting ourselves in a decent and fitting way, then we do not know what scorn, and eventually what rudeness of behaviour, will come into being. Paul therefore lays down certain things, which have to do with ordering things in public, and that in itself makes for enhancing the tone of gatherings for worship (*quo sacri coetus ornantur*). But, so that he might make them all the readier to do what he says, Paul begins by praising their obedience in the past, for they had indeed kept to the arrangements he had given them. For, having begotten that church for the Lord, he had handed over to them a certain organization for running it. Since they had maintained this, the Corinthians gave him grounds for hoping that they would also be open to instruction for the future.

But it is a strange thing that when he had taken them to task for so many things before, he is now praising them. More than that, indeed, if we think about the state of that church, as it was described in the earlier part of the letter, they were far from deserving commendation like this. To such an objection I reply that some of them were afflicted with those sins, which Paul mentions before, indeed some with one, some with another. At the same time, however, the form, which he had commended to them, had been preserved by the whole body. Now there is no inconsistency in this situation: that a great many sins, and of different kinds too, hold sway over a certain people, so that some of them are cheating, others robbing, some are full of envy, others quarrelling, and still others committing fornication, while, at the same time, as far as the public form of the Church is concerned, the institutions of Christ and the apostles are kept in being.

That will be clearer if we keep to what Paul means by παραδόσεις (traditions). Apart from this, something must be said about this word in answer to the Papists, who arm themselves with this verse, in order to defend their view of traditions. It is a well-worn principle of theirs, that the teaching of the apostles consists of two parts, writings and traditions. Under this second class they include not only all sorts of absurd superstitious beliefs and childish rites which they have in super-abundance, but all sorts of stupid abominations which are contrary to the plain word of God, and, finally, tyrannical laws of their own devising which simply torture the consciences of men. Thus there is nothing so foolish, nothing so absurd, in fact nothing so monstrous, that it may not shelter under this umbrella, or, if you like, be tarred with this brush. Therefore, since Paul mentions traditions here, they seize upon this little word in their usual way, in order to make Paul the inventor of all the abominations, which we, on our part, refute by appealing to the clear evidence of Scripture.

Now, I do not deny that some of the traditions of the apostles were not written down, but I do not agree that they were elements of doctrine, and that they had to do with things necessary for salvation. What then had they to do with? The answer is, matters affecting order and polity. We know that each church is free to set up the form of polity that suits its circumstances, and is to its advantage, because the Lord has not given any specific directions about this. So it was that Paul, the first to lay the foundations of the church at Corinth, had given shape to it by means of good, sound directions (*institutis quoque piis et honestis*) so that everything might be done there decently and in order, as he enjoins in chapter 14.40.

But what has this to do with the pointless, nonsensical ceremonies, which we come face to face with in Popery today? What has it to do with a superstition that exceeds that of the Jews? What, indeed, has it to do with a tyranny like that of Phalaris, by which they torture the consciences of wretched people? What has it to do with so many signs of idolatry? For, if people are going to give rules to others, the right way to do it is to practise the same moderation as Paul, so as not to force people to accept their decisions, when all the time they are making up whatever suits themselves, but rather to ask that they imitate them, as they are *imitators of Christ*. Under these circumstances, where people have had the effrontery to produce the inventions of their own fancy, it is certainly going beyond a joke when they demand obedience from everybody else. Finally, we must realize that Paul is commending their earlier obedience, in order to make them more open to instruction for the future.

3. *But I would have you know.* The old proverb says: 'Good laws are born of bad manners.' Since no question had yet been raised about the practice (*ritus*), which is dealt with here, Paul had made no pronouncement about it. The error of the Corinthians now gave him an opening for teaching what was the right way to act in this connexion. In order to prove that it is unbecoming for women to appear in a public gathering for worship with their heads uncovered, and, on the other hand, for men to pray or prophesy with their heads covered, Paul starts off with the arrangements which God has appointed.

What he says is this: 'As *Christ* is under *God*, as His *Head*, so the man is subject to Christ, and the woman to the man.' We shall see later how Paul concludes from that, that women ought to be veiled. In the meantime let us grasp these four levels to which he refers. God, then, keeps His pre-eminence; Christ has the second place. How is this so? The answer is, since He has made Himself subject to the Father in our flesh, for, apart from that, being of one essence with the Father, He is equal with Him. Let us bear in mind, therefore, that this is said about Christ the Mediator. My point is that He is inferior to the Father, because He has clothed Himself with our nature, so that He might be the first-born among many brothers.

There is rather more difficulty in what follows. Here, the man is placed in an intermediate position between Christ and the woman, so that Christ is not the Head of the woman. Yet it is the same apostle who teaches in Galatians 3.28 that '*in Christ* . . . there is no male or female'. Why has he kept this difference here, when he has cut it out of the other passage? My answer to that is that the solution depends on the contexts of the two passages. When Paul says that there is no difference between man and woman, he is speaking about the spiritual Kingdom of Christ, where the outward characteristics (*personae*), count for nothing, and are not taken into consideration, for it has nothing to do with the body, nothing to do with men's physical relationships with each other (*ad externam hominum societatem*), but it is concerned wholly with the spirit. That is why Paul declares that there is even no difference between 'a slave' and 'a free man'. At the same time, however, he leaves intact the civil order (*civilem ordinem*) and also the distinctions in honours, for ordinary everyday life cannot get on without these. But here, Paul is concerned with what is honourable and seemly, and belongs to the sphere of ecclesiastical polity. Therefore, so far as spiritual union (*ad spiritualem coniunctionem*) is concerned, in the eyes of God, and inwardly in their conscience, Christ is the head of both the man and woman without any distinction, because, in the spiritual realm, no consideration is given to male or female. On the other hand, as far as external connexions and social propriety are concerned, the man takes his lead from Christ, and the woman from the man, so that they do not stand on the same level, but this inequality exists.

If anyone asks how marriage stands in relation to Christ, I reply that Paul is speaking here about the sacred union (*de sancto coniugio*) of believers, the union of which Christ is the officiating priest (*antistes*) and which is consecrated in His name.

4. *Every man praying.* Of the two statements that now follow, the first has to do with the *man*, and the second with the *woman*. Paul says that the man offers an insult to Christ, his Head, if he prays or prophesies with his head covered. Why is this? Because he is made subject to Christ, and that includes the condition that he take first place in the control of the household and its affairs. For in his own home the father of the family is like a king. Therefore he reflects the glory of God, because of the control which is in his hands. If he covers his head, he brings himself down from that pre-eminence in which God has placed him, to be under authority to others. So damage is done to the honour that belongs to Christ. For example, if anyone whom a prince has appointed to act on his behalf does not know how to keep his place, but cheapens his position, so that it becomes a laughing-stock to even the humblest people, does that man not bring discredit upon his prince? Similarly, if the man does not keep his place, if he is not under Christ's authority in such a way as to exercise his own authority in the oversight of his family, he is, to that extent, obscuring the glory of Christ, which is reflected in the well-constituted order of marriage. Finally, the covering or veil, as we shall see is the symbol of an authority interposed in their midst.

I take prophesying to mean here, explaining the mysteries of God, for the enlightening of those who hear, as we find in chapter 14. Similarly, praying means thinking out the form which the prayer will take, and giving a lead, so to speak, to all the people; and that is the function of the public teacher, for Paul is not discussing prayer in general here, but prayer in public worship. But let us remember that here the extent of their error is that seemliness is spoiled, and the difference in standing, imposed by God, is blurred. For we should not be so hide-bound by conscientious principles as to think that a teacher is doing anything wrong in wearing a skull-cap on his head, when he is speaking to the people from the pulpit. But all that Paul is after is that it may be made clear that the man is in authority, and that the woman is in subjection to him, and that is done when the man uncovers his head in the sight of the congregation, even if he puts his skull-cap on again afterwards so as not to catch cold. To sum up, the one guiding principle is τὸ πρέπον, propriety; if that is preserved, Paul asks for no more.

5–6. *But every woman praying or prophesying.* The second proposition is that women ought to have their heads covered when they pray or prophesy, otherwise they dishonour their head. For the man does honour to his head by making it plain to everyone that he is independent; similarly the woman does so by showing that she is under subjection. Conversely, therefore, if the woman uncovers her head, she shakes herself free of subjection, and shows contempt for her husband at the same time. But it seems to be unnecessary for Paul to forbid a woman to prophesy bare-headed, since in I Tim. 2.12 he debars women from speaking in the church altogether. Therefore they would have no right to prophesy, even with their heads covered, and the obvious conclusion is that it is a waste of time for Paul to be discussing the question of head-covering here. The answer can be given that when the apostle disapproves of the one thing here, he is not giving his approval to the other. For when he takes them to task because they were prophesying bare-headed, he is not giving them permission, however, to prophesy in any other way whatever, but rather is delaying the censure of that fault to another passage (chapter 14.34 ff). That is a perfectly adequate answer. However it might meet the situation quite well to say that the apostle expects this unassuming conduct from women, not only in the place where the whole congregation is assembled, but also in any of the more formal gatherings, either of matrons or of men, such as sometimes meet in private houses.

For it is one and the same thing as if she were shaven. Paul now uses other reasons to press home his point that bare-headedness is unbecoming in women. Nature itself holds it in horror, he says. A woman with her head shaved is a loathsome, indeed an unnatural sight. We assume from this that the woman is given her hair as a natural covering. If anyone should now raise the objection that her hair, being her natural covering, is therefore all that is needed, Paul says that it is not, for it is a covering of such a kind that it requires another one to cover it! And from this we can hazard the likely conjecture that women, who had lovely hair, were in the habit of doing without any covering in order to show off its beauty. Therefore Paul intentionally remedies this fault, by bringing forward a view quite the opposite to theirs, that, instead of this making them attractive to men, and awakening men's lust, it only makes themselves spectacles of unseemliness.

7. *A man ought not to have his head veiled, forasmuch as he is the image.*
The same question can now be raised about the *image*, as was raised
before about the head. For both sexes were created according to the
image of God (*ad imaginem Dei*), and Paul urges women, as much as
men, to be re-formed according to that *image*. But when he is speaking
about image here, he is referring to the conjugal order (*ad ordinem
coniugalem*). Accordingly it has to do with this present life, and, on the
other hand has nothing to do with conscience. The straightforward
solution is this, that Paul is not dealing here with innocence and holiness, which women can have just as well as men, but about the pre-
eminence which God has given to the man, so that he might be superior
to the woman. The glory of God is seen in the higher standing which
the man has, as it is reflected in every superior authority.

The woman is the glory of the man. There is no doubt that the woman
is a splendid adornment to the man's life. For God has greatly honoured
her in appointing her to be the man's companion and helper for life,
and in putting her under him, as the body to the head. For Solomon's
description (in Prov. 12.4) of the conscientious wife as the crown of her
husband, is true of the whole sex, if we think about the ordering of
God; for that is what Paul is endorsing here, showing that the woman
was created for the express purpose of greatly enriching the man's life.[1]

8–9. *For the man is not of the woman.* Paul now makes use of two
arguments to support the superiority which he had attributed to men
over women. The first is that the woman took her origin from the
man, and that therefore she has a lower standing. The second is that
the woman has been created for the sake of the man, and therefore she
is subject to him, as a finished article depends on what goes to its
making. That the man is the source of the woman, and the end for
which she is made, is plain from the law: 'It is not good that the man
should be alone. Let us make for him etc.' Further, 'God took one
of Adam's ribs, and formed Eve' (Gen. 2.21, 22).

10. *For this cause ought the woman to have a sign of authority on her head.*
From that authoritative source Paul produces evidence in support of
outward seemliness. 'She has been put in subjection', he says, 'therefore
let her wear the token of subjection.' Metonymy is used in the word
authority, because Paul means a symbol by which she makes known
the fact that she is under the power of her husband; and it is in fact a
covering, either a robe, or linen cloth, or some other kind of covering.

Someone asks if Paul is speaking of married women only. It is true
that some restrict what Paul teaches here to married women, because
subjection to the authority of a husband does not apply in the case of

---

[1] Tholuck's reading *ut insigne sit viri ornamentum* is followed instead of that of
C.R. which has *Dei* instead of *viri*.

virgins. But these people are only showing their ignorance; for Paul looks higher, viz. to the eternal law of God, which has made the female sex subject to the authority of men. Therefore all women are born to submit to the pre-eminence of the male sex. If that were not so, the principle which Paul has derived from nature would be beside the point, viz. his saying that it is just as improper for a woman to have her head uncovered as to have it shaved, because this applies to virgins as well.

Because of the angels. Various explanations are given of this phrase. Because the prophet Malachi calls priests, 'angels of God' (2.7), some think that Paul is speaking about them. But ministers of the Word are never described in this way alone, that is to say, without the addition of something else; and besides, that interpretation would be very forced. Therefore I take it in its normal sense. But someone will ask why he wanted women to have their heads covered because of the angels. What has this to do with them? Some answer that by saying that angels are present when believers are praying, and are therefore witnesses of any unseemliness, that may be allowed to creep into their meetings. But what need is there for such subtle thinking? We know that the angels are always waiting upon Christ, as their Head also, and serving Him. Therefore when women go so far as to presume to do what they like, and, against the Law of both God and men, appropriate the sign of power for themselves, they let the angels see how unseemly they are. Therefore this phrase is given by way of amplification, as if he had said: 'If women do away with their veils, it is not only Christ, but all the angels as well, who will be witnesses of the ruinous result.' And this interpretation fits in very well with the apostle's purpose. He is dealing here with the standing people have. And he says that when women rise to a higher place than they are entitled to, all that their efforts amount to is that they let the angels of heaven know how presumptuous they are.

11. *But neither is the man without the woman.* This is added, partly to restrain men from treating women badly, partly to give encouragement to women, so that their subjection may not be a source of annoyance to them. Paul is saying: 'The male sex has a superiority over the female, but on this condition, that they ought to be bound together in mutual goodwill; for the one cannot get on without the other. Should they be separated they are like mutilated parts of a mangled body. Let them, then, be tied to each other by this bond of mutual service.'

By saying, 'in the Lord', Paul is calling believers back to what the Lord has appointed; whereas the only thing that unbelievers look to is the pressure of necessity. For if ungodly men find no difficulty in living a single life, then they look with contempt upon the whole sex, and pay no attention to the fact that the appointment and decree of God puts them under obligation to it. But believers are well aware that the male sex is only one half of the human race. They ponder the meaning for them of the words: 'God created man (*hominem*) . . . male and female created he them' (Gen. 1.27 and 5.2). So they freely acknowledge that they owe something to the weak sex. Believing women similarly think about what their duty is. Thus the man has no life without the woman, because that would mean a head cut off from the body; nor has the woman any existence without the man, for that would be a body without the head. Let the man therefore carry out his function as the head, having supremacy over her; let the woman perform her function as the body, giving help to him. Let that be the rule not only for married people, but also for the unmarried; for I am not concerned with marriage here, but with public obligations, which also have a place in the lives of people who are not married. If it is your opinion that this should rather be made to apply to the whole sex, I do not protest. All the same, just as Paul is addressing himself to individuals, so he seems to be pointing out what the special function of each person is.

12. *For as the woman is of the man.* If one of the reasons why the man enjoys superiority is that the woman has been taken out of him, in the same way a reason for their amicable relationship lies in the fact that men are not able to look after and maintain themselves without the help of women. For it still remains an undeniable fact that 'it is not good that the man should be alone' (Gen. 2.18). What Paul says here can certainly be taken as referring to propagation, since children are not produced by men on their own, but by men and women together. But I also take it to mean that a woman is an indispensable help to a man, because a solitary life is not good for men. This principle of God gives us encouragement to do all we can to share our lives with each other.

But all things are of God. God is the source of both sexes. Therefore both of them ought humbly to accept and preserve the part given them by God. Let the man exercise his authority with moderation, and not ill-treat the woman, who has been given to him as his companion. Let the woman be content in her position of subjection, and not feel indignant because she has to play second fiddle to the superior sex. Otherwise they will both throw off the yoke of God, who has made those differences in their positions, that they might be beneficial to them. Moreover, it is a far more serious thing to say that when the man and woman cease fulfilling their obligations to each other, they are rebelling against the authority of God, than if Paul had said that they are doing injury to each other.

14. *Doth not even nature itself.* Paul again sets *nature* before them as the teacher of what is proper. Now, he means by 'natural' what was accepted by common consent and usage at that time, certainly as far as the Greeks were concerned. For long hair was not always regarded as a disgraceful thing in men. Historical works relate that long ago, i.e. in the earliest times, men wore long hair in every country. Thus the poets are in the habit of speaking about the ancients and applying to them the well-worn epithet 'unshorn'. In Rome they did not begin to use barbers until a late period, about the time of Africanus the Elder [born 235 B.C.]. When Paul was writing these words, the practice of cutting hair had not yet been adopted in Gaul and Germany. Yes, and more than that, indeed, it would have been a disgraceful thing for men, just as much as women, to have their hair shaved or cut. But since the Greeks did not consider it very manly to have long hair, branding those who had it as effeminate, Paul considers that their custom, accepted in his own day was in conformity with nature.

16. *But if any man seems.* A contentious man is one who takes a delight in stirring up quarrels, and gives no consideration at all to the place of truth. Included in this category are all those who destroy good and useful customs where there is no need to do so; who raise controversies about matters which are as clear as day; who will not listen to reason; who cannot endure anyone getting the better of them. This class of people also includes the unsocial (ἀκοινώνητοι) who have a strange outlook, which leads them to some new, extraordinary way of life. Paul does not think that these people deserve any answer, because contention is a harmful thing, and for that reason it ought to be kept out of the churches. From this Paul is teaching us that those who are obstinate and fond of a quarrel should be authoritatively checked, rather than proved to be in the wrong by means of lengthy debates. For there will never be an end to disputes if you mean to contend with a quarrelsome person until you get the better of him; for even if he is refuted a hundred times he will go on arguing, fresh as ever.

Let us pay close attention to this verse, therefore, so that we may not allow ourselves to be carried away by useless arguments. However there is always the proviso that we must know how to pick out contentious people. For the man who does not agree with our opinions, or is bold enough to oppose us, must not always be thought of as a contentious person. But when wilfulness and obstinacy stare us in the face, then let us say with Paul that 'contentions are not in keeping with the ways of the Church'.

But in giving you this charge, I praise you not, that ye come together not for the better but for the worse. For first of all, when ye come together in

*the church, I hear that divisions exist among you; and I partly believe it.
For there must be also heresies among you, that they which are approved
may be made manifest among you. When therefore ye assemble yourselves together, it is not possible to eat the Lord's supper: for in your
eating each one taketh before other his own supper; and one is hungry,
and another is drunken. What? have ye not houses to eat and to drink
in? or despise ye the church of God, and put them to shame that have
not? What shall I say to you? shall I praise you in this? I praise you
not.* (17-22)

Paul's censure of the fault described in the earlier part of the chapter
was merely a mild and friendly rebuke, because the Corinthians were
committing their offence out of ignorance, and so it was only fair that
they should be readily forgiven. At the beginning of the chapter Paul
had praised them because they had faithfully kept the instructions
which he had given them. Now he begins a more penetrating attack,
because they were committing certain offences which were of a more
serious nature; and there was no question of their ignorance this time.

17. *But, denouncing this, I am not praising.* This is my solution of the
difficulty here, for Paul seems to have interchanged the participle and
the verb. Erasmus' interpretation is not suitable, when he translates
παραγγέλειν as 'to give instructions'. But the verb 'to denounce',
would suit the context better. However I do not make an issue of this.

There is a contradiction between this phrase and what he says at the
beginning of the chapter. He might have put it like this: 'Because I
have praised you, do not get it into your heads that there is no qualification to it, for I have something to take you to task about, something
that deserves reproof indeed.' But, in my view, this is not concerned
with the Lord's Supper alone, but also with other sins, which Paul will
mention. Let us therefore think of this as a general statement, when
he says that the Corinthians are reprimanded, because they come together not for the better but for the worse. The particular results of
this evil will be dealt with later.

Paul's first complaint against them is that they do not come together
for the better; his second that they do so for the worse. The second is
certainly the more serious. But the first one must not be put up with
either; for if we pay attention to what takes place in Church, not a
single meeting of the people ought to be fruitless. For there we listen
to God's teaching, we offer prayers, and celebrate the mysteries. The
Word bears fruit when trust in God, and fear of Him, grow in us; when
we make progress in the life of holiness; when, more and more, we put
off the old man; when we go on in newness of life. The purpose of the
mysteries is to give us practice in devotion and love. The prayers also

ought to be effective for doing all those things. Besides all this, the Lord works efficaciously by His Spirit, because He does not want the things, which He has appointed, to be fruitless. Therefore if we derive no benefit from the gatherings for worship, and we are not made better men as a result of them, it is our ingratitude that is to blame, and therefore we deserve to be reproached. For we ourselves cause it to happen that the things, which, by their very nature and by the appointment of God, ought to bring benefits to us, leave us without profit.

We now turn to the second fault, that *they come together for the worse.* This is a far more serious matter, yet it is nearly always the consequence of the first. For if we derive no profit from the things which God has provided, the way He punishes our indolence is by letting us become worse. And it is generally the case that neglect causes many corruptions; and in particular this is so because people do not give a thought to using things in the way they ought to be used, with the almost inevitable result that they quickly lapse into making up things that are harmful.

18. *When ye come together in the church, I hear there are divisions.* Some think that divisions and heresies refer to that badly disciplined conduct (ἀταξία) about which he will be speaking shortly. I think that they cover more than that. Indeed it is unlikely that he would have used terms like these, which are not suitable and apposite for describing that disorder. Those people maintain that Paul has used sterner language in order to make the seriousness of their sin stand out all the clearer. I would grant as much, if the meaning of the words fitted in with it. His reproof here is, therefore, in general terms, to the effect that they were not in harmony, as Christians ought to be, but in fact everyone was far too much bound up in his own affairs to make the slightest effort to accommodate himself to others. That was the root of that particular abuse, which we will learn about almost at once; that was the root of their vanity and arrogance, so that each one was putting himself on a pedestal and looking down his nose at others; that was the root of their neglect of edification, and their desecration of the gifts of God.

Paul says that he partly believes it, so that they might not all make up their minds that he is laying such a serious offence as this one at the door of every one of them, without distinction, and so get the chance to complain that they were being accused of something of which they were innocent. At the same time, however, he is hinting that this had reached his ears, not by a mere, vague rumour, but by a more definite report, the trustworthiness of which he could not completely set aside.

19. *For there must be also heresies among you.* He had spoken of divisions already. Now he speaks of heresies, to make things still

clearer. In addition, we gather that from his use of the word *also*, for it is inserted by way of amplification (πρὸς αὔξησιν).

It is well known in what sense the fathers used these two terms and what sort of distinction they made between heretics and schismatics. They maintained that *heresy* consists in disagreement about doctrine; and *schism* consists rather in an alienation of spirits as, for example, when anyone left the Church because of a grudge he bore, or dislike of the ministers, or inability to get on with others. Despite the fact that bad teaching can only lead to the splitting of the Church, so that heresy is the root and source of schism; and despite the fact that jealousy or pride is the mother of nearly every heresy, it is, nevertheless, a valuable thing to have this distinction between the two.

But now let us see what Paul means by them. I have already rejected the view of those who explain the heresy as the separation which occurred at the table, in that the rich did not share their supper with the poor; for it was Paul's intention to point out something which was more offensive still. But, setting aside other people's views, I take schism and heresy here as being a matter of degree, where one goes further than the other. Thus schisms are to be found either where there are secret animosities, with not a sign of that agreement which there ought to be among believers, or, where conflicting interests are making their presence felt, every one thinking his own way to be right, and having nothing to do with all that the others say or do. Heresies appear when the evil goes so fast and so far that hostility breaks out into the open, and men are quite deliberate about dividing themselves up into conflicting groups.

Paul does not want the faithful to be disheartened by the sight of the Corinthians making heavy weather of it because of their divisions. So the apostle throws quite a different light on this thing that is a cause of offence, by saying that what is rather happening is that the Lord is putting the perseverance of His own people to the test by trials like these. What glorious comfort! Paul says: 'When what we see in the Church is not full unity but, instead, certain signs of brokenness, springing from the fact that people do not agree properly together, then there should be no question of our being disturbed or ready to give in; on the contrary, even if sects come into the open we ought to remain steadfast and constant. For in this way not only are hypocrites brought to light, but also, and on the other hand, the sincerity of the faithful is proved. For as, on the one hand, this makes plain to us the fickleness of those who have not been rooted in the Word of the Lord, and the dishonesty of those who had been making a show, by pretending to be good men; so, on the other hand, it enables the good to give clearer evidence of their steadfastness and sincerity.'

But notice that Paul says *there must be*, for by using that word he means that this situation does not arise by chance, but by the reliable providence of God, because He wants to test His own people, like gold in the furnace. Now if God is satisfied with this, it means that it is something beneficial to us. Yet that must not give us grounds for entering into thorny arguments, or rather for getting confused in a labyrinth, about the question of the necessity of fate. We know that there will never be a time in which there will not be many false people. We know that they are controlled by the spirit of Satan, and that evil holds them well and truly captive. We know that Satan constantly leaves no stone unturned in order to break up the unity of the Church. That is the source of the necessity, of which Paul is speaking, not fate. We also know that in His wonderful wisdom the Lord turns the pernicious contrivances of Satan to the salvation of the faithful. So there comes about the result, which Paul describes, 'that those who are upright may be seen all the more clearly'. For it is not the case that a blessing, such as this, ought to be thought of as coming from heresies, which, being bad in themselves, cannot produce anything but evil; but as coming from God, who changes the nature of things by His infinite goodness, so that the very things which Satan had devised for the destruction of the elect, turn out to be for their advantage.

Now Chrysostom maintains that the particle ἵνα indicates not cause, but result. That is not of much importance. For the cause is the secret purpose of God, by which evil things are manipulated in such a way that everything turns out well. Finally, we know that the ungodly are pressed by Satan in such a way that they are moved to do things, and also do things, of their own free will! Therefore they are left without a leg to stand on.

20. *It is not to eat the Lord's Supper.* Paul now turns to condemn the abuse which had crept into the Corinthians' observance of the Lord's Supper, viz. that they were mixing up ordinary banquets with the feast that is holy and spiritual; and along with that went contempt for the poor. Paul says that when this is done it is not the Lord's Supper that they are eating; not because one particular abuse would completely destroy, and reduce to nothing, the most sacred institution of Christ, but because they were desecrating the sacrament by observing it in the wrong way. In ordinary conversation we are accustomed to say that a thing is not done, unless it is done right. Now, this was not an insignificant corruption, as we shall see later.

If you take the words 'it is not' in the sense 'it is not allowed', as some people do, there will be no difference in the meaning, viz. that the Corinthians are not ready for eating the Lord's Supper, because they are so divided. Nevertheless, what I have just stated is simpler,

viz. that Paul condemns the inclusion of common things which have
no relation to *the Lord's Supper*.

21. *For everyone takes his own supper first.* It is a very wonderful
thing, and almost like a miracle that Satan was able to do so much in
such a short space of time. This serves as an example to warn us, what
something that is old can do when it is unsupported by any reason; in
other words, how much weight a well-established custom has, when
the word of God itself provides not a shred of evidence to justify it.
Since they had become used to this, they held it to be legitimate. At
that time Paul was available to step in. But what was the position after
the death of the apostles? We can imagine how Satan was allowed to
run riot just as much as he liked! Yet this is the strongest foundation
on which the Papists build: 'Here is something ancient; it was done
long ago; therefore let it be as authoritative as an oracle from heaven.'

But we cannot say for certain what gave rise to this abuse, or what
caused it to emerge so quickly. Chrysostom thinks that it took its
origin in the love-feasts (ἀπὸ τῶν ἀγαπῶν), the situation being that, while
the rich had been in the habit of bringing food from their homes, and
eating along with the poor, without making any difference between
them, they later began to cut the poor out, and to guzzle their delicacies
on their own. And there is no doubt, for Tertullian makes it plain,
that that was a very ancient practice. Now they used to describe as
agapae (ἀγάπαι) those common meals, which they held among themselves, because they symbolized their brotherly love, and consisted of
what they contributed. And I am quite sure that the origin of it lay
in the sacrificial rites common to both Jews and Gentiles. For I am
aware that the Christians usually corrected the defects in those rites,
but in such a way that they still retained a certain resemblance to them.
It is very likely that, when they saw that both the Jews and the Gentiles
were supplementing their sacrifice by a feast, but that they both sinned
through vanity, over-indulgence and intemperance, they instituted a
form of feast, which would rather discipline them in sobriety and
moderation. At the same time the fact of their sharing with each other
would give it the aspect of a spiritual meal. For the poor were fed
there at the expense of the rich, and they all sat at the same table. But
whether they had lapsed into this worldly and corrupt practice right
at the start, or whether an institution, which was otherwise not so bad,
had degenerated into this state with the passage of time, Paul does not
want this spiritual feast to be mixed up with ordinary feasts in any way.
It is certainly a fine thing to see both the poor and the rich eating together of the foods which have been contributed, and the rich sharing
their abundance with the needy; but we should not put such emphasis
on anything that it leads to our desecrating the holy sacrament.

And this one is hungry. One bad aspect of the situation was that the rich, by making sumptuous provision for themselves, seemed, in a way, to be casting their extreme poverty in the teeth of the poor. When Paul says that some are drunk, and others are hungry, he is using hyperbole to bring out their inequality; for some had food enough to stuff themselves full, while others had barely enough to keep body and soul together. Thus the poor were made the laughing-stock of the rich, or at least were made to feel ashamed. It was therefore an unsavoury spectacle, and not in keeping with the Lord's Supper.

22. *Have ye not houses?* This lets us see how thoroughly dissatisfied the apostle was with this custom of theirs, of feasting, even if there had never been that abuse which has just been mentioned. For though it seems quite acceptable for the whole Church to eat the Supper at one common table, yet, on the other hand, it is definitely wrong to turn the gathering for worship into other practices, that are quite foreign to its nature. We know what the Church ought to meet together to do; to hear teaching; to pour out prayers and sing hymns to God; to celebrate the mysteries; to make confession of our faith; to take part in religious rites and other godly exercises. Anything else that is done there is out of place. Each person has a home of his own, which is intended for him to eat in and drink in; it is therefore improper to do these things in the gathering for worship.

What shall I say to you? Having dealt with the matter, he now puts it to them to consider whether they deserve to be praised, for they could not defend such an obvious abuse. But he exerts further pressure on them by putting questions like these to them: 'What else was I to do? Will you say that there are no grounds for condemning you?'

Some manuscripts connect the words 'in this' with the verb which follows, in this way: 'Shall I praise you? In this I do not praise you'; but in the Greek manuscripts the other reading is more usually found, and it is more suitable.

For I received of the Lord that which also I delivered unto you, how that the Lord Jesus in the night in which he was betrayed took bread; and when he had given thanks, he brake it, and said, This is my body, which is broken for you: this do in remembrance of me. In like manner also the cup, after supper, saying, This cup is the new covenant in my blood: this do, as oft as ye drink it, in remembrance of me. For as often as ye eat this bread, and drink the cup, ye proclaim the Lord's death till he come. Wherefore whosoever shall eat the bread or drink the cup of the Lord unworthily, shall be guilty of the body and the blood of the Lord. But let a man prove himself, and so let him eat of the bread, and drink of the cup. For he that eateth and drinketh, eateth and drinketh judgement unto himself, if he discern not the body. (23–29)

Up to this point Paul has been showing what was wrong; now he begins to teach them the best way to rectify matters. For the institution of Christ is a fixed standard, so that the slightest deviation from it means that you fall into error. Since the Corinthians had departed from this standard, he calls them back to it. This passage ought to be carefully studied, for it shows that the only remedy for removing and correcting corruptions is to get back to the unadulterated institution of God. That is what our Lord Himself did when he was speaking about marriage (Matt. 19.3). The scribes made reference to custom and also to the concession which Moses allowed, but He Himself only brought forward His Father's institution; because it is an inviolable principle. When we do this today, the Papists make loud protest that we are tampering with and spoiling everything. We make it quite clear that it is not just that they have departed from the primary institution of our Lord in one way only, but that they have corrupted it in a thousand ways. Nothing is more obvious than that their Mass is poles apart from the Holy Supper of Our Lord. I go a step further. We point out that it is swarming with wicked abominations. It therefore stands in need of correction. Our demand is this, and it is clear that Paul had to make it too, that the institution of our Lord be the common standard for us, and that both sides be in agreement about that. They make violent protest against that. Now you know the nature of the controversy about the Lord's Supper in our own day.

23. *I have received from the Lord.* By these words Paul means that the only authority that carries any weight in the Church is that of the Lord. For he might have put it this way: 'I have not delivered to you something I have made up. When I came to you, I had not invented a new supper, the product of my own imagination; but I regard Christ as its originator, and from Him I have received what I have personally delivered to you. Return therefore to this fundamental source.' Therefore, when we have turned our backs on the rules which men make, the authority of Christ alone will remain, unshaken.

On the night in which he was betrayed. The reference to the time reminds us that the purpose of the mystery is that we may be confirmed in the blessing that the death of Christ gives. For the Lord could have entrusted the covenant to the disciples on some earlier occasion, but He was waiting for the time of His sacrifice, so that the apostles would not have long to wait before seeing what he had foreshadowed in the bread and wine actually fulfilled in His body.

If anyone infers from this that we therefore ought to celebrate the

Supper at night, and after eating an ordinary meal, I answer that when we look at our Lord's actions, we must consider what He intended us to do. It is certain that He had no intention of delivering instruction to them about nocturnal rites, something like those of Ceres, and also that He did not mean to invite His people to His spiritual feast after they had eaten a hearty meal. Such actions of Christ as we are not asked to imitate should not be regarded as belonging to His institution. That is why there is no difficulty about refuting the cunning arguments of the Papists, by which they evade what I have already said about retaining and preserving what Christ actually instituted, and only that. 'Therefore', they say, 'we will only receive the Lord's Supper at night, and after we have dined, not after fasting.' Such talk, I say, is a waste of breath; because it is an easy matter to determine what the Lord did for the express purpose that we should follow His example; one should rather say, what He did in order to direct us to do it also.

24. *When he had given thanks.* Paul says in I Tim. 4.5 that every gift we receive from God's hand is sanctified to us through the Word of God and prayer. Nowhere, therefore, do we read of our Lord eating with His disciples, without the fact that He gave thanks being recorded. There is no doubt that He has taught us, by His own example, to do the same thing. Yet this thanksgiving goes deeper than that, for Christ is giving thanks to His Father for His mercy towards the human race, and His priceless gift of redemption; and He encourages us, by His example, so that, as often as we approach the Holy Table, we may lift up our hearts in acknowledgement of the boundless love of God towards us, and be inflamed with true gratitude to Him.

Take, eat, this is my body. Since it was Paul's intention here to teach us about the right way to observe the sacrament, and since he does it briefly, we should, on our part, study what he has to say with careful attention, not passing over anything lightly, in view of the fact that everything that he says very much needs to be known, and deserves the closest consideration.

In the first place let us note that here Christ divides the bread among the disciples so that they may all eat it together; and in this way all may share and share alike. Therefore when a common table is not prepared for all who believe, when they are not invited to the common breaking of bread, when, in short, the faithful do not share with each other, there are no grounds for describing the proceedings as the Lord's Supper. But why do they call people together for the mass? Perhaps the answer is that they may be sent away again unsatisfied, after seeing a pointless show. It has, therefore, nothing in common with the Supper.

From this verse we also gather that the promise of Christ no more applies to the mass than to the feast of the college of priests of Mars. For when Christ promises that He will give us His body, He similarly commands us to take the bread and eat it. If we do not obey this commandment of His, all our boasting about having His promise is to no avail. Let me put this in another way, in language that is more customary: the promise is bound up with the commandment, as if the latter were a condition; the promise therefore only becomes effective if the condition is fulfilled. To take an example, it is written (Ps. 50.15), 'Call upon me: I will hear you.' What we have to do is to obey God's commandment so that He may carry out what He has promised us; otherwise we deprive ourselves of its fulfilment. But what about the Papists? They ignore the question of sharing, and consecrate the bread for a totally different purpose, at the same time making it their boast that they have the body of the Lord. Since they cause an ungodly divorce, in separating the things which Christ has joined together, it is plain that their boasting is a hollow thing. Therefore, as often as they quote the words, 'This is my body', we must retort with the other words, which precede them, 'take', and 'eat'. For the meaning of the words is: 'By sharing in the breaking of bread, according to the order and rite which I have commanded, you will also be sharing in my body.' Thus when a person eats it on his own, the promise is non-effective in that case. Besides, these words teach us what the Lord wants us to do. 'Take', he says. Therefore, those who sacrifice to God take their lead from some other teacher than Christ, for He does not give us instructions in these words to carry out a sacrifice.

But what do the Papists actually say about the Mass? At first they were presumptuous enough to allege that it was right and proper for it to be called a sacrifice. They now admit that it is a commemorative sacrifice indeed, but in this way, that by their daily offering the blessing of redemption is brought to the living and the dead. Whatever it may be, they certainly present something that looks like a sacrifice (*immolationis spectaculum*). In the first place it is a high-handed thing to do, seeing that there is no command of Christ to justify it. But they commit a still more serious sin in doing this, because, while Christ intended that the purpose of the Supper should be that we take and eat, they have corrupted it to serve exactly the opposite purpose.

This is my body. I shall not go over once again the unhappy battles which have been disturbing the Church in our time, over the meaning of these words. I only wish it were possible to bury all remembrance of them in everlasting oblivion! I shall give my own views about the words, not only sincerely and honestly, but also, without any reservation, as I usually do.

Christ calls the bread His body. I reject, without further argument, the absurd notion that our Lord did not show the bread to the apostles, but His own body, which was plain before their eyes; for immediately afterwards there come the words, 'This cup is the new covenant in my blood.' Let there be no further questioning of the fact that here Christ is referring to the bread.

But now we turn to the question, what does He mean when He refers to the bread? In order to arrive at the meaning we must bear in mind that He is speaking figuratively; and he would be an exceedingly bold man who would deny that. Why, then, is the term body applied to the bread? I think everybody would agree that it is for the same reason as John calls the Holy Spirit a dove (John 1.32). So far we are in agreement. Further, in the case of the Spirit the reason was that He had appeared in the form of a dove; therefore the name, Spirit, is transferred to the visible sign. Is there any reason why we should not say that metonymy is used here in a similar way, and the name body given to the bread, because it is a sign or symbol of the body? If any disagree with me they will perhaps pardon me; but it seems to me that it is only causing trouble to persist in arguing about that. I am therefore quite clear in my own mind that this is a sacramental way of speaking (*sacramentalem loquendi modum*), when the Lord applies to the sign the name of the reality signified (*rei signatae*).

We must now go a step further, and ask why metonymy is used. My answer to that is that the name of the reality signified is not given to the sign simply because it stands for it (*sit figura*); but rather because it is a symbol by which the reality is held out to us (*exhibetur*). For I do not accept the comparisons which some people make with secular or worldly things, for they are in a different category from the sacraments of our Lord. The statue of Hercules is called 'Hercules'; but it is nothing else but a bare, empty representation (*figura*). But the dove is described as the Spirit, because it is a definite pledge (*tessera*) of the presence of the invisible Spirit. Therefore the bread is the body of Christ, because it bears indubitable witness to the fact that the very body, which it stands for, is held out to us; or because, in offering us that symbol, the Lord is also giving us His body at the same time; for Christ is not one to deceive us, and make fools of us with empty representations. Accordingly, it is as clear as day to me that here the reality is joined to the sign; in other words, we really do become sharers in the body of Christ, so far as spiritual power is concerned, just as much as we eat the bread.

We must now look into the mode of participation. The Papists press their doctrine of transubstantiation upon us. They hold that, when the consecration has taken place, the substance of the bread no longer remains, but only the accidents. Over against this fabrication we set, not only the plain words of Scripture, but also the very nature of the sacraments. For what will the signification (*significatio*) of the Supper be, if there is no analogy between the visible sign and the spiritual reality (*si nulla sit inter signum visibile et rem spiritualem analogia*)? They think that the sign has the false and misleading appearance (*speciem*) of bread. What, then, about the reality signified? It can only be a mere piece of make-believe. Therefore, if there ought to be a corresponding relationship (*convenientiam*) between the sign and the reality (*veritate*) behind it, then the bread must be real (*verum*) bread, not imaginary, in order to represent the real (*verum*) body of Christ. Besides, this verse shows that it is not just that the body of Christ is given to us, but that it is given to us as food. Now, it is not the colour at all, but the substance of the bread, that nourishes us. To put it in a nutshell, if the reality itself is to be a genuine reality, the sign must also be a genuine sign.

Therefore, having rejected the nonsense of the Papists, let us see the way in which the body of Christ is given to us. Some people's explanation is that it is given to us when we are made sharers in all the benefits, which Christ procured for us in His own body; by that I mean, when, by faith, we embrace Christ, crucified for us and raised from the dead, and, in that way, come to share effectively in all His benefits. Those who think like this, have every right to their point of view. But I myself maintain that it is only after we obtain Christ Himself, that we come to share in the benefits of Christ. And I further maintain that He is obtained, not just when we believe that He was sacrificed for us, but when He dwells in us, when He is one with us, when we are members of His flesh, when, in short, we become united in one life and substance (if I may say so) with Him. Besides, I am paying attention to the implication of the words, for Christ does not offer us only the benefit of His death and resurrection, but the self-same body in which He suffered and rose again. My conclusion is that the body of Christ is really (*realiter*), to use the usual word, i.e. truly (*vere*) given to us in the Supper, so that it may be health-giving food for our souls. I am adopting the usual terms, but I mean that our souls are fed by the substance of His body, so that we are truly (*vere*) made one with Him; or, what amounts to the same thing, that a life-giving power from the flesh of Christ (*vim ex Christi carne vivificam*) is poured into us through the medium of the Spirit, even although it is at a great distance from us, and is not mixed with us (*nec misceatur nobiscum*).

Only one problem remains: how is it possible for His body, which is in heaven to be given to us here on earth? Some people think that the body of Christ is boundless, and is not confined to any one place, but fills both heaven and earth, like the essence of God. That notion is so absurd that it does not need to be refuted. The Schoolmen discuss the question of His body of glory with more acuteness, but all their teaching simply amounts to this, that Christ is to be found in the bread, as if He were shut up (*inclusus*) in it. The outcome is that men look with amazement upon the bread, and give adoration to it as if it were Christ. Should anyone ask them whether it is the bread they worship, or its appearance (*speciem*), they are certain to answer him with a firm 'neither', but all the same, when they are going to give Christ their adoration, they turn in the direction of the bread. By that I mean that it is not merely a matter of turning their eyes and their whole body, but also their thoughts. Now, what else is this but pure idolatry? But the sharing in the Lord's body, which, I maintain, is offered to us in the Supper, demands neither a local presence, nor the descent of Christ, nor an infinite extension of His body, nor anything of that sort; for, in view of the fact that the Supper is a heavenly act, there is nothing absurd about saying that Christ remains in heaven and is yet received by us. For the way in which He imparts Himself to us is by the secret power of the Holy Spirit, a power which is able not only to bring together, but also to join together, things which are separated by distance, and by a great distance at that.

But to be capable of this impartation, we must rise up to heaven. In this connexion our physical senses are of no avail to us, and so it is faith that must come to our help. When I speak of 'faith', I do not mean any kind of opinion, which depends upon what men make up, since there are many people constantly boasting about their 'faith', and who are extremely wide of the mark on the point at issue here. What then? You see bread, and nothing else, but you hear that it is a sign of the body of Christ. Be quite sure that the Lord will really carry out what you understand the words to mean: that His body, which you do not see at all, is spiritual food for you. It seems unbelievable that we are fed by the flesh of Christ, which is so far away from us. Let us remember that it is a secret and wonderful work done by the Holy Spirit, and it would be sinful of you to measure it by the little standard of your own understanding. In the meantime, however, get rid of stupid notions, which keep your eyes glued on the bread. Let Christ keep His flesh, which is real flesh (*veram carnis naturam*), and do not hold the mistaken view that His body stretches all over heaven and earth. Do not tear Him into pieces by your fanciful ideas, and do not worship Him in this place or that according to your carnal apprehension (*pro carnali tuo sensu*). Let Him remain in His heavenly glory; and aspire to reach heaven yourself, that, from it, He may impart Himself to you.

These few thoughts will satisfy the minds of right-minded, humble people. My advice to the inquisitive is to look elsewhere for the satisfaction of their craving for information.

Which is broken for you. Some think that this refers to the distribution of the bread, because it was necessary that Christ's body be preserved intact, to conform with the prediction in Exodus 12.46: 'not a bone of him shall be broken.' For myself, while acknowledging that Paul has made allusion to the breaking of the bread, yet I take broken to be used here in the sense of sacrificed; certainly this is not the proper use of the word, but it is not out of place. For even if 'not a bone of him' was damaged, yet, since His body was exposed first of all to so much torture and suffering, and then to the punishment of death in its cruellest form, it cannot be said that it was uninjured. That is what Paul means by its being broken. This, however, is the second part of the promise, and it must be not passed over lightly. For the Lord does not offer His body to us, just His body with nothing else said about it, but His body as having been sacrificed for us. The first part, then, tells us that His body is held out to us; this second part brings out what we come to enjoy through it, viz. a share in redemption, and the application to us of the benefit of His sacrifice. That is why the Supper is a mirror which represents Christ crucified to us, so that a man cannot receive the Supper and enjoy its benefits, unless he embraces Christ crucified.

This do in remembrance of me. The Supper is therefore a memorial (μνημόσυνον) provided to assist our weakness; for if we were otherwise sufficiently mindful of the death of Christ, this help would be superfluous. This applies to all the sacraments, for they help us in our weakness. But we shall soon learn what sort of memorial of Himself Christ wanted us to keep in the Supper.,

Some draw the inference from this phrase that, in these circumstances, Christ is not present in the Supper, because there can only be a memorial (*memoria*) of something that is absent. That can be easily answered: according to this way of thinking of the Supper as remembrance (*recordatio*), Christ is indeed absent from it. For Christ is not visibly present, and is not seen by our eyes as are the symbols, which, by representing Him, stir us up to remember Him. Finally, in order to be present with us, He does not change His place, but from heaven He sends down the efficacy of His flesh to be present in us.

25. *The cup, after they had taken their supper.* The apostle seems to suggest that there was a certain interval of time between the giving out of the bread and the cup; and the Evangelists do not make it quite clear if the whole was a continuous action. Indeed that does not matter very much, because it may well have been that the Lord gave some discourse, which would have come in between His giving out of the bread and the cup. But, since He was doing and saying nothing that was unrelated to the mystery, there is no need for us to say that its administration was disorganized or broken up.

248

I did not want to adopt Erasmus' rendering, 'when supper was over', because ambiguity should be avoided in a matter of such great importance.

This cup is the new covenant. What is predicated of the *cup* applies also to the bread; and so He is using these words to express what He had already said more briefly, that the bread is His *body.* For we have it for this reason, that it may be a covenant in His body, i.e. a *covenant* which has been once for all ratified by the sacrifice of His body, and is now confirmed by eating, viz, when believers eat that sacrifice. And so, where Paul and Luke speak of the *covenant in my blood* Matthew and Mark speak of *the blood of the covenant*, which amounts to the same thing. For the blood was poured out to reconcile us to God, and now we drink it spiritually in order to have a share in that reconciliation. Therefore, in the Supper we have both the covenant (*foedus*) and a reinforcing pledge of the covenant.

If the Lord spares me I shall speak about the word covenant or testament (*testamentum*) in the commentary on the Epistle to the Hebrews. But it is well known that sacraments are described as 'testaments', because they provide us with 'testimonies' of God's goodwill, in order to make our minds all the surer of it. For the Lord deals with us in a similar way to men, who make their covenants with each other with solemn rites. This way of speaking is by no means unsuitable, because, by reason of the connexion between word and sign, the covenant of the Lord really is bound up with the sacraments, and the term covenant (*foedus*) bears a relation to us, or embraces us. This will be of great value for understanding the nature of the sacraments, for, if they are covenants, then they contain promises, which may awaken men's consciences to an assurance of salvation. It follows from this that they are not only outward signs of the faith we profess, for men to see, but also aids to our own inner life of faith.

This do, as oft as ye drink. Christ has therefore instituted a twofold sign in the Supper. Those things which God hath joined together, let not man put asunder. Therefore to distribute the bread without the cup is to mutilate the institution of Christ. For we are listening to the words of Christ. As He commands us to eat the bread, so He commands us to drink of the cup. Complying with one half of the commandment, and disregarding the other, is nothing else but making a mockery of what He has laid down. But debarring the people from the cup which Christ gives to everybody, as happens under the tyranny of the Pope, is without a doubt a diabolical presumption. Their quibble that Christ was speaking to the apostles, and not to the ordinary people, is exceedingly childish, and is easily refuted from this very passage; for here Paul is addressing himself to men and women without distinction, and to the whole Church in fact, and says that he has delivered this to them in accordance with the Lord's commandment. By what spirit will those who have dared to annul this institution allege they were directed? And yet this gross corruption is also doggedly defended in our own day. Little wonder that they are brazen enough to use speeches and writings in an attempt to justify something which they are defending by fire and sword in such a cruel way!

26. *For as often as ye eat.* Paul now adds a description of the way in which the memorial ought to be kept, viz. with thanksgiving. It is not that the memorial depends completely upon the confession of our lips, for the main point is that the power of the death of Christ should be sealed upon our consciences. But this knowledge ought to move us to praise Him openly, so as to let men know, when we are in their company, what we are aware of within ourselves in the presence of God. The Supper, is therefore, if I may say so, a kind of memorial (*quoddam memoriale*) which must always be maintained in the Church until the final coming of Christ; and which was instituted for this purpose, that Christ may remind us of the benefit of His death, and that we, on our part, may acknowledge it before men. That is why it is called the *Eucharist.* Therefore, in order that you may celebrate the Supper properly, you must bear in mind that you will have to make profession of your faith.

This shows us quite clearly how impudently they make a mockery of God, who boast that in the Mass they have something answering to the nature of the Supper. For what is the Mass? They admit (for I am not speaking about the Papists, but about the would-be followers of Nicodemus) that it is packed full of detestable superstitions, to which they pretend to be giving their approval by their outward posture. What sort of way is this to proclaim the death of Christ? Are they not rather abandoning it?

Until he come. Since we always stand in need of an aid such as this, as long as we are living in this world, Paul points out that we have been entrusted with this act of remembrance (*recordationem*) until Christ appears for judgement. For, in view of the fact that He is not present with us in a visible form, we need to have some symbol of His spiritual presence, with which to occupy our minds.

27. *Wherefore whosoever shall eat the bread . . . unworthily.* If the Lord expects gratitude from us when we receive this mystery; if He wants us to acknowledge His grace with our heart and make it known with our lips, then the man who has offered Him insult rather than honour will not escape without punishment; for the Lord will not tolerate the despising of His commandment.

Now, in order to grasp the meaning of this verse, we must know what 'eating unworthily' means. Some people make it apply only to the Corinthians, and to the corruption which had got such a hold in their midst. But my own view is that Paul, as he usually does, moves from that particular suggestion to general teaching, or from one example to a whole class. The Corinthians had one particular fault. Paul takes advantage of this to speak of every kind of fault to be found in the administration or receiving of the Supper. He says: 'God will not allow this mystery to be desecrated without punishing it severely.'

Therefore, to 'eat unworthily' is to ruin the pure and proper use by our own abuse. That is why there are various degrees of unworthiness, so to speak; and some people sin more seriously, while others do so only slightly. Any fornicator, perjurer, drunkard or cheat, without a shred of penitence, may force his way in. Since reckless contempt such as that bears the mark of a cruel insult to Christ, there is no doubt that anyone like that receives the Supper to his own destruction. Another will come who is not in the grip of any obvious or perceptible fault, but all the same is not as prepared in his heart as he ought to be. Since this complacency or carelessness is a sign of irreverence, it also deserves the punishment of God. Thus, since there are various degrees of eating unworthily, the Lord inflicts lighter punishments on some, severer on others.

Now this verse has given rise to the question, which some people later went on to debate far too hotly, whether people who eat unworthily are in fact eating the body of Christ at all. For some people were so carried away by the controversy as to say that it is received by good and bad alike; and in our own day many loud-mouthed persons are doggedly maintaining that in the very first Supper Peter received no more than Judas. I am indeed reluctant to enter upon a rather fierce debate with anyone about this matter, which, in my opinion, is a peripheral one. But as others take it upon themselves to adopt the attitude of a schoolmaster, and, without any justification, to declaim what suits themselves, and to shout down anyone offering the slightest suggestion of the opposite point of view, we will therefore be pardoned if we quietly give reasons to support what we consider to be the truth.

It is an axiom to me, and I will not allow myself to be shifted from it, that Christ cannot be separated from His Spirit. That convinces me that when we receive His body, it is neither His dead, passive body, nor His body divorced from the grace and power of His Spirit. I will not spend much time in proving what I have just said.

Now if a man has not a vestige of a living faith or of repentance, and nothing of the Spirit of Christ, how can he receive Christ Himself? More than that, since he is completely under the control of Satan and sin, how will he be fit to receive Christ? Therefore, on the one hand,

I grant that there are persons who truly receive Christ in the Supper and are yet, at the same time, unworthy. Many of the weak, for example, are in that category. On the other hand I do not take the view that those who bring simply a faith in the historical events of the Gospel (*fidem historicam*),[1] without a lively awareness of repentance and faith, receive only the sign. For I cannot bear to tear Christ apart, and I am horrified at the absurd notion that to unbelievers He gives Himself to be eaten in a lifeless form, as it were. And Augustine is thinking along these lines when he says that the wicked receive Christ in the Supper in so far as it is a sacrament (*sacramento tenus*). He puts that more clearly in another passage, when he teaches that, while the rest of the apostles ate the bread, i.e. the Lord (*panem Dominum*), Judas however ate only the bread of the Lord (*panem Domini*).

But the objection is made here that the efficacy of the sacraments does not depend upon the worthiness of men, and that the promises of God are not in the least impaired or destroyed by the badness of men. I agree with that, and for that very reason I say further, and in explicit terms, that the body of Christ is offered to bad men just as much as to good, and that is all that is required so far as the effect of the sacrament and the faithfulness of God are concerned. For, in the Supper God does not cheat the wicked by a mere representation of the body of His Son, but really does hold it out to them; and the bread is not an empty sign for them, but a pledge (*tessera*) of His faithfulness. Their rejecting it does not damage or alter the nature of the sacrament in any way whatever.

We must still deal with an objection arising from what Paul says in this passage. 'Paul says the unworthy are guilty, because they do not discern the Lord's body, therefore they do receive His body in it.' I say that that conclusion is wrong. For, apart from their rejecting it, it is right to call them guilty, because they desecrate and dishonour what is offered to them by the way they use it, as if they were throwing it on the ground and trampling it underfoot. Do you call that an insignificant sacrilege? So I see no difficulty in what Paul says, so long as you pay attention to what God is offering and holding out to the wicked, and not to what they receive.

28. *But let a man prove himself.* The following exhortation is drawn from the threat that has just been given. If those who eat unworthily are guilty of the body and blood of the Lord, then let no-one approach the table without being well and truly prepared. Let everyone, therefore, take care not to fall into this sacrilege through neglect or indifference.

---

[1] French text: 'a historical faith, as it is called, i.e. just assenting to the Gospel story.'

But the question is now asked: when Paul summons us to an examination, what ought the nature of it to be? The Papists think that it consists in auricular confession. They order all those who are about to receive the Supper to examine their lives carefully and anxiously, so that they may unburden all their sins in the ear of a priest. That is their method of preparation! But I myself maintain that the holy examination of which Paul is speaking is far removed from torture. Those people think that they are clear after they have tortured themselves with their thoughts for a few hours, and have let the priest into the secret of their shamefulness. It is another kind of examination that Paul requires here, one corresponding to the proper use of the Holy Supper.

This is the quickest or easiest method of preparation for you. If you want to derive proper benefit from this gift of Christ, you must bring faith and repentance. Therefore, so that you may come well prepared, the examination is based on those two things. Under repentance I include love, for there is no doubt that the man, who has learnt to deny himself in order to devote himself to Christ and His service, will also give himself whole-heartedly to the promotion of the unity which Christ has commended to us. Indeed it is not perfect faith or repentance that is asked for. This is said because some people, by being far too insistent upon a perfection which cannot be found anywhere, are putting a barrier between every single man and woman and the Supper for ever. But if you are serious in your intention to aspire to the righteousness of God, and if, humbled by the knowledge of your own wretchedness, you fall back on the grace of Christ, and rest upon it, be assured that you are a guest worthy of approaching this table. By saying that you are worthy, I mean that the Lord does not keep you out, even if in other respects you are not all you ought to be. For faith, even if imperfect, makes the unworthy worthy.

29. *He who eats unworthily, eats judgement to himself.* Paul had already clearly pointed out the seriousness of the offence, in saying that those who 'eat unworthily shall be guilty of the body and blood of the Lord'. Now he is giving them cause for alarm by the threat of punishment. For many people are not disturbed by the sin itself, but only if they are visited by the judgement of God. So that is what Paul is doing when he declares that this food, which is otherwise beneficial, will be turned into poison and cause the destruction of those who eat unworthily.

Paul adds the reason for this, viz. because they do *not discern the Lord's body*, as something that is holy and not common. What he means is that they handle the sacred body of Christ with unclean hands, and, worse, they treat it as if it were worthless, giving not a thought to its great value. They will therefore pay the penalty for desecrating it so much. But let my readers bear in mind what I said a little ago, that the body of Christ is *offered* to them, even if their unworthiness prevents them from sharing in it.

For this cause many among you are weak and sickly, and not a few sleep. But if we discerned ourselves, we should not be judged. But when we are judged, we are chastened of the Lord, that we may not be condemned with the world. Wherefore, my brethren, when ye come together to eat, wait one for another. If any man is hungry, let him eat at home; that your coming together be not unto judgement. And the rest will I set in order whensoever I come. (30–34)

30. *For this cause etc.* Having dealt in general terms with the matter of eating unworthily, and the kind of punishment awaiting those who desecrate this mystery, Paul now speaks about the punishment which they were undergoing at that very time. We do not know if a plague was raging there at the time, or whether they were afflicted by other kinds of diseases. Whatever it was, we gather from what Paul says, that the Lord had sent some scourge to discipline them. And when Paul says that they are being punished because of eating unworthily, he is certainly not hazarding a guess, but is asserting something of which he is very well aware. So he says that many lay sick, that many were in the grip of a lingering state of weakness, and many had died, because of their abuse of the Supper, by which they had offended God. He is pointing out in this way that we are given a warning by diseases and other scourges of God, so that we might think about our sins; for, since God finds no pleasure in our afflictions, He does not hurt us unless there is good reason for doing so.

This is a big and many-sided subject; but let a very brief comment on it suffice here. If, in Paul's time, an abuse of the Supper, which was not of the most serious kind, could stir up the wrath of God against the Corinthians, so that He punished them so severely, what are we to think about the situation in our own day? Throughout the range of Popery we see not only horrible desecrations of the Supper, but also a profane and detestable thing set up in its place.

(1) In the first place, it is prostituted to sordid gain and money-making. (2) It is a mutilated thing, because the cup has been taken away. (3) Its form has been quite changed, since it has become the custom for each one to have his feast on his own, so that sharing with each other is done away with. (4) No explanation of the mystery is given in it, but all that is to be heard is a murmuring, which is more like the incantations of magicians, or the horrible sacrifices of the heathen, than our Lord's institution. (5) There are countless ceremonies, abounding not only in senseless things, but also in superstition, and, on that account, obvious corruptions. (6) There is the devilish

invention of sacrifice, which amounts to a wicked blasphemy against the death of Christ. (7) It is well designed for causing wretched men to become drunk with a carnal confidence, when they set it before God as an expiation, and think that by this charm they are driving away everything that could hurt them, and that without faith and without penitence. Yes, and more than that, when they are so sure that they are armed against the devil and death, and that, as far as God is concerned, they are securely protected against Him, they make so bold as to sin with much greater freedom, and they grow in stubbornness. (8) In it an idol is worshipped in the place of Christ. In short, it is swarming with all sorts of abominations.

Now, we administer the Supper in its purity, after it has been restored to us as though it had come back from exile. But even among us how much irreverence there is! How much hypocrisy there is in the case of many people! What a shocking mix-up there is, when no distinction is made, and scoundrels and people who are openly dissolute push their way in, people whom no decent or respectable person would have anything to do with in ordinary social relations! And still we wonder what is the reason for so many wars, so many plagues, so many failures of the harvest, so many disasters and calamities, as if the cause was not in fact as plain as a pikestaff. And we certainly cannot look for an end to misfortunes, until we have removed their cause by correcting our faults.

31. *For if we were to judge ourselves.* Here we have another remarkable statement: that God does not become angry with us all of a sudden, punishing us as soon as we go wrong, but for the most part it is because of our negligence that He is almost forced to punish us, i.e. when He sees that we are unconcerned and apathetic, and deluding ourselves so far as our sins are concerned. Thus we turn away or mitigate punishments which threaten us, if we first of all take stock of ourselves, and, full of penitence, ward off God's anger by praying earnestly to Him, and by inflicting punishments on ourselves of our own free will. In a word, believers forestall the judgement of God by penitence, and the only remedy by which they can obtain acquittal in the sight of God is by voluntarily condemning themselves.

However, you are not to understand (as the Papists usually do) that there is a kind of transaction between us and God in this connexion, so that, by inflicting punishment on ourselves of our own accord, we make amends to Him, and in some sense redeem ourselves from His hand. We do not therefore turn aside the judgement of God in advance because we bring something of a compensating nature, which might appease Him. The reason for it is that when God punishes us, He intends to shake us out of our lethargy, and stir us up to penitence. If we do that of our own accord there is no longer any reason for Him to proceed with carrying out His judgement against us. But if anyone who had begun to be dissatisfied with himself and to practise penitence is, nevertheless, still pursued by God's scourging, we should realize that his repentance is not so complete and strong that he does not stand in need of some reproof to help develop it still further. Note how repentance forestalls the judgement of God as a suitable remedy, but not as something that replaces it.

32. *But when we are judged.* Here we have much-needed comfort. For if anybody in trouble thinks that God is angry with him, he will be broken in spirit rather than stirred up to penitence. Paul therefore says that when God shows His anger to believers He does it in such a way that He does not forget His mercy at the same time; and even more than that, he says that when He punishes them it is out of His particular concern for their salvation. It is an inestimable comfort that the punishments by which our sins are corrected are proofs, not of the wrath of God for our destruction, but rather of His Fatherly love; and that, at the same time, they help us to recover our salvation for God is angry with us as sons, whom He does not want to perish.

When Paul says *that we may not be condemned with this world* he is meaning two things. The first is that when the children of this world are contented and untroubled, lulled to sleep by their own pleasures, they are being fattened like pigs for the day of slaughter. For even although the Lord does sometimes summon the ungodly also to repentance by scourging them, yet He often passes them by as strangers, and allows them to take their downward way unchecked, until they have filled the measure of their final condemnation to the full. This privilege, of being called back from destruction by punishments, is therefore one that belongs only to believers.

The second thing he means is that punishments are remedies which believers need, for otherwise they themselves would also rush onwards to eternal destruction, if they were not held in check by temporary punishments.

Those thoughts should help us, not only to be patient, so that we may endure calmly the afflictions laid upon us by God, but also to be grateful, so that giving thanks to God our Father, we may submit ourselves to His discipline in willing obedience. There are many other ways in which they can be of use to us: for they make our punishments salutary things for us, so long as they are teaching us to mortify the flesh, and to be humble before God; they make us accustomed to obeying God; they convince us of our own weakness; they set our hearts aflame with an eagerness for prayer; they give hope something to work on; so that the long and short of it is that whatever severity there may be in these thoughts is all absorbed in spiritual gladness.

33. *Wherefore, my brethren.* From dealing with teaching of a general nature Paul now returns to the particular instance, with which he had begun. He now ends up by saying that equality must be preserved in the Lord's Supper so that there may be the genuine sharing which there ought to be, and that each person may not celebrate his supper on his own; and finally that this sacrament should not be mixed up with ordinary feasts.

34. *And the rest I will set in order.* It is likely that there were some other matters besides this, which it would be worth while changing for the better; but because they were of far less importance the apostle puts off their amendment until he visits the Corinthians. Although it could well be that nothing of that sort actually existed there, yet, because a person has a clearer knowledge of what is needed when he is on the spot, Paul retains for himself the freedom to arrange things personally, according to the demands of the actual situation which he will find.

Papists take up this against us also as a shield for the defence of the mass. For they explain that as the 'setting in order' which Paul is promising here; as if, indeed, he would have taken it upon himself to interfere with the unchangeable institution of Christ, which he so clearly endorses in this passage. For what resemblance has the mass to the institution of Christ? But let us hear no more of such nonsense, since there is no doubt that Paul is speaking only of the propriety of outward behaviour. But as that is a matter which is left to the discretion of the Church, so, in regulating it, circumstances of times, places, and people ought to be taken into consideration.

CHAPTER TWELVE

Now concerning spiritual gifts, brethren, I would not have you ignorant. Ye know that when ye were Gentiles ye were led away unto those dumb idols, howsoever ye might be led. Wherefore I give you to understand, that no man speaking in the Spirit of God saith, Jesus is anathema; and no man can say, Jesus is Lord, but in the Holy Spirit. Now there are diversities of gifts, but the same Spirit. And there are diversities of ministrations, and the same Lord. And there are diversities of workings, but the same God, who worketh all things in all. But to each one is given the manifestation of the Spirit to profit withal. (1-7)

1. *Now concerning spiritual things.* Paul passes on to correct another fault. Since the Corinthians made wrong use of the gifts of God for ostentation and display, there was little or no concern for love. Paul now teaches them that the reason for believers being enriched with spiritual gifts by God is for the upbuilding of their brothers. But Paul breaks down the principle into two parts. In the first place he points out that God is the source of the gifts; then, having laid that down, he goes on to discuss their purpose. From their own experience he proves that the things in which they were boasting come to men from the graciousness of God; for he reminds them how ignorant, stupid and spiritually blind they were before God called them. Therefore it is plain that it was not nature that provided them with these gifts, but God in His gratuitous kindness.

As far as the words are concerned, when he says, 'I would not have you ignorant', we must supply 'of what is right', or 'of where your duty lies', or something of that sort. And by spiritual things he means spiritual gifts, as we shall see later.

In what follows there are two possible readings; some manuscripts have ὅτι only, others add ὅτε. They use ὅτι in the sense of the explanatory 'that'. ὅτε means 'when', and that reading is far more suitable. That variation apart, the construction is confused in other ways; but the meaning is clear enough. Quite literally it reads: 'You know that when you were Gentiles, following after dumb idols, just as you were led.' But in my own translation I have kept faithfully to what Paul intended to say.

By *dumb idols* he means that they could neither think nor move about.

This verse brings home to us how great the blindness of man's mind is, when he lacks the illumination of the Holy Spirit; because he gapes in wonder at dumb idols, and cannot rise any higher than that in his search for God; and more than that, indeed, he is driven by Satan like a beast.

Paul uses the word Gentiles here with the same meaning as in Ephesians 2.12. There he says: 'You were at that time Gentiles, without God, strangers to the hope of salvation, etc.' Perhaps Paul is also arguing from the opposite: What if now, after God has taken them under His protection, to be directed by His Word and Spirit, they show less willingness to follow His instructions, than their readiness in the old days to give in to Satan's suggestions and carry them out.

3. *Wherefore I give you to understand.* Having pointed a lesson from their own experience, Paul goes on to give instruction of a general nature but based upon it. For what had been the Corinthians' experience is something that all men share in, viz. wandering in error, before being brought back to the truth by God in His graciousness. Therefore, if we are not to be going wrong for ever, we must be under the direction of the Spirit of God. From this it also follows that everything which is concerned with the true knowledge of God is a gift of the Holy Spirit.

Paul also argues from opposite causes to opposite effects. For no-one speaking by the Spirit of God can curse Christ; so, on the other hand, no-one can honour Christ except by the Spirit of God. To say that Jesus is anathema means to use blasphemy against Him. To say that Jesus is Lord means to speak of Him with honour and reverence, and to extol His majesty.

At this point someone asks whether unbelievers have the Spirit of God, when on occasion they sing the praises of Christ in glowing terms. I reply that there is no doubt that they have Him, in so far as that effect is concerned; but the gift of regeneration is one thing, the gift of mere factual knowledge (*intelligentiae*) is another, for even Judas was endowed with that when he preached the Gospel.

We also discover from this just how powerless we are, for we cannot employ our tongues to give praise to God unless they are governed by the Holy Spirit. The Scriptures frequently remind us of this (David bears witness of this when he prays for this gift: 'Lord, open thou my lips' (Ps. 51.15)), and on all sides the saints acknowledge that, unless the Lord opens their mouths, they are not capable of being heralds for Him. Among others, Isaiah says in chapter 6.5, 'I am a man of unclean lips' etc.

4. *Now there are diversities of gifts.* The harmony of the Church lies in the fact that it is, so to speak, a unity of many parts; in other words, when the different gifts are all directed to one and the same end, just

as in music different parts are adjusted to each other and combined so well that they produce one harmonious piece. It is only right, therefore, that *gifts* should be distinguished from each other just as much as offices, and that they should, nevertheless, be all combined in a unity.

Paul speaks in support of this variety of gifts in Romans chapter 12, so that nobody may obscure the distinction which the Lord has made, by boldly usurping somebody else's place. Paul therefore urges individuals to be content with their gifts, and to make the most of them. He forbids them to overstep their own bounds by selfishly striving to get something else. In a word he encourages each one to consider how much he has been given, the nature of his allotted share, and what he has been called to do.

Here, on the other hand, he is instructing individuals to bring whatever they have as a contribution to the common stock, and not to keep the gifts of God to themselves, which would mean that the benefits of each person's gifts would be restricted to himself alone, instead of being shared with others; but to work harmoniously together for the edification of all. In both passages Paul uses the analogy of the human body, but, obviously enough, for different reasons. What he says amounts to this: that gifts are not distributed to believers in such variety, in order that they may be kept in isolation from each other; but there is a unity in difference, because One Spirit is the source of all the gifts, One God is Lord of all the ways of serving (*ministeriorum*), and the originator of all the activities. But God who is the originator ought also to be the goal.

One Spirit. Careful attention should be given to this verse in order to counter fanatics, who think that the name Spirit does not refer to anything *essential*, but only to the gifts or activities of divine power. But Paul shows quite clearly here that there is *one essential* power of God, from which all His activities proceed. The name Spirit is certainly very often transferred by metonymy to the gifts themselves, and so we read of the Spirit of understanding, judgement, might, moderation. But Paul makes it quite plain here that judgement, and understanding, and gentleness and all the rest proceed from the one source. For it is the function of the Holy Spirit to send out the power of God, and keep it at work, by bestowing these gifts on men, and distributing them among them.

5. *One Lord.* The fathers used these verses against the Arians as evidence in support of the Trinity of Persons. For here the Spirit is named, then the Lord, and finally God, and one and the same activity is ascribed to the Three. That means they take Lord to mean Christ. But although I have no objection to this interpretation of the verses, yet I am sure that this is too shaky an argument for anyone wanting to

put Arians to silence; for there is a relation between the words 'services' and 'Lord'. Paul says that the services are different, but there is one God whom we are bound to serve, no matter what service we are engaged in. This opposite view gives a straightforward meaning, letting us see that to make the words refer to Christ alone is too forced.

6. *One God who worketh.* The Greek for the word which is rendered *facultates* (powers, faculties) by me is ἐνεργήματα, a word which is connected with the verb 'to work' (ἐνεργεῖν: *operare*); just as in Latin the noun 'effect' corresponds to the verb 'to effect'. Paul means that even if believers are well equipped with different powers, yet all these powers have their source in the single power of God. In the same way the words in this verse, 'worketh all things in all', are not traced back to God's general providence, but to the generosity which He shows us in thinking everyone worthy of some gift. What it amounts to is that men have nothing good or praiseworthy except what comes from God alone. For that reason it is beside the point here to ask how God acts in Satan and the reprobate.

7. *But to each one is given the manifestation of the Spirit.* Paul now reveals the purpose which God has meant His gifts to serve, for He does not lavish them upon us for nothing, and He does not intend them to be used for show. Therefore we must ask, what purpose do they serve? Paul's answer is πρὸς τὸ συμφέρον, 'for giving benefit', i.e. so that the Church may derive benefit from them.

The manifestation of the Spirit can be taken passively, just as well as actively. It can be read passively because where there is prophecy, or knowledge, or any other gift, there the Spirit of God is manifest. It can be taken as active because, when the Spirit of God provides us with any gift, He unlocks His treasures, in order to reveal to us things, which would otherwise be hidden and beyond our reach. The second is the better interpretation.

Chrysostom's view is rather awkward and forced, viz. that the word 'manifestation' is used because the only way that unbelievers come to know God is by visible miracles.

For to one is given through the Spirit the word of wisdom; and to another the word of knowledge, according to the same Spirit: to another faith, in the same Spirit; and to another gifts of healings, in the one Spirit; and to another workings of miracles; and to another prophecy; and to another discernings of spirits: to another divers kinds of tongues; and to another the interpretation of tongues: but all these worketh the one and the same Spirit, dividing to each one severally even as he will. For as the body is one, and hath many members, and all the members of the body, being many, are one body; so also is Christ. For in one Spirit were we all

*baptized into one body, whether Jews or Greeks, whether bond or free;
and were all made to drink of one Spirit.* (8-13)

8. *For to one.* Paul now goes on to add a list, that is to say, he details
particular kinds of gifts, not all gifts of course, but sufficient for his
present purpose. He says: 'Believers are richly equipped with different
gifts, but let every one acknowledge that the Spirit of God has given
to him whatever he has, for He pours out His gifts, as the sun spreads
its beams all over the land.'

As far as the difference between these gifts is concerned, knowledge
or comprehension (*scientia vel cognitio*) and wisdom are used in various
ways in the Scriptures, but here I understand them as expressing a
difference of degree, as in Col. 2.3, where they are also in conjunction,
and where Paul teaches that 'all the treasures of wisdom and knowledge
are hidden in Christ'. Accordingly I take knowledge to mean an
understanding of holy things; but wisdom a thorough-going grasp of
them. Prudence is sometimes given a kind of intermediate position
between them, and then it means skill in turning knowledge to some
practical purpose. Those two words are indeed very closely related
to each other, but all the same one can see a difference between them,
when they are set side by side. Let *knowledge* therefore be understood
as the ordinary grasp of things, but *wisdom* as including an insight, by
their unveiling, into things of a more secret and lofty nature.

9. The word *faith* is used here for a particular kind of faith, as the
context will soon make plain. This is the type of faith, which does not
lay hold of Christ in His wholeness for redemption, justification and
sanctification, but only in so far as miracles are performed in His name.
Judas had faith like that, and even he carried out miracles by it.
Chrysostom makes a slightly different distinction, calling it the 'faith
relating to miracles' (*signorum*), and not to Christian teaching (*dogma-
torum*), but there is not much divergence between that and the interpretation, which I have just given.

Everyone knows what is meant by the *gift of healings.*

10. There is not the same certainty about *powers to effect miracles* (*de
facultatibus potentiarum*), or, as others render it, 'the workings of powers'
(*operationibus virtutum*). I am however inclined to think that it is the
power (*virtutem*) which is exercised against demons, and also hypocrites.
Thus when Christ and the apostles authoritatively subdued demons or
put them to flight, that was ἐνεργήμα, effective working. Other instances are when Paul brought blindness upon the magician (Acts
13.11); and when Peter caused Ananias and Sapphira to fall dead upon
the ground simply by speaking to them (Acts 5.1-11). Therefore the
gifts of healing and miracles are both channels of God's goodness to

262

us; but in His severity He uses miracles for the destruction of Satan.

I take the term *prophecy* to mean that unique and outstanding gift of revealing what is the secret will of God, so that the prophet is, so to speak, God's messenger to men. My reasons for thinking so will be given more fully later.

The *discerning of spirits* was an acuteness in weighing up men who were making out that they were people of consequence. I am not speaking about the normal common-sense, which we make use of in forming judgements; but this was a special perspicuity, bestowed on a few people as a gift of God. This spiritual judgement was used, not simply to prevent their being deceived by the lying faces or false airs, but rather to enable them to make out the difference between the true ministers of Christ and the false, as if they had marks to distinguish them.

The *interpretation of tongues* was different from the knowledge of tongues, for those who had the latter gift often did not know the language of the people with whom they had to have dealings. Interpreters translated the foreign languages into the native speech. They did not at that time acquire these gifts by hard work or studying; but they were theirs by a wonderful revelation of the Spirit.

11. *The one and the same Spirit dividing to each one.* From all that it follows that people are in the wrong, who do not care a straw about sharing, but break up that holy harmony, where all the parts blend well together—something that can only exist when all, under the direction of the same Spirit, work together in agreement. Paul is again calling the Corinthians back to unity, when he reminds them that they have all obtained whatever gifts they have, from the one source; but at the same time he shows that no-one has so much as to be self-sufficient, and not need the help of other people. For that is what he means by saying, 'dividing to each one severally even as he will'. The Spirit of God therefore distributes these gifts among us, so that we may all make our contribution to the common good. He does not lavish everything on any individual, in order to prevent anyone from being so satisfied with his lot, as to cut himself off from others, and live to himself alone. The adverb 'severally' is used for the same purpose, because it is particularly important that the difference from one another, by which God binds us in dependence on each other, be properly preserved by us.

Now, when 'willing' is predicated of the Spirit, along with power at that, it is permissible to draw the conclusion that the Spirit is truly and properly God.

12. *For as the body is one.* Paul now introduces the simile of the human body, which he also uses in Romans 12.4, but for a different

purpose, as I have already pointed out. There he is directing each person to be content with his own calling, and not to trespass on other people's territory, for ambition, inquisitiveness or some other self-seeking motive drives many people into grasping more than is good for them. But in this passage Paul is urging believers to bind themselves together by pooling their gifts for the benefit of each other; for their gifts were given them by God, not for every individual to nurse his own to himself, but so that they might help one another.

Besides, it is quite a common thing for any association or company of men to be called a body, as, for instance, the body-politic, the governing body, and the body of the people. Once, long ago, when Menenius Agrippa wanted to reconcile the Roman people to the senate, against whom they were rebelling, he told a fable,[1] which bore some resemblance to what Paul is teaching here. But the situation is entirely different in the case of Christians, for they do not constitute a mere *body*-politic, but are the spiritual and mystical body of Christ, as Paul himself adds.

The meaning therefore is this: even if there are different members in the body, with different functions, yet they are connected together in such a way as to form a unity. Therefore, we who are members of Christ, even if we are equipped with different gifts, ought nevertheless to be concerned about that union with each other, which we have in Christ.

So also is Christ. The name of Christ is substituted for that of the Church, for the comparison (*similitudo*) was to be applied, not to the only-begotten Son of God, but to us. But because Paul calls the Church 'Christ' this verse is full of rare comfort. For Christ invests us with this honour, that He wishes to be discerned and recognized, not only in His own Person, but also in His members. So the same apostle says in Ephesians 1.23 that the Church is His fullness (*complementum*), as if He would be mutilated in some way, were He to be separated from His members. And indeed, as Augustine neatly puts it somewhere in his writings, 'Since in Christ we are a fruitful vine, *out of Christ what are we but withered little branches?*' Our comfort lies in this truth, that as He and the Father are one, so we are also one with Him. That is why He shares His name with us.

13. *For in one Spirit were we all baptized.* Proof of this is provided by the effect of baptism. Paul says: 'By baptism we are ingrafted into the body of Christ, so that we are bound together, joined each to the other as members, and live the one life. Therefore he who wants to remain in the Church of Christ must necessarily devote himself to this fellowship.'

---

[1] His fable was that of the belly and the limbs: Livy, 2.16.7; 2.32.8; 2.33.10.

Paul of course is speaking about the baptism of believers, which is efficacious through the grace of the Spirit. For to many people baptism is merely a formality, a symbol without any effect; but believers actually do receive the reality with the sacrament. So, as far as God is concerned, it always holds true that baptism is an ingrafting into the body of Christ, because everything that God shows forth to us in baptism, He is prepared to carry out, so long as we, on our part, are capable of it. And the apostle is keeping things in proper perspective here, in teaching that it is undoubtedly of the essence of baptism to incorporate us into the body of Christ. However, so that no-one might suppose that this is effected by the outward symbol, Paul adds that it is the work of the Holy Spirit.

Whether Jews or Greeks. Paul mentions these two classes in order to point out that the difference in people's condition is no obstacle to that sacred unity, which he is commending. The addition of this phrase is appropriate and timely, for two things could have given rise to bad feeling at that time. The first was that the Jews were reluctant to put other peoples on the same level as themselves. The other situation liable to cause jealousy was where all the people who had outstanding gifts were keeping themselves quite apart from their brothers, by maintaining an attitude of superiority.

And were all made to drink of one Spirit. The literal rendering of the Greek is, 'we have been made to drink into one Spirit'. It seems, however, that in order to prevent the two words ἐν (in) and ἕν (one) coming one before the other, Paul purposely changed ἐν to εἰς (into), as he is accustomed to doing quite often. He does not therefore mean that 'we have drunk of the same Spirit', but rather is pointing out once again that it is by the power of the Spirit of Christ that we are made to drink.

Then, it is not certain whether here he is speaking about baptism or the Lord's Supper. I am rather of the opinion that he should be understood as referring to the Supper, because he mentions drink, for I have no doubt that he intended an allusion to the analogy of the sign (*ad signi analogiam*). Drinking has certainly no connexion at all with baptism. But even if the cup is only half of the Supper, that does not cause any difficulty however, for it is quite a common practice in the Scriptures to use synecdoche when speaking of the sacraments. In chapter 10 he mentioned the bread only, omitting any reference to the cup. The meaning, therefore, will be that the purpose for which we share in the cup is that we may all drink the same spiritual drink. For in it we drink the life-giving blood of Christ, so that we may have life in common with Him; and that really happens when He dwells in us by His Spirit. Furthermore that Spirit is One. Paul therefore

teaches that as soon as believers are initiated by the baptism of Christ
they are already filled with zeal for cultivating unity with each other;
then afterwards, when they receive the Holy Supper, they are again
led, step by step, to the same unity, because they are all being revived
by the same drink at the same time.

*For the body is not one member, but many. If the foot shall say, Because
I am not the hand, I am not of the body; it is not therefore not of the body.
And if the ear shall say, Because I am not the eye, I am not of the body;
it is not therefore not of the body. If the whole body were an eye, where
were the hearing? If the whole were hearing, where were the smelling?
But now hath God set the members each one of them in the body, even as
it pleased him. And if they were all one member, where were the body?
But now they are many members, but one body. And the eye cannot say
to the hand, I have no need of thee: or again the head to the feet, I have
no need of you. Nay, much rather, those members of the body which
seem to be more feeble are necessary: and those parts of the body, which
we think to be less honourable, upon these we bestow more abundant
honour; and our uncomely parts have more abundant comeliness;
whereas our comely parts have no need: but God tempered the body
together, giving more abundant honour to that part which lacked; that
there should be no schism in the body; but that the members should have
the same care one for another. And whether one member suffereth, all
the members suffer with it; or one member is honoured, all the members
rejoice with it. Now ye are the body of Christ, and severally members
thereof.* (14–27)

15. *If the foot were to say.* This is the development ($\epsilon\pi\epsilon\xi\epsilon\rho\gamma\alpha\sigma\iota\alpha$) of
the preceding sentence; or, to put it in another way, Paul elaborates
and amplifies, in order to elucidate what he has just compressed into
a few words. Again, everything in this section corresponds to the
fable of Menenius Agrippa. If a rebellion were to break out in the
body, the feet saying that they were not obliged to do anything for the
rest of the body, and not only they, but the stomach, eyes and hands
as well, what would the result be? Would it not be the destruction of
the whole body? Yet, Paul is pressing one point here, viz. that each
member should be content with its own place and relative position,
and not be envious of others, since he makes a comparison between the
superior members and those which have a lower value. For the eye
takes a place of greater honour in the body than the hand, and the hand
than the foot. But would nature tolerate it, if the hands were spurred
on by jealousy to refuse to do their work? Will another assent to the
demand of the hand to cut itself off from the rest of the body?

Not to be of the body means here, to have no dealings with the rest of the members, but to live for itself, suiting its own convenience. Paul asks: 'Because the hand is jealous of the eyes, does that give it any right to deny the other members its services?'

These things are said of the physical body, but they ought to be applied to the members of the Church, so that self-seeking, or distorting jealousy and envy may not give rise to bad feeling in our midst, with the consequence that someone occupying an inferior position is unwilling to give his services to those who are his superiors.

17. *If the whole body were an eye.* Paul dismisses that foolish straining after equality by showing that it is impossible. He says: 'If all the members were eager to have the honour that belongs to the eye, the inevitable result would be the destruction of the whole body. For it is impossible for the body to remain healthy and sound, unless its members have different functions, and perform services for each other. Equality is therefore in conflict with the well-being of the body, because it gives rise to confusion, which in turn leads to instant disaster. What a piece of folly it would be, then, if one member, rather than give way to another, were to be responsible for bringing about not only its own ruin, but that of the body as well!'

18. *But now hath God set.* This is another argument based on what God has ordained. It seemed good to God that the body should be composed of different members, and that they should be supplied with different functions and gifts. Therefore any member that is dissatisfied with its own position, is waging war with God like the giants. Let us bow our heads, then, to the order that God Himself has established, so that we will not be wasting our efforts by opposing what He wants.

19. *If they were all one member.* Paul means that God did not bestow different gifts on the members of the body without any purpose or reason, but that He did so because it had to be like that for keeping the body in being; for if such a well-balanced arrangement were done away with, then there would be the confusion and disintegration of chaos. We ought to be all the readier to submit ourselves to the providence of God, therefore, seeing it has made everything serve our common interests so well.

'One member' is taken to mean a uniform mass, unrelieved by any variations. If God were to give our body the shape of a mass like that, it would be a useless lump.

20. *Many members, but one body.* Paul drives this home so often because the heart of the whole matter lies in these words; viz. the unity of the body is of such a kind as can only be preserved by having a variety of members; and, on the other hand, while the members differ from each other in their functions and abilities, it is in such a way that they are nevertheless connected to each other in order to preserve the

unity of the body. Paul is therefore teaching that no body can continue to exist as such, unless its many parts combine in harmony, so that we may know that each of us is consulting the common good as well as his own, by carrying out his own particular function.

21. *The eye cannot say to the hand.* Up to this point Paul has been showing what the duty of the less honourable members is, viz. to give their services to the body, and not to be envious of the more outstanding members. Now, on the other hand, he is instructing the worthier members not to despise the inferior ones, for they cannot do without them. The eye is a superior part to the hand, yet it cannot treat it with disdain, or scoff at it as a useless thing.

22. Paul also argues, by appealing to their usefulness, that that is how it ought to be. Those that are considered not so valuable are the more necessary; therefore, for the sake of the well-being of the body, they ought not to be despised.

Paul uses the word 'weaker' here for 'contemptible', as he does in II Cor. 12.9, when he says that he *glories* in his weaknesses, meaning by this word, things which were bringing contempt and humiliation upon him.

23. *And our uncomely parts.* This is a second argument, to the effect that the shame connected with one member spreads to include the whole body; and that is apparent from the care we take to cover our uncomely parts. Paul says: 'Our *comely* parts do not require any assumed adornment, but we are much more concerned about looking after the parts, that we are modest about, or that are not so presentable. The reason why we do that is that their shame would bring disgrace upon the whole body.'

To bestow honour is to put on a covering for the sake of adornment, so that the parts whose exposure would be a shameful thing are decently hidden.

24. *But God has adjusted the body.* Paul repeats what he had said once before, but more explicitly, viz. that God has ordained this harmonious arrangement, and for the benefit of the whole body at that, because it could not continue to exist otherwise. For why is it that all the members are spontaneous in their concern for the reputation of a member, which is not sufficiently presentable, and unite to cover its shame? The instinct to do this has been given to them by God, because, if there was not this way of keeping things in balance, disagreement would soon break out in the body. It is apparent from this that as soon as someone wrongfully claims more than his allotted share, not only is the body destroyed and the natural arrangement turned upside down, but also that the authority of God is openly rejected.

26. *If one member suffers.* In the human body there exists a sympathy

of such a kind that, if one member suffers any misfortune, all the rest share in its affliction; just as they share in its happiness when something good comes its way. Therefore there is no room for envy or scorn in it.

To be 'honoured' is used in a broad sense here for being in favourable and happy circumstances. Now there is nothing that makes for the fostering of harmony better than this feeling for each other, where each one realizes that he is enriched by the benefits of others every bit as much as they, and that when they suffer loss, he is impoverished along with them.

27. *Now you are the body of Christ.* It follows that all that has been said about the nature and characteristics of the human body, ought to be applied to us, for we are not just a civil society, but, having been ingrafted into the body of Christ, we really are members one of another. Therefore every one of us should realize that whatever his gift, it has been given to him for the upbuilding of all the brethren; with that in mind he should devote it to the common good, and not suppress it, burying it within himself so to speak, or use it as if it were his private possession. A man who stands out because he has greater gifts, should not become swollen-headed, and look down upon others, but he should ponder the fact that there is nothing so insignificant that there is no use for it. To take an example, even the least significant of believers does in fact bear fruit relative to his slender resources, so that there is no such person as a useless member of the Church. Those who are not blessed with such great distinction should not envy those who are superior to them, nor refuse to obey them, but they should keep the position in which they have been placed. Let there be love for each other, sympathy (συμπάθεια) with each other, and consideration for each other. Let it be the common good that influences us, so that we may not ruin the Church by spite, or jealousy, or pride, or any discord; but let every single person rather devote all his energy to its consecration.

This is a rich and splendid theme, but I have confined myself to pointing out how the preceding analogy (*similitudo*) ought to be applied to the Church.

And severally members thereof. Chrysostom thinks that this phrase was added because the Corinthians were not the Church Universal. That interpretation is, to my mind, rather forced. I once thought that it was an indication of some impropriety—'after a fashion' (*quodammodo*), to use the Latin idiom. But when I take everything into closer consideration I rather think it refers to the differences among the members, which Paul had mentioned. Therefore, they are members 'in part', inasmuch as each one has had allocated to him his own share and his precise duties. The context itself leads us to that meaning. So, 'in part' or 'individually', and 'as a whole' will be correlatives.

And God hath set some in the church, first apostles, secondly prophets, thirdly teachers, then miracles, then gifts of healings, helps, governments, divers kinds of tongues. Are all apostles? are all prophets? are all teachers? are all workers of miracles? have all gifts of healings? do all speak with tongues? do all interpret? But desire earnestly the greater gifts. And a still more excellent way shew I unto you. (28–31)

At the beginning of the chapter Paul had spoken about 'powers' (*facultatibus*); now he takes up the discussion of offices. We ought to pay particular attention to this order of things. For the Lord only appointed ministers after first providing them with the requisite gifts, and making them fit for the duties they had to carry out. We must infer from that that people with absolutely no qualifications, who force themselves upon the Church, are fanatics, driven by an evil spirit. There are many, for instance, who boast that they are moved to action by the Spirit, and pride themselves in a secret call of God, when all the time they are unlearned and totally ignorant. But in reality the natural order is that the gifts come before the actual office. Therefore, just as he has already shown that whatever individuals have received from God ought to be given as a contribution to the common good, so Paul now reminds them that the offices are apportioned in such a way that by their combined efforts they may all build up the Church, each person making his own particular contribution at the same time.

28. *First apostles.* Paul does not include every kind of office in his list. Indeed that was not necessary, for all that he wanted to do was to cite examples. In Ephesians 4.11 there is a fuller list of the offices, which are constantly needed for the government of the Church. I shall give the reason for this when I deal with that passage, if the Lord will let me get as far as that; although not even there does he mention all of them.

As far as the verse before us is concerned, we must note that some of the offices, to which Paul is referring, are permanent, while others are temporary. The permanent offices are those which are necessary for the government of the Church. The temporary ones, on the other hand, are those which were designed, at the beginning, for the founding of the Church, and the setting up of the Kingdom of Christ; and which ceased to exist after a while.

The office of teacher (*officium doctoris*) belongs to the first class, that of apostle to the second. For the Lord appointed (*creavit*) the apostles, so that they might spread the Gospel throughout the whole world. He did not assign any particular boundaries or parishes to them but wanted them to act as ambassadors for Him, wherever they went, among people of every nation and language. In that respect they differ from the pastors, who are bound, so to speak, to their own churches. For the pastor does not have a mandate to preach the Gospel all the world over, but to look after the church, that has been committed to his charge. In Ephesians 4.11 Paul includes evangelists in the list, after the apostles, but he omits them here, for he passes from the highest order (*a primo gradu*) straight on to the prophets.

I am certain, in my own mind, that he means by prophets, not those endowed with the gift of foretelling, but those who were blessed with the unique gift of dealing with Scripture, not only by interpreting it, but also by the wisdom they showed in making it meet the needs of the hour. My reason for thinking so is that Paul prefers prophecy to all the other gifts, because it is a greater source of edification, a statement that can hardly be made to apply to the prediction of future events. Again, when he defines the work of the prophet, or at least deals with the main things which he ought to be doing, he says that he devotes himself to consolation, encouragement and teaching. But these activities are quite distinct from predictions. From this verse let us therefore learn that prophets are (1) outstanding interpreters of Scripture; and (2) men endowed with extraordinary wisdom and aptitude for grasping what the immediate need of the Church is, and speaking the right word to meet it. That is why they are, so to speak, messengers who bring news of what God wants.

This difference between them and teachers can be pointed out, that the task of teachers consists in preserving and propagating sound doctrines (*sana dogmata*) so that purity of religion may remain in the Church. Nevertheless, this title is also used in different ways, and perhaps rather refers to the pastor here; unless you may prefer to take it in a general sense for all who are gifted with the ability to teach, as is the case in Acts 13.1, where Luke also brackets them with prophets. I have a reason for not sharing in the opinion of those who confine the task of the prophet to the interpretation of the Scriptures. It is that Paul directs that only two or three of them ought to speak, and in turn at that, and that does not harmonize with their doing nothing else but interpreting the Scriptures. In a word my view is that the prophets referred to here are those who are skilful and experienced in making known the will of God, by applying prophecies, threats, promises, and all the teaching of Scripture to the current needs of the Church. Should anyone be of a different opinion, I am willing to acknowledge that there is room for it, and will not pick a quarrel with him because of it. For it is difficult to make up one's mind about gifts and offices, of which the Church has been deprived for so long, except for mere traces or shades of them, which are still to be found.

As far as miracles and the gift of healing are concerned, I have already spoken about them in chapter 12. Only, it must be observed that Paul is not speaking about the gifts themselves so much as the exercise of them.

Because the apostle is detailing offices here, I do not accept Chrysostom's view that the word ἀντιλήμψεις (i.e. supports or helps) means upholding the weak. What does it mean, then? Surely either it refers to something which was both an office, and a gift, in the Church of long ago, but of which we have no knowledge now; or, it has to do with the work of the diaconate, that is to say, the care of the poor. I prefer the second explanation. But Paul mentions two kinds of deacons in Romans 12.8, and I have spoken about them in the relevant commentary.

I take *governments* to mean elders (*seniores*), who were responsible for discipline. For the early Church had its 'Council of the Elders' (*Senatus*) to keep the people in uprightness of life. Paul reveals that in I Tim. 5.17, where he refers to a twofold order (*duplicem ordinem*) of Presbyters.[1] Government was therefore carried out by presbyters who surpassed others in gravity, experience and authority.

Paul includes under *kinds of tongues* both the knowledge of languages, and the gift of interpreting them. But they were two distinct gifts, because sometimes a person, who spoke many languages, did not, however, know the tongue of the actual church, that he had to deal with; and interpreters made up for such a deficiency.

29. *Are all apostles?* Of course it can happen that one person may be endowed with many gifts, and hold two of the offices to which Paul has referred; and there is really nothing out of place about that. But what Paul is after is to show, first of all, that nobody is so fully equipped with everything, as to be replete in himself, and not feel the need of other people's help. Secondly, he wants to show that offices, just as much as gifts, are distributed in such a way, that no single member constitutes the entire body. For Paul's intention in this passage is to stamp out anything giving cause for pride, distorting jealousies, arrogance and contempt of the brethren, ill-will, self-seeking, and everything of that sort.

31. *Desire earnestly the greater gifts.* This could also be translated 'value highly', and that would fit the context quite well. All the same it does not make much difference to the meaning. For Paul is urging the Corinthians to value or strive after, above all, those gifts which are the most effective for upbuilding. For the fault of caring more for ostentation rather than beneficial things, was rife among them. That is why they were neglecting prophecy. At the same time the whole place echoed with tongues; and though they made a great fuss about

1 French text: 'deux ordres de Prestres, c'est à dire d'Anciens'.

that, there was in fact little to show for it all. Yet Paul is not addressing himself to individuals, as though he wanted each person to aim at being a prophet, or teacher, but all that he is doing is to urge that they should be concerned about upbuilding each other, hoping that they might thus devote themselves all the more earnestly to the things which are the most effective for upbuilding.

CHAPTER THIRTEEN

*If I speak with the tongues of men and of angels, but have not love, I am
become sounding brass, or a clanging cymbal. And if I have the gift of
prophecy, and know all mysteries and all knowledge; and if I have all
faith, so as to remove mountains, but have not love, I am nothing. And
if I bestow all my goods to feed the poor, and if I give my body to be
burned, but have not love, it profiteth me nothing.* (1-3)

And I show you a still more excellent way.[1] I could not do anything
else but change such a senseless division of the chapter, especially since
I find it impossible to expound it properly otherwise. For what was
there to gain by hacking off a sentence and tacking it on to the previous
chapter, when it agrees so well with what follows, and is indeed
expanded and completed by it? It is likely that it happened through a
mistake on the part of the copyists.

Be that as it may, after Paul had directed that particular attention be
paid to upbuilding, he now promises to show them something of still
greater value, viz. that everything must be put to the test of the rule
of love (*caritas*). The most excellent way then is where love is the
controlling power in all our actions. And indeed he begins right away
by affirming that all virtues count for nothing without love. For there
is nothing, no matter how wonderful or extraordinary it may be, that
is not ruined, from God's point of view, by the absence of love. And
what Paul teaches here echoes what he asserts elsewhere, that love is
'what the law is aiming at' (I Tim. 1.5), and 'the bond of perfectness'
(Col. 3.14); and also when he grounds the holiness of believers entirely
in love; for what else does God ask of us in the whole of the second
table of the Law? It is not therefore to be wondered at that all our
actions are to be judged by the standard of whether they show signs of
springing from love. Nor is it to be wondered at that gifts, which are
otherwise excellent, only realize their true value when they are related
to love.

1. *If I speak with the tongues of men.* Paul begins with eloquence,
which is certainly an excellent gift in itself, but when it is divorced from
love it is no help for procuring a man favour with God. In speaking
of tongues of angels he is using hyperbole for something remarkable
or rare. Yet I prefer to give it a precise interpretation as referring to the
different kinds of languages. For the Corinthians, who assessed the

---

[1] Calvin makes the last phrase of chapter 12 part of verse 1.

value of everything by the reputation it could give them, and not by the results it produced, were setting great store by the ability to speak many languages. Paul is saying, 'You may have a grasp of all the languages, not only those of all men, but of the angels over and above. Do not however get the impression that God will think any more highly of you than of a cymbal, that is to say, if you do not have love'.

2. *And if I have the gift of prophecy.* Paul also reduces the value of this gift to nothing, even though he had rated it above all others, if it is not subject to love. To *know all mysteries* may seem to have been added to prophecy by way of explanation; but, because knowledge comes immediately after it, and he made separate mention of knowledge in an earlier context, one should consider whether the knowledge of mysteries is not used here instead of wisdom. While I would not go so far as to be dogmatic about it, I am yet much attracted to that view.

The *faith*, of which he is speaking here, is of a special kind, as is obvious from the words that go with it, 'so as to remove mountains'. Therefore the quibblers are wasting their time, in misrepresenting this verse so as to take away from the power of *faith*. Therefore, in view of the fact that the word 'faith' has many shades of meaning (πολύσημον) the discerning reader should note the sense in which it is used here. Now Paul is his own interpreter (as I have already said), for he limits faith here to miracles. It is what Chrysostom calls 'the faith of signs or miracles', and we, a 'particular faith', because it does not lay hold of Christ in His wholeness, but only of His power in effecting miracles. That is why men can sometimes have that, when they do not have the Spirit of sanctification, as was the case with Judas.

3. *And if I bestow all my goods.* Considered in itself this certainly deserves the highest praise. But since the giving away of things often has its roots in self-seeking, and not in true generosity; or, again, because a man, who is generous, is often destitute of the other aspects of love (since even a generous feeling is only one element in love), it can happen that an action, so praiseworthy in other respects, may be looked upon by men as a really splendid thing, and made the object of their praises, and yet count for absolutely nothing in the eyes of God.

And if I give my body. There is no doubt that Paul is speaking about martyrdom here, which is the finest and supreme action of all. For what is more admirable than that unconquerable firmness of character, where a man has no hesitation about pouring out his life for his witness to the gospel? But even this God also regards as nothing, if the heart is bare of love. At that time the kind of punishment, which he mentions, was not the one usually inflicted upon Christians. For we read that in those days tyrants who aimed at the destruction of the Church proceeded against them with the sword rather than fire, with the exception of Nero, who, in his madness, also resorted to burning. But the Spirit seems to have been predicting, through the medium of Paul, the persecutions that were to come. But that is incidental. The point of this verse is that, because love alone is the rule governing our actions, and the only guide as to the right way to use the gifts of God, God approves of nothing that lacks it, no matter how magnificent men may think it. For without it the fairness of all virtues is mere veneer, it is empty jangling, it is not worth a straw, in short it is rank and offensive.

Now the Papists infer from this that love is therefore of more value for justifying us than faith. But I shall refute that later on. In the meantime let us carry on with the passage.

> *Love suffereth long, and is kind; love envieth not; love vaunteth not itself, is not puffed up, doth not behave itself unseemly, seeketh not its own, is not provoked, taketh not account of evil; rejoiceth not in unrighteousness, but rejoiceth with the truth; beareth all things, believeth all things, hopeth all things, endureth all things. Love never faileth: but whether there be prophecies, they shall be done away; whether there be tongues, they shall cease; whether there be knowledge, it shall be done away.* (4–8)

4. *Love is patient.* Paul now lets us know how excellent love is, by showing us its effects, or fruits. However, these descriptions do not simply aim at making it attractive, but at making the Corinthians understand the way it expresses itself in action, and its nature. But the main object is to show how necessary it is for preserving the unity of the Church. And I have no doubt that Paul intended to reprimand the Corinthians in an indirect way, by confronting them with a situation quite the reverse of their own, so that they might recognize their own faults by their contrast with what they saw.

The first description of love is that by patiently enduring many things it strengthens the peace and harmony of the Church. Love's second quality is very similar, viz. gentleness and considerateness, for that is what the Greek verb means (χρηστεύεσθαι). The third quality is that it corrects emulation, which is the root cause of all disputes. He includes envy in emulation, for it is very like it; or, rather he means the kind of emulation which is linked with envy and more often than not springs from it. It follows that where envy holds sway, where each one is eager to be first, or to appear to be first, love cannot thrive.

The Greek behind my rendering, 'does not act insolently', is περπερεύεται. Erasmus translates it as 'is not shameless'. It is well known that the word (περπερεύεσθαι) has different meanings, but since it is sometimes used for 'being unruly, or becoming haughty, because of self-confidence', this meaning seems to suit this verse better. Paul therefore is claiming a moderating influence for love, and shows that it is a bridle for holding men in check, and preventing them from lapsing into ferocity, so that they may rather live together in a quiet and ordered way. Finally, he adds that love is a stranger to pride. Therefore, any man who is under the control of love, is not puffed up with pride, looking down his nose at others in his self-satisfaction.

5. *It does not act in an unbecoming way* (οὐκ ἀσχημονεῖ). Erasmus translates this as 'it is not disdainful', but since he cites no authority in support of this meaning, I preferred to retain its proper and usual significance. My explanation, then, is this: that love does not take delight in meaningless ostentation, or does not make a great fuss, but always acts in a moderate and seemly way. And in this way Paul is once again censuring the Corinthians in an indirect way, because they were so indecently proud that they had no qualms about abandoning all graciousness.

Seeketh not its own. It can be inferred from this that love is not innate in us, for we all have a natural tendency to love and care for ourselves, and to seek our own interests; indeed it is truer to say that we cannot attend to them fast enough! Love is the only cure for such a perverted tendency, for it makes us ignore our own circumstances, and be really concerned about our neighbours, loving and caring for them. Besides, 'to seek one's own things' is to be devoted to oneself, and to be completely taken up with looking after one's own interests. The question whether it is permissible for a Christian to be concerned about his own advantage, is solved by that definition. For Paul does not mean that we must have no care and anxiety about our own affairs at all; but he is condemning excessive care and anxiety about them, which, in turn, spring from excessive blind love of ourselves. But the excessiveness actually consists in neglecting others through thinking about ourselves, or being distracted by concern for our own interests from that consideration, which God commands us to have for our neighbours.

Paul adds that love is also a bridle for putting a check on disputes; and that follows from the first two statements in this verse. For people who are gentle and tolerant do not suddenly flare up in anger, and are not easily roused to engage in controversies and battles.

7. *Bears all things.* Paul means by all the descriptions in this verse that love is neither impatient nor malicious. For it is of the essence of tolerance to bear and to endure all things, while it is of the essence of sincerity and humanity to believe and hope all things. We are naturally too devoted to ourselves, and that fault makes us irritable and complaining. As a result what happens is that everyone wants other people to carry his burdens, at the same time refusing to assist them in any

way. Love is the cure for this disease, for love makes us servants to our brothers, and teaches us to carry their burdens on our shoulders. Again, because we are naturally malicious, we are also suspicious, and take the wrong meaning out of nearly everything. But love is calling us back to humanity so that we may think of others in a kindly and sincere way.

By Paul's reference to 'all things' we must understand things that must be endured, and in the right way. For we are not to put up with vices, either by showing approval of them with flattering talk, or by lending support to them through conniving at them by our indifference. Again, this endurance does not cut out disciplinary measures and punishments which are deserved. The same thing applies in regard to humanity in forming judgements.

Love believeth all things. Not that a Christian knowingly and intentionally allows himself to be imposed upon; not that he strips himself of wisdom and discernment so as to let people find it easier to cheat him; not that he has forgotten how to distinguish black from white! What then? As I have already said, what Paul is asking for here is sincerity and humanity in forming judgements; and here he affirms that these two virtues constantly go hand in hand with love. What that will mean in practice is that a Christian will consider it better to be taken in through his own kindness and good-nature than to cause harm to his brother through ill-founded suspicion.

8. *Love never fails.* Another of the outstanding features of love is that it lasts for ever. A quality like that, which will never come to an end, is certainly worth striving after. Love is therefore to be preferred before all temporary and perishable gifts. Prophecies pass away; tongues cease; knowledge comes to an end. Therefore, love stands so high above them all just because it survives after they have ceased to exist.

The Papists twist this verse in order to support the dogma which, without any scriptural authority, they have invented, viz. that the souls of the departed are praying for us to God. For they reason in the following way: 'Praying is an eternal service that love undertakes; love lasts on in the souls of the saints who have died; therefore they are praying for us.' Although I have no wish to make too keen an issue of this matter, yet, in order that they may not get the impression that they have gained a good deal of advantage by that concession of mine, I am making a brief reply to their opposing standpoint.

In the first place, even if love never ends the immediate consequence is not that it remains continually at work, as they say. For what is to stand in the way of the saints, now enjoying their peace and rest, from not making use of love in the duties they now have to discharge? I ask you, what incongruity is there for the Papists to find in that? In the second place, were I to say that the duty of love to make intercession for the brethren is not an everlasting one, how are they to succeed in proving the opposite? Knowledge of people's needs is necessary for intercession. If we are allowed to hazard a guess about the state of the dead, it is a more likely conjecture that the blessed departed do not know what is happening here, than that they are aware of what our needs are. The Papists imagine, indeed, that they see the whole world in the reflected light which they have from the presence of God. But that is an impious and utterly pagan supposition, which smacks more of Egyptian theology than it agrees with Christian thinking. Therefore, in the light of the ignorance of the saints as to our circumstances, suppose I were to say that they are not concerned about us, what argument would the Papists press upon me, in order to force me to abandon my point of view? Supposing I were to maintain that they are so gripped, and as it were absorbed, by the vision of God, that they can think of nothing else at all, how will they prove that this is not a reasonable point of view? Supposing I were to say quite explicitly that the everlastingness of love, which the apostle refers to here, will come into being after the Last Day, and has nothing at all to do with the intervening time? Supposing I were to say that the responsibility for mutual intercession has been entrusted only to the living, to those on their pilgrimage through this world, and for that reason does not involve the dead at all?

But I have already said more than enough; for the very point for which the Papists fight so strongly I leave undecided, so as not to provoke controversy over a matter that is pointless. It was however worth while noting, in passing, how little support this verse does, in fact, afford them, when they themselves think that it provides them with such a powerful weapon. Let it be enough for us that their assertion is unsupported by any scriptural evidence, and therefore in maintaining it they are both audacious and unthinking.

Whether knowledge, it will be destroyed. The meaning of these words is already quite clear; but they give rise to a question, which is by no means a trivial one, viz. whether those who, in this world, are outstanding in so far as learning or other gifts are concerned, will have the same standing as ignorant people in the Kingdom of God. In the first place, I would like to advise my readers, who are believers, not to torture themselves by probing into these matters too much. They should seek the way by which they may attain to the Kingdom of God, rather than ask questions about the conditions which will prevail in it; for by maintaining silence on these matters Himself, our Lord has also taught us not to indulge in such curiosity. But now I answer the question, as far as I can conjecture, and also from the scanty information I can glean from this passage. Since learning, knowledge of languages, and similar gifts serve the needs of this life, it does not seem to me that they will remain in existence when that time comes. The learned will, however, not be impoverished in any way, despite the destruction of their gifts, because they will receive the fruition of them, and that is far more desirable.

For we know in part, and we prophesy in part: but when that which is perfect is come, that which is in part shall be done away. When I was a child, I spake as a child, I felt as a child, I thought as a child: now that I am become a man, I have put away childish things. For now we see in a mirror, darkly; but then face to face: now I know in part; but then shall I know even as also I have been known. But now abideth faith, hope, love, these three; and the greatest of these is love. (9-13)

Paul now shows that prophecy and all the other gifts of that sort are destroyed, because they are bestowed upon us to help us in our weakness. But one day our imperfection will come to an end; therefore the use of those gifts will also stop at the same time. Because it would be absurd for them to continue when there will be no need for them, they will, therefore, perish. Paul pursues this argument right to the end of the chapter.

9. *We know in part.* Most people explain this verse in the wrong way, viz. that our knowledge is not yet perfect, but that we are making daily progress in it; and that the same thing applies to prophecy. But Paul's meaning is that the fact that we have knowledge and prophecy is precisely because we are imperfect. Therefore 'in part' means that we are not yet made perfect. Knowledge and prophecy will therefore have a place in our lives, so long as imperfection clings to us, for they help us in our incompleteness. It is certainly true that we are required to make progress throughout our life, and anything that we have is only in an unfinished state. But we must realize what Paul wants to point out, viz. that the gifts in question are only temporary. But the reason why he points that out is that the benefit of them is only effective so long as we are moving on to the goal, by making progress every day.

10. *When that which is perfect is come.* Paul might have put it this way: 'When we have reached the winning-post, then the things that helped us on the course will be finished with.' But he uses the same way of expressing himself as before, in setting perfection in contrast with what is in part. He is saying: 'When perfection comes it will abolish everything that gives aid to our imperfections.' But when will that perfection come? It begins, indeed, at death, because then we put off many weaknesses along with the body; but it will not be completely

established until the day of judgement, as we shall soon learn. We conclude from that, that it is stupid of people to make the whole of this discussion apply to the intervening time.

11. *When I was a child.* Paul illustrates what he said by a comparison. For many things which are appropriate to childhood disappear later on, when we come to maturer years. For example, when we are children we need to go to school, but that would be ridiculous for a grown man. Now, as long as we are living in this world, we need some instruction; for we are still far short of the fullness of wisdom. Therefore the perfection, which will be a kind of maturity in spiritual age, will put an end to instruction, and all the things that go with it. In the letter to the Ephesians (4.14) Paul urges us to be no longer children, but he has a different object in view there, and we shall speak about it, when dealing with that passage.

12. *For now we see in a mirror.* Now we come to the application of the comparison: the mode of knowledge which we now have is appropriate to our imperfect state, and what you might call our childhood; because we do not yet have a clear insight into the mysteries of the Kingdom of Heaven, and we do not yet enjoy the unclouded vision. In order to bring that out Paul uses yet another comparison, viz. that the only way we see now is as in a mirror, and therefore blurred. He conveys that indistinctness by the use of the word 'enigma'.

In the first place there is no doubt that he is comparing the ministry of the Word, and the aids needed for exercising it, to a mirror. For God, who is otherwise invisible, has appointed these as means for revealing Himself to us. Of course this can also be made to embrace the whole structure of the universe, in which the glory of God shines out for us to see, as we find expressed in Rom. 1.20 and Heb. 11.3. The apostle describes the created things as mirrors in which God's invisible majesty is to be seen, but since Paul is dealing particularly here with spiritual gifts, which are of assistance to the ministry exercised by the Church, and go along with it, we shall not digress further.

I say that the ministry of the word is like a mirror. For the angels do not need preaching, or other inferior aids, or sacraments. They have the advantage of another way of seeing God, for God does not show them His face merely in a mirror (*in speculo*), but He presents Himself openly before them (*palam se illis praesentem exhibit*). But we, who have not yet scaled such heights, look upon the likeness of God (*imaginem Dei speculamur*) in the Word, in the sacraments, and, in short, in the whole ministry of the Church.

Paul here speaks of the vision which we have as 'obscure' (*aenigmaticam*), not because there is any question of its being dubious or misleading, but because it is not so clear as it will eventually be at the

Last Day. He teaches the same thing in a different way in II Cor. 5.6–7: 'While we are at home in the body, we are absent from the Lord, for we walk by faith, not by sight.' Therefore our faith now looks upon God, who is so to speak absent (*tanquam absentem*). How is this so? Because it does not see His face, but is satisfied with the likeness in the mirror (*in speculi imagine*). But when we leave the world behind, and depart to Him, faith will look upon Him, as it were, at close quarters and revealed before its very eyes.

Therefore we must understand it in this way: that the knowledge of God, which we now derive from His Word, is undoubtedly reliable and true, and there is nothing muddled, or unintelligible or dark about it; but when it is called 'obscure' (*aenigmaticam*) it is in a relative way, because it falls a long way short of that clear revelation to which we look forward, when we shall see face to face. So this verse is not in conflict in any way with others, which speak of the clarity, sometimes of the law, sometimes of the whole of Scripture, and most of all of the Gospel. For there is an open and naked revelation of God in the Word (enough to meet our needs), and there is nothing recondite (*involutum*) about it, as unbelievers imagine, to keep us in a state of uncertainty. But how small a share this is of the vision toward which we reach out! Therefore it is described as 'obscure' only in comparison with the other.

The adverb 'then' indicates the last day, rather than the time immediately after death. But even if fullness of vision will be delayed until the day of Christ, we will begin to have a closer view of God as soon as we die. Our souls will then be set free from our bodies, and will have no further need of either the external ministry or other inferior aids. But Paul (as I pointed out before) is not anxious to discuss the state of the dead, because knowledge about that is of little value for godliness.

Now I know in part, that is to say, the knowledge we now have is incomplete. John says the same thing in his letter (I John. 3.2): 'We know that we are indeed the children of God; but it is not yet made manifest, until we shall see God as He is.' Then we shall see God not in His reflection (*imagine*) but in Himself, so that there will be, so to speak, a mutual seeing.

13. *But now abideth faith, hope, love*. What all the foregoing amounts to is that love stands high above all the other gifts, but instead of the list of gifts which Paul had given earlier, he now puts faith and hope alongside love, for all the others are summed up in these three. For what purpose does the whole ministry serve, but that we may be trained in these three gifts?

So *faith* has a wider range of meaning here than in earlier instances of its use. For it is as though Paul said, 'There are indeed many and

differing gifts, but they are all looking to and making for this one end.'
Therefore, 'to remain' means that this is the amount left over, after
everything has been deducted, as when an account is made up in book-
keeping. For faith does not continue after death, as the apostle contrasts it with sight elsewhere, and teaches that it lasts only so long as
we are absent from the Lord. We now understand what is meant by
faith in this verse, viz. the knowledge of God and His will, which we
obtain through the ministry exercised by the Church; or, if you prefer
it, faith understood in its fullness, and in its proper sense.

Hope is nothing else but perseverance in faith. For once we have
come to believe in the Word of God, after that we have still to go on
until all things are brought to completion. Therefore, as faith is the
mother of hope, it is also sustained by it to keep it from perishing.

The greatest of these is love. We will find that that is so if we assess its
excellence by the effects it has, as they have already been detailed by
Paul, and if we also take its everlastingness into consideration. Each
person derives personal blessing from his own faith and hope, whereas
love is poured out for the good of others. Faith and hope are the con-
comitants of our imperfect state, but love will continue even in the
conditions of perfectness.

For, if we examine the results of faith, one by one, and compare
them, we will find that faith is in many ways superior. Yes, and even
love itself, according to the testimony of the same apostle (I Thess. 1.3),
is a product of faith; and the effect is, without a doubt, inferior to its
cause. In addition, a remarkable tribute is paid to faith, which does
not apply in the case of love, when John (I John 5.4) says of faith, that
'it is our victory, which overcomes the world'. Finally it is by faith
that we are born again, become the sons of God, obtain eternal life, and
Christ dwells in us. I make no mention of countless other blessings,
but those few examples will be enough to bring out what I mean when
I say that faith is superior to love in many of its effects. It is clear from
that, that love is said to be greater here, not in every respect, but
because it will last for ever, and now has a primary role in keeping the
Church in being.

But it is strange how self-satisfied the Papists are, in proclaiming in
tones of thunder, that, if faith justifies, therefore love, which is described as greater, does it much more. Now there is already a clear
answer to this contention in what I have said. But supposing we grant
that love is pre-eminent in every way, what are we to say to this kind
of argument, that says that because it is greater, it is more effective for
justifying men? According to that way of thinking, a king will plough
the land better than a farmer, and will make a better job of a shoe than
a shoemaker, because he is a man of nobler birth than both of them

together. Similarly, a man will run faster than a horse, and will carry
a bigger load than an elephant, because he is a superior being to them!
Again, on the same principle, the angels will give better light to the
earth than the sun and moon, because they are so much above them!
If the power to justify depended on the worth or merit of faith, perhaps
we ought to pay heed to what they say. But we do not teach that faith
justifies because it is more valuable, or holds a more honoured place,
but because it receives the righteousness which is offered freely in the
Gospel. Greatness, or worth, has no part to play in this, and counts for
nothing here. That is why this verse affords no more assistance to the
Papists than if the apostle had actually placed faith before everything
else.

CHAPTER FOURTEEN

Follow after love; yet desire earnestly spiritual gifts, but rather that ye may prophesy. For he that speaketh in a tongue speaketh not unto men, but unto God; for no man understandeth; but in the spirit he speaketh mysteries. But he that prophesieth speaketh unto men edification, and comfort, and consolation. He that speaketh in a tongue edifieth himself; but he that prophesieth edifieth the church. Now I would have you all speak with tongues, but rather that ye should prophesy; and greater is he that prophesieth than he that speaketh with tongues, except he interpret, that the church may receive edifying. But now, brethren, if I come unto you speaking with tongues, what shall I profit you, unless I speak to you either by way of revelation, or of knowledge, or of prophesying, or of teaching? (1-6)

Just as he had previously urged them to desire earnestly the greater gifts, so now he advises them to *follow after love*; for that was the supreme power which he had undertaken to show them. They will therefore keep their gifts well under control, so long as love has an honoured place in their dealings with each other. For Paul is tacitly taking them to task for the lack of love, which had been apparent up to then in the way they were abusing their gifts. And he infers from things that happened in the past that, when they are not giving the first place to love, they are not making serious and proper efforts to lay hold of what is really the finest thing to have. He therefore points out to them how senseless a thing their self-seeking is, when it makes shipwreck of their hopes and longings.

1. *Follow after love.* In case the Corinthians might raise the objection that God would be insulted if they despised His gifts, the apostle anticipates it by asserting that he does not mean to deny them those gifts, which they had been using in the wrong way. On the contrary he encourages them to be eager for those gifts, and wishes them to have a place in the Church. And there is no doubt that, because they were given for the benefit of the Church, the way that men mishandled them ought not to have meant their being tossed aside as useless or harmful. But all the same Paul approves of prophecy more than all the other gifts, since it was the one that gave the greatest benefit. Paul deals with the question most reasonably, by not rejecting anything that was of some use, but at the same time by encouraging them not to let a perverted zeal make them rate minor things above those of primary

285

importance. But he establishes prophecy in the leading place. Therefore, 'desire earnestly spiritual gifts', he says. In other words, 'Do not disregard any gift, for I urge you to strive after all of them, so long as prophecy retains pride of place.'

2. *For he that speaketh in a tongue speaketh not unto men.* Paul now gives the reason, based on actual experience, why he preferred prophecy to other gifts. He compares it with the gift of tongues. It is likely that the Corinthians were giving undue attention to the gift of tongues, because it was more showy, for it is the case that, when people hear somebody speaking in a foreign language, they are usually moved to wonderment. Paul, working on accepted principles, therefore shows how perverted that is, since it does nothing at all in the way of upbuilding the Church. His first point is that a person 'speaking in a tongue is speaking not to men but to God'. In other words (as the proverb goes), 'he preaches to himself and the walls'. There is no pleonasm in the use of the word 'tongue', as there is in these examples, 'she spoke with her mouth, as follows . . .' and 'I heard his voice with these ears';[1] but it means a foreign language. The reason why 'he is not speaking to men' is that 'nobody understands', i.e. words he can distinguish. For they all hear a sound, but do not understand what he is saying.

He speaks in the Spirit. i.e. 'by a spiritual gift' (for that is the way I explain it, along with Chrysostom), 'he speaks mysteries and things which remain secret, and which, therefore, bring no benefit'. Chrysostom takes 'mysteries' in a good sense here, as extraordinary revelations from God. But I interpret it in a bad sense, as unintelligible, baffling, enigmatic sayings; as if Paul had written, 'Nobody understands a word he says.'

3. *He that prophesieth, speaketh unto men.* Paul says that prophecy enriches everybody, while 'a tongue' is treasure buried in the ground. How stupid it is therefore to waste all one's time on something that is useless, and to neglect what is obviously the most valuable thing of all! 'To speak for edification' is to give teaching suitable for upbuilding. For I take this term to mean teaching which trains us in religion, in faith, in the worship and fear of God, and in the responsibilities of holiness and righteousness. But since most of us need incentives, while others are beset by troubles, or handicapped by weakness, he mentions comfort and consolation in addition to teaching. It is clear from this verse, and from the foregoing, that prophecy is not the gift of foretelling; but since I have spoken about this once before, I will not repeat myself.

4. *He that speaketh in a tongue edifieth himself.* Paul had said in verse 2

[1] Virgil, *Aeneid*, 4.359.

that the person with this gift 'speaks to God', but now he says that 'he speaks to himself'. But anything that is done in the Church ought to be for the good of all. Let there be no more, then, of this misleading self-seeking, which causes obstacles to be put in the way of all the people deriving benefit! Besides, Paul is speaking by way of concession; for when ambition pours out a flood of bombast like that, the heart lacks any desire to be helpful; but in fact it is as though Paul were ordering those ostentatious people, who are concerned only for themselves, to have nothing more to do with believers, when they assemble together.

5. *Now I would have you all speak with tongues.* Paul reiterates that he is not giving the preference to prophecy in such a way as to leave no room for tongues. We must pay particular attention to this, for God has bestowed no gift on His Church without there being some purpose for it; and tongues were of some use at that time. But, granted that, through their misguided zeal for showiness, the Corinthians were turning that gift into something that was, to some extent, superfluous and valueless, and to some extent even harmful, yet, by correcting this fault, Paul is giving his approval to tongues none the less. Thus you see that there is no question of his wanting to abolish tongues, or keep them out of the Church.

In our own day when there is a crying need for the knowledge of tongues, and when, at our stage in history, God in His wonderful kindness has rescued them from darkness and brought them to light, there are great theologians who, faced with that situation, are loud and violent in their protests against them. Since there is no doubt that the Holy Spirit has bestowed undying honour on tongues in this verse, it is easy to deduce what sort of spirit moves those critics who make strong attacks against the study of languages with as much insulting language as they can muster. Yet they are dealing with different things. For Paul is referring to all languages, without distinction, which were such a great help in proclaiming the Gospel among all the nations. On the other hand those present-day critics are condemning the languages from which the pure truth of Scripture is to be drawn as from fountains.

However a qualification follows: that we must not spend so much time on tongues, that we give rather scant attention to prophecy, when it ought to have priority.

Except he interpret. For, if interpretation is added, then there will be prophecy. Do not, however, imagine that Paul is here allowing anybody to waste the time of the Church by muttering foreign words. For how ridiculous it would be to proclaim the same thing in many languages, when there is no need to do so! But it often happens that the use of a foreign language is timely. Finally, let our only aim be that what we do may make for the upbuilding of the Church.

6. *But now if I come.* Paul takes himself as an example, because his own situation illustrated what he had to say particularly well. The Corinthians were aware of the rich fruit his teaching yielded. He therefore asks them what use it would be to them if he were to employ strange languages when speaking to them. By this appeal to experience he is pointing out to them that it is far better to pay attention to prophecies. Moreover he was not giving the same cause for offence in condemning stupid behaviour like this on his own part, rather than that of somebody else.

Now, Paul gives four ways of edifying: *revelation, knowledge, prophesying* and *teaching.* Since interpreters take different views about them, I may be allowed to say what I think they mean also. But because it is only a conjectural point of view, I leave my readers to make up their minds about it.

I bracket revelation and prophesying together, and I think that prophesying is the servant of revelation. I take the same view about knowledge and teaching. Therefore whatever anyone has obtained by revelation he gives out in prophesying. Teaching is the way to pass on knowledge. So a prophet will be the interpreter and minister of revelation. This supports, rather than conflicts with, the definition of prophecy which I gave earlier. For I said that prophesying does not consist in the simple or bare interpretation of Scripture, but also includes the knowledge for making it apply to the needs of the hour, and that can only be obtained by revelation and the special influence of God.

Even things without life, giving a voice, whether pipe or harp, if they give not a distinction in the sounds, how shall it be known what is piped or harped? For if the trumpet give an uncertain voice, who shall prepare himself for war? So also ye, unless ye utter by the tongue speech easy to be understood, how shall it be known what is spoken? for ye will be speaking into the air. There are, it may be, so many kinds of voices in the world, and no kind is without signification. If then I know not the meaning of the voice, I shall be to him that speaketh a barbarian, and he that speaketh will be a barbarian unto me. So also ye, since ye are zealous of spiritual gifts, seek that ye may abound unto the edifying of the church. Wherefore let him that speaketh in a tongue pray that he may interpret. For if I pray in a tongue, my spirit prayeth, but my understanding is unfruitful. What is it then? I will pray with the spirit, and I will pray with the understanding also: I will sing with the spirit, and I will sing with the understanding also. Else if thou bless with the spirit, how shall he that filleth the place of the unlearned say

*the Amen at thy giving of thanks, seeing he knoweth not what thou
sayest? For thou verily givest thanks well, but the other is not
edified.* (7-17)

7. *Even inanimate things.* Paul introduces the similes, first, of musical
instruments, and then of the general nature of things, for every sound
has its own peculiar quality enabling it to be distinguished. Paul says,
'Even the very inanimate things teach us a lesson.' Of course there are
many noises or crashes to be heard by chance, which have no musical
significance. But Paul is speaking here about sounds which are the
products of a certain technical skill, as though he said: 'A man cannot
give life to a harp or flute, but he produces sounds, which are adjusted
in such a way that they can be picked out. How absurd then that
actual men, endowed as they are with intelligence, should utter in-
distinguishable and unintelligible sounds!'

All the same we must not go into the matter of musical harmonies
too closely here, because Paul is only touching on what everybody is
aware of, the sound of the trumpet, for example, which he refers to in
verse 8. For the trumpet is designed to stir the blood in such a way
that it excites not only men but horses also. That is why, as the
historical records relate, the Spartans preferred to use the flute, when
they were joining battle, so that in the first assault the army might not
rush upon the enemy in too violent a fury.

Finally, we all know from experience how great a power music has
for moving men's feelings, so that Plato teaches, quite rightly, that in
one way or another music is of the greatest value in shaping the moral
tone of the state.

Speaking into the air is *beating the air.* It is as though he said: 'Your
voice will reach neither God nor men, but will vanish into thin air.'

10. *None of them mute.* Paul now speaks more generally; for he now
brings in the natural sounds of all the animal kingdom. He uses the
word mute here for *unintelligible*, i.e. as opposed to a clear, distinct
sound. For the barking of dogs is different from the neighing of
horses; the roaring of lions from the braying of asses. Every single
type of bird has its own particular way of singing or chirping. The
whole of the natural order, which God has ordained, therefore calls
for the making of distinguishable sounds.

11. *I shall be to him that speaketh a barbarian.* Our speech ought to be
the reflection of our minds; not only as the proverb observes, but as
Aristotle teaches at the beginning of his *On Interpretation.* It is therefore
pointless and absurd for a man to speak in a gathering of people, when
the hearer understands not a word of what he says, and cannot even
catch the slightest inkling, to show him what the speaker means. Paul

is therefore quite right in regarding it as the height of absurdity that a man should prove to be a 'barbarian' to his audience, because he talks away in an unknown language. At the same time he makes fine fun of the Corinthians' stupid ambition, for, by doing this very thing, they were eager for people to praise them and think them wonderful. Paul tells them: 'All the reward you will get for your pains is that you will be a barbarian.'

For the name 'barbarian', whether it is a 'manufactured' one (as Strabo thinks), or has some other derivation, is taken in a bad sense. So the Greeks, who looked upon themselves as the only people who were good speakers and had a refined language, called all the other peoples, barbarians, because of their rough and boorish way of speaking. But, in fact, no matter how cultivated a language may be, even it can be described as 'barbarous' when nobody can understand it! 'The hearer', Paul says, 'will be a barbarian to me, and *vice versa*'. He means by those words, that if anyone speaks in an unknown language he is not sharing in the fellowship of the Church, but is rather separated from it; and that the others are quite right to have a poor opinion of anyone who does this sort of thing, seeing that he thinks very little of them in the first place.

12. *Since you are eager for spirits (spirituum)*. Paul concludes by saying that the gift of tongues was not given in order to give a few people the chance to show off, without contributing anything to the benefit of the Church. He says: 'If spiritual gifts are a source of delight to you, see that they are directed to upbuilding. It is only when the Church obtains benefit from you that you will be really outstanding and deserving of praise.' But that does not mean to say that Paul is allowing people to have a passion for outshining others, even if they do benefit the Church in the process; but, by correcting that fault, he shows how far short they fall of what they are aiming at. At the same time he indicates who should be thought the most highly of. The more anxious a person is to devote himself to upbuilding, the more highly Paul wishes him to be regarded. However, as far as we are concerned, this must be our one aim, here and now, that the Lord may be the conspicuous and outstanding person, and that His rule may be extended daily.

Paul uses the word 'spirits' by metonymy here for 'spiritual gifts', in the same way as the Spirit of teaching, or of understanding, or of judgement, stands for spiritual teaching, or understanding, or judgement. Yet we must remember what he taught before, that it is 'one and the same Spirit who distributes different gifts to individuals according to His will' (12.11).

13. *Wherefore let him that speaketh in a tongue*. Here Paul is replying, by way of anticipation, to a question which could easily have been put

to him: 'Does that mean, then, that if anyone knows a foreign language, his gift will be useless? And why should something which could be brought into the light and be a means of glorifying God be kept a dark secret?' Paul provides the remedy. 'Let him ask God for the gift of interpretation also. If he does not have that, let him refrain, in the meantime, from giving an ostentatious performance.'

14. *For if I pray in a tongue.* Even if this does also serve as a suitable example to confirm what he has been urging up to this point, I think, however, that it is a new subject. For it is likely that the Corinthians also went wrong in this respect, that, just as they were in the habit of speaking in foreign languages, so they were also using them in prayer. All the same, both abuses sprang from the same source, for they belonged to one and the same class.

The meaning of *praying in a tongue* is clear from the preceding verses of the chapter, viz. to express a prayer in a foreign language. On the other hand it is not so easy to explain what is meant by 'spirit' here. Ambrose's reference to the Spirit which we receive in baptism has no foundation at all, or anything resembling a foundation. Augustine rather more subtly takes it to mean the apprehension which grasps ideas and the signs of realities (*signa rerum*), so that it is a faculty of the soul inferior to mental intelligence. Those who understand it as the breathing of the throat, in plainer terms the breath, hold a more likely view. But the way that Paul constantly uses the word in this discussion conflicts with that interpretation. Further than that, indeed, the word appears to have been repeated so often by way of concession. For they were taking a pride in that honourable description, which Paul certainly allows them to have; but he, on the other hand, is pointing out how dangerous it is to make wrong use of a good and wonderful thing. It is as if he said: 'You are boasting to me about this spirit of yours. But why, if it is a useless thing?' That is why I am led to agree with Chrysostom's understanding of this word, for he gives it the same meaning as it had before, a spiritual gift. Thus 'my spirit' will mean exactly the same as 'the gift conferred on me'.

But here a new question is raised. For it is incredible (at least we do not read of any instance) that there were any people who spoke by the influence of the Spirit, in a language they did not know themselves. For the gift of tongues was not bestowed merely for the purpose of making a noise, but rather for the purpose of communication, of course. For how laughable it would have been had the tongue of a Roman been directed by the Spirit of God to utter Greek words, when he himself had no knowledge of Greek whatever. He would have been like the parrots, magpies and crows which men train to make human sounds! But if somebody endowed with the gift of tongues spoke sensibly and intelligently, it would have been pointless for Paul to say that 'the spirit prays but the understanding is unfruitful', for the understanding must have been acting together with the spirit.

My answer to that is that for the sake of illustration Paul is taking a purely hypothetical situation, as follows: 'If the gift of speaking in a tongue is kept distinct from the understanding, so that the speaker is a foreigner to himself, as well as to others, what good will he do by stammering along like that?' For it is not correct to describe the *understanding* as ἄκαρπον, unfruitful, on the grounds that the Church derives no benefit, in view of the fact that Paul is speaking about the private prayers of individuals here. Let us therefore remember that things which are really bound together are kept separate here for the sake of teaching, and not because it can or usually does fall out that way. The meaning is now plain. 'If I devise prayers in a language that is unknown to me, and the spirit provides me with a rich flow of words, it is clear that the spirit itself, which controls my tongue, will indeed be praying, but my understanding will be wandering elsewhere, or at any rate will not be involved in the prayer.'

We should note that Paul thinks it a great fault if the understanding takes no part in prayer. No wonder! For what else do we do in praying but pour out our thoughts and desires before God? Again, in view of the fact that spiritual prayer is a means of worshipping God, what is more out of keeping with its very nature than its coming only from the lips, and not from the innermost recesses of the soul? Everybody would have been thoroughly familiar with all these things, if the devil had not so deprived the world of its senses that men believe that they are praying properly, when they make their lips move!

And the Papists are so obstinately stupid that not only do they make excuses for praying without understanding what you say, but they also prefer the ignorant to mutter and murmur in words that are unknown to them. At the same time they mock God with a sharp piece of sophistry, saying that 'the final intention' is enough. Let me illustrate that. Suppose a Spaniard curses God in German, when he is in a state of mental upheaval because of many worldly cares, then, so long as he makes use of a formal prayer, and makes peace with God with a passing thought, it is, in their view, worship acceptable to God.

15. *I will pray with the spirit.* In case anyone should protest, 'Will the spirit, then, be of no value in prayer?' Paul teaches that it is certainly in order to pray with the spirit, so long as the mind, i.e. the understanding, is also brought into play. He therefore allows and approves of the use of the spiritual gift in prayers; but he insists that the mind should not be inactive, and that, of course, is the main point.

When he says, 'I shall sing the Psalms,' or *I shall sing*, he is speaking specifically instead of generally. For, since the Psalms had as their themes the praises of God, he uses 'singing psalms' (ψάλλειν) for *blessing* or giving thanks to God. For in our prayers we either ask something from God, or acknowledge the blessing He has bestowed upon us.

From this verse we also gather, however, that at that time the custom of singing was already in use among believers. That is also established by Pliny, who, writing at least forty years or so after the death of Paul, tells us that the Christians were in the habit of singing hymns to Christ before daylight. And indeed I have no doubt that from the very beginning they adopted the usage of the Jewish Church in singing psalms.

16. *Else if thou bless with the spirit.* Up to this point Paul has been showing that the prayers of each one of us will be futile and fruitless, if the mind and voice do not work together. He now goes on to deal with public prayers also. If the man who composes and says prayers on behalf of the people, is not understood by the congregation, how will the ordinary people share in it properly, and be able to indicate at the end that the prayer includes what they themselves want? For people are not taking part in the prayers, unless they are all in complete agreement about what they want. The same thing applies in regard to blessing, in which we give thanks to God.

Now Paul's way of speaking reveals that one of the ministers repeated or offered the prayers in a distinct voice, and that the whole congregation followed in their own minds what that one person was saying, until he drew to a close, when all of them, it is certain, said *Amen,* in order to indicate openly that the prayers made by him were the prayers of all of them. It is known that the Hebrew word *Amen* is derived from the same root as gives us the word for 'trustworthiness' or 'truthfulness'. It therefore indicates the confirmation not only of things we affirm in prayer, but also of what we ask for. Further, since the Jews were familiar with the word through long usage, the result was that it passed from them to the Gentiles, and the Greeks used it just as if it were part of their own language. It therefore became a common term among all the nations. Paul now says, 'If in public prayer you use a foreign language, which is not understood by the uneducated and ordinary people, in whose presence you are speaking, nobody will be sharing in your prayer, and your prayer, or blessing, will no longer be public.' 'Why?' 'Nobody,' Paul says, 'can add his *Amen* to a prayer or psalm unless he understands it.'

But the very thing that Paul rejects out of hand, the Papists look upon as a sacred and legitimate practice. This only serves to show their amazing impudence. More than that indeed, this is a shining example, which lets us see the way in which Satan has been given a free hand to wage his offensive in Papist circles. For what is clearer than these words of Paul, that an uneducated person cannot take part in public prayer, unless he understands what is being said? What is plainer than this prohibition, 'thanksgivings or prayers should not be repeated in public except in the language everyone understands, the native tongue'? When every day they do what Paul says should not, or even cannot, be done, are they not treating Paul as if he were an uneducated person himself? When they are so scrupulous about observing what He forbids, are they not openly defying God? So we see how Satan amuses himself among them with impunity. But their devilish obstinacy is betrayed by the fact that, even after being warned, so far are they from being repentant, that they actually defend a corruption, as serious as this, with fire and sword.

I thank God, I speak with tongues more than you all: howbeit in the church I had rather speak five words with my understanding, that I might instruct others also, than ten thousand words in a tongue. Brethren, be not children in mind: howbeit in malice be ye babes, but in mind be men. In the law it is written, By men of strange tongues and by the lips of strangers will I speak unto this people; and not even thus will they hear me, saith the Lord. Wherefore tongues are for a sign, not to them that believe, but to the unbelieving: but prophesying is for a sign, not to the unbelieving, but to them that believe. If therefore the whole church be assembled together, and all speak with tongues, and there come in men unlearned or unbelieving, will they not say that ye are mad? But if all prophesy, and there come in one unbelieving or unlearned, he is reproved by all, he is judged by all; the secrets of his heart are made manifest; and so he will fall down on his face and worship God, declaring that God is among you indeed. (18-25)

18. *I thank God etc.* Many people belittle other people's abilities simply because they themselves cannot be outstanding in them. Paul did not want to give the impression that he is decrying the gift of tongues through ill-will or jealousy, and so he anticipated a suspicious attitude of that sort, by saying that he himself stands out above them all. He says: 'You should realize that what I am saying ought not to give you grounds for suspicion, as if I would depreciate something that I personally lack, for if we had a contest about languages not one of you would be able to hold a candle to me. But while I could make a good showing in that sort of thing, I am more concerned about upbuilding.' Paul's teaching is given a good deal of weight by the fact that he is not thinking of his own reputation at all. But in order not to give the impression of being too insolent by putting himself in

front of others, he ascribes it all to God as His gift. So he tempers his boasting with modesty.

19. *I had rather speak five words.* This is hyperbole, unless you take 'five words' to mean five sentences. But since Paul, who, if he liked, could have spoken in tongues and made a dazzling show of himself, voluntarily refrains, and quietly makes upbuilding his one and only aim, in this way he clearly shows up the inflated ambition of those who are so very eager to draw attention to themselves with what is merely empty jingling. At the same time the authority of the apostle ought to have no little influence in drawing them away from vanity of that sort.

20. *Brethren be not children in mind.* Paul goes a step further, for he shows that the Corinthians are silly enough, not only to be responsible for bringing on themselves what the Lord threatens to send, when it is His intention to inflict the heaviest punishment on His people; but also to be reaching out for it as if it were something specially worth having. What sheer folly this is, to be putting all your heart into the pursuit of something which God looks upon as accursed.

But in order to understand Paul's meaning better, we should note that this sentence depends on the testimony of Isaiah (28.11), which he adds immediately after. But since interpreters have been misled through not noticing such a connexion, and in order to clear away all erroneous views, we shall first of all give an explanation of the Isaianic passage, and then deal with Paul's words.

In that chapter the prophet makes a strong attack upon the ten tribes, which had given themselves up to all sorts of vile practices. The only consolation is that God still had an unsullied people in the tribe of Judah, but soon he is bewailing its corruption also, and all the more bitterly because there was no hope of their improvement. For he speaks in God's name, saying, 'whom shall I teach knowledge? them that are weaned from the milk, and drawn from the breasts?' He means that they are no more capable of instruction than newly weaned infants.

Then follows: 'Precept upon precept, instruction upon instruction, command upon command, direction upon direction, here a little, there a little.'[1] By these mimicking words he brings out the slowness and stupidity which were keeping them back. It is as though he said:

[1]
CALVIN	VULGATE (Clem.)

Isaiah 28.10

CALVIN	VULGATE (Clem.)
Praeceptum ad praeceptum,	*Quia manda, remanda;*
instructio ad instructionem,	*manda, remanda;*
mandatum ad mandatum,	*exspecta, reexspecta;*
directio ad directionem,	*exspecta, reexspecta;*
paululum ibi, paululum ibi.	*modicum ibi, modicum ibi.*

'I am only making a pretence of working when I teach them, for they are making no progress, and that is because they are unbelievably backward, and what they had been laboriously taught over a long period of time they forget in a moment.'

Again there follows: 'The one who speaks to that people is, as it were, one who speaks with stammering lips, and in a foreign language.'[1] This is the verse which Paul is quoting. Now its meaning is that the people are afflicted with such blindness and folly that when God speaks to them they understand Him no better than they would any barbarian or foreigner, making unintelligible sounds in an unknown language; and that is a dreadful curse. But Paul has not quoted the prophet's words exactly, because it was enough for him to point out the verse, so that the Corinthians having been reminded of it, might study it more closely.

As to his saying that 'it is written in the law' this is not inconsistent with the usual way of speaking. For the prophets did not have a ministry that was unconnected with the law, but were in fact interpreters of the law, and all their teaching is something like a supplement to it. That means that the *law* covers the whole body of Scripture which existed until the time of Christ.

Now the conclusion that Paul draws from this verse is: 'Brethren, beware of being like children, a situation which the prophet condemns so severely, for it means that the voice of God resounds in your ears with no result. Indeed, when you reject prophecy, which is made to sound in your very ears, and you prefer to be struck dumb with astonishment by what is no more than an empty noise, does that not mean that, on your own responsibility, you are heading straight for the curse of God?'

Further, in case the Corinthians might protest that elsewhere it is regarded as a praiseworthy thing to be children spiritually, Paul anticipates them, and indeed urges them to be 'children in malice', but to take care not to be 'children in their thinking'. We may infer from that just how insolent are the people who make the simplicity of Christians to consist in ignorance. Paul wants all believers to be, as far as possible, mature in their thinking. Since it is easier to lead asses than

---

[1]   CALVIN   VULGATE (Clem.)
                        Isaiah 28.11

Text:
Alienis linguis et labiis   In loquela enim labii
alienis loquar, populo huic.   et lingua altera
Commentary: loquetur ad populum istum.
Qui loquitur ad populum istum,
est quasi qui utitur balbis
labiis et lingua peregrina.

men, the Pope, pleading the excuse of simplicity, directs that all his people should remain in ignorance. Because of this we should make a comparison between what lies under the Pope's direction, and what Christ has instituted, and see how they agree.

22. *Wherefore tongues are for a sign.* This verse can be explained in two ways, depending on whether 'therefore' is taken as referring only to the preceding sentence, or in a general way to the whole of the foregoing discussion. If it is a particular connexion with the sentence before, the meaning will be: 'You realize, brethren, that the thing you are wanting so eagerly, is not a benefit which God gives to believers, but a punishment with which He takes vengeance on unbelievers.' When it is understood in this way, Paul would not be taking into account the permanent use of tongues, but would be referring only to an actual situation that arose just once. However, if anyone wants to widen it to include the whole discussion, I have no quarrel with him, although I am quite satisfied with the explanation which I have just given.

If we take it in a general way, the meaning will be: 'Tongues in so far as they are given as a sign, i.e. as a miracle, are meant, strictly speaking, not for believers, but for unbelievers.' Tongues were useful in many ways. They met the needs of the actual situation, so that the difference in languages did not prevent the apostles from spreading the Gospel through the whole world; and there was therefore no nation to which they could not communicate it. Tongues were also useful for moving or frightening unbelievers by confronting them with a miracle. For this miracle, just like the others, aimed at the preparing of those, who were still strangers to Christ, for obedience to Him. Believers, who had already devoted themselves to the teaching of Christ, did not need preparation like that to the same extent. Therefore the Corinthians were wrong in giving undue emphasis to that gift, while they set prophecy aside and neglected it. Prophecy was, of course, set apart specially and particularly for believers and for that reason they ought to be familiar with it; for, as far as tongues were concerned all that the Corinthians were concerned about was their miraculous element.

23. *If therefore the whole church be assembled together.* They were not aware of their own fault, because their minds were completely taken up by a foolish and misleading desire. Paul therefore warns them that they will be making themselves the laughing-stock of unbelievers or the uninformed, should they come into their gathering and hear them uttering sounds, but not speaking intelligibly. For will somebody who is ignorant of all this not think people mad, who utter a meaningless noise instead of normal speech, and spend their time in a futile way

like that, when they are supposed to have met together to hear God's teaching? There is much sting in this sentence: 'In your own hearts you are highly delighted with yourselves; but unbelievers and the uninformed are laughing at all your nonsense. It means that you are not aware of something, which is perfectly obvious to those who have no knowledge about all this, and do not believe.'

Chrysostom raises a problem here: if it is the case that tongues were given as a sign to unbelievers, why is Paul now saying that these same people will scoff at them? His own answer is that as a sign their purpose is to fill them with amazement, and not to be a means of instructing them, or reforming them. He also adds, however, that it is because of their own sinfulness that they think of the sign as madness. That explanation of his does not meet with my approval. Granted that an unbelieving or ignorant person may be moved by the miracle, and stand in awe of this gift of God, that does not make him cease, all the same, from ridiculing and condemning the wrong use of the gift at the wrong time. Further, he will think within himself: 'What are these men aiming at, by wearying themselves and others to no purpose? What on earth is the use of speaking and saying nothing?' Paul's meaning therefore is that the Corinthians can be highly pleased with themselves, but the unbelieving and uninformed will be perfectly justified in condemning them for behaving in a senseless way.

24. *But if all prophesy.* Just as he had previously shown how prophecy is more beneficial than tongues to those who are of the household of faith, so now he teaches that it would also be of value to outsiders. This is a most powerful argument for showing the Corinthians that they are in the wrong. For it was extremely perverse of them to make light of a gift, that is of the greatest benefit to those who are outside the Church, as well as those who are inside it; and to be fascinated by another gift that is useless for those who belong to the household, and also puts a stumbling-block in the way of those who are outside it. He points out the effect that prophecy has, viz. it summons the consciences of unbelievers to the judgement seat of God, and imbues them with such a lively realisation of the judgement of God, that somebody who, in his indifference, used to despise sound teaching, is forced to glorify God.

But we will find it much easier to understand this verse if we compare it with another, Hebrews 4.12. 'For the word of God is living and active, and sharper than any two-edged sword, and piercing even to the dividing of soul and spirit, of both joints and marrow, and the discerner of the thoughts of the heart.' For in both places the Word of God is said to have the same sort of efficacy, but in the Hebrews passage it is described more fully and clearly. As far as the verse before us is concerned there is no difficulty now in understanding what being reproved and being judged mean. The consciences of men are sleepy and inactive, and untroubled by a sense of dissatisfaction with their sins, so long as they are enveloped in the darkness of ignorance. In a word, unbelief is like drowsiness which makes un insensitive. But the Word of God penetrates to the innermost corners of the mind, and, by bringing light, so to speak, dispels the darkness, and drives out that deadly lethargy. Therefore that is the way in which unbelievers are reproved, because, as soon as they realize that it is God they have to deal with, they are seriously perturbed, and really frightened. In the same way they are judged, because, while they were previously surrounded by darkness, and then had no idea of their wretchedness and shameful lives, now they are brought into the light, and compelled to bear witness against themselves.

When Paul says that they are judged and reproved by all, we should take him to mean, by all who prophesy, for he had said at the beginning of the verse, if all prophesy. He has purposely made use of the general word 'all' in order to remove their contempt for prophecy. The unbeliever is reproved, I maintain, not because the prophet pronounces judgement upon him either in his secret, unexpressed opinion of him, or in what he actually says in explicit terms, but because, when he listens, his conscience accepts its own judgement through what is taught. He is judged because he goes down into the depths of his own being, and after examining himself, he comes to a realization of what he is like, a knowledge which was denied him before. There is a Word of Christ's which refers to the same thing: The Spirit 'when he is come will convict the world in respect of sin' (John 16.8). Immediately afterwards Paul adds this: 'The secrets of his heart are made manifest.' For, in my opinion at any rate, he does not mean that it is made plain to the others what sort of person he is, but rather that his conscience is stirred so that he knows his sins, which were hidden from him before.

At this point Chrysostom asks a question again: how is it consistent to say that prophecy is so effective in influencing unbelievers, when Paul had said a little before that it was not given for them? His own answer is that it is given to them not as a useless sign, but as a means of instructing them. I myself feel it would be simpler and therefore more appropriate were we to say, that it is not given to unbelievers who are perishing, whose minds Satan has blinded to keep them from seeing the light shining in it. And it will suit better still if this sentence is linked up with the prophecy of Isaiah (28.11); because there the prophet is speaking about unbelievers, in whose case prophecy is futile and unproductive.

25. *Falling on his face he will worship.* For it is the knowledge of God,

and nothing else, which can bring down the pride of the flesh. Prophecy causes that to happen to us. By its very nature it is peculiarly effective for bringing men down from their pinnacles, to lie prostrate in adoration of God. Yet even prophecy is of no value to many people; indeed they are made worse by listening to it. Moreover, in attributing this power to prophecy, Paul did not intend to imply that it is invariably operative. He simply wanted to point out what a great benefit is derived from it, and the nature of its function. It therefore speaks volumes for it that it forces unbelievers to confess that God is present with His people, and His majesty is reflected in their gathering.

> *What is it then, brethren? When ye come together, each one hath a psalm, hath a teaching, hath a revelation, hath a tongue, hath an interpretation. Let all things be done unto edifying. If any man speaketh in a tongue, let it be by two, or at the most three, and that in turn; and let one interpret: but if there be no interpreter, let him keep silence in the church; and let him speak to himself, and to God. And let the prophets speak by two or three, and let the others discern. But if a revelation be made to another sitting by, let the first keep silence. For ye all can prophesy one by one, that all may learn, and all may be comforted; and the spirits of the prophets are subject to the prophets; for God is not a God of confusion, but of peace; as in all the churches of the saints.* (26–33)

26. *What is it then, brethren?* Paul now shows them a way to rectify these evils. In the first place there must be room for every single gift, but in its turn, and in due proportion. Further, the Church must not be devoting itself to useless and futile practices, but whatever is done must be done for edification. But he begins by defining edification in this way: 'Everyone who is provided with some gift should take pains to employ it for the good of all.' For the word 'everyone' ought to be understood like that, so that no-one may take it in a universal sense, as if all of them to a man were endowed with some such gift.

27. *If any man speaks in a tongue.* Paul now gives an outline of the order and lays down the mode to be followed. 'If you intend to speak in tongues, only two of you should speak, and anyhow not more than three, and an interpreter should be present at the same time. Languages are useless without an interpreter, and so they should not be employed in that event.' It should be observed that Paul is not issuing a command; he is merely giving permission. For the Church can do without tongues, and suffer no inconvenience, except where they are helpful for prophesying, as for example Hebrew and Greek are today. But Paul makes this concession so as not to give the impression of keeping back any gift of the Spirit from the congregation of the faithful.

It might appear, however, that there is an inconsistency here also, since he had said before that in so far as tongues are a sign they are suitable for unbelievers. My answer to that is that, even if a miracle is performed especially for the benefit of unbelievers, it does not follow, however, that it may not effect believers in some respects. If you take it that an unknown language is a sign to unbelievers, in the sense that the words of Isaiah bear, then the method, which Paul outlines here, is different. For he allows room for languages, so long as interpretation goes along with them, which means of course that nothing is left obscure. Therefore when Paul corrects the fault of the Corinthians he uses a very well-balanced mixture. On the one hand he rejects no gift of God, no matter what it is, so that all the blessings which He bestows may be seen in the company of believing people. On the other hand he imposes restrictions to prevent ambition stealthily taking the place that belongs to the glory of God, and to prevent any less important gift from standing in the way of the principal ones. And he adds flavouring to it so that there may not be ostentation only, without any results.

28. *Let him speak to himself and to God.* Paul is saying: 'Let him enjoy his gift in his own heart, and let him give thanks to God.' For I take 'speaking to himself and to God' to mean thinking within himself about the gift graciously conferred upon him, and giving silent thanks for it, and enjoying it as if it were his own private possession, when there is no opportunity for using it publicly. For Paul contrasts this speaking in secret with that done publicly in Church; and the latter is forbidden by him.

29. *Let the prophets speak by two or three.* Paul imposes restrictions on prophecy as well, because 'too many cooks spoil the broth', as the common saying has it. This is true, for our everyday experiences bring it home to us. He does not limit the number so precisely as he did in the case of tongues, however, for there is not the same danger, if they were to give more time to prophecies; and indeed the ideal thing would be to give constant attention to them; but at the same time Paul has taken into account what men can cope with in their weakness.

We have still to ask, however, why he limits both prophecies and languages to the same number, except that in the case of the latter he expressly adds, 'at the most three'; for if languages are not so valuable, surely it is right that they should be used more sparingly? I answer that prophecy is included in languages, in the way that Paul understands the word, for languages were used either for discourses or for praying. In the discourses the interpreter took the place of the prophet, and so that was the chief, and the more frequent, way in which languages were employed. He puts a restriction on it only to prevent it becoming degraded because of pride, and to prevent those who were less able from depriving the better qualified of their turn and opportunity for speaking. For he surely intends that those to whom he assigns the task of speaking should be drawn from the cream of them, and appointed by common assent. But of course there are none readier to push themselves to the front than those who have a slight smattering of merely commonplace knowledge, so that the proverb is proved true, 'fools rush in where angels fear to tread' (*audax inscitia*). Paul intended to counteract this evil, when he allotted the task of speaking to two or three.

Let the others discern. So as not to give the others a chance to protest, thinking he wanted the gift of God suppressed, and put an end to in their case, Paul shows them how it is possible to use it for the good of the Church, even when they have to keep quiet, viz. if they are weighing up, in their own minds, what is said by others. For it is an inestimable benefit that there are some who are experienced in judging, so as not to allow sound teaching to be corrupted by the deceiving ways of Satan, or to be spoiled in any other way by worthless nonsense. Therefore Paul is pointing out that even by remaining silent the rest of the prophets will be rendering service to the Church.

But it may seem odd that men are allowed to make judgements concerning the teaching of God, which ought to be established beyond any dispute. My answer to that is that the teaching of God is not subjected to the judgement of men, but their task is simply to judge, by the Spirit of God, whether it is His Word which is declared, or whether, using this as a pretext, men are wrongly parading what they themselves have made up; as we will learn again soon.

30. *But if a revelation is made to another sitting by.* It is also all to the good that the opportunity of speaking will be given to them, whenever they have something worth-while to say; and so they will have no further cause to complain that the Spirit is bound, or His voice silenced. For when the situation demands it, all are given opportunity and freedom to speak. The one proviso is that no-one must push himself forward out of turn, satisfying his own self-esteem rather than meeting people's need. On the other hand Paul requires all of them to practise this self-restraint, by each of them (when actually speaking) giving way to somebody else who has something better to impart. For genuine freedom of the Spirit does not consist in each one being allowed to blurt out anything he likes at random, but only in all, from the most to the least important, being quite willing to take their turn, and in listening to the one Spirit, no matter by whose voice He speaks. As far as the reliability of this revelation is concerned, we shall soon learn about that.

31. *For ye all can prophesy one by one.* In the first place, when Paul says 'all' he does not include the whole of the faithful, but only those who had been endowed with this gift. Further, he does not mean that they should all have equal turns, but that individuals should come forward to speak more or less often, depending on whether it is for the people's benefit. Paul might have put it like this: 'nobody will stand and wait for ever, but the opportunity of speaking will present itself sometimes to some, sometimes to others.'

He adds, *that all may learn,* because, even though this applies to the whole of the people, yet it is appropriate to the prophets, and, in fact, Paul is meaning them especially. For no man will ever be a good teacher, if he does not show that he himself is teachable, and is always ready to learn; and the man will never be met who is so self-sufficient in the fullness and completeness of his knowledge that he would gain nothing by listening to other people. All should, therefore, carry out their duties as teachers in such a way as not to decline to take their turn as learners, or to be annoyed at having to do so, whenever others are given the opportunity of giving instruction to the Church.

In the second place Paul says that *all may be comforted.* We must infer from that, that, so far from being jealous, ministers of Christ should rather rejoice wholeheartedly that they are not the only ones who excel, but that there are others who share the same gift. The sacred records tell us that Moses had an attitude like that. For when Moses' minister (Joshua) was aflame with foolish jealousy, and indignant that the gift of prophecy was conferred on others also, he rebukes him, saying: 'No! rather my wish is that the whole people shared in this superb gift along with me' (Num. 11.28). And indeed it is particularly encouraging to conscientious ministers to see the Spirit of God, whose instruments they themselves are, at work in others. That is a great source of re-assurance to them. It is also a heartening thing that the spread of the word of God is greatly helped, when there are many ministers and witnesses of it.

But because the verb παρακαλεῖσθαι, which Paul uses here, is ambiguous, it can also be translated, 'they may receive an exhortation'. That is quite suitable, for it is sometimes good for us to listen to others, in order to be given an incentive to do our duty with greater eagerness.

32. *And the spirits of the prophets.* Another of the reasons why it is necessary for them to take it in turns is because it will sometimes be the case that the other prophets may find fault with something in the teaching given by one of their number. Paul says: 'It is not fair that anyone should be above the risk of criticism. So what in fact will happen is that opportunities for speaking will sometimes come round again to somebody who was sitting in silence among the congregation.'

Some people have misunderstood this verse, as if Paul was saying that the prophets of the Lord are not like 'men possessed', who, once an ecstatic influence (ἐνθουσιασμός) had laid hold of them, lost their self-control. It is certainly a fact that the prophets of God were not beside themselves, but that has nothing to do with this verse of Paul's. For its meaning (as I have already said) is that nobody is exempt from the criticism of others, but that all must be given a hearing, with the stipulation that their teaching must, at the same time, be subjected to criticism.

Of course that is not without its difficulty, for the apostle tells us that their *spirits are subject*. Although he is speaking about gifts, how can prophecy, a gift of the Holy Spirit, be judged by men, without the Spirit Himself being subject to their judgement? According to this way of thinking he will be subjecting even the word of God, which is revealed by the Spirit, to scrutiny. There is no need to point out how intolerable that would be, because it is self-evident. But I deny that either the Spirit, or the word of God, is to be controlled by criticism of that sort. My contention is that the Holy Spirit maintains His majesty unimpaired, so that He 'judges everything, while He is judged by nobody'. The holy Word of God also continues to be respected, so that it is accepted without dispute, as soon as it is presented.

'What is subject to examination, then?' you will ask. I answer that if anyone had a full revelation, there is no doubt that that person, and his gift as well, would be above all criticism. I maintain that there is no question of subjection where there is fullness of revelation. But because God has distributed His Spirit to each person to a limited extent only, so that even where His outpouring is at its greatest there is always something lacking, it is not to be wondered at if not a single person is raised to such a high position as to look down upon everybody from his eminence, and to be spared having anybody to criticize him.

We now see that without insulting the Holy Spirit in any way, His gifts may stand scrutinizing. And more than that, when everything has been investigated, and nothing is found to need correction, there will be something, all the same, which could do with improving. What it amounts to, therefore, is that the gift is subjected to examination in this way, that the prophets weigh up what is said, to see if it has come from the Spirit of God, for if it is established that the Spirit is the source of it, there is no need for further perplexity.

However, another question is asked: by what standard is the examination to be made? Part of the answer is given from the lips of Paul himself, who, in Romans 12.6, measures prophecy 'according to the analogy of faith' (*ad analogiam fidei*). But as far as the actual judging is concerned, there is no doubt that it ought to be controlled by the Word and Spirit of God, so that only what is perceived to be from God receives approval, that nothing is condemned except by means of His Word, and, in short, that God alone is in charge of the judgement, and that men are simply His heralds.

We may gather from this passage of Paul's how that church was flourishing with a remarkable wealth and variety of spiritual gifts. For there were colleges of prophets, so that it would have been quite a task to allocate their turns. There was so great a variety of gifts that there was some redundancy. Today we see our own slender resources, our poverty in fact; but this is undoubtedly the punishment we deserve, as the reward for our ingratitude. For God's riches are not exhausted, nor has His liberality grown less; but we are not worthy of His largess, or capable of receiving all that He generously gives. However, we have still enough and to spare of light and teaching, so long as there is no neglect of the practice of godliness and the results it produces.

33. *For God is not of confusion.* A word like 'author' must be understood. This is a most valuable sentence for it teaches us that the only way we can serve God is by being people who love peace, and are eager to have it. So where people want to quarrel, we can be quite sure that God is not reigning there. But how easy it is to say that! Isn't it constantly on people's lips? At the same time, indeed, most people make trouble about nothing, or cause an upheaval in the Church when they want to make themselves conspicuous by some means or other, and to have an air of importance.

Therefore, when we are forming judgements about the servants of Christ, let us bear in mind that attention must be given to this standard, whether they are anxious for peace and concord, and whether by behaving in a peaceable way, they are avoiding quarrels as far as they possibly can. Of course there is the proviso that we must understand by peace, the peace of which the truth of God is the bond. For if we have to fight against godless teachings, then, even if it is necessary to move heaven and earth, we must persevere, nevertheless, in the struggle. We must certainly make it our primary concern to see that the truth of God is maintained without any controversy; but if unbelievers resist, we must struggle against them, and we must not be afraid that we will be blamed for the disturbances. For the peace, of which rebellion against God is the token, is an accursed thing; whereas the struggles, which are necessary for the defence of the Kingdom of Christ, are blessed.

As in all the churches. The comparison does not refer merely to the first part of this verse, but to all he has outlined above. It is as though he said: 'So far I have given you no directions, which are not followed in all the churches, and that is how those same churches are kept together in peace. Therefore you should be borrowing what other churches have found by experience make for their well-being, and are most valuable for preserving peace.'

Paul makes particular mention of *the saints* for the sake of emphasis, as if to free all properly organized churches from any undeserved stigma.

> *Let the women keep silence in the churches: for it is not permitted unto them to speak; but let them be in subjection, as also saith the law. And if they would learn anything, let them ask their own husbands at home; for it is shameful for a woman to speak in the church. What? was it from you that the word of God went forth? or came it unto you alone? If any man thinketh himself to be a prophet, or spiritual, let him take knowledge of the things which I write unto you, that they are the commandment of the Lord. But if any man is ignorant, let him be ignorant. Wherefore, my brethren, desire earnestly to prophesy, and forbid not to speak with tongues. But let all things be done decently and in order.* (34–40)

It appears that the Corinthian church was also spoiled by this fault, that when they met together, there was a place for the chattering of women, or rather it was allowed great liberty. Paul accordingly forbids them to speak in public, either by way of teaching or prophesying. But we should understand this as referring to the situation where things can be done in the regular way, or where the Church is well established. For a situation can arise where there is a need of such a kind as calls for a woman to speak. But Paul is confining himself to what is fitting in a properly organized congregation.

34. *Let them be in subjection, as also saith the law.* What has the subjection, under which the law places women, to do with what Paul is teaching now? For someone will say: 'What is there to prevent them teaching even although they are in subjection?' I reply that the task of teaching is one that belongs to someone with oversight, and is for that reason inconsistent with being in subjection. For how unsuitable it would be for a woman, who is in subjection to one of the members, to be in an authoritative position over the whole body! It is therefore an argument based on incompatibilities; because, if the woman is under subjection, she is therefore debarred from having authority to teach in public. And there is no doubt that wherever natural propriety itself has had its effect, women in all ages have been excluded from the control of public affairs. And common sense tells us that the rule of women is improper and defective. Furthermore, while at one time in Rome they were allowed to plead in court, the impudence of Caia Afrania resulted in their being forbidden to do even that. But Paul's

reasoning is straightforward: that authority to teach is out of keeping with the woman's role, because, if she does teach, she is set over all the men, whereas she should properly be under subjection.

35. *And if they would learn anything.* So that he might not give the impression, by speaking like this, of closing the door of learning on women, he instructs them to make their inquiries in private, if they are in doubt about anything, to prevent their initiating any discussion in public. Although he says 'husbands', he is not forbidding the women from consulting the prophets themselves, if necessary; for all husbands are not capable of giving an answer.

But as he is discussing the external organization (*externa politia*) here, it is enough for his purpose to point out what is unseemly, so that the Corinthians might avoid it. However, the discerning reader should come to the decision, that the things which Paul is dealing with here, are indifferent, neither good nor bad; and that they are forbidden only because they work against seemliness and edification.

36. *What? was it from you that the word of God went forth?* This rebuke is a bit sharper, but it was needed to curb the pride of the Corinthians. For they were inordinately pleased with themselves, and would not tolerate fault being found in any way with themselves or anything connected with themselves. So Paul inquires if they are the only, indeed, if they are the first and the last, Christians in the world. He asks: 'Do you mean to say that it was from you that the Word of God went forth? In other words, did it originate with you? Did it come to an end with you? That is, will it not be spread any further?' In admonishing them, what Paul is after is this, that, having ignored the practices of others, they may not rest content with their own devices or customs.

But this teaching is of a general nature, for no church ought to be turned in on itself, to the neglect of others. But, on the contrary, all of them should be extending the right hand to each other, to promote their fellowship with each other; and, as the concern for unity demands, they should be adjusting themselves to one another.

But at this point it is asked whether any church which was established before another one (*ordine praecessit*) can for that reason also make it accept its institutions. For Paul seems to imply as much by what he is saying. For example, Jerusalem was the mother of all the churches, because the Word of the Lord had originated there. Could she use that to claim a privileged position for herself, and put all the others under an obligation to do what she did? I reply that here Paul does not use an argument with a universal bearing, but one that was especially applicable to the Corinthians, something he is often in the habit of doing. Therefore he is thinking of particular parties rather than of this particular problem. That is why it does not necessarily follow that churches, which are later in origin, must be forced to adopt, in every detail, the practices of those which were set up earlier. Indeed Paul himself serves as an example, for he did not bind himself by this principle, so as to force on other churches the usages that were adopted at Jerusalem. Let there be no self-promotion, no stubbornness, no pride or contempt for other churches; but, on the contrary, let there be an eagerness for upbuilding, let there be moderation and common sense; and, when that happens, even where there are a great many different practices, there will be nothing calling for reproof.

Let us remember, then, that it was the pride of the Corinthians that was being taken to task here. For they were considering their own interests in isolation. Because of that they did not defer to the older churches from which they had received the Gospel, and they did not trouble to adapt themselves to other churches, to which the Gospel had spread after them. How I wish that in our own day there was no Corinth, as far as both this and other faults are concerned! Yet we see how cruel men, who have never tasted the Gospel, cause disturbances in the faithful churches by enforcing their own laws like tyrants.

37. *If any man thinketh himself to be a prophet.* Bear in mind the duty of judging which Paul had earlier entrusted to the prophets, viz. that they are to accept what they recognize as coming from God. But he is not telling them to make investigations as they would into something which they are doubtful about, but to embrace his teaching as the undoubted Word of God; because if they judge aright they will recognize it as the Word of God. In addition, it is in virtue of his apostolic authority that he takes it upon himself to give them instructions about what decision they ought to reach.

He shows even more confidence in saying immediately afterwards, *if any man is ignorant, let him be ignorant.* This was certainly legitimate in Paul's case, for he had no doubt at all in his own mind about the revelation he had received from God; and also, he ought to have been well known to the Corinthians, so that they should have regarded him as an apostle of the Lord, and in no other way. But everyone cannot make such a claim for himself; or, if he does do so, people will only laugh at him, and quite rightly, for showing off; for there is room for confidence like Paul's only when the words that are on the lips of men are borne out by facts. Paul was stating no more than the truth in saying that his injunctions were those of the Lord; many, on the other hand, will allege the same thing without any warrant. The whole thing hinges on the fact that it is clear that a man is speaking by the Holy Spirit, and is not expressing his own ideas, when he cannot bear to be called to order. But the man who is a genuine instrument of the

Holy Spirit, and nothing else, will, like Paul, dare to make the confident assertion that those who will reject his teaching are not prophets or spiritual people. And he will be within his rights in doing so, according to what we read at the beginning of this letter, 'he that is spiritual judgeth all things' (2.15).

But at this point it can be asked how Paul asserts that they are the injunctions of the Lord, for there is no corroboration of them in the Scriptures. And still another problem presents itself, that, if they are the commandments of the Lord, then they are bound to be observed, and bind men's consciences; and yet they are administrative arrangements, and there is not the same compulsion for us to observe them. But all that Paul is saying is that he is laying down nothing but what is agreeable to the will of God. Further, God informed him of His counsel so that he might recommend that way of ordering outward things (*ordinem istum in rebus externis*) at Corinth and elsewhere, not that it might be an inviolable law, like those which deal with the spiritual worship of God, but a useful form for all the children of God, and one not at all to be ignored.

38. *If any man is ignorant.* The Vulgate reads, 'if any man is ignorant, he will not be known', but that is wrong. For it was not Paul's intention to give any opportunity to the quarrelsome people, who are never done disputing, and under the pretext of inquiring at that, as if something was not yet clear to them; or at any rate he is pointing out, in general terms, that he has no time for all who called in question what he said. It is as if he said: 'If anyone does not grasp this, I have no time for his uncertainty; for that will not impair the certainty of my teaching in the slightest. Let me therefore have nothing to do with a man like that, no matter who he is. As for you, do not let that in any way shake your confidence that Christ is speaking through me.' In short, he means that sceptics, the quarrelsome, and hair-splitters by their questionings, do not in the slightest degree lessen the authority of sound teaching, and of that truth, about which believers ought to have no doubts whatever. At the same time he warns us not to let their uncertainty cause any hindrance to us. But greatness of mind like that, which despises all human judgements, ought to be based on assured truth. Therefore, just as, on the one hand, it would be perverse and stupid, once you have adopted a certain point of view, either to stick to it stubbornly, even although everybody else disagrees with you; or to cling to it defiantly when they have their doubts about it; so, on the other hand, when we are quite sure that it is God who is speaking, let us leap confidently over all human barriers and all difficulties.

39. *Wherefore my brethren.* This is the conclusion in connexion with the main question, that prophecy should be preferred to other gifts,

because it is the most useful gift of all, and yet at the same time the others ought not to be neglected. But we must pay attention to the way he puts it. For he is pointing out that prophecy is worth aspiring to earnestly and eagerly, on the part of all. At the same time he urges them not to begrudge the rarer gift of *tongues* to others, for it is not to be sought after so much; yes, and more than that, he tells them to get rid of all jealousy, and give them the praise they deserve.

40. *Let all things be done decently and in order.* This conclusion is more general, for not only does it sum up the whole situation in a few words, but also the different aspects of it. And more than that, it provides us with a suitable standard for assessing everything connected with external organization (*ad externam politiam*). Since he had dealt with rites in various passages, he wanted, at this point, to sum everything up very briefly, viz. that seemliness should be preserved, and disorder should be avoided. This statement shows that he was not willing to put people's consciences under obligation to the instructions he gave above, as if they were binding for their own sake, but only in so far as they make for seemliness and peace. From this we acquire (as I have said) a general principle, which tells us the purpose which the organization of the Church (*Ecclesiae politia*) ought to be serving.

The Lord allows us freedom in regard to outward rites, in order that we may not think that His worship is confined to those things. At the same time, however, He has not allowed us unlimited and unbridled liberty, but has, so to speak, put railings round about it; or at any rate He has restricted the freedom, which He has given us, in such a way that it is only from His Word that we can make up our minds about what is right. Therefore when this passage is considered properly, it will reveal a difference between the tyrannical edicts of the Pope, which crush the consciences of men in a detestable form of slavery, and the godly laws of the Church, which preserve its discipline and order. Furthermore, we may easily infer from this, that the Church's laws are not to be regarded as mere human traditions, seeing that they are based on this general injunction, and clearly give the impression of being approved, as it were, from the mouth of Christ Himself.

CHAPTER FIFTEEN

Now I make known unto you, brethren, the gospel which I preached unto you, which also ye received, wherein also ye stand, by which also ye are saved; I make known, I say, in what words I preached it unto you, if ye hold it fast, except ye believed in vain. For I delivered unto you first of all that which also I received, how that Christ died for our sins according to the scriptures; and that he was buried; and that he hath been raised on the third day according to the scriptures; and that he appeared to Cephas; then to the twelve; then he appeared to above five hundred brethren at once, of whom the greater part remain until now, but some are fallen asleep; then he appeared to James; then to all the apostles; and last of all, as unto one born out of due time, he appeared to me also. For I am the least of the apostles, that am not meet to be called an apostle, because I persecuted the church of God. But by the grace of God I am what I am: and his grace which was bestowed upon me was not found vain; but I laboured more abundantly than they all: yet not I, but the grace of God which was with me. (1-10)

1. *Now I make known unto you.* Paul now takes up another theme, the resurrection, for the Corinthians' belief in this had been shaken by some unbelieving people. But it is not clear whether they were in doubt only about the resurrection of the body at the last, or the immortality of the soul also. It is quite well known that there were various mistaken views in this connexion. Certain philosophers contended that men's souls are immortal, but the question of the resurrection of the body never entered the head of one of them. The Sadducees, again, had a grosser outlook, for it was limited to this present life, and besides that, they thought that the soul of man is a mere breath, lacking any substance.

Therefore it is not at all clear to us (as I have already said) whether the Corinthians had at that time reached such a stage of foolishness that they gave up having any confidence in a future life, or whether they merely denied the resurrection of the body; but the arguments, which Paul uses, seem to imply that they were completely fascinated by the Sadducees' nonsense. For example, when he says, 'What is the use of being baptized for the dead; would it not be better to eat and drink; why do we stand in jeopardy every hour?' and the like, it would have been easy to reply, following the lines of the philosophers, 'Because our souls survive after death'. Accordingly some people make the

whole of Paul's argument in this chapter refer to the immortality of
our souls. But while I myself leave undecided the question of what the
error of the Corinthians actually was, yet I cannot be persuaded to
make the words of Paul apply to anything else but the resurrection of
the body. Therefore let it be settled once and for all that he is dealing
with that, and nothing else, in this chapter.

But how if the unorthodoxy (*impietas*) of Hymenaeus and Philetus
had penetrated as far as Corinth, for those two said that the resurrection
is past already and that there would be no future one? There are also
fanatics like them in our own day, or, one should rather say, demons
under the influence of other demons, who call themselves Libertines.
But it certainly seems to me to be nearer the truth to hazard the guess
that they have been misled by some imaginary notion, which cut away
their hope of the future resurrection, in the same way as the Libertines
by imagining some sort of symbolical resurrection, do away with the
real one, which has been promised to us.

Whatever the situation was, it surely provides a dreadful example,
and something in the nature of a warning to us, that people who had
been under the instruction of so outstanding a teacher, could have
forsaken him so soon for such grossly mistaken views. But is there any
cause for wonder, when in the Church of Israel the Sadducees had the
audacity to profess openly that man is no different from a beast, as far
as the essential nature of the soul is concerned, and that he has no more
happiness than what the animals have? Let us take note however that
blindness like that is the just judgement of God, for those who do not
acquiesce in the truth of God, are driven hither and thither by the
deceptive tricks of Satan.

But someone asks why Paul has deferred, or put off, to the end of this
letter, a subject which deserved precedence over everything else. Some
people's answer to that is that Paul did so, to let it make a deeper
impression on their memories. I rather think that Paul intended to
make no mention of such an important matter, until he had vindicated
his authority, which to some extent had lost its influence among the
Corinthians, and until he had subdued their pride and made them
willing to receive his teaching.

Now I make known unto you. To *make known* does not mean here to
teach something of which they had no knowledge at all, but to remind
them of what they had heard before. It is as if he said: 'Take a
fresh look, along with me, at that Gospel, with which you had
become acquainted, before you were led away from the right path.'
Paul refers to the doctrine of the resurrection as the Gospel, so that
they might not imagine that it is in order for anyone to entertain
any views he likes on it, and get away with it, as a person may

well do with other subjects, with no adverse effect on his salvation.

Paul amplifies that by adding, *which I preached unto you*, as though he said: 'You recognize me as an apostle, don't you? Then there is no doubt that it was on those lines that I myself taught you.' The second amplification is to the effect that they had already believed it, so that, if they now allow themselves to be convinced to the contrary, they will have to be accused of being fickle. A third amplification is to the effect that up to now they had persevered in that belief with a firm and unwavering resolution, which is saying a good deal more than that they had held that belief once upon a time. But the most important of these amplifying statements is that Paul declares that it is precisely in this very thing that their salvation consists. For the conclusion to be drawn from that is, that if the resurrection is cut out, then they have no religion left, no assurance of faith left, and, in fact, no faith left at all.

Others take 'standing' differently, as meaning 'being supported or kept up'. But the interpretation I have given is nearer the truth.

2. *If you hold it fast, except ye believed in vain.* These two conditional clauses have a sharp sting in them. In the first he is condemning their indifference or changeableness, because a collapse as sudden as theirs was proof that they had never grasped what had been taught them, or that their knowledge had been only a frail, fragile thing, when it had faded away so quickly. In the other phrase he warns them that they have been wasting their time and breath in professing allegiance to Christ, if they do not hold on to this fundamental principle of the faith.

3. *For I delivered unto you first of all.* Paul now supports what he had said already by showing that the resurrection had been preached by him, and as one of the principal and fundamental elements in the Gospel indeed. 'First of all', he says, meaning that it is like the foundation which we normally lay when putting up a building.

And at the same time he strengthens the authority of his preaching by adding, that he delivered nothing but what he had received. For he means that he recounted, not merely what others reported to him, but also what the Lord had entrusted to him. For the word ought to be explained in light of the context. Now it is the duty of an apostle to make known publicly only what he has received from the Lord, so that he is directly (*de manu, quod aiunt, in manum*) responsible for giving out (*administret*) the pure Word of God to the Church.

That Christ died etc. You can now see more clearly where he received it from, for he quotes the Scriptures as evidence. In the first place he mentions the death of Christ, and indeed his burial as well, so that we may conclude that as He was like us in both of them, the same thing applies in regard to resurrection. Therefore He Himself has entered into death along with us, that we might rise along with Him. The reality of death, which He has shared with us, is brought out more vividly by mentioning His burial also. Again, the death and resurrection of Christ were foretold in many passages of Scripture, but in none more clearly than Isaiah 53, Daniel 9.26, and Psalm 22.

For our sins. That is to say, He took our curse upon Himself, in order to deliver us from it. For what else was the death of Christ, but a sacrifice for the expiation of our sins; an atoning punishment (*poena satisfactoria*) through which we are reconciled to God; the condemnation of one person to procure our acquittal? Paul says the same sort of thing in Rom. 4.25 also; but there, on the other hand, he says that the resurrection produces another effect, in that it confers righteousness upon us. For, as sin was destroyed by the death of Christ, so righteousness was procured by His resurrection. This distinction should be carefully noted, so that we may know what to expect from the death of Christ, and what from His resurrection. Finally, when other passages of Scripture refer to His death only, we should realize that in those instances His resurrection is included in His death; but when they are mentioned separately, the commencement (*initium*) of our salvation is in His death, as we see here, and its completion (*complementum*) in His resurrection.

5. *That he appeared to Cephas.* Paul now cites eye-witnesses (αὐτόπτας) as they are called in Luke 1.2, who saw the fulfilment of what the Scriptures had foretold would take place. He does not give a complete list, however, for he omits the women. When he says, therefore, that He appeared to Peter first of all, we must understand that he is the first among the men, so that Mark's statement (16.9) that He appeared first to Mary is not inconsistent with it in any way.

But how can he say that he appeared to the twelve, when there were only eleven of them left after the death of Judas? Chrysostom thinks that this happened after Matthias had been elected in his place. Others preferred to correct the figure, as if it was a mistake. But when we realize that it was by Christ's own ordering that twelve of them were set apart, even though one of them would be struck off the list, it does not strike us as strange that the term was retained. It was for the same reason that the body of men at Rome were called the Hundred, although there were actually one hundred and two of them, for the use of the name had persisted there too. Therefore you should simply take the twelve to mean the chosen apostles here.

It is not quite clear when that appearance to 'more than five hundred' took place, except that it is possible that such a great company had been gathered together at Jerusalem, when He showed Himself visibly to them. For Luke (24.33) speaks in general terms of disciples who had met along with the eleven, but he does not say how many there were. Chrysostom makes it refer to the Ascension, and explains ἐπάνω as 'from above'. This could certainly have been after the Ascension, in view of the fact that Paul tells us that He appeared to James on his own.

By all the apostles I understand, not only the twelve, but also the disciples to whom He had entrusted the task of preaching the Gospel. In view of the fact that our Lord intended that His resurrection should have many eye-witnesses, who would tell of it again and again, we should therefore bear in mind that our faith in it should be all the more assured. And since the apostle proves the resurrection of Christ from the fact that He appeared to many people, he is pointing out in that way that this was no 'symbolical' resurrection, but a genuine and physical (*naturalem*) one, for our eyes cannot be witnesses of a 'spiritual' resurrection.

8. *Last of all as unto one born out of due time . . . to me.* Paul now adds himself to the number of the other witnesses, for to him also Christ had shown Himself alive in His glorious state. Because this appearance was no hallucination it should also have been valuable for strengthening belief in the resurrection; and that is the use Paul makes of this evidence in Acts 26.8.

But because it was very important that his authority should carry the greatest possible weight among the Corinthians, he inserts, in passing, something that says a great deal in his own favour. But he tones it down in such a way that, although he is making a tremendous claim for himself, he is very modest at the same time. Therefore, in case anyone should challenge him, saying, 'Who are you, that we should give credence to you?' he freely acknowledges his own unworthiness. In the first place, indeed, he compares himself to a premature child, and (in my opinion) that is a reference to his sudden conversion. For just as babies do not come forth from the womb until they have been in it for the proper period of time and been fully formed, so our Lord followed a suitable time-table in creating, fostering and shaping the apostles. Paul, on the other hand, had been pushed out of the womb, before the living spirit had scarcely had time to be properly conceived in him.

Some people take it that the term *one born out of due time* stands for 'one born after his father's death'. But the former is much more suitable, because he was begotten, born and a mature man all in one moment. Besides, this abortive birth makes the grace of God all the more evident in Paul's case than if he had grown up in Christ little by little, step by step.

9. *For I am the least.* It is not certain whether his enemies told people this in order to weaken their trust in him, or whether he made this

confession entirely of his own free will. While I do not doubt that he
never had the slightest hesitation about being prepared and even glad
to belittle himself, in order to magnify the grace of God, yet I suspect
that in this verse he intended to meet false charges against him. There
were people at Corinth who made it their business to undermine his
authority by maliciously speaking against him. That fact we can
gather from many of the preceding passages, and also from a comparison
that he introduces a little later on, one that he would certainly never
have made, if he had not been forced to do so by the wickedness of
certain people. He might have put it like this: 'Insult me as much as
you like, I will not mind being made lower than the very dust, I will
not mind if I count for nothing, so that the goodness of God towards
me may be all the more apparent. Let me therefore be regarded as the
least of the apostles; indeed I know that I am not even worthy of that
position. For what merits had I that would enable me to reach it?
When I used to persecute the Church of God, what did I deserve then?
But there is in fact no need for you to determine my worth, for the
Lord paid no attention to the kind of man I was, but by His grace made
another man of me.'

What it amounts to is this, that Paul does not object to being the
meanest of them all, almost a nonentity in fact, so long as being looked
down upon like that does not hinder his ministry in any way, and does
not detract one whit from his teaching. He is quite content, as far as
he himself is concerned, to be regarded as unworthy of any honour,
provided that he may commend his apostleship, because of the grace
which was bestowed upon him. And God certainly did not honour
him with such outstanding gifts in order that His grace might be buried
in oblivion, but His intention had been to make Paul's apostleship a
notable and most valuable one.

10. *And his grace . . . was not vain.* The people who set free will in
opposition to the grace of God, fearing that we may make Him wholly
responsible for whatever good we do, twist these words to suit their
view, as though Paul were boasting that by his own efforts he had
taken care to prevent God conferring His grace on him to no purpose.
Accordingly they come to the conclusion that grace is certainly offered
by God, but the right use of it is something that man has in his own
power, and the responsibility for preventing it lying dormant is his.
But I deny that these words of Paul give any support to their mistaken
point of view, for in this verse he is not claiming anything as his own,
as though, independently of God, he had done something praiseworthy.
What, then, does he mean? So as not to give the impression of making
an empty boast, that is all words, lacking support in reality, he is saying
that he is telling of what is there for everyone to see. Finally, granted

that these words show that Paul did not make wrong use of the grace of God, and did not render it useless by his own idleness, yet I hold that we have no justification, on that account, for apportioning between him and God the praise which ought to be ascribed altogether to God, in view of the fact that He bestows upon us, not only the ability to do well, but also the will to do so, and the result of our efforts.

More abundantly. Some make this apply to braggarts who, by belittling Paul, were pushing themselves and their own interests forward, because, according to their view at any rate, it would not be fitting for Paul to wish to enter into rivalry with the apostles. But, when he does compare himself to the apostles, he does so because of ungodly people, who were in the habit of confronting him with them, in order to lower his reputation, as we see in the Letter to the Galatians (1.11). So it is quite probable that he is speaking about the apostles, when he rates his own efforts above theirs. And it is certainly true that he stood out above the rest, not only by enduring many hardships, by undergoing many testing experiences, by abstaining from many things he was at liberty to use, by constantly despising dangers of every kind; but also because the Lord was crowning his efforts with a greater measure of success. For I take 'labour' to mean the results that were to be seen for his labour.

Not I but the grace of God which was with me. By omitting the relative the Vulgate has given those who do not know Greek an opportunity of going wrong. Because it renders it, 'Not I but the grace of God with me', they have come to think that only half the credit is to be given to God, while the other half is kept for man. Therefore their understanding is that Paul did not work on his own, because he could do nothing without co-operating grace, while at the same time his own free will and his own efforts had their own part to play. But his words strike quite a different note, for having said that something was applicable to himself, he corrects that and transfers it entirely to God; entirely, I insist, and not just a part of it; for he affirms that whatever he may have seemed to do was in fact totally the work of grace. This is indeed a remarkable verse, not only for bringing down human pride to the dust, but also for making clear to us the way that the grace of God works in us. For, as though he were wrong in making himself the source of anything good, Paul corrects what he had said, and declares that the grace of God is the efficient cause of everything. We should not imagine that Paul is merely simulating humility here. He is speaking as he does from his heart, and because he knows that it is the truth. We should therefore learn that the only good we have is what the Lord has given us gratuitously; that the only good we do is what He does in us; that it is not that we do nothing ourselves, but that we act only when we have been acted upon, in other words under the direction and influence of the Holy Spirit.

Whether then it be I or they, so we preach, and so ye believed. Now if Christ is preached that he hath been raised from the dead, how say some among you that there is no resurrection of the dead? But if there is no resurrection of the dead, neither hath Christ been raised: and if Christ hath not been raised, then is our preaching vain, your faith also is vain. Yea, and we are found false witnesses of God; because we witnessed of God that he raised up Christ: whom he raised not up, if so be that the dead are not raised. For if the dead are not raised, neither hath Christ been raised: and if Christ hath not been raised, your faith is vain; ye are yet in your sins. Then they also which are fallen asleep in Christ have perished. If in this life only we have hoped in Christ, we are of all men most pitiable. (11–19)

11. *Whether I or they.* Having compared himself with the rest of the apostles, Paul now puts himself alongside them, and them alongside himself, because of their agreement about the subject matter of their preaching. It is as if he said: 'I am saying no more about myself; but all of us have been at one in teaching, and are still continuing to teach, these things.' For the verb κηρύσσομεν (we preach) is in the present tense, indicating continuous action, or persistence in teaching. 'If the truth is different from what we say then our apostleship is finished and done with; and in addition, since you have believed what we told you, therefore your religion collapses also.'

12–13. *Now if Christ.* Paul now begins to prove the resurrection of all of us from the resurrection of Christ. For a mutual and reciprocal result is established from the one side and from the other, one that is both affirmative and negative. First of all, if you take 'from Christ to us', it is as follows: 'If Christ has risen, then we shall rise. If Christ has not risen, then we shall not rise.' Conversely, take 'from us to Christ', as follows: 'If we rise, therefore Christ has risen. If we do not rise, then Christ has not risen.'

Now take them in their order. This is the reasoning behind the argument that is to be drawn 'from Christ to us': 'Christ did not die or rise again for Himself, but for us, therefore His resurrection is the substance (*hypostasis*) of ours; and that which was effected in Him must be brought to completion in us also.' In negative form, on the other hand, it is this: 'There would otherwise have been no reason or purpose for His rising again, because the result of it is not to be sought in His own person, but in His members.'

On the other hand, the reasoning behind the foregoing conclusion, that is to be drawn by arguing 'from us to Him', is: 'For the resurrection is not a natural thing, and comes from no other source but Christ alone. For in Adam we die; only in Christ do we gain life again. It follows from that that His resurrection is the basis of ours, so that if His is taken away there will be none for us.' The reasoning behind the negative conclusion has already been given; for since He had to rise again for our sake alone, then, if there was no benefit for us, there would be no resurrection on His part.

14. *Then is our preaching vain*, not simply because it includes a certain element of falsehood, but because it is worthless and misleading through and through. For what is there left if Christ has been devoured by death, if He has been annihilated, if He has been crushed by the curse of sin, if, finally, He has surrendered to Satan? In a word, once that fundamental principle has been done away with, everything that remains will be valueless.

For the same reason he adds that their faith will be vain; for how will there be any firmness of faith, when no hope of life presents itself? But in the mere death of Christ we can discover nothing but grounds for despair; for someone who has been completely conquered by death cannot effect the salvation of others. Let us therefore remember that the main foundation of the whole Gospel is the death and resurrection of Christ; so that we must devote special attention to them, if we want to make good and regular progress in the Gospel, or rather, if we do not want to remain ineffective and unfruitful.

15. *Yea and we are found false witnesses*. The other bad results which he has just recounted are certainly serious enough, as far as we are concerned: that faith dies away, that the whole teaching of the Gospel is useless and valueless, that we have been deprived of all hope of salvation. But it is also no trivial and laughing matter that the apostles, who had been appointed by God to be the heralds of His eternal truth, are found out to be men who have been deceiving the world with their lies; for that turns back on God and shows Him in the worst possible light.

We can take the phrase, *false witnesses of God*, in two ways: either that they were lying by making wrong use of God's name, merely as a pretext; or that people discovered that they were liars when they testified as to what they had received from God. The second one appeals to me more, because it is a far more serious matter than the other; and Paul had already spoken about how it affected men. He now warns that if the resurrection of Christ is denied, then God is guilty of lying, in the person of witnesses who had been brought forward at His instigation. The reason which is added also agrees very well with that, because they had made a false assertion, not on their own initiative, but on God's.

I am aware that other people explain the preposition κατά in a different way. The Vulgate translates it *adversus*, 'against'; while Erasmus renders it *de*, 'concerning'. But since it also bears the sense of ἀπό, i.e. 'from', in Greek, that meaning seemed to me to be more in agreement with the apostle's intention. For he is not dealing here with men's reputation (as I have already stated), but with the fact that God will be exposed to the charge of lying, since what they are proclaiming had its origin with Him.

17. *Ye are yet in your sins.* For although Christ has made atonement for our sins, so that they might no longer be laid to our charge in the judgement of God, and He has crucified our old man, that its passions might reign no longer in us, and, finally, He has by His own death destroyed the power of death, and the devil himself, yet there would be none of these things if He had not emerged the victor by rising again. So, if the resurrection is done away with, the tyranny of sin is being set up anew.

18. *Then they which are fallen asleep.* Since Paul wanted to prove that, if the resurrection of Christ is cut out, our faith is useless, and Christianity merely a deception, he had said that the living would remain in their sins; but, because the dead provide an even clearer illustration of what the consequences would be, he now introduces a reference to them.

'What benefit would it be to the dead that they had once been Christians? Therefore our brothers, who are already dead, lived in the faith of Christ for nothing.' But if it is granted that the soul is immortal in its nature, this reasoning seems, at first glance, to be weak; for it can easily be protested that the dead have not perished, because their souls are living, apart from their bodies. Some fanatics conclude from this verse that there is no life in the intermediate period of time between death and resurrection. But there is no difficulty in refuting their ‚nonsense. For although the souls of the dead are now living and enjoying blessed rest, yet the completion of their happiness and consolation depends on the resurrection alone; because it is well with them for this, and no other, reason, that they are waiting for that day, in which they will be summoned to possess the Kingdom of God. That is why the hope of the dead is in vain, if that day does not come sooner or later.

19. *If in this life only we have hope in Christ.* Here is another incongruous situation, not only that we are spending our time and effort in vain when we believe, in view of the fact that the benefit derived from our faith perishes at death; but that it is even better not to believe at all, for unbelievers would be in a stronger and more desirable position. To believe, 'in this life only', means here, to confine the benefits derived

from our faith to this world, so that our faith no longer looks or extends beyond the bounds of this present life. This verse makes it clearer that the Corinthians had been taken in by some misleading and fanciful notion of a symbolical resurrection, such as Hymenaeus and Philetus were alleging at that time, as if the final benefit from our faith will be held out to us in this world. For, in view of the fact that resurrection means the completion of our salvation, and is the culminating point, as it were, of all our blessings, the man who says that our resurrection has already taken place, leaves us with nothing better to hope for after death. Be that as it may, this verse, however, gives no support at all to the nonsense of those who imagine that our souls sleep along with our bodies until the Resurrection Day. For they object that, if our souls continue to live after they are separated from our bodies, Paul would not have said that, if the resurrection were done away with, we would have hope only in this life, seeing that our souls would still have some sort of happiness left them. My answer to that is that Paul was not dreaming of Elysian fields, and silly nonsense of that kind, but that he has taken it as an undoubted fact that Christians direct their hope entirely to the Day of the Last Judgement; that believing souls today also rejoice in precisely the same expectation; and, for that reason, everything is lost to us, if an assurance of that sort is playing us false.

But why has he said that we would be *of all men most wretched*, as though a Christian's lot is worse than that of an unbeliever? 'For all things come alike to . . . the good and the bad,' as Solomon says in Eccles. 9.2. I reply that all men, whether they are good or bad, are undoubtedly equally exposed to similar calamities, and experience alike the same frustrations and the same misfortunes; but there are two reasons why Christians fare worse in all ages; and there was also another reason which belonged peculiarly to Paul's time.

The first reason is that, while the Lord may frequently also punish unbelievers with His lashes, and begin to carry out His judgements against them, yet He particularly afflicts His own people, and that in different ways. He does so, in the first place, because those whom He loves, He disciplines, and, secondly, in order to train them in endurance, to test their obedience, and to prepare them, step by step, by the way of the Cross for a real renewal. Be that as it may, the following always hold true as far as believers are concerned: 'For the time is come for judgement to begin at the house of God' (I Pet. 4.17); again, 'we are counted as sheep for the slaughter' (Ps. 44.22); and again, 'ye died, and your life is hid with Christ in God' (Col. 3.3). In the meantime the circumstances of unbelievers are usually richer because the Lord fattens them like pigs for the day of slaughter.

The second reason is that believers, even if they have an abundance of riches and goods of every kind, yet do not run riot with them, and do not gorge themselves in a light-hearted way. In a word they do not enjoy the world, as unbelievers do, but move on their way with anxious hearts, sighing all the time, partly because they are aware of their own weakness, and partly because they are longing for the life to come. Unbelievers, on the other hand, are completely absorbed in the intoxicating delights of this present life.

The third reason, which, as I said before, was peculiar to Paul's own day, was that the name 'Christians' was at that time so hateful and disreputable, that nobody could give his allegiance to Christ, without exposing himself to the immediate risk of death. Paul has therefore good cause for saying that Christians would be 'the most wretched of men' if their assurance was limited to this world.

But now hath Christ been raised from the dead, the firstfruits of them that are asleep. For since by man came death, by man came also the resurrection of the dead. For as in Adam all die, so also in Christ shall all be made alive. But each in his own order: Christ the firstfruits; then they that are Christ's, at his coming. Then cometh the end, when he shall deliver up the kingdom to God, even the Father; when he shall have abolished all rule and all authority and power. For he must reign, till he hath put all his enemies under his feet. The last enemy that shall be abolished is death. For, He put all things in subjection under his feet. But when he saith, All things are put in subjection, it is evident that he is excepted who did subject all things unto him. And when all things have been subjected unto him, then shall the Son also himself be subjected to him that did subject all things unto him, that God may be all in all. (20-28)

20. *But now hath Christ been raised.* Having shown how everything would be completely upset if we deny the resurrection of the dead, Paul this time takes for granted what he had fully proved before, that 'Christ has risen again', and he adds that He is the firstfruits, a metaphor borrowed (it would seem) from the ancient practice under the law. For just as the whole year's crop was dedicated in the firstfruits, so the power of Christ's resurrection is extended to all of us; or you may prefer a simpler explanation, that in Him the first fruit of the resurrection was gathered. However I myself prefer to understand the verse in this sense, that the rest of the dead will follow Him, in the same way as the whole harvest does the firstfruits; and this is confirmed by the next verse.

21-22. *Since by man came death.* Paul needs to prove that Christ is the firstfruits, and on the other hand that He was not raised up from the dead as an isolated individual. He makes his proof from contrasts; because death is not something natural, but is due to the sin of man. Therefore just as Adam did not die for himself alone, but for us all, so it follows that Christ, who is the antitype, did not rise again merely for Himself. For He came to restore everything which had been brought to ruin in Adam.

But the nature of this argument of his must be noted, because he does not join issue with the use of a figure of speech, or an example, but he relies on opposite causes to prove opposite effects. The cause of death is Adam, and we die in him; therefore Christ, whose function it is to restore what we have lost in Adam, is the cause of life for us; and His resurrection is the foundation (*hypostasis*) and pledge of ours. And just as Adam is the originator of death, so Christ is the one with whom life has its origin. In the fifth chapter of Romans he uses the same contrast, but with this difference, that there he is dealing with spiritual life and death, but here the point at issue is the resurrection of the body, which is the reward of the spiritual life.

23. *But each in his own order.* He deals with a question which someone might raise: 'If the life of Christ draws ours along with it, why do we have no visible evidence of this? Instead, although Christ has risen from the tomb, we rot in it.' Paul's answer is that God has appointed another way of ordering things. Let it therefore be enough for us that we now have the firstfruits in Christ, but the time for our resurrection will be when He comes. For our life must still be hid with Him, because He has not yet appeared. It would therefore be quite wrong to want to anticipate that day when Christ will be revealed.

24. *After that the end, when he shall deliver up.* Paul put a bridle on men's impatience, by asserting that the time would not be ripe for our new life until the coming of Christ. But because this world is like a stormy sea, in which we are constantly being tossed·about, and because our lot is so uncertain, or rather full of troubles, and because everything is subject to sudden change, weak minds could be thrown into a state of agitation by these things. Therefore Paul now calls our attention back to that day, saying that everything will be put in order then. Therefore the end will be then, in other words, the goal of our course, the peaceful haven, the situation immune from change of every kind. At the same time he warns us that we must wait for that end, because it is not appropriate for us to receive the crown in the middle of the race.

It will be explained a little later on how *Christ will deliver up the kingdom to the Father.* When he says, 'to God, even the Father', that can be taken in two ways; either that God the Father is called the God and Father of Christ; or that the name 'Father' is added by way of explanation. In the latter case the conjunction 'even' will mean 'namely'. As far as the former is concerned, there is nothing incongruous or unusual in saying that Christ is in subjection to God, as far as His human nature is concerned.

When he shall have abolished all rule. Some take this as referring to the powers which are in opposition to Christ Himself. For they take into account what follows in the next verse, 'till he hath put all his enemies under his feet'. But this clause reflects what he said at the beginning of the verse, that Christ will not deliver up the Kingdom before the end. Therefore there is no reason why we should limit this clause in the way these people suggest. Therefore I explain it in a general way, and understand by the word, the legitimate powers, which have been ordained by God.

In the first place, the prophets speak of the darkening of the sun and the moon (Isa. 13.10; Ezek. 32.7), so that God alone may be conspicuous. Now although that has begun to be fulfilled under the rule of Christ, it will not, however, be brought to absolute completeness until the last day. It will then be necessary for every exalted thing to come to an end, so that the glory of God may alone be resplendent. Further, we are aware that all earthly rules and positions of authority have to do only with the maintaining of life as we know it here, and are, for that reason, an integral part of this world, and, it follows from that, in turn, that they are temporary things.

Therefore, as the world will come to an end, so also will polity, magistracy, laws, distinctions in order, degrees of honour and everything of that sort. No longer will the servant be different from his master, the king from the ordinary man, and the magistrate from the private citizen. Furthermore, there will then be an end both to the rule which angels exercise in heaven, and to the offices of ministers and overseers in the Church, so that God alone may exercise His own power and dominion through Himself, not through the hands of men or angels. Of course there will still be angels, and they will also retain their superiority (*excellentia*). The righteous will also be resplendent, each one according to his measure of grace. But the angels will give up the rule, which they now exercise in the name, and by the commandment, of God. Bishops, teachers and prophets will sustain their roles no longer, and will lay down the office which they are now discharging. *Rule* and *authority* and *power* mean much the same thing in this verse; but these three words are in conjunction with each other in order to make the meaning plainer.

25. *For he must reign.* Paul shows that it is not yet the time for Christ to deliver up the Kingdom to the Father, in order to bring out at the same time that the end has not yet come, when everything will be

restored to its true condition and to a peaceful state, because Christ has not yet subdued all His enemies. But that must take place, because the Father has placed Him at His right hand on condition that He does not surrender the authority which He has received, until they have all been brought under His sway. This has also been said for the comfort of believers, so that they may not grow impatient because the coming of the resurrection is so long delayed.

This verse is taken from Psalm 110.1. But Paul seems to make more subtle play with the word 'until' than its simple and natural meaning requires. For in that verse the Spirit is announcing, not what will occur after the end, but only what had to happen beforehand. My answer to that is that Paul does not argue that Christ will hand back the Kingdom to the Father, because that is foretold in this Psalm, but he has made use of the evidence of the Psalm merely for the purpose of proving that the day for delivering up the Kingdom has not yet arrived, because Christ has still to deal with His enemies. Finally, Paul explains, in passing, what is meant by 'Christ sitting at the right hand of the Father', for, instead of that metaphorical expression, he uses the simple word reigning.

26. *The last enemy . . . death.* We are aware that there are still many enemies resisting Christ, and obstinately opposing His rule. But death will be the last enemy to be destroyed, and so Christ must still be the administrator of His Father's Kingdom. Believers should therefore take heart, and not lose hope, until all the things which ought to come before the resurrection are actually fulfilled.

But somebody is asking what exactly he means by saying that death will be destroyed last of all, when it has been destroyed already by the death of Christ, or at any rate by His resurrection, which is the victory over death, and the attainment of life? I reply that it has been destroyed in such a way as to be no longer fatal for believers, but not in such a way as to cause them no trouble. It is true that the Spirit of God, who dwells in us, is life; but all the same we still have a mortal body. The 'stuff' of death in us will one day be taken away, but that has not happened yet. We have been born again of incorruptible seed, but we have not yet reached maturity of growth (*perfectionem*). Or, to epitomize the matter in a simile, the sword of death used to be able to pierce right to the heart, but now it is blunt. It wounds still, of course, but without any danger; for we die, but, in dying, we pass over into life. Finally, as Paul teaches in Romans 6.12-14 about sin, we must look upon death in this light, that it undoubtedly dwells in us, but that it has no dominion over us.

27. *For He put all things in subjection under his feet.* People think that this piece of evidence is taken from Psalm 8.7, and I am quite in agree-

ment with that, although there would be nothing out of place in saying that this is a conclusion that Paul has reached by considering the nature of the rule of Christ. But let us take up the more widely accepted point of view.

Paul shows, from the Psalm, that God the Father has handed over to Christ power over everything, because it is said, 'Thou hast put all things under his feet.' The words themselves are plain enough, if two difficulties did not present themselves. The first is that the prophet is speaking there not of Christ only, but of the whole human race. The second is that by 'all things' he means only those things which serve the purpose of benefiting our physical existence, as we find in Genesis 2.19.

The first difficulty is easily solved, for, since Christ is the firstborn of all creation (Col. 1.15) and the heir of all things (Heb. 1.2), God the Father has not given the human race the use of all created things in such a way as to interfere with the chief power and, so to speak, the direct lordship remaining in the hands of Christ. We know, moreover, that Adam lost the right that had been bestowed upon him, so that we can no longer call anything 'ours', for the ground was cursed, and everything in it, and it is by Christ alone that we recover what we had been deprived of. There is therefore every justification for this statement that the Father has put all things under His feet being made to apply particularly to the person of Christ, seeing that we have no right to possess anything, except in Him. For how can we be heirs of God unless we are sons? And by whom are we made His sons but by Christ?

This is the solution to the second difficulty. The prophet indeed makes specific mention of the birds of the air, the fish of the sea, and beasts of the field, because this kind of lordship is there to be seen, and is perfectly obvious. But at the same time this general statement embraces much more than that, viz. heaven and earth, and all that they contain. Now, the thing subjected ought to be suited to the person of the ruler; i.e. its condition must resemble and correspond to his. But Christ does not require animals for food, or other created things to meet any need of His at all. Therefore He rules so that all things may serve His glory. Because He chooses us to share in His dominion, we plainly see the results of this in the shape of created things; but believers are aware in their own hearts and consciences of something else that springs from it, something that has a far wider application, as I have already said.

All things . . . he is excepted who did subject all things unto him. Paul drives home two points: (1) that all things must be brought into subjection to Christ, before He hands back His sovereignty over the world to the Father; and (2) that the Father has handed everything over to the Son, but so as to keep the chief authority in His own hands.

It follows from the first that the hour of final judgement has not yet struck; and from the second that Christ is now the intermediary between us and the Father, so that He may bring us to Him in the end. And so Paul goes on at once to draw the conclusion that 'after all things have been subjected to Him, then the Son Himself will subject Himself to the Father' (v. 28). It is as if he said: 'Let us calmly wait until Christ is victorious over all His enemies and brings us, along with Himself, under the sovereignty of God, so that the Kingdom of God may be brought to complete fullness in us.'

But what various parts of the Scriptures assert about the eternity of the Kingdom of Christ seems to conflict with this sentence. For how will these statements harmonize with each other: 'Of his kingdom there will be no end '(II Pet. 1.11), and 'He will also be subjected' (Phil. 2.8)? By answering this problem we will see more clearly what Paul meant. In the first place we must observe that all power was handed over to Christ, in that He was manifested in the flesh. Such great majesty would not be appropriate for a mere man, but nevertheless the Father exalted Him in the self-same nature in which He was humbled, and gave unto Him the name before which every knee should bow etc. (Phil. 2.8). Further, we must note that He has been appointed Lord and supreme King so that He may be the Father's Viceregent, so to speak, in the governing of the world. It is not the case, however, that He does all the work, while the Father does nothing. (For how could that be, seeing that He is the wisdom and counsel of God, that He is of one essence with Him, and is therefore also God?) But the reason why Scripture bears witness to the fact that Christ now holds the sovereignty over heaven and earth in place of the Father, is that we may not think of anyone else as ruler, lord, defender, or judge of the living and the dead, but that we keep our eyes fixed on Him and Him alone. Of course we acknowledge that God is the Ruler, but His rule is actualized in the man Christ (*sed in facie hominis Christi*). But Christ will then hand back the Kingdom which He has received, so that we may cleave completely to God. This does not mean that He will abdicate from the Kingdom in this way, but will transfer it in some way or other (*quodammodo*) from His humanity to His glorious divinity, because then there will open up for us a way of approach, from which we are now kept back by our weakness. In this way, therefore, Christ will be subjected to the Father, because, when the veil has been removed, we will see God plainly, reigning in His majesty, and the humanity of Christ will no longer be in between us to hold us back from a nearer vision of God.

28. *That God may be all in all.* Does that mean the devil and the disobedient as well? Not at all!—unless we are perhaps disposed to

take the verb 'to be' as meaning 'to be known and to be seen openly.' In that case the meaning will be: 'Since the devil is now fighting against God, since the wicked upset the order instituted by Him, throwing it into chaos, since countless things that offend us are staring us in the face, it can hardly be said that it is obvious that God is all in all. But when Christ has carried out the judgement which the Father has entrusted to Him, and overthrown Satan and all the disobedient, then the glory of God will be seen in their destruction. The same thing can also be said about authorities, which are sacred and lawful in their own character, for in a sense they hold us back, so that God may not now appeal to us properly as He is in Himself. But then God will be governing heaven and earth by Himself, without any intermediary, and then in that way He will be all; and in consequence He will finally be in all, and not in all persons only, but in all created things as well.'

This is a faithful interpretation, and, because it agrees quite well with what the apostle had in mind, I am willing to accept it. But it will not be out of place if this phrase is taken as referring to believers only, in whom God has already begun His Kingdom, and will then bring it to completion, and in such a way that they will cleave to Him entirely.

Either of these interpretations is enough in itself to repel the impious and nonsensical views of certain people, who make wrong use of this verse to prove what they are maintaining. Some imagine that God will be all in all in the sense that everything will vanish, and dissolve into nothingness. But the only meaning that the words of Paul bear is that all things must be restored to God as their one and only beginning and end, so that they may be bound closely to Him. Others infer from this that the devil and all the disobedient will be saved, as if God would not in fact be all the better known in the destruction of the devil, than if He were to make a friend of him, and make him one with Himself. So we see how impudent madmen of that sort are, when they twist this saying of Paul's to support their own blasphemies.

Else what shall they do which are baptized for the dead? If the dead are not raised at all, why then are they baptized for them? Why do we also stand in jeopardy every hour? I protest by that glorying in you, brethren, which I have in Christ Jesus our Lord, I die daily. If after the manner of men I fought with beasts at Ephesus, what doth it profit me? If the dead are not raised, let us eat and drink, for to-morrow we die. Be not deceived: Evil company doth corrupt good manners. Awake up righteously, and sin not; for some have no knowledge of God: I speak this to move you to shame. (29–34)

29. *Else what shall they do?* Paul reverts once again to the absurd consequences of the error under which the Corinthians were labouring.

He had started to deal with these right at the beginning, but he inserted teaching and consolation, and so broke the thread of the argument for a little; so he takes it up again now.

In the first place, he protests that the baptism, which is received by people who are regarded as dead already, will be useless, if in fact there is no resurrection.

Before I explain this verse, it is worth while refuting the usual exposition, which is supported by the authority of the Fathers, and to which nearly everybody assents. Thus Chrysostom and Ambrose, followed by others, think that when anyone had been deprived of baptism by sudden death, the Corinthians were in the habit of substituting a living person for the dead one, to be baptized at his grave. Indeed they do not deny that this custom was a perversion, and full of superstition. But they also say that, in order to refute the Corinthians, Paul relied on this one argument, that while they were denying the resurrection, they were yet making it quite plain that they did believe in it. But, as far as I am concerned, nothing induces me to give credence to this, for it is hard to believe that people who were denying the resurrection were at one and the same time making use of a rite like this, along with others. But this retort would, therefore, have been made to Paul at once: 'Why do you put pressure on us with this old wives' superstition, when in fact you do not approve of it yourself?' Again, if they had practised this, they had a ready answer: 'If we have been in error in doing this up to now, it would be better for the error to be corrected than that it should be made use of for proving something of the greatest importance.'

But supposing their argument was sound, are we to think, however, that, if a practice as corrupt as this had prevailed among the Corinthians, the apostle would have said nothing about it, seeing that he took them to task for nearly every single one of their faults? He condemned, in previous chapters, certain practices, which were not as serious as this. He had no hesitation about issuing directions about women covering their heads and other similar matters. He did not merely disapprove of their faulty administration of the Supper, but was very penetrating in his criticism. At the same time would he say not a word about such a horrible profanation of baptism, when it was a far more serious matter than the other one was? He has been very vehement in his attack on those who were giving their tacit approval to the superstitious beliefs and practices of the heathen by frequenting their feasts. Would he have allowed this abominable heathen superstition to be carried on openly in the very Church under the name of Holy Baptism? But even allowing that he could have kept quiet about it, what are we to say when he actually makes specific mention of it? I ask you, is it likely that the apostle would adduce, as an argument, a sacrilege by which baptism was corrupted and turned into a completely magical abuse, and have not even a single syllable to say in condemnation of its offensiveness? When dealing with things which are not of primary importance, he nevertheless interjects the parenthesis, that he is speaking as a man. Would this not have been a more appropriate and suitable place for such a parenthesis? Would anyone not take the fact, that he mentions it now without a single word of censure, to mean that it is a legitimate practice? I certainly understand Paul to be speaking here about the regular use of baptism, and not a corruption of it like that.

Now let us find out what the meaning is. I used to think that Paul was pointing out the all-embracing end of baptism here, for the benefit of baptism is not confined to our life here. But afterwards, when I gave more careful consideration to the words, I saw that Paul is dealing with one particular aspect here. For he is not speaking about everybody, when he says what will they do who are baptized etc. Moreover I do not like interpretations which are clever rather than sound. What does it mean then? I maintain that the people who are baptized for the dead are those who are thought of as dead already, and who have given up hope of life altogether. And so the preposition ὑπέρ will have the meaning of the Latin *pro* (as), for example in the expression *habere pro derelicto*, to regard as abandoned. That meaning is not forced.

Or there is another way of looking at it, which you may prefer: to be baptized for the dead will mean to be baptized so as to get the benefit when dead, and not when alive. For it is well known that in the early days of the Church, when people who were still unbaptized beginners in the faith (*catechumeni*) had fallen ill, and if they were clearly in imminent danger of death, they were in the habit of asking for baptism, so that they might not depart from this world before they had professed Christ, and also that they might carry the seal of their salvation with them.

It appears from the writings of the Fathers that superstition afterwards infiltrated into this practice also, for they inveigh against those who were postponing their baptism until death, so that, once they had been purified of all their sins, they might come to the judgement of God. This is indeed a stupid error, which sprang partly from great ignorance, and partly from hypocrisy. But here Paul is merely touching on a custom that was sacred and in accordance with our Lord's institution, viz. that if a catechumen who had already accepted the Christian faith in his heart saw that death was drawing near, he asked for baptism, partly for his own comfort, and partly for the strengthening (*aedificationem*) of his brethren. For it is no little comfort to bear the proof of this salvation sealed on one's own body. There is also a strengthening, which should not be overlooked, in making confession of one's faith. So those people were baptized for the dead, because it would have been no advantage to them in this world, and the fact that they despaired of life was the very reason why they were asking for baptism when they did.

We now see that it was not pointless for Paul to ask what they would do if there was nothing to hope for after death. This verse is also a proof that those impostors, who had been upsetting the faith of the Corinthians, had concocted a symbolical resurrection, making the ultimate goal for believers to lie in this world. He gives greater emphasis to his question by repeating it in this form, 'why then are they baptized for the dead?' It is as though he said: 'It is not only the people who think that they have their lives before them who are baptized, but also those whom death is staring in the face; and the latter are baptized so that they may reap the benefit of their baptism after they have died.'

30. *Why do we also stand in jeopardy?* If resurrection and final happiness are in this world, why then do we, of our own free will, abandon it, and gladly submit to death? His reasoning could also be explained in this way: it would be futile for us to be in peril every hour if a better life were not waiting for us after we have encountered death. But he is speaking about the risks to their lives, which believers run of their own free will, because they confess Christ. This nobleness of mind, in despising death, I maintain, would be set down to foolhardiness rather than self-possession if the saints perished when they died, for it is madness, born of the devil, to purchase undying fame by dying.

31. *I die daily.* Paul says that he himself has such a contempt for death, so that he might not give the impression of being courageous when he is in no personal danger. He says: 'Every single day I am under the constant threat of death in many forms. What a fool I would be to bring so much unhappiness on myself, if there was no reward stored up in heaven for me! Yes, and more than that, if my glory and blessedness lie in this world, why do I not enjoy it rather than give it up of my own accord?' He says that he dies daily because he was constantly assailed by dangers that were so great and so pressing, that death was, in a sense, staring him in the face. It is the same sort of thing as is spoken about in Psalm 44.23, and we shall come across in the next letter.

By our glory. The Vulgate has 'on account of', but that is obviously due to the ignorance of the copyists, for there is no ambiguity about the Greek particle. Therefore it is an oath, by which he intended to stir up the Corinthians, to pay more attention to what he has to say in connexion with this particular point. He might have expressed himself like this: 'My brothers, I am no philosopher pouring out a torrent of words in the study. Since I expose myself to death every day it is imperative for me to think in earnest about the life of heaven. Believe, therefore, a man who is thoroughly experienced!'

And he uses an unusual form of oath, but one that is suitable for the subject he is dealing with. That well-known oath of Demosthenes, which Fabius quotes, is like it; when he swore by the shades of the men who had met their death in the battle of Marathon, but his real intention was that other people would be incited to defend the Republic. So Paul swears here 'by the glory which Christians have in Christ', but that glory is in heaven. He is showing, therefore, that what they were calling in question is in fact something he is so sure of that it has the force of a sacred oath. The skilful way he handles this deserves particular attention.

32. *If after the manner of men.* Paul mentions a notorious form of death; and it may be clear from its very nature that he would have been worse than a fool in facing it, if a better life was not awaiting us after death; for he exposed himself to a kind of death that was looked upon as a disgrace. He is saying: 'What use was there in gaining a bad name for myself, and in undergoing the cruellest of deaths at the same time, if all my hopes were confined to this world?'

After the manner of men means, in this verse, within the limits of this mortal life, so that we get our reward in this world.

Those who were *fighting with wild beasts* are not those who were thrown to the wild beasts, as Erasmus has supposed in error, but those who were condemned to provide a spectacle for the people by being set to fight with wild beasts. There were, therefore, two quite distinct kinds of punishment, to be thrown to the wild beasts, and to fight with them. For those who were thrown to those animals were instantly torn to pieces; while those who were fighting with them used to advance armed into the arena, so that if they had the advantage of strength and courage and nimbleness they could escape by killing the beasts. Furthermore, there was a school for training those who fought with the beasts, just as there was for the gladiators. Very few of them used to escape, however, because a man who despatched one animal was forced to fight with a second, until the cruelty of the spectators had been glutted, or, one should rather say, until it was changed to mercy. And yet there were men to be found, who were so hopeless and desperate that they offered themselves for this purpose. And, let me say in passing, that this is the 'hunting spectacle' which is punished so severely by the ancient canons, as well as being branded as infamous by the civil laws.

I return to what Paul has to say. We see the pass to which God allowed His servant to come, and how marvellously He also rescued him. But Luke makes no mention of this contest; and from that we may infer that Paul went through many things, which have not been committed to writing.

Let us eat and drink. This is the cry of the Epicureans, who take the view that man's greatest good consists in having pleasure here and now. Isaiah also asserts (22.13) that this is said by dissolute men, when the prophets of God threaten them with ruin, in order to summon them to repentance. For, scoffing at these threats, they give themselves up to self-indulgence and unrestricted pleasure; and in order to demonstrate their high-handed independence they say: 'Since we have to die, let us enjoy the time we now have, and do not let us torture ourselves with shadowy fears before the hour strikes.' On the other hand, look at what a certain commander said to his army: 'Comrades in arms, let us break our fast with a glad heart, for this day we shall dine in the underworld.' Now that was an exhortation to meet death undaunted, and has nothing to do with the theme of this verse. I think that Paul borrowed a catch-phrase which was in common use among dissolute and shameless good-for-nothings; or (to be brief) a common maxim of the Epicureans, which amounted to this: 'If death means man's annihilation, he can do no better than indulge in pleasure, without bothering his head about anything as long as he draws breath.' Such sentiments often recur in Horace.

33. *Be not deceived, bad conversations corrupt good manners.* Because there is nothing easier than to fall into the method of making irreverent speculations, while pretending to be making inquiries, Paul meets this danger by warning that the imparting of wrong information is more effective than we may realize in contaminating our minds and corrupting us morally. To do so he makes use of a saying of the poet Menander; for we are at liberty to borrow from any source anything that has come from God. And as all truth emanates from God, there is no doubt that the Lord has even put into the mouth of unbelievers whatever contains genuine and sound teaching; but I prefer that we look to Basil's *Oration to Young Men* for the treatment of this theme. Therefore since Paul knew that this saying was familiar to the Greeks he chose to make use of it, rather than express the same idea in his own words, so that they might listen to him more readily. For it was easier for them to receive something to which they were accustomed; and we ourselves can assent to that from our own experience with well-worn sayings.

But this is a sentence that particularly deserves our attention, because, when Satan cannot make a direct attack upon us, he deceives us by pretending that there is nothing wrong in our starting all sorts of speculations for the sake of finding out what the truth is. Therefore, speaking from the opposite standpoint, Paul protests against that strongly, saying that we must be on our guard against the imparting of wrong information, as we would against poison that can kill at once; for it steals its way secretly into our minds, and soon afterwards corrupts the whole of our being. Let us therefore note that there is nothing more harmful than bad teaching and ungodly speculations, which make us deviate, even in the slightest degree, from an orthodox and pure faith. For it is not without good cause that Paul exhorts us not to be deceived.

34. *Awake up righteously.* Since he realized that the Corinthians had, so to speak, fallen into a drunken sleep through an unduly false sense of security, Paul shakes them out of their torpor. But by adding the word 'righteously' he makes it clear what kind of state he wants them to be in when they do wake up. For they were alert and clear-headed enough as far as their own affairs were concerned; and, further, there is no doubt that they prided themselves in their keenness; but yet they were sluggards in connexion with something which, more than anything else, demanded that they should be wide awake. That is why he says awake righteously; in other words, 'Turn all your thoughts, and give your devotion, to things that are good and holy.'

He also gives a reason for doing so, saying, 'Some of you have no knowledge of God.' It was necessary for this to be said, for otherwise they would have looked upon his warning as uncalled for, since they were exceedingly wise in their own eyes. But he accuses them of ignorance of God, so that they might know they were lacking in what was the most important thing of all. This is valuable as a warning against those who are adepts at flying through the air, but, at the same time, are blind to what lies before their feet; and who are stupidly dull when they ought to be as keen-witted as possible.

To shame, i.e. in the way fathers make their children feel ashamed by rebuking them for their wrongdoings, in order that by shame they may cover their shame. On the other hand, when he said, earlier, that he had no intention of bringing shame upon them, he meant that he did not wish to let them be disgraced by his making a public exposure of their offences in a hostile and disagreeable way. But at this point it was in their own interest that they should be reproached in severer terms, since they were still taking a delight in such great evils. Indeed when Paul charges them with ignorance of God, he leaves them with no honour to their name.

But some one will say, How are the dead raised? and with what manner of body do they come? Thou foolish one, that which thou thyself sowest is not quickened, except it die: and that which thou sowest, thou sowest not the body that shall be, but a bare grain, it may chance of wheat, or of some other kind; but God giveth it a body even as it pleased him, and to each seed a body of its own. All flesh is not the same flesh: but there is one flesh of men, and another flesh of beasts, and another flesh of birds, and another of fishes. There are also celestial bodies, and bodies terrestrial: but the glory of the celestial is one, and the glory of the terrestrial is another. There is one glory of the sun, and another glory of the moon, and another glory of the stars; for one star differeth from another star in glory. So also is the resurrection of the dead. It is sown in corruption; it is raised in incorruption: it is sown in dishonour; it is raised in glory: it is sown in weakness; it is raised in power: it is sown a natural body; it is raised a spiritual body. If there is a natural body, thare is also a spiritual body. So also it is written, The first man Adam became a living soul. The last Adam became a life-giving spirit. Howbeit that is not first which is spiritual, but that which is natural; then that which is spiritual. The first man is of the earth, earthy: the second man is of heaven. As is the earthy, such are they also that are earthy: and as is the heavenly, such are they also that are heavenly. And as we have borne the image of the earthy, we shall also bear the image of the heavenly. Now this I say, brethren, that flesh and blood cannot inherit the kingdom of God; neither doth corruption inherit incorruption. (35–50)

35. *How will the dead be raised?* Nothing is more repugnant to human reason than this tenet of the faith. For nobody else, except God, can convince us that after our bodies, which are already subject to corruption, have rotted away, or been consumed by fire, or been torn to pieces by wild animals, they will be restored in their wholeness, but in a far better nature. Does not our whole cast of mind reject it as incredible, even as absurd in the extreme? In order to do away with this appearance of absurdity Paul makes use of *anthypophora,* that is to say, as though from the lips of an opponent, he makes an objection which seems, at first sight, to conflict with the teaching about the resurrection. For this particular question is not that of someone who is asking because he is in doubt about the way it happens; but of someone who declares that he cannot believe what is said about the resurrection, because it is something that cannot possibly happen. That is why, in his reply, Paul rebuts that sort of objection rather roughly. Let us therefore take note that those who are represented as speaking here are people who want to mock at belief in the resurrection, and use insulting gestures, on the ground of its impossibility.

36. *Thou foolish one, that which thou thyself sowest.* The apostle could have retorted that, although the way it happens is something beyond

our comprehension, it is nonetheless easy to God. Accordingly this is not something that must be decided upon on the basis of what we ourselves understand, but the honour for doing this must be ascribed to the wonderful, secret power of God, so that we may believe that it will achieve what we cannot grasp.

But Paul adopts another method. For he shows that, far from it being the case that the resurrection is contrary to nature (*naturae adversitur*), we can find a clear example of it every day of our lives in a process of nature itself, in the way the fruits grow. For where do the fruits that we gather from the earth have their origin, but in rottenness? For, once the seed has been sown, nothing will spring up, unless the grains die. Therefore in the fact that corruption is the origin and cause of reproduction, we have a kind of representation of the resurrection. It follows, therefore, that our appraisal of the power of God is far too spiteful and ungrateful, if we do not ascribe to Him, what is already plain before our eyes.

37. *Thou sowest not the body that shall be.* This comparison has two parts (1) that it is not to be wondered at that bodies rise again out of rottenness, in view of the fact that the same thing happens in the case of the sown seed; (2) that it is not contrary to reason that our bodies should be restored in another state, since from the bare grain God brings forth so many ears, perfect products of a skill that calls for wonder, and bursting with grains of a superior quality.

But, because, by speaking in this way, he might appear to be suggesting that many bodies will therefore spring up from one body, he qualifies what he has said by something else, viz. that God forms the kind of body that He wants, meaning that in that also there is a difference in quality. He adds, to each seed a body of its own, and that phrase qualifies what he had said about the other body; for he says that it is not so different, that it does not retain its own appearance (*speciem*).

39. *All flesh is not the same flesh.* This is another comparison, but one that serves the same purpose; even although others may give a different explanation of it. For, in saying that the term flesh covers the body of both man and beast, and that each has yet a different kind of flesh, Paul means that there is really one substance (*unam substantiam*) but a difference in quality (*in qualitatem*). What it amounts to is this, that whatever diversity we perceive in any particular kind (*in quoqua specie*) is a sort of foreshadowing of the resurrection, because God makes it quite plain that it is not difficult for him to renew our bodies by changing their present state.

41. *There is one glory of the sun, and another glory of the moon.* Not only is there a difference between heavenly and earthly bodies, but even the heavenly bodies are not equal in glory; for the sun outshines the moon,

and the other stars differ from each other. Accordingly this dissimilarity appears in the resurrection of the dead. But an error is usually made in the application of this, for people think that Paul meant to say that after the resurrection there will be different degrees of honour and glory for the saints. That is, of course, perfectly true, and other passages of Scripture bear witness to it; but it has nothing to do with what Paul has in mind here. For he is not discussing how the saints will differ from each other in their condition after the resurrection, but how the bodies, which we now have, differ from those which we shall receive at the last.

He is therefore removing any suggestion of absurdity by the use of this simile: the sun and moon are of one substance, but they differ greatly from each other in honour and splendour. Therefore is there any cause for wonder if our body puts on a more splendid quality? And it is as though he said: 'I teach that nothing will take place in the resurrection that has not been presented to the eyes of everyone already.' It is plain from the context that that is the meaning of the words. For what would cause Paul, and what purpose would it serve, to make this sudden jump, if indeed he was now comparing the saints with each other in their different states, when up to this point he has been comparing the present state of all with their future one, and when he carries on with that comparison in the verses which follow?

43. *It is sown in corruption.* In case any doubt remains Paul makes himself clear, by setting out the difference between our present state and that which will follow the resurrection. What sort of consistency would his treatise have, if earlier he had intended to make a distinction between the degrees of glory that the saints will have? Therefore there is no doubt that up to this point he has been pursuing a single theme.

He now reverts to the first simile which he had used, but makes it fit his purpose more closely. Or, if you prefer it, retaining that simile, he compares the time of this present life metaphorically to seed-time, and that of the resurrection to the harvest; and he says that now our body is indeed subject to death and dishonour, but then it will be glorious and incorruptible. He says the same thing in different words to the Philippians (3.21): 'Christ will fashion anew the body of our humiliation, that He may make it like the body of His glory.'

44. *It is sown a natural body.* Because he could not enumerate every single aspect, he embraces them all in one word, saying that the body is now *natural* (*animale*) and then it will be *spiritual* (*spirituale*). Further the name *natural* (*animale*) is given to that which is determined (*informatur*) by the soul (*anima*); the name *spiritual* (*spirituale*) to that which is determined by the Spirit. For it is the soul which gives life to the body, and prevents it from becoming a corpse; and so it is only right

that it should be described in terms of the soul (*anima*). But after the resurrection that life-giving power which it receives from the Spirit will be more predominant.

But let us always remember what we have seen already, that there is but one and the same substance of the body, and that it is only the quality which is referred to here. To make it quite clear, let the present quality of the body be called 'animation'; and its future quality, 'inspiration'. For as far as the soul's giving of life to the body now is concerned, that involves the intervention of many aids; for we need drink, food, clothing, sleep and other things like them. That proves to us beyond the shadow of a doubt how frail a thing 'animation' is. But the power of the Spirit for giving life will be much fuller, and for that reason independent of necessities of that sort. This is the straightforward, natural meaning of the apostle's words; and should prevent people getting lost any longer in airy speculations. That is what happens to those who think that the substance of the body will be spiritual; when the fact is that no mention is made of its substance, and it will undergo no change.

45. *As also it is written, The first man Adam became a living soul.* So that what he has said about the 'natural' body might not appear to be a new idea Paul quotes the scriptural passage which says that Adam became a living soul (Gen. 2.7), meaning that his body was now informed by a soul, so that he became a living man. Someone asks what the word 'soul' means here. It is well known that the Hebrew word, נֶפֶשׁ (*nephesh*) which Moses uses, has many shades of meaning; but in this verse it is taken to mean the life-principle (*pro motu vitali*), or the essence of life itself (*ipsa vita essentiale*); and the latter indeed appeals to me more. I notice that the same thing is said about the animals, that they became a living soul. But while the 'soul' of every living creature ought to be considered according to its own genus (*secundum genus suum*), there is nothing to prevent one kind of soul being common to all of them, viz. the life-principle (*motus vitalis*); and the soul of man yet having something peculiar and proper to it, namely, what is essentially immortal, for instance, the light of understanding, and reason.

The last Adam. This expression is not found written anywhere in Scripture. Therefore when he says, 'it is written', that must be understood as referring only to the first part of this verse; but after citing the scriptural evidence the apostle now begins to make his own independent contrast of Christ with Adam. It is as if he said: 'Moses states that Adam was given a living soul; but Christ, on the other hand, is endowed with a life-giving Spirit. And it is a far greater thing to be Life, or the source of life, than just to have life.'

But we must take note that Christ was also a living soul like ourselves, but over and above His soul, the Spirit of the Lord was poured out upon Him, that by the power of the Spirit He might rise from the dead, and raise up others. Attention must be paid to this, so that no-one might think that the Spirit took the place of the soul in Christ, as Apollinaris once imagined. And, apart from that, the meaning of this verse can be found in Romans chapter 8, where the apostle declares that 'the body is indeed dead because of sin', and we carry in ourselves what makes for death; but 'the Spirit of Christ, who *raised Him* up from the dead dwells' also in us; and that He is Life, to raise us up from the dead also at the last. You see from this that we have living souls since we are men, but that the life-giving Spirit of Christ is poured out upon us through the grace of regeneration. In short, Paul's meaning is that the condition which we acquire through Christ is far better than the situation of the first man, because a living soul was given to Adam for himself and for his posterity, but Christ, on the other hand, has brought us the Spirit who is Life.

Paul's reason for calling Christ *the last Adam* is that, as the human race had been brought into being in *the first man*, so it was restored in Christ. I shall repeat that in a simpler way. All men were brought into being in the first man, because God had bestowed on him whatever He was intending to give to all, so that the circumstances of the whole human race were determined by the person of that one man. By his fall he brought ruin on himself and those belonging to him, because he dragged them all with him into disaster at the same time. Christ came to restore our nature from its catastrophic downfall, and raise it up to a better state. Adam and Christ are therefore, as it were, the two origins, or roots, of the human race. That is why there is every justification for calling Adam the first man, and Christ the last.

But this provides no support for the fanatics who make a Christ out of each one of us, as if there were, and had always been, only two men; and as if, on the other hand, this multitude of people, which we see with our eyes, were a meaningless illusion.

There is a similar comparison in Romans 5.12.

46. *But that is not first which is spiritual.* Paul is saying: 'It is necessary that we take our origin from Adam and be like him, before we are renewed in Christ. That is why it should be no surprise to us that we begin with a living soul, for, in the order of things, being born precedes being born again, and similarly living comes before rising again.'

47. *The first man is of the earth, earthy.* The 'natural life' comes first, because the earthy man is first. The spiritual life will follow, as Christ, the Man from heaven, came after Adam.

Again, the Manichaeans misinterpret this verse, with their desire to prove that Christ brought a body from heaven into the womb of the Virgin. But they went wrong in thinking that Paul is speaking here about the substance of the body, when he was dealing rather with its characteristic or quality. Therefore, even if the first man had an immortal soul, and it was not derived from the earth at all, he yet smacked of the earth, from which his body had its origin, and on which he had been set to live. Christ, on the other hand, has brought us the life-giving Spirit from heaven, in order that He might regenerate us into a life that is better and higher than that on earth. In short, our life in this world we owe to Adam, as branches to the root; Christ, on the other hand, is the originator and source of the life of heaven.

But someone will make this inference: it is said that Adam is from the earth, Christ from heaven. The nature of the relationship between them requires that Christ should have a body from heaven, just as Adam's body was formed from the earth; or, at least, that the soul of the man should have sprung from the earth, while Christ's soul, on the other hand, should have come from heaven. To that I answer that Paul did not make his comparison of the two men as detailed and close as all that—for there was no need for that. But since he was discussing the nature of Christ and Adam, he made a passing reference to the creation of Adam, saying that he had been formed from the earth; and, at the same time, in order to let us see how valuable Christ is, he states that He is the Son of God, who has come down to us from heaven, and, for that reason, retains His heavenly nature and power. That is the straightforward meaning; on the other hand the subtlety of the Manichaeans is nothing else but a misrepresentation.

But a reply must be given to yet another objection. For as long as Christ was in the world, He lived a life in common with us, and, therefore, earthy; therefore this is not a proper contrast. The answer to this problem will help still further in refuting the fanciful notion of the Manichaeans. For we know that the body of Christ was subject to death, and that it was delivered from corruption, not by some inherent property of its own (*essentiali proprietate*), to use the accepted term, but by the providence of God and nothing else. Therefore not only, as regards the substance of His body, was He earthy, but for a time He also shared in our earthy condition. For before the power of Christ could show itself by conferring the life of heaven on us, it was necessary for Him to die in the weakness of the flesh. But it was in the resurrection that this heavenly life first appeared, that He might give life to us also.

49. *And as we have borne the image.* Some people have thought that Paul has digressed here to make a call for a godly and holy life; and because of that they have changed the verb from the future tense to the

hortatory subjunctive. Furthermore some Greek manuscripts read φορέσωμεν. But since that does not fit in so well let us rather keep to what is appropriate to the context and Paul's immediate purpose. To begin with, let us note that this is not an exhortation, but teaching, pure and simple; and that Paul is not dealing with newness of life here, but is continuing, without a break in the thread of his argument, his discussion of the resurrection of the body. This, therefore, will be the meaning: Since the 'animal nature', which we have first of all, is the image of Adam, so we will conform to Christ in His heavenly nature; and when that happens our restoration will be complete. For we now begin to bear the image of Christ, and we are daily being transformed into it more and more; but that image depends upon spiritual regeneration. But then, it will be restored to fullness, in our body as well as our soul; what has now begun will be brought to completion, and we will obtain in reality what as yet we are only hoping for.

Now, if someone still prefers the other reading, this verse would have had the effect of disturbing the Corinthians; and, if they had been really alive in their thinking about godliness and new life, it could have inflamed them with the hope of heavenly glory at the same time.

50. *Now this I say.* This phrase indicates that what follows is an explanation of the preceding statement. And it is as though Paul said: 'What I mean by saying that we shall bear the image of the heavenly Adam is this, that our bodies need to be renewed because they are subject to corruption, and cannot, as such, gain possession of God's incorruptible Kingdom. Therefore, the only way we can enter into the Kingdom of Christ is by Christ's renewing us according to His own image.'

Finally, we must understand *flesh and blood* to mean flesh and blood as they are at present constituted; for our flesh will share in the glory of God, but only after it has been renewed and restored to life by the Spirit of Christ.

Behold, I tell you a mystery: We shall not all sleep, but we shall all be changed, in a moment, in the twinkling of an eye, at the last trump: for the trumpet shall sound, and the dead shall be raised incorruptible, and we shall be changed. For this corruptible must put on incorruption, and this mortal must put on immortality. But when this corruptible shall have put on incorruption, and this mortal shall have put on immortality, then shall come to pass the saying that is written, Death is swallowed up in victory. O death, where is thy victory? O death, where is thy sting? The sting of death is sin; and the power of sin is the law: but thanks be to God, which giveth us the victory through our Lord Jesus Christ. Wherefore, my beloved brethren, be ye stedfast, unmoveable, always abounding in the work of the Lord, forasmuch as ye know that your labour is not vain in the Lord. (51-58)

Up to this point Paul's argument consisted of two parts. He has shown, first of all, that there will be a resurrection of the dead; and, secondly, what the nature of it will be. But he now goes on to give a fuller description of how it will take place, calling his description a *mystery*, because there was not the same clarity about this, as in the case of the other two aspects, in the absence, so far, of any revelation of God on the subject. He does this in order to make them give more attention to what he has to say. For that wicked doctrine had gained strength from the fact that they were discussing this subject in a careless and light-hearted way, as if it were something that afforded them not the slightest difficulty. Therefore, by using the word 'mystery', Paul is warning them that they are to become acquainted with something, not only about which they, as yet, know nothing, but also which must be regarded as part of God's heavenly secrets.

51. *We shal certainly not all sleep.* There is no variant in the Greek manuscripts, but there are three different readings in the Latin. The first is: 'We shall all die indeed, but we shall not all be changed.' The second is: 'We shall all rise again indeed, but we shall not all be changed.' The third is: 'We shall certainly not all sleep, but we shall all be changed.' My guess is that these differences arose from the fact that some readers, who were rather obtuse, and who found the true reading distasteful, took it upon themselves to substitute what they thought was a more likely one. For, on the face of it, it seemed inconsistent to them that 'we shall not all die', when Hebrews 9.27 states that 'it is appointed unto men once to die'. They therefore altered it to mean 'all are not to be changed', although 'all will rise again', or 'all will die', and by being changed they mean the glory which only the sons of God will obtain. But we can decide from the context what the true reading is.

Paul's purpose is to explain what he had said, viz. that we will be made like Christ, because 'flesh and blood cannot inherit the kingdom of God'. But that gave rise to the question: what then will be the fate of those who will survive until the Day of the Lord? Paul answers that, although they do not die, they will all, nevertheless, be renewed, so that mortality and corruption will be done away with. But we must note that he is speaking about believers only; for, although there will be a resurrection, even a changing of unbelievers, yet, in view of the fact that they are passed over in silence here, we should make all that is said apply to the elect alone. We now see how well this sentence fits in with the preceding one, for, having said that we shall bear the image of Christ, he now makes it plain that that will happen, when we shall be changed, so that what is mortal will be swallowed up by life, and he also shows that it will make no difference to this change, that the coming of Christ will overtake some who are still alive at that time.

But we have still to find a solution to the problem that 'it is appointed unto all men to die'; and it is not such a difficult task indeed. Since the change cannot take place without the destruction of the nature that existed previously, such a change is quite rightly regarded as a kind of death; but since there is no separation of the soul from the body, it is not to be thought of as an ordinary death. It will be death, then, in that our corruptible nature will be destroyed; it will not be falling asleep, because the soul will not depart from the body; but there will be a sudden transition from our corruptible nature to blessed immortality.

52. *In a moment.* Paul is still speaking in general terms; in other words this covers everybody. For a change will take place in everybody, suddenly, instantaneously, because Christ's coming will be sudden. And to stress the quickness of it, he then employs the phrase, the winking or flicker of an eye, for there are two readings in the Greek, ῥοπῇ or ῥιπῇ (wink, or quiver). However, it makes no difference to the sense. Paul chose a particular movement of the body, that surpasses all the others in speed; for there is nothing swifter than the movement of the eye. At the same time, however, he is making an allusion to being asleep, as the contrast to the twinkling of the eye.

With the last trump. Although the repetition of the word 'trumpet' seems to make it quite definite that it is to be taken literally here, yet I prefer to regard it as a metaphor. In I Thessalonians 4.16 he links the 'voice of the archangel' with 'the trump of God'. As a commander summons his army to battle with the notes of a trumpet, so Christ will call the dead to Him, by His resounding proclamation, which will be heard distinctly all over the world. Moses tells us about the kind of sounds that echoed out when the law was promulgated, and how loud they were. What a very different situation it will be when not a single nation but the whole world is to be summoned to the tribunal of God! And it is not only the living who are to be called together, but the dead are also to be summoned from their graves. More than that, even, a command will have to be issued to dry bones and dust, so that, recovering their earlier form, and getting back their spirit, they may immediately appear as living men in the presence of Christ.

The dead will rise. Having spoken in general terms about all, Paul now explicitly shows how it applies to both the dead and the living. Therefore this division is nothing else but an explanation of the previous sentence, 'we shall not all die but we shall all be changed.' Paul

is saying: 'Those who are already dead, will rise again incorruptible.'
Take note of the change that the dead undergo! Then he says: 'Those
who will still be alive will also be changed.' There you are—both are
covered! And now you realize that everybody will undergo the same
change, but it is by no means the case that everybody will fall asleep.

But when he says *we shall be changed*, he counts himself among those
who will be alive at the coming of Christ. Since it was already the
last times, the saints were to expect that day every single hour. Although in his letter to the Thessalonians he makes that remarkable
prophecy about the scattering of the Church that would occur before
the coming of Christ, that does not prevent him from confronting the
Corinthians with the event here and now, as it were, and being able to
put himself and them alongside those who would be alive when the
day came.

53. *For this corruptible.* Take note that our body as well as our soul
will share in the life of the Kingdom of God; and yet it remains true
that flesh and blood cannot inherit the Kingdom of God, for they will
first be freed from corruption. Therefore our nature, corruptible and
mortal as it is, is not fitted for the Kingdom of God, but when it has
shed its corruption and been clothed with incorruption, then it will
enter into it. And this verse plainly confirms that we shall rise in the
very same flesh that we have now, for the apostle has assigned it a new
quality, as if it were a garment. If he had said, 'This corruptible ought
to be renewed,' he would not have so clearly and effectively disposed
of the error of those fanatics who invent the notion that men are to be
given new bodies. But when he says here that this corruptible is to be
clothed in glory, there is no more room left for argument.

54–55. *Then shall come to pass this saying.* This is not merely an
amplification (ἐπεξεργάσια), but a confirmation of the previous
sentence, for what the prophets have foretold is bound to be fulfilled.
But this prophecy will not be implemented until our bodies have laid
aside their corruption and put on incorruption, and so the latter is also
something that must necessarily take place.

Now, *come to pass* is taken here in the sense of being fully accom-
plished; for what Paul mentions, has already begun in us, and also
makes daily progress towards completion, but it will not have its
proper fulfilment until the last day.

Further, it is not really very clear what the source of this quotation
is, because there are many passages in this vein in the prophets. One
can only say that it is quite likely that the first phrase has been taken
from either of two sources. The first passage is Isaiah 25.8, where it is
said, 'The Lord hath swallowed up death for ever.' The other likely
passage (and this is the preference of a great many, indeed nearly

everybody) is Hosea 13.14, where the prophet, deploring the stubborn-ness and wickedness of Israel, complains that Israel was like a premature child, who is struggling against the efforts of his mother in labour, so as not to emerge from the womb. And from this the prophet concludes that Israel had no-one but herself to blame for the fact that she was not delivered from death.

He says:[1]

> 'I will redeem them from the power of the underworld;
> I will rescue them from death.'

But it does not matter very much whether you take those verbs in the future indicative or the subjunctive, because either way the meaning comes to this, that God was prepared to give them the blessing of His salvation, provided that they were willing to accept it; and that it was therefore their own fault if they perished.

He then adds:[2]

> 'I will be your ruin, O death;
> I will be your destruction, O underworld!'

By these words God means that He saves His faithful people only when death and the underworld are reduced to nothing. For everybody will agree that that verse gives us a description of a completed state of salvation. Therefore so long as we do not see death destroyed like that, it follows that we cannot yet enter upon that fullness of salvation which God promises to His people, and which is deferred until that day, for the same reason. Accordingly it is then that death will be swallowed up, that, in other words, it will be reduced to nothing; so that we may have a complete and thorough victory over it.

As far as the second part of the saying is concerned, in which Paul taunts death and the underworld, it is not certain whether he is using his own words, or whether he intended to quote the words of the prophet there also. For where we have rendered it,

> 'I will be your ruin, O death;
> I will be your destruction, O underworld!'

the Greek (i.e. LXX) translation is:

> 'Where is your indictment, O death?
> Where is your sting, O underworld?' (Hos. 13.14)

---

[1] So Calvin: *De potestate inferni redimam eos, a morte eruam eos.*
   Vulgate (Clem.):   *De manu mortis liberabo eos,*
                    de morte redimam eos.

[2] Calvin here: *Ero exitium, o mors,*
                     Excisio tua, o inferne.
   Vulgate (Clem.):   *Ero mors tua, o mors,*
                    morsus tuus ero, inferne! (Hos. 13.14)

But although the error of the Greek writers can be excused on account of the similarity of the words,[1] anyone studying the context carefully will see how far they have wandered from what the prophet had in his mind. The true meaning, therefore, is that the Lord will destroy death and put an end to the underworld. Yet, there is a possibility that as the Greek translation was in common use, Paul was alluding to it; and there is nothing wrong with that suggestion. However he did not even quote it word for word, for, instead of 'victory', it used a legal 'cause', or 'action'. I am quite clear in my own mind that he did not really intend to use the prophet's testimony here, so as to take advantage of his authority, but, in passing, simply adapted to his own purpose a saying which had passed into common currency, since, apart from that, it was of a religious nature. What is most important is that we should realize that, with this ringing cry of assurance, Paul intended to put heart into the Corinthians, as though confronting them with the reality of the resurrection there and then. But although we do not yet see the victory with these eyes of ours, and the day of triumph has not yet dawned, but, on the contrary, we have still to endure war and its dangers every day; that does not however shake the assurance of faith in the slightest, as we shall point out soon.

56. *The sting of death is sin*, that is to say, 'Death has no other weapon except sin, with which to wound us, since death comes from the wrath of God. But God is angry only with our sins; do away with sin then, and death will not be able to harm us any more.' This is in line with what he said in Romans 6.23, that 'the wages of sin is death'. But he uses another metaphor here, for he compares sin to a sting, as the only thing with which death is equipped for inflicting a fatal wound upon us. If that is taken away then death is disarmed, and can inflict no further injury. Now, Paul will soon explain why he says this.

The power of sin is the law. It is the *Law* of God that gives that sting its deadly power, because, of course, it not only lays bare our guilt, but also increases it. A clearer interpretation of this saying is to be found in Romans 7.9, where Paul shows us that we are alive, so long as we 'do not have the law', because there is nothing wrong with us in our own eyes, and we have no awareness of our wretched condition, until the Law summons us before the judgement of God, and makes our conscience smart with the sense of eternal death. Again, he teaches that sin has been, in a sense, lulled to sleep, but it is roused by the Law, only to grow more outrageous and high-handed. At the same time however he protects the Law from misrepresentation, by saying that it is holy and good and righteous, and that in itself it is neither the producer of sin, nor the cause of death. And so his conclusion is that

---

[1] *νίκη* victory, and *δίκη* a law-suit.

the blame for whatever evil there is must be laid at our own door, since it is obvious that it comes from the corruption of our nature. The Law therefore only provides the means by which harm is done; the real cause of the trouble lies in ourselves. The reason why he calls the Law, in this verse, the force or *power* of sin, is that it carries out the judgement of God upon us. At the same time he is not denying that sin inflicts death even on those who are ignorant of the Law, but says that in their case it is not so violent in the exercise of its domineering sway. For the Law came that sin might increase, or that it might become sinful beyond measure.

57. *But thanks be to God.* This makes it plain why he mentioned both sin and the Law when dealing with death. Death has no sting for hurting us except sin, and to this sting the Law adds its deadly power. But Christ has conquered sin, and by His conquest has obtained the victory for us, and redeemed us from the curse of the Law. It follows therefore that we are no longer lying under the power of death. Accordingly, even if all that those blessings involve has not yet been revealed to us, we may confidently glory in them; because what has been completed in the Head must of necessity be brought to completion in the members. We have every right then, to taunt death as a conquered power, because Christ's victory is our victory.

Therefore when Paul says that 'the victory has been given to us', we must understand, first of all, that in His own person Christ has destroyed sin, met the requirements of the Law, endured the curse, appeased the wrath of God, and procured life; and secondly, that He has begun to make us sharers in all those blessings already. For, although we are carrying about the remnants of sin, it does not reign in us; even if it still wounds us, yet its stabs are not fatal, because its point has been blunted, so that it might not penetrate to the vital parts of the soul. Although the Law is still threatening, yet, on the other hand, we have the benefit of the liberty which Christ has procured for us, and that counteracts the terrors of the Law. Even if the remnants of the flesh still dwell in us, yet the Spirit, who raised Christ from the dead, is life, because of righteousness.

58. *Wherefore, my brethren.* Having satisfied himself that he had explained the belief in the resurrection sufficiently, Paul now closes his discussion with an exhortation; and that is much more effective, than if he had drawn to a close in the ordinary way, confirming what he had said.

He says: 'Since your labour is not vain in the Lord, be steadfast, and abound in good works.' The reason why he says that their labour is not vain is that God has a reward in store for them. That is the one and only hope that encourages believers at the start, and sustains them later on, so that they do not fall out of the race. So he charges them to remain steadfast, because they are resting on an unshakeable foundation, when they know that a better life is ready, waiting for them, in heaven.

He adds *abounding in the work of the Lord*, for the resurrection hope has the effect of making us not grow tired of doing good, as Paul teaches in Colossians 1.10. For, in face of the obstacles which we are constantly meeting, who would not lose heart, or be forced off the road, were it not that, by thinking of a better life, he is kept, in that way, in the fear of God? But, on the other hand, he is pointing out that if the resurrection hope is taken away, the whole structure of religion would collapse in ruins, as if the foundation had been torn out. There is no doubt that if the hope of reward is removed and destroyed, the eagerness to continue running will not merely flag, but will fade away altogether.

CHAPTER SIXTEEN

Now concerning the collection for the saints, as I gave order to the churches of Galatia, so also do ye. Upon the first day of the week let each one of you lay by him in store, as he may prosper, that no collections be made when I come. And when I arrive, whomsoever ye shall approve by letters, them will I send to carry your bounty unto Jerusalem: and if it be meet for me to go also, they shall go with me. But I will come unto you, when I shall have passed through Macedonia; for I do pass through Macedonia; but with you it may be that I shall abide, or even winter, that ye may set me forward on my journey whithersoever I go. For I do not wish to see you now by the way; for I hope to tarry a while with you, if the Lord permit. (1-7)

1. *But concerning the collection.* Luke tells us in Acts 11.28 that the prophecy of Agabus, to the effect that there would be a famine in the reign of the Emperor Claudius, provided the saints with the opportunity of collecting alms for the assistance of the brethren at Jerusalem. For, although the prophet had declared that almost the whole world would share in this disaster, yet, because the people in Jerusalem were oppressed by greater poverty, and because all the Gentile churches, if they wanted to avoid the charge of being extremely ungrateful, were under an obligation to help the place from which they had received the Gospel, the result was that people were forgetting about themselves, and were making up their minds to give assistance to Jerusalem. That they were hard pressed by dire need at Jerusalem is evident from the letter to the Galatians 2.10, where Paul states that the apostles had entrusted him with the task of encouraging the Gentiles to provide assistance. But the apostles would never have given him such a commission if necessity had not driven them to it. Further, this verse bears out the truth of what Paul also asserts in that other passage, that he had taken pains to encourage the Gentiles to give relief for necessity of that sort. But he now gives instructions about the way they were to give help. In order that the Corinthians may fall in with it all the more readily, he mentions that he had already prescribed it to the churches of Galatia; for an example ought to have had a greater effect in influencing them, seeing that we are naturally inclined to have nothing to do with something which has not been tried out very often as yet. Now follows the method, by which he meant to get rid of all delays and hindrances.

2. *On one of the sabbaths.* What Paul is aiming at is that they should

have their alms ready in time. He therefore tells them not to await his arrival, because anything done without warning and in a hurry is not done well; but to contribute what they thought proper, each one according to his ability, on the sabbath, in other words, on the day in which they met together for worship.

Chrysostom explains the phrase κατὰ μίαν σαββάτων, as 'on the first sabbath.' I do not agree with him; for Paul's meaning is rather that one person should contribute on one sabbath, another on another sabbath; or even every one of them on every sabbath, if they so wished. For he is thinking, in the first place, in terms of convenience; and secondly that the gathering for worship, where believers rejoice in the communion of saints, could be an additional incentive to them.

No more do I accept the same Chrysostom's opinion that sabbath has been substituted here for the *Lord's Day*; for it is very likely that at the beginning the apostles retained the day with which they were already familiar, but that afterwards the scrupulous observances of the Jews forced them to have done with it, and substitute another. Now the Lord's Day was chosen in preference to all the others, because the resurrection of our Lord put an end to the shadows of the Law. Therefore that day is a reminder to us of our Christian freedom.

Finally, it is easy for us to infer from this verse that the faithful always had a particular day for resting from their work, not because inactivity is a way of serving God, but because it is of importance for preserving common concord, that a particular day should be appointed for meeting together for worship, since it cannot be done every day. For, while Paul, in another passage, forbids that any distinction be made between one day and another, we should understand him to do so in the interests of religion, and not for the sake of polity and external order.

Treasuring up. I preferred to retain the Greek participle (*thesaurizans*) because it seemed to me to express the idea much more emphatically. For although θησαυρίζειν means 'to hoard', in my opinion, however, Paul intended to point out to the Corinthians that whatever they might contribute to the saints would be the best and securest treasure they could have. For if it was possible for a heathen poet to say: 'The riches you have given away are the only ones you will have for ever', should that principle not have even greater influence among us, for we do not depend upon the gratitude of men, but we have God, who substitutes Himself for the poor man as the debtor, so that He may one day restore to us, with full interest, whatever we give away? That is why this word of Paul's echoes the saying of Christ: 'Provide for yourselves treasure in heaven, so that it may not be exposed either to thieves or moths' (Matt. 6.19).

As he may prosper. Instead of this the Vulgate has 'according to his own discretion', the translator no doubt having been misled by the similarity of the word.[1] Erasmus, on the other hand, has 'what will have been convenient'. Neither of these has satisfied me, because the proper meaning of the word is much more apposite, viz. 'to get on and prosper'. Paul therefore makes a fresh appeal to everyone to consider what he can afford. He might have said: 'Let each of you give to the poor from his income in proportion as God has blessed him.'

3. *And when I arrive.* Because we are readier to give when we have definite knowledge that our gifts will be well looked after, Paul shows the Corinthians how they can be certain that their gifts will be in good and trustworthy hands, viz. by their choosing men whose worth has already been proved, and entrusting them with their business. More than that, even, he offers his own services, should they desire them; and that goes to show that this is something that Paul has at heart.

5. *For I am going to pass through Macedonia.* The generally accepted view is that this letter was sent from Philippi. If you wanted to make the journey from there to Corinth by the land route it was necessary to go through Macedonia; for the colony of Philippi was situated in the remotest corner facing the Macedonian mountains. Paul could, of course, have gone there by sea instead of travelling overland, but he wanted to go and see the churches of Macedonia, and encourage them by visiting them *en route*. That is the usual way of looking at it.

But to me it seems more likely that the letter was written from Ephesus, for a little afterwards he says that 'he will stay there until Pentecost.' Also, he greets the Corinthians, not on behalf of the Philippians but of the churches of Asia. Moreover he states quite plainly in the second letter that, after he had sent this letter, he crossed over to Macedonia. And, after going through Macedonia, he would have been well clear of Ephesus, but, on the other hand, next door to Achaia. Therefore I have no doubt that he was at that time in Ephesus. From there one could make a direct sea-crossing to Achaia; while anyone visiting Macedonia had to take a long, roundabout, and more difficult route. Paul is therefore letting them know that he will not come to them by the direct route, because he has 'to go through Macedonia'.

But, in addition, he promises the Corinthians that he will spend quite a long time with them; and in that way he shows the love (*amorem*) he has for them. For what other reason would cause him to make an extended visit except that he was concerned about their welfare? On the other hand he is showing how he is convinced beyond

[1] Reading εὐδοκεῖ (it seems good) for εὐοδῶται (he prospers).

the shadow of a doubt of the affection (*caritate*) that they, on their part, have for him, when he takes it altogether for granted that they will do him the kindness of escorting him further on his way; for he says that because he is confident of their friendship.

But after saying all that he qualifies it with, *if the Lord permit*. Believers ought to add this proviso to all their plans and intentions. For it is very rash to undertake, and make definite arrangements for, many future events, seeing that we do not have even a single moment under our own control. But although the most important thing is to submit all our intentions to God in our own hearts; yet, at the same time, it is right that we should become accustomed to using expressions like this, so that whenever we are dealing with future events, we may make everything depend upon the will of God.

> *But I will tarry at Ephesus until Pentecost, for a great door and effectual is opened unto me, and there are many adversaries. Now if Timothy come, see that he be with you without fear; for he worketh the work of the Lord, as I also do: let no man therefore despise him. But set him forward on his journey in peace, that he may come unto me: for I expect him with the brethren. But as touching Apollos the brother, I besought him much to come unto you with the brethren: and it was not at all his will to come now; but he will come when he shall have opportunity.*
> (8–12)

8. *I will tarry.* I have used this verse in support of my argument that this letter was sent from Ephesus rather than Philippi. For it is likely that the apostle is referring to a place in which he was living at the time of writing, rather than to one which he would have to reach by a very roundabout way. In addition, to pass through Macedonia, it would have been necessary to turn away from Corinth, when coming close to it, and take ship across the sea, in order to reach Ephesus. Paul is therefore telling them in advance that he will remain at Ephesus until Pentecost; and another reason for doing so was to make them wait for him all the more patiently.

Erasmus preferred 'until the fiftieth day'. In adopting this reading he was influenced by worthless guesses rather than any solid reasoning. He protests that the day of Pentecost, as now observed, had not yet been established as a Christian festival. I agree with him as far as that is concerned. He denies that this should be understood as referring to the Jewish festival, because, more than once, Paul condemns and renounces scrupulous observance of days. But I concede to him, not that Paul kept that day at Ephesus because he was bound by scrupulous regard for it; but rather that he did so because there would be a greater gathering of people then, and so he hoped that he would be presented with an opportunity of spreading the Gospel. Similarly when he was eager to get to Jerusalem, the reason he gave for his haste was that he might reach there by Pentecost. But while others went there to offer sacrifices according to the rites of the Law, he went with a different purpose in mind, thinking that the greater the numbers present, the greater effectiveness his ministry would have. But it would really be quite pointless to suggest that Paul is meaning an exact period of fifty days here. And since he clearly says τὴν Πεντηκοστήν (the Pentecost), this can only be taken to mean a specific day. If you wish to know about this festival see Leviticus 23.16.

9. *For a great door . . . is opened.* Paul gives two reasons for staying longer at Ephesus; (1) because he is being given an opportunity of spreading the Gospel there; and (2) because his presence is particularly necessary due to the presence of a great number of adversaries. It is, therefore, as if he said: 'By prolonging my stay here a little longer I shall do a lot of valuable work, whereas, if I were not on the spot, Satan would do a very great deal of damage.'

In the first part of this verse he uses a fairly common metaphor, by taking the word 'door' to mean an opportunity, for the Lord was opening up an 'entrance' for him to spread the Gospel. He calls this door 'great', because he was able to win many people. He calls it 'effectual' because the Lord was blessing his labour, and making his teaching efficacious by the power of His Spirit. We see, therefore, that this holy man sought the glory of Christ everywhere, and did not choose a place that would suit his own convenience or pleasure; but his only concern was where could he be of the greatest use, and where could he serve the Lord and have more to show for his labours.

He adds to this that he did not run away from troubles by any means, but voluntarily placed himself where he saw that the battle would have to be fought more sharply, and would be heavier. For he was remaining because he was threatened by many adversaries, and since he was so well equipped to withstand their attack, he was bound to be all the more prepared and willing to do so.

10. *Now if Timothy come.* Paul speaks as if he is not yet certain that Timothy will come. But he commends Timothy to them, so that he might come to no harm among them, not because they would endanger his life, but because he would encounter the opposition of many enemies of Christ. He therefore wants them to take great care that no harm befall him.

He gives the reason: 'for he worketh the work of the Lord.' We gather from this that the Church of Christ ought to be concerned about preserving the lives of her ministers; and it is no doubt right that the richer anyone is in the higher gifts, that make for the upbuilding of the faithful, and the more strenuously he devotes himself to it, the more precious is his life to us.

The phrase, 'as I also do', has been added, either to bring out his worthiness; or simply to point out that they were both carrying out the same sort of task, labouring in the Word.

11. *Let no man therefore despise him.* Here he gives them a further charge about Timothy: not to despise him; perhaps because he was still a young man, and young men are not usually respected so highly. Paul therefore wanted them to watch out that nothing might stand in the way of a faithful minister of Christ being given the honour he deserves. Of course it may have been that Paul considered that, if they were not concerned about his life as they ought to have been, that in itself was a sign of their contempt for him. This piece of advice seems to go further than that however, and to mean also that they were not to think little of Timothy because it so happened that they knew nothing of his worth.

In the third place he instructs them to conduct him on his way in peace, that is, safe from all harm. For 'peace' means safety here.

12. *As far as Apollos our brother is concerned.* Apollos had succeeded Paul in the task of building up the Corinthians, and so Paul spoke of him earlier, as the one carrying out the task of watering. He now apologizes for Apollos not coming with the others, and he does so in order that the Corinthians might not suspect that he had kept him back. For, since Apollos was so well known to them, they were all the more attached to him; and it was easy for them to suppose that, because Paul was offended with them, it had all been purposely arranged that Apollos should not come to them. They could certainly have been asking each other the question: 'Why has he sent them to us rather than Apollos?' Paul replies that it was certainly not his own fault, because he had urged him to go, but Apollos himself promises to come as soon as the opportunity presents itself.

Watch ye, stand fast in the faith, quit you like men, be strong. Let all that ye do be done in love. Now I beseech you, brethren (ye know the house of Stephanas, that it is the firstfruits of Achaia, and that they have set themselves to minister unto the saints), that ye also be in subjection unto such, and to every one that helpeth in the work and laboureth. And I rejoice at the coming of Stephanas and Fortunatus and Achaicus: for that which was lacking on your part they supplied. For they refreshed my spirit and yours: acknowledge ye therefore them that are such. The churches of Asia salute you. Aquila and Prisca salute you much in the Lord, with the church that is in their house. All the brethren salute you. Salute one another with a holy kiss. The salutation of me Paul with mine own hand. If any man loveth not the Lord, let him be anathema. Maranatha. The grace of the Lord Jesus Christ be with you. My love be with you all in Christ Jesus. Amen. (13-24)

13. *Watch etc.* This is a brief exhortation but a very important one· He orders them to watch, so that Satan might not take them by surprise when they were off their guard. For, as warfare goes on without a break, so the watch must be maintained uninterrupted. But we are mentally alert when we are not hampered by earthly cares, and are free to meditate on the things of God. For as the body is weighed down with dissipation and drunkenness, and becomes fit for nothing, so the cares and passions of the world, sloth or indifference, are like a spiritual drunkenness, which overpowers the mind.

The second call to them is to continue steadfastly in the faith, or to keep hold of the faith, so that they stand firm, because it is the foundation on which we rest. But he is clearly pointing out the way to continue steadfastly; it is by resting on God with unshakeable faith.

In the third place comes something that is closely related to that, for he encourages them to be manly and courageous.

And because we are naturally weak he urges them, in the fourth place, to be strengthened, or to obtain strength. For where we translate 'be strong' Paul uses only one word, which is equivalent in meaning to 'be strengthened' (*roborari*).

14. *Let all that ye do be done in love.* Paul again repeats the rule that should govern all our dealings with each other. So his wish is that love should be in control, because the biggest fault of the Corinthians was that each one was concerned with his own affairs, to the neglect of others.

15. *You know the household of Stephanas.* We know from our everyday experience what a good thing it is that those, whom God has equipped with the more outstanding gifts, have the greatest authority. Therefore if we want to look to the Church's well-being let us always take care that honour is given to good men. Let their advice have the greatest weight. Let the rest give way to them, and allow themselves to be guided by their wisdom. Paul is doing that in this verse, when he advises the Corinthians to show respect towards the household of Stephanas. For God is revealing Himself to us, where the gifts of His Spirit are in evidence. Therefore, if we do not want to give the impression of being people who treat God with contempt, let us, of our own accord, submit ourselves to all on whom God has bestowed the richer gifts.

Now, so that they might be all the readier to honour that household (for it certainly seems to me that the addition of the other name is not genuine, in this verse at any rate), he reminds them that they were 'the firstfruits of Achaia'; in other words, that the members of the household of Stephanas were the first to embrace the Gospel. It is not always the case, of course, that the man who is first on the field is better than the rest; but where perseverance goes along with it, those who have, in a sense, paved the way for the Gospel by the readiness with which they believed, deserve to be held in honour. But we must note that the people whom he thinks worthy of this honourable description are those who had dedicated their services and resources for the benefit of believers. For the same reason he speaks well of Fortunatus and Achaicus a little after, viz. that the better a man is, the more highly regarded he should be, in order that he might be able to be of even greater service. Moreover, in order that the Corinthians might feel more inclined to love them, he says that these men had compensated for the failure of their entire church by the services they rendered on their behalf.

19. *With the church that is in their household.* What a wonderful thing to be put on record!—that the name '*Church*' is applied to a single family; and yet it is fitting that all the families of believers should be organized in such a way as to be so many little churches. On the other hand, the word 'congregation', which Erasmus preferred, is not in line with what Paul had in mind. For he did not mean to describe a mere crowd of people, and use an ordinary word to do so, but to speak with great respect about the organization of a particular Christian household (*de Christiana oeconomia*).

The fact that he sends them greetings on behalf of Aquila and Priscilla confirms what I pointed out already, that this letter was written from Ephesus rather than Philippi. For Luke informs us that, when Paul left Ephesus to go elsewhere, they took his place there.

20. *Greet one another with a holy kiss.* Kissing was a very common custom among the Jews, as the Scriptures make plain to us. In Greece, while the custom was not so customary and common, yet it was not unknown. But Paul is probably speaking here about a ceremonial kiss, with which they greeted each other when they gathered for worship. For I could well believe that from the time of the apostles a kiss was already used in connexion with the administration of the Supper. But among nations who had no wish at all to adopt the practice of kissing there crept in, in its place, the custom of kissing the paten. Be that as it may, because it was a sign of mutual love, I have no doubt that Paul meant to encourage them to cultivate goodwill among themselves, not only in their hearts and in the duties which they were bound to perform, but also with that sign, so long as it was *holy*, that is to say, not lustful

or sham; although 'holy' can also be taken as referring to an act of worship.

22. *If anyone does not love the Lord Jesus.* The conclusion of the letter consists of three parts. He prays that the Corinthians may have the grace of Christ. He declares the love that he himself bears towards them. And he uses the severest of threats in an attack upon those who were making a false profession of the name of Christ, when they did not love Him from the heart. For Paul is not referring to outsiders, who were quite open about their dislike of the name 'Christian', but to deceivers and hypocrites, who were causing disorder in the churches, when all they were concerned about was their own material gain, and being able to make an empty show. He pronounces a curse of excommunication on such people, and invokes further evil on them as well. But it is not clear whether he desires that they be destroyed in the presence of God, or wishes them to be hateful, I should rather say, accursed in the eyes of believers. For instance, in Galatians 1.8, when he affirms that somebody preaching a corruption of the Gospel is to be accursed he does not mean him to be rejected or condemned by God, but that he should be detested by us. Let me put it in this simple way: 'Let them be rooted out and perish, for they are pests in the Church.' And indeed there is nothing more pernicious than the kind of people who take advantage of the profession of religion for the sake of their own corrupt desires. Paul certainly puts his finger on the source of this evil, when he says that they do not love Christ, for a genuine and earnest love for Christ will prevent us from causing any offence to our brothers.

The word *maranatha*, which he adds immediately afterwards, is a little more difficult. Nearly all the Fathers agree that they are Syriac words. Jerome however explains it as 'The Lord has come', while others render it 'when the Lord comes', or 'until the coming of the Lord'. But I think that it is perfectly plain to anyone how pointless and silly it is, to think that the apostle spoke to the Greeks in Syriac, when he wanted to say, 'The Lord has come'. Those who translate it as 'when the Lord comes' are only hazarding a guess, for that meaning is not even very plausible. Is it not much more likely that this was a formula which the Jews were in the habit of using when they wanted to anathematize someone? For the apostles never express themselves in words of a foreign language, except when they are reporting what another person said, for instance, *Eli, Eli, lama sabachthani; Talitha cumi; Ephphatha*; or when they employ a word that has passed into general use, such as *Amen* and *Hosanna*. Let us therefore see if *Maranatha* suits excommunication. Now Bullinger has pointed out, on the authority of Theodore Bibliander, that in Aramaic, *Maharamata* is the same as the

Hebrew חֵרֶם (*chērem*, i.e. ban, curse); and Wolfgang Capito, that man of blessed memory, once gave me corroboration of that. But it is not unusual for the apostles to write these words differently from the way they are pronounced in their own language; and that is plain even in the above examples. Therefore, after Paul had condemned with an anathema those who do not love Jesus Christ, he was disturbed by the seriousness of the matter, and, as though he felt that he had not said enough, he added a term that was in common use among the Jews, when they passed the sentence of anathema. It is as though I were to say, 'I excommunicate you'; but, if I were to add, 'and I declare you to be accursed or anathema', I would be giving more forcible expression to my feelings.

INDEX OF SCRIPTURE REFERENCES

INDEX OF SCRIPTURE REFERENCES

INDEX OF SCRIPTURE REFERENCES

INDEX OF SCRIPTURE REFERENCES

INDEX OF NAMES

GENERAL INDEX

Adoption, 23f, 30, 57, 59, 60
Adultery, 145f
Agapae (Love-feasts), 240
Ages, Ends of the, 212
Amen, 293
Analogy, 135, 191, 246, 260, 265, 269, 304
Angels, 96, 119, 233, 281, 324
Anxieties (in marriage), 160-2
Apostle, 15f, 93, 183-6, 270, 313
Apostolic succession, 16, 186, 192
Assurance, 58, 59, 212f

Baptism, 29ff, 152, 200ff, 264f, 291
Baptism for 'the dead', 329ff
Barbarian, 290
Body, The, 129-33, 199, 260, 263f, 266ff, 335-41, 343f
Body of Christ (The Church), *see* under 'Church'
Body of Christ (in the Lord's Supper), 246f, 248, 251, 253
Bread (in the Lord's Supper), 216f, 243-8, 250-2
'Burning', Sexual, 144

Call, and Calling, 15, 18, 23, 43f, 85, 152f, 157, 192
Carnal, 65ff, 207
Catechumens, 330
Celibacy, 134, 138, 140ff, 156f, 158, 160f, 163f, 165, 167
Centumviri ('The Hundred'), 208, 314
Chastity, Garland of, 158, 168
Christ
    Adam and, 319, 322f, 326, 339-41
    Ascension, 315
    Benefits of, 46, 60, 127, 205, 209, 246, 248, 347
    and His Brothers, 185

Our Cleansing, 74, 127
Death of, 127, 248, 250, 313f, 320, 347
Divinity of, 19
Eternity of, 209, 327
Example of, 226f, 243
Father, Relation to, 83, 175, 229, 323f, 325ff
Final Coming of, 250, 343
Firstfruits, The, 322f
Foundation of Church, 73ff
Head of Church, 28, 29, 91, 92f, 210, 230, 347
Humanity of, 83, 339f
Judge, Our, 22, 87, 118
Justification, Our, 262
Lordship of, 19, 27, 175, 259, 326, 327
Mediator, 209, 229, 327
Passover, Our, 110f
Redemption, Our, 46, 74, 132, 179, 262
Resurrection of, 127, 318-22, 323
Righteousness, Our, 46, 74, 127
Rock, The, 204f
Sanctification, Our, 46, 74, 127, 262
Supper, In the, 205, 246f, 248, 250, 251-4
Teacher, Our, 82
Union with, 18, 24, 45, 83, 97, 129ff, 216, 230, 246, 264
Victory of, 347
Wisdom, Our, 22, 45f, 74, 94
Church, The
    Body of Christ, 18, 21, 28, 90, 129-31, 216, 260f, 262-6, 269, 347
    Discipline, 102f, 106ff, 114f
    Dispensation, In Old, 200-13
    Divisions in, 25, 26-30, 67, 71, 237-9
    Founded on Christ, 73ff
    Head is Christ, 28, 29, 91, 92f, 210, 230, 347

365

GENERAL INDEX

GENERAL INDEX

CALVIN'S
NEW TESTAMENT
COMMENTARIES

A NEW TRANSLATION

This volume is the second in a completely new translation into modern English of Calvin's commentaries on the New Testament. Those familiar with the previous translations have frequently discovered that they failed to reveal the close coherence of Calvin's ideas, missed many of his characteristic images, and often translated whole passages poorly or omitted them altogether. Dr. Paul T. Fuhrmann, Professor of Church History at Columbia Theological Seminary, says, "Most of Calvin's works were translated into English over one hundred years ago. Such translations were naturally influenced by the mind current in those days. Since then better editions of the original works of Calvin have been made available to scholars; important books on him have been written; an immense literature about the Reformer has piled up, so that Calvin's concepts as well as his use of Latin and French words are better understood today than one hundred years ago. In the light of these facts it is no exaggeration to state that this new translation of Calvin's N.T. Commentaries under the editorship of Thomas F. Torrance and David W. Torrance is truly an event in the English-speaking world."

Dr. Fuhrmann goes on to say, "Thousands of volumes, telling us of times and circumstances, take us for trips around the Bible, but how many writers today can penetrate,